AMERICAN POLITICAL, ECONOMIC, AND SECURITY ISSUES

# U.S. POLITICAL PROGRAMS: FUNCTIONS AND ASSESSMENTS

# AMERICAN POLITICAL, ECONOMIC, AND SECURITY ISSUES

AMERICAN POLITICAL, ECONOMIC, AND SECURITY ISSUES

# U.S. POLITICAL PROGRAMS: FUNCTIONS AND ASSESSMENTS

JULIANNA M. MORETTI

AND

KAREN J. CHORDSTRON

EDITORS

Nova Science Publishers, Inc.
*New York*

For permission to use material from this book please contact us:
Telephone 631-231-7269; Fax 631-231-8175
Web Site: http://www.novapublishers.com

**NOTICE TO THE READER**

The Publisher has taken reasonable care in the preparation of this book, but makes no expressed or implied warranty of any kind and assumes no responsibility for any errors or omissions. No liability is assumed for incidental or consequential damages in connection with or arising out of information contained in this book. The Publisher shall not be liable for any special, consequential, or exemplary damages resulting, in whole or in part, from the readers' use of, or reliance upon, this material. Any parts of this book based on government reports are so indicated and copyright is claimed for those parts to the extent applicable to compilations of such works.

Independent verification should be sought for any data, advice or recommendations contained in this book. In addition, no responsibility is assumed by the publisher for any injury and/or damage to persons or property arising from any methods, products, instructions, ideas or otherwise contained in this publication.

This publication is designed to provide accurate and authoritative information with regard to the subject matter covered herein. It is sold with the clear understanding that the Publisher is not engaged in rendering legal or any other professional services. If legal or any other expert assistance is required, the services of a competent person should be sought. FROM A DECLARATION OF PARTICIPANTS JOINTLY ADOPTED BY A COMMITTEE OF THE AMERICAN BAR ASSOCIATION AND A COMMITTEE OF PUBLISHERS.

Additional color graphics may be available in the e-book version of this book.

**LIBRARY OF CONGRESS CATALOGING-IN-PUBLICATION DATA**

U.S. political programs : functions and assessments / editors, Julianna M. Moretti and Karen J. Chordstron.
p. cm.
  Includes bibliographical references and index.
  ISBN 978-1-61209-448-9 (hbk. : alk. paper)
 1.  United States--Economic policy--21st century. 2.  United States--Social policy--21st century. 3.  United States--Foreign relations--21st century. 4. United States--Politics and government--21st century. I. Moretti, Julianna M. II. Chordstron, Karen J.
 HC106.84.U17 2011
 320.60973--dc22
2011003975

*Published by Nova Science Publishers, Inc. † New York*

# CONTENTS

# PREFACE

This new book presents and discusses various economic policies in North America. Topics discussed include the Manhattan Project, the Apollo Program and Federal Technology R&D programs; the Millennium Challenge Corporation and the Technology Innovation Program; America COMPETES Act and the FY2010 budget; employment-based health coverage and health reform; senate consideration of presidential elections; the National Security Council and the Global Peace Operations Initiative.

Chapter 1 – Article II, Section 2 of the Constitution provides that the President shall appoint officers of the United States "by and with the Advice and Consent of the Senate." This report describes the process by which the Senate provides advice and consent on presidential nominations, including receipt and referral of nominations, committee practices, and floor procedure.

The vast majority of presidential appointees are confirmed routinely by the Senate. A regularized process facilitates quick action on thousands of government positions. The process also allows for lengthy scrutiny of candidates when necessary. Each year, a few hundred nominees to high-level positions are subject to Senate investigations and public hearings.

Committees play the central role in the process through investigations and hearings. Senate Rule XXXI provides that nominations shall be referred to appropriate committees "unless otherwise ordered." The Senate rule concerning committee jurisdictions (Rule XXV) broadly defines issue areas for committees, and the same jurisdictional statements generally apply to nominations as well as legislation. A committee often gathers and reviews information about a nominee either before or instead of a formal hearing.

A committee considering a nomination has four options. It can report the nomination to the Senate favorably, unfavorably, or without recommendation, or it can choose to take no action at all. It is more common for a committee to fail to take action on a nomination than to reject a nominee outright.

The Senate handles executive business, which includes both nominations and treaties, separately from its legislative business. All nominations reported from committee are listed on the Executive Calendar, a separate document from the Calendar of Business, which lists pending bills and resolutions. Generally speaking, the majority leader schedules floor consideration of nominations on the calendar. Nominations are considered in "executive session," a parliamentary form of the Senate in session that has its own journal and, to some extent, its own rules of procedure.

The question before the Senate when a nomination is called up is "will the Senate advise and consent to this nomination?" Only a majority of Senators present and voting, a quorum being present, is required to approve a nomination. Because nominations are vulnerable to filibusters, however, stronger support may be necessary. Cloture may be invoked to bring debate on a nomination to a close.

Nominations that are pending when the Senate adjourns or recesses for more than 30 days are returned to the President unless the Senate, by unanimous consent, waives the rule requiring their return (Senate Rule XXXI, clause 6). If a nomination is returned, and the President still wants a nominee considered, he must submit a new nomination to the Senate.

Chapter 2 – Some policymakers have concluded that the energy challenges facing the United States are so critical that a concentrated investment in energy research and development (R&D) should be undertaken. The Manhattan project, which produced the atomic bomb, and the Apollo program, which landed American men on the moon, have been cited as examples of the success such R&D investments can yield. Investment in federal energy technology R&D programs of the 1970s, in response to two energy crises, have generally been viewed as less successful than the earlier two efforts. This report compares and contrasts the three initiatives.

In 2008 dollars, the cumulative cost of the Manhattan project over 5 fiscal years was approximately $22 billion; of the Apollo program over 14 fiscal years, approximately $98 billion; of post-oil shock energy R&D efforts over 35 fiscal years, $118 billion. A measure of the nation's commitments to the programs is their relative shares of the federal outlays during the years of peak funding: for the Manhattan program, the peak year funding was 1% of federal outlays; for the Apollo program, 2.2%; and for energy technology R&D programs, 0.5%. Another measure of the commitment is their relative shares of the nation's gross domestic product (GDP) during the peak years of funding: for the Manhattan project and the Apollo program, the peak year funding reached 0.4% of GDP, and for the energy technology R&D programs, 0.1%.

Besides funding, several criteria might be used to compare these three initiatives including perception of the program or threat, goal clarity, and the customer of the technology being developed. By these criteria, while the Manhattan project and the Apollo program may provide some useful analogies for thinking about an energy technology R&D initiative, there are fundamental differences between the forces that drove these historical R&D success stories and the forces driving energy technology R&D today.

Critical differences include (1) the ability to transform the program or threat into a concrete goal, and (2) the use to which the technology would be put. On the issue of goal setting, for the Manhattan project, the response to the threat of enemy development of a nuclear bomb was the goal to construct a bomb; for the Apollo program, the threat of Soviet space dominance was translated into a specific goal of landing on the moon. For energy, the response to the problems of insecure oil sources and high prices has resulted in multiple, sometimes conflicting, goals. Regarding use, both the Manhattan project and the Apollo program goals pointed to technologies primarily for governmental use with little concern about their environmental impact; for energy, in contrast, the hoped-for outcome depends on commercial viability and mitigation of environmental impacts from energy use.

Although the Manhattan project and the Apollo program may provide some useful analogies for funding, these differences may limit their utility regarding energy policy. Rather, energy technology R&D has been driven by at least three not always commensurate goals—resource and technological diversity, commercial viability, and environmental protection—which were not goals of the historical programs.

Some policymakers have concluded that the energy challenges facing the United States are so critical that a concentrated investment in energy research and development (R&D) should be undertaken. The Manhattan project, which produced the atomic bomb, and the Apollo program, which landed American men on the moon, have been cited as examples of the success such R&D investments can yield.

Investment in federal energy technology R&D programs of the 1970s, in response to two energy crises, have generally been viewed as less successful than the earlier two efforts. This report compares and contrasts the goals of, and the investments in, the three initiatives, which may provide useful insights for Congress as it assesses and debates the nation's energy policy.

Chapter 3 – The Technology Innovation Program (TIP) at the National Institute of Standards and Technology (NIST) was established in 2007 to replace the Advanced Technology Program (ATP). This effort is designed " ... to support, promote, and accelerate innovation in the United States through high- risk, high-reward research in areas of critical national need," according to the authorizing legislation. Grants are provided to small and medium-sized firms for individual projects or joint ventures with other research organizations.

While similar to the Advanced Technology Program in the promotion of R&D that is expected to be of broad-based economic benefit to the Nation, TIP appears to have been structured to avoid what was seen as government funding of large firms that did not necessarily need federal support for research. The committee report to accompany H.R. 1868, part of which was incorporated into the final legislation, stated that TIP replaces ATP in consideration of a changing global innovation environment focusing on small and medium-sized companies. The design of the program also "acknowledges the important role universities play in the innovation cycle by allowing universities to fully participate in the program."

The elimination of ATP and the creation of TIP have renewed the debate over the role of the federal government in promoting commercial technology development. In arguing for less direct federal involvement, advocates believe that the market is superior to government in deciding technologies worthy of investment. Mechanisms that enhance the market's opportunities and abilities to make such choices are preferred. It is suggested that agency discretion in selecting one technology over another can lead to political intrusion and industry dependency. On the other hand, supporters of direct methods argue that it is important to focus on those technologies that have the greatest promise as determined by industry and supported by matching funds from the private sector. They assert that the government can serve as a catalyst for cooperation. As the 111th Congress makes budget decisions, the discussion may serve to redefine thinking about governmental efforts in facilitating technological advancement in the private sector.

Chapter 4 – In a speech on March 14, 2002, President Bush outlined a proposal for a major new U.S. foreign aid initiative. The Millennium Challenge Corporation (MCC) provides assistance through a competitive selection process to developing nations that are pursuing political and economic reforms in three areas: ruling justly, investing in people, and fostering economic freedom.

The MCC differs in several respects from past and current U.S. aid practices:

- the competitive process that rewards countries for past and current actions measured by 17 objective performance indicators;
- the pledge to segregate the funds from U.S. strategic foreign policy objectives that often strongly influence where U.S. aid is spent; and
- the requirement to solicit program proposals developed solely by qualifying countries with broad-based civil society involvement.

As announced by the President Bush in March 2002, the initial plan had been to fund the MCC annually at $5 billion by FY2006, but this figure has never been reached. The Administration has sought a combined $15.0 billion for the MCC program, FY2004-FY2009, while Congress appropriated $8.3 billion, or little more than half of the total sought (55%). Under the FY2009 Omnibus appropriations (P.L. 111-8), Congress provided $875 million to the MCC. On May 7, 2009, the Administration issued its FY20 10 budget request, providing $1 .425 billion for the MCC.

Congress authorized the MCC in P.L. 108-199 (January 23, 2004). Since that time, the MCC's Board of Directors has approved 18 Compacts: with Madagascar (April 2005), Honduras (June 2005), Cape Verde (July 2005), Nicaragua (July 2005), Georgia (September 2005), Benin (February 2006), Vanuatu (March 2006), Armenia (March 2006), Ghana (August 2006), Mali (November 2006), El Salvador (November 2006), Mozambique (July 2007), Lesotho (July 2007), Morocco (August 2007), Mongolia (September 2007), Tanzania (September 2007), Burkina Faso (June 2008), and Namibia (July 2008). In June 2009, the Madagascar Compact was terminated early, as were uncontracted components of the Nicaragua Compact. A suspension of the roads portion of the Armenia Compact has been continued.

MCC implementation matters continue to unfold, including the relationship of MCC and USAID, sectors chosen, and the impact of rising costs on country programs. A growing question raised by some Members of Congress concerns the level of funding to support MCC programs. Some fear that insufficient funds might force the MCC to reduce the number of recipients or the size of the grants. Others, however, support reductions in the MCC budget, disturbed by the slower-thananticipated pace of Compact agreements and lack of concrete results to date.

Chapter 5 – The 111th Congress will face a number of issues regarding the development of civilian capabilities to carry out stabilization and reconstruction activities. In September 2008, Congress passed the Reconstruction and Stabilization Civilian Management Act, 2008, as Title XVI of the Duncan Hunter National Defense Authorization Act for Fiscal Year 2009 (S. 3001, P.L. 110-417, signed into law October 14, 2008). This legislation codified the existence and functions of the State Department Office of the Coordinator for Reconstruction and Stabilization (S/CRS) and authorized new operational capabilities within the State Department, a Civilian Response Corps of government employees with an active and a standby component, and a Civilian Reserve Corps.

S/CRS was established in 2004 to address longstanding concerns, both within Congress and the broader foreign policy community, over the perceived lack of the appropriate capabilities and processes to deal with transitions from conflict to stability. These capabilities and procedures include adequate planning mechanisms for stabilization and reconstruction operations, efficient interagency coordination structures and procedures in carrying out such tasks, and appropriate civilian personnel for many of the non-military tasks required. Effectively distributing resources among the various executive branch actors, maintaining clear lines of authority and jurisdiction, and balancing short- and long-term objectives are major challenges for designing, planning, and conducting post-conflict operations, as is fielding the appropriate civilian personnel.

Since July 2004, S/CRS has worked to establish the basic concepts, mechanisms, and capabilities necessary to carry out such operations. Working with a staff that has slowly grown from a few dozen to 112 individuals from the State Department, other executive branch agencies, and on contract as of January 30, 2009, S/CRS has taken steps to monitor and plan for potential conflicts, to develop a rapid-response crisis management "surge" capability, to improve interagency and international coordination, to develop interagency training exercises, and to help State Department regional bureaus develop concepts and proposals for preventive action.

In June 2008, Congress specifically provided $65 million for S/CRS and USAID S&R activities, including the establishment and implementation of civilian response capabilities, in the Supplemental Appropriations Act, 2008 (P.L. 110-252). Congress provided another $75 million in FY2009 appropriations in the Omnibus Appropriations Act, 2009 (P.L. 111-8).

On March 7, 2009, the Obama Administration requested $323.3 million in FY20 10 funds to continue the development of the Civilian Response Corps (CRC) active and standby components, formally launched in July 2008, and the establishment of a 2,000-member civilian reserve component. In addition, the Administration requested a $40 million Stabilization Bridge Fund under the Economic Support Fund (ESF) to fund activities of deployed CRC members responding to urgent needs until other funds are reprogrammed, transferred, appropriated, or otherwise made available for that purpose. Among the issues that Congress will face regarding the development of civilian capabilities are the means to support, maintain, and deploy the civilian response and reserve corps.

In action on the Foreign Relations Authorization Act, Fiscal Years 2010 and 2011 (H.R. 2410), the House authorized the Administration's CSI FY2010 funding request of $323.3 million and "such sums as may be necessary for fiscal year 2011." In floor action, the House incorporated an amendment to expand the categories of persons who would be permitted to participate in the CRC.

Chapter 6 – The America COMPETES Act (P.L. 110-69) became law on August 9, 2007. The act is intended to increase the nation's investment in research and development (R&D), and in science, technology, engineering, and mathematics (STEM) education. It is designed to focus on two perceived concerns believed to influence future U.S. competitiveness: inadequate R&D funding to generate sufficient technological progress, and inadequate numbers of American students proficient in STEM or interested in STEM careers relative to other countries.

The act authorizes funding increases for the National Science Foundation (NSF), National Institute of Standards and Technology (NIST) laboratories, and the Department of Energy Office of Science (DOE SC) over FY2008-FY2010. If maintained, the increases would double the budgets of those entities over seven years. The act establishes the Advanced Research Projects Agency – Energy (ARPA-E) within DOE, designed to support transformational energy technology research projects with the goal of enhancing U.S.

economic and energy security. A new program, Discovery Science and Engineering Innovation Institutes, would establish multidisciplinary institutes at DOE National Laboratories to "apply fundamental science and engineering discoveries to technological innovations," according to the act.

Among the act's education activities, many of which are focused on high-need school districts, are programs to recruit new K-12 STEM teachers, enhance existing STEM teacher skills, and provide more STEM education opportunities for students. The new Department of Education (ED) Teachers for a Competitive Tomorrow and existing NSF Robert Noyce Teacher Scholarship (Noyce) programs provide opportunities, through institutional grants, for students pursuing STEM degrees and STEM professionals to gain teaching skills and teacher certification, and for current STEM teachers to enhance their teaching skills and understanding of STEM content. The act also authorizes a new program at NSF that would provide grants to create or improve professional science master's degree (PSM) programs that emphasize practical training and preparation for the workforce in high-need fields.

The America COMPETES Act is an authorization act. New programs established by the act will not be initiated and authorized increases in appropriations for existing programs will not occur unless funded through subsequent appropriation acts. The 110th Congress provided FY2008 appropriations to establish ED's Teachers for a Competitive Tomorrow program, and NIST's Technology Improvement Program (TIP), which replaced the existing Advanced Technology Program. The 111th Congress provided FY2009 appropriations, supplemented by the American Recovery and Reinvestment Act (ARRA), to establish DOE's ARPA-E and NSF's PSM program. Although some America COMPETES Act research and STEM education programs received appropriations at authorized levels in FY2009, others did not.

As Congress deliberates the FY2010 budget, an issue for Congress is what level, if any, it will appropriate funds for America COMPETES Act programs. Although the Obama Administration requested FY2010 funding for most America COMPETES Act R&D programs at levels below that authorized, it contends that FY2009 (due to ARRA funding), and if approved as requested, FY20 10 appropriations would fund federal R&D programs at the highest levels in U.S. history. Several programs newly authorized in the act have never been appropriated funds and the Obama Administration has not proposed funding them. An issue for these programs is whether or not they will receive the funding necessary to establish them. The America COMPETES Act provides authorization levels only through FY2010.

Chapter 7 – It is estimated that nearly 170 million individuals have employer-based health coverage. As part of a comprehensive health care reform effort, there has been support (including from the Obama Administration) in enacting comprehensive health insurance reform that retains the employer- based system. This report presents selected legal considerations inherent in amending two of the primary federal laws governing employer-sponsored health care: the Employee Retirement Income Security Act (ERISA) and the Internal Revenue Code (IRC).

ERISA may be a key part of the health reform discussion in two main ways. The first way is if Congress desires to amend the employer-based system, for example, to require financing or benefits for group health plans as provided by employers. If a national proposal were to require employers to provide or contribute to the payment of health benefits or to provide specific benefits as part of group health plans, ERISA could be a vehicle for this type of proposal. Second, if Congress were to amend the role of states in regulating employment-based health benefits, ERISA's express preemption provision, § 514, would likely be implicated. Section 514 of ERISA is commonly seen as a barrier for states in enacting health reform that affects the employer-based system. This report provides an overview of ERISA preemption and analyzes some of the current issues dealing with the extent to which ERISA can preempt state health reform efforts, as well as issues that may be considered in a national health reform effort.

While the current tax treatment of employer-provided health insurance is not technically an obstacle to health reform, various health reform proposals have included amendments to these tax provisions. The value of employer-provided health insurance is generally not subject to income or payroll taxes. This effectively results in the subsidization of employer-provided health insurance by the federal government. Some have argued that this subsidization is partly responsible for increasing costs of health insurance, as it gives participants an inaccurate sense of the true cost of their health care and leads to increased utilization of health care resources. Therefore, some have proposed reducing or eliminating this exclusion in order to provide individuals with a more accurate economic picture of their health care choices, while simultaneously raising federal revenue to pay for other aspects of health care reform. This report discusses the legal framework underlying the current tax treatment of employer-provided health care.

Chapter 8 – Science and engineering activities have always been international. Scientists, engineers, and health professionals frequently communicate and cooperate with one another without regard to national boundaries. This report discusses international science and technology (S&T) diplomacy, instances when American leadership in S&T is used as a diplomatic tool to enhance another country's development and to improve understanding by other nations of U.S. values and ways of doing business. According to the National Research Council, five developmental challenges where S&T could play a role include child health and child survival, safe water, agricultural research to reduce hunger and poverty, micro-economic reform, and mitigation of natural disasters.

Title V of the Foreign Relations Authorization Act, FY1 979 (P.L. 9 5-426) provides the current legislative guidance for U.S. international S&T policy. This act states that Department of State (DOS) is the lead federal agency in developing S&T agreements. The National Science and Technology Policy, Organization, and Priorities Act of 1976 (P.L. 94-282) states that the director of the White House Office of Science and Technology Policy (OSTP) is to advise the President on international S&T cooperation policies and the role of S&T considerations in foreign relations. DOS sets the overall policy direction for U.S. international S&T diplomacy, and works with other federal agencies as needed. OSTP acts as a interagency liaison. A number of federal agencies that both sponsor research and use S&T in developing policy are involved in international S&T policy.

A fundamental question is why the United States should invest in international S&T diplomacy instead of domestic research and development (R&D) and science, technology, engineering, and mathematics education (STEM) activities, which are facing budget constraints. If Congress should decide that funding international S&T activities is important, agreeing on a policy goal beyond enhancing the country's development, such as improving U.S. relations with other countries, or enhancing popular opinion of the United States may help set priorities.

Policy options identified for Congress by expert committees who have assessed U.S. international S&T diplomacy efforts include ensuring a baseline of science, engineering, and technical (SET) literacy among all appropriate DOS personnel, increasing the presence overseas of personnel with significant SET expertise, and expanding the Department's engagement within global SET networks through exchanges, assistance, and joint research activities addressing key global issues. Other proposed actions include increasing USAID support that builds S&T capacity in developing countries, and orienting other departments and agencies S&T developing country programs to support the development priorities of the host countries. Another proposal would establish a new U.S. government organization called the "Development Applications Research Institute" (DARI) to develop and apply innovative technologies to development problems. In all of these efforts, Congress might wish to consider enhancing the prominence of the STAS, and coordination among S&T leaders at OES, STAS, and OSTP.

On June 4, 2009, President Obama announced several international S&T diplomacy programs in Muslim-majority countries including a new fund for technological development in these countries, establishing centers of scientific excellence, and appointing new science envoys. On June 8, 2009, the House passed the International Science and Technology Cooperation Act of 2009 (H.R. 1736), which would require the OSTP Director to establish an interagency committee to identify and coordinate international science and technology cooperation.

Chapter 9 – The National Security Council (NSC) was established by statute in 1947 to create an interdepartmental body to advise the President with respect to the integration of domestic, foreign, and military policies relating to the national security so as to enable the military services and the other departments and agencies of the Government to cooperate more effectively in matters involving the national security. Currently, statutory members of the Council are the President, Vice President, the Secretary of State, and the Secretary of Defense; but, at the President's request, other senior officials participate in NSC deliberations. The Chairman of the Joint Chiefs of Staff and the Director of National Intelligence are statutory advisers. In 2007 the Secretary of Energy was added to the NSC membership.

The President clearly holds final decision-making authority in the executive branch. Over the years, however, the NSC staff has emerged as a major factor in the formulation (and at times in the implementation) of national security policy. Similarly, the head of the NSC staff, the National Security Adviser, has played important, and occasionally highly public, roles in policymaking. This report traces the evolution of the NSC from its creation to the present.

The organization and influence of the NSC have varied significantly from one Administration to another, from a highly structured and formal system to loose-knit teams of experts. It is universally acknowledged that the NSC staff should be organized to meet the particular goals and work habits of an incumbent President. The history of the NSC provides ample evidence of the advantages and disadvantages of different types of policymaking structures.

Congress enacted the statute creating the NSC and has altered the character of its membership over the years. Congress annually appropriates funds for its activities, but does not, routinely, receive testimony on substantive matters from the National Security Adviser or from NSC staff. Proposals to require Senate confirmation of the Security Adviser have been discussed but not adopted.

The post-Cold War world has posed new challenges to NSC policymaking. Some argue that the NSC should be broadened to reflect an expanding role of economic, environmental, and demographic issues in national security policymaking. The Clinton Administration created a National Economic Council tasked with cooperating closely with the NSC on international economic matters. In the wake of the 9/11 attacks, the George W. Bush Administration established a Homeland Security Council. The Obama Administration has combined the staffs of the Homeland Security Council and the National Security Council, while retaining the two positions of National Security Adviser and Homeland Security Adviser. Although the latter has direct access to the President, the incumbent is to organizationally report to the National Security Adviser.

Chapter 10 – In its May 2009 budget request for FY2010, the Obama Administration has requested $96.8 million for the Global Peace Operations Initiative (GPOI). GPOI was established in mid-2004 as a five-year program with intended annual funding to total $660 million from FY2005 through FY2009. (Actual funds allocated to the GPOI program from FY2005 through FY2009 totaled, as of April 2009, some $480.4 million.) The centerpiece of the Bush Administration's efforts to prepare foreign security forces to participate in international peacekeeping operations, GPOI's primary purpose has been to train and equip 75,000 military troops, a majority of them African, for peacekeeping operations by 2010. In October 2008, the National Security Council's Deputies Committee approved a five-year renewal of GPOI's mandate. Congressional approval of the FY2010 budget request would provide funding for the first year of this extension.

To date, GPOI also provides support for the Center of Excellence for Stability Police Units (CoESPU), an Italian "train-the-trainer" training center for gendarme (constabulary police) forces in Vicenza, Italy. In addition, GPOI promotes the development of an international transportation and logistics support system for peacekeepers, and encourages information exchanges to improve international coordination of peace operations training and exercises. Through GPOI, the United States supports and participates in a G* Africa Clearinghouse and a G8++ Global Clearinghouse, both to coordinate international peacekeeping capacity building efforts.

GPOI incorporates previous capabilities-building programs for Africa. From FY1997 to FY2005, the United States spent just over $121 million on GPOI's predecessor program that was funded through the State Department Peacekeeping (PKO) account: the Clinton Administration's African Crisis Response Initiative (ACRI) and its successor, the Bush Administration's African Contingency Operations Training and Assistance (ACOTA) program. (ACOTA is now GPOI's principal training program in Africa.) Some 16,000 troops from ten African nations were trained under the early ACRI/ACOTA programs. Some $33 million was provided from FY1998 to FY2005 to support classroom training of 31 foreign militaries through the Foreign Military Financing account's Enhanced International Peacekeeping Capabilities program (EIPC).

Within a year after GPOI was initiated in late 2004, the Administration began expanding its geographical scope to selected countries in Central America, Europe, and Asia. In 2006 and 2007, the program was further expanded to countries in Asia, South Asia, and the Pacific. GPOI now includes 53 "partner" countries and two partner organizations throughout the world, although the emphasis is still on Africa. According to figures provided by the State Department, almost 57,600 peacekeeper trainees and peacekeeper trainers were trained as of January 31, 2009..

Congress has tended to view the concept of the GPOI program favorably, albeit sometimes with reservations. Over the years, the State Department has addressed various congressional concerns. In a June 2008 report, the Government Accountability Office (GAO) recommended several further improvements (GAO-08-754).

In its first action on GPOI during the 111th Congress, the House passed legislation authorizing the Secretary of State to carry out and expand GPOI programs and activities (Section 1108 of the Foreign Relations Authorization Act, Fiscal Years 2010 and 2011, H.R. 2410, passed June 10, 2009).

Chapter 11 – Health care reform has become an issue in the 111th Congress, driven by growing concern about millions of people without insurance coverage, continual increases in cost and spending, and quality shortcomings. Commonly cited figures indicate that more than 45 million people have no insurance, which can limit their access to care and ability to pay for the care they receive. Costs are rising for nearly everyone, and the country now likely spends over $2.5 trillion, more than 17% of gross domestic product (GDP), on health care services and products, far more than other industrialized countries. For all this spending, the country scores but average or somewhat worse on many indicators of health care quality, and many may not get appropriate standards of care.

These concerns raise significant challenges. Each of the concerns is more complex than might first appear, which increases the difficulty of finding solutions. For example, by one statistical measure, far more than 45 million people face the risk of being uninsured for short time periods, yet by another, substantially fewer have no insurance for long periods. Insurance coverage and access to health care are not the same, and it is possible to have one without the other. Having coverage does not ensure that one can pay for care, nor does it always shield one from significant financial loss in the case of serious illness. Similarly, high levels of spending may be partly attributable to the country's wealth, while rising costs, though difficult for many, may primarily mean that less money is available for other things.

Solutions to these concerns may conflict with one another. For example, expanding coverage to most of the uninsured would likely drive up costs (as more people seek care) and expand public budgets (since additional public subsidies would be required). Cutting costs may threaten initiatives to improve quality. Other challenges include addressing the interests of stakeholders that have substantial investments in present arrangements and the unease some people have about moving from an imperfect but known system to something that is potentially better but untried. How much reform might cost and how to pay for it is also an issue.

Health care reform proposals will likely rekindle debate over perennial issues in American health care policy. These include whether insurance should be public or private; whether employment- based insurance should be strengthened, weakened, or left alone; what role states might play; and whether Medicaid should be folded into new insurance arrangements. Whether changes to Medicare should occur at the same time may also be considered. Concerns about coverage, cost and spending, and quality are likely to be addressed within the context of these issues.

The committees of principal jurisdiction for health care are working on comprehensive reform proposals. The Senate HELP Committee released a draft on June 9th, while a coordinated measure by three House committees (Education and Labor, Energy and Commerce, and Ways and Means) was released on June 19th. The Senate Finance Committee has no draft available to the public, though it has released policy option documents. A dozen other comprehensive bills were introduced by the end of June.

This report does not discuss or even try to identify all of the concerns about health care in the United States that are prompting calls for reform. Other concerns may also be important, at least to some, and will likely contribute to the complexity of the reform debate.

Versions of these chapters were also published in *Current Politics and Economics of the United States, Canada, and Mexico,* Volume 12, Numbers 1-4, edited by Frank Columbus, published by Nova Science Publishers, Inc. They were submitted for appropriate modifications in an effort to encourage wider dissemination of research.

In: U.S. Political Programs: Functions and Assessments ISBN: 978-1-61209-448-9
Editors: Julianna M. Moretti and Karen J. Chordstron © 2011 Nova Science Publishers, Inc.

*Chapter 1*

# SENATE CONSIDERATION OF PRESIDENTIAL NOMINATIONS: COMMITTEE AND FLOOR PROCEDURE[*]

*Elizabeth Rybicki*

## ABSTRACT

Article II, Section 2 of the Constitution provides that the President shall appoint officers of the United States "by and with the Advice and Consent of the Senate." This report describes the process by which the Senate provides advice and consent on presidential nominations, including receipt and referral of nominations, committee practices, and floor procedure.

The vast majority of presidential appointees are confirmed routinely by the Senate. A regularized process facilitates quick action on thousands of government positions. The process also allows for lengthy scrutiny of candidates when necessary. Each year, a few hundred nominees to high-level positions are subject to Senate investigations and public hearings.

Committees play the central role in the process through investigations and hearings. Senate Rule XXXI provides that nominations shall be referred to appropriate committees "unless otherwise ordered." The Senate rule concerning committee jurisdictions (Rule XXV) broadly defines issue areas for committees, and the same jurisdictional statements generally apply to nominations as well as legislation. A committee often gathers and reviews information about a nominee either before or instead of a formal hearing.

A committee considering a nomination has four options. It can report the nomination to the Senate favorably, unfavorably, or without recommendation, or it can choose to take no action at all. It is more common for a committee to fail to take action on a nomination than to reject a nominee outright.

The Senate handles executive business, which includes both nominations and treaties, separately from its legislative business. All nominations reported from committee are listed on the Executive Calendar, a separate document from the Calendar of Business, which lists pending bills and resolutions. Generally speaking, the majority

---

[*] This is an edited, reformatted and augmented edition of a United States Congressional Research Service publication, CRS Report RL31980, dated May 8, 2009.

leader schedules floor consideration of nominations on the calendar. Nominations are considered in "executive session," a parliamentary form of the Senate in session that has its own journal and, to some extent, its own rules of procedure.

The question before the Senate when a nomination is called up is "will the Senate advise and consent to this nomination?" Only a majority of Senators present and voting, a quorum being present, is required to approve a nomination. Because nominations are vulnerable to filibusters, however, stronger support may be necessary. Cloture may be invoked to bring debate on a nomination to a close.

Nominations that are pending when the Senate adjourns or recesses for more than 30 days are returned to the President unless the Senate, by unanimous consent, waives the rule requiring their return (Senate Rule XXXI, clause 6). If a nomination is returned, and the President still wants a nominee considered, he must submit a new nomination to the Senate.

## INTRODUCTION

Article II, section 2 of the Constitution provides that the President shall appoint officers of the United States "by and with the Advice and Consent of the Senate." The method by which the Senate provides advice and consent on presidential nominations, referred to broadly as the confirmation process, serves several purposes. First, largely through committee investigations and hearings, the confirmation process allows the Senate to examine the qualifications of nominees and any potential conflicts of interest. Second, Senators can influence policy through the confirmation process, either by rejecting nominees or by extracting promises from nominees before granting consent. Also, the Senate sometimes has delayed the confirmation process in order to increase its influence with the executive branch on unrelated matters.

Senate confirmation is required for several categories of government officials. Military appointments and promotions make up the majority of nominations, approximately 65,000 a Congress, and most are confirmed routinely. Each Congress also considers close to 4,000 civilian nominations, and, again, many of them, such as appointments to or promotions in the Foreign Service and the Public Health Service, are routine. Civilian nominations considered by the Senate also include federal judges and specified officers in executive departments, independent agencies, and regulatory boards and commissions. Some categories of civilian nominations are treated specifically and in greater depth in other Congressional Research Service (CRS) reports [1]

Approximately 99% of presidential appointees are confirmed routinely by the Senate. With tens of thousands of nominations each Congress, the Senate cannot possibly consider them all in detail. A regularized process facilitates quick action on thousands of government positions. The Senate may approve en bloc hundreds of nominations at a time, especially military appointments and promotions.

Although most nominees are swiftly and routinely confirmed by the Senate, the process also allows for close scrutiny of candidates when necessary. Each year, a few hundred nominees to high-level positions are regularly subject to Senate investigations and public hearings. Most of these are routinely approved, while a small number of nominations are disputed and receive more attention from the media and Congress. Judicial nominations, particularly Supreme Court appointees, are generally subject to greater scrutiny than nominations to executive posts, partly because judges serve for life [2]. Among the executive branch positions, nominees for policymaking positions are more likely to be examined closely, and are slightly less likely to be confirmed, than nominees for non-policy positions [3]

There are several reasons for the high percentage of confirmations. Most nominations and promotions are not to policymaking positions and are of less interest to the Senate. In addition, some sentiment exists in the Senate that the selection of persons to fill executive branch positions is largely a presidential prerogative. Historically, the President has been granted wide latitude in the selection of his Cabinet and other high-ranking executive branch officials [4].

Another important reason for the high percentage of confirmations is that Senators often are involved in the nomination stage. The President would prefer a smooth and fast confirmation process, so he may decide that it is in his interest to consult with Senators in his party prior to choosing a nominee. Senators most likely to be consulted, typically by White House congressional relations staff, are Senators from a nominee's home state, leaders of the committee of jurisdiction, and leaders of the President's party in the Senate. Senators of the President's party are sometimes invited to express opinions or even propose candidates for federal appointments in their own states [5]. There is a long-standing custom of "senatorial courtesy," whereby the Senate will often decline to proceed on a nomination if a home-state Senator expresses opposition [6]. Positions subject to senatorial courtesy include U.S. attorneys, U.S. marshals, and U.S. district judges.

## RECEIPT AND REFERRAL

The President customarily sends nomination messages to the Senate in writing. Once received, nominations are numbered by the executive clerk and read on the floor. The clerk actually assigns numbers to the presidential messages, not to individual nominations, so a message listing several nominations would receive a single number. Except by unanimous consent, the Senate cannot vote on nominations the day they are received, and most are referred immediately to committees.

Senate Rule XXXI provides that nominations shall be referred to appropriate committees "unless otherwise ordered." In a few instances, by unanimous consent, the Senate has confirmed nominations without referral to a committee, particularly when the nominee is a current or former Senator. Formally the presiding officer, but administratively the executive clerk's office, refers the nominations to committees according to the Senate's rules and precedents.

The Senate rule concerning committee jurisdictions (Rule XXV) broadly defines issue areas for committees, and the same jurisdictional statements generally apply to nominations as well as legislation [7]. An executive department nomination can be expected to be referred to the committee with jurisdiction over legislation concerning that department or to the committee that handled the legislation creating the position. In some instances, the committee of jurisdiction for a nomination has been set in statute [8].

The number of nominations referred to various committees differs considerably. The Committee on Armed Services, which handles all military appointments and promotions, receives the most. The two other committees with major confirmation responsibilities are the Committee on Judiciary, with jurisdiction over the confirmation of judges, U.S. attorneys, and U.S. marshals, and the Committee on Foreign Relations, which considers ambassadorial and other diplomatic appointments.

Occasionally, nominations are referred to more than one committee, either jointly or sequentially. A joint referral might occur when two committees each have a claim to a nomination. Both committees must report on the nomination before the whole Senate can act on it, unless the Senate discharges one or both committees. If two committees have unequal jurisdictional claims, then the nomination is more likely to be sequentially referred. In this case, the first committee must report the nomination before it is sequentially referred to the second committee. The second referral often is subject to a requirement that the committee report within a certain number of days. Typically, nominations are jointly or sequentially referred by unanimous consent. Sometimes the unanimous consent agreement applies to all future nominations to a position or category of positions [9]

## COMMITTEE PROCEDURES

### Written Rules

Most Senate committees that consider nominations have written rules concerning the process. Although committee rules vary, most contain standards concerning information to be gathered from a nominee. Many committees expect a biographical resumé and some kind of a financial statement listing assets and liabilities. Some specify the terms under which financial statements will or will not be made public.

Committee rules also frequently contain timetables outlining the minimum layover required between committee actions. A common timing provision is a requirement that nominations be held for one or two weeks before the committee proceeds to a hearing or a vote, permitting Senators time to review a nomination before committee consideration. Other committee rules specifically mandate a delay between steps of the process, such as the receipt of pre-hearing information and the date of the hearing, or the distribution of hearing transcripts and the committee vote on the nomination.

Some of the written rules also contain provisions for the rules to be waived by majority vote, by unanimous consent, or by the chair and the ranking minority member [10].

### Investigations

Committees often gather and review information about a nominee either before or instead of a formal hearing. Because the executive branch acts first in selecting a nominee, congressional committees are sometimes able to rely partially on any field investigations and reports conducted by the Federal Bureau of Investigation (FBI). Records of FBI investigations are provided only to the White House, although a report or a summary of a report may be shared, with the President's authorization, with Senators on the relevant committee. The practices of the committees with regard to FBI materials vary. Some rarely if ever request them. On other committees, the chair and ranking member review any FBI report or summary, but on some committees these materials are available to any Senator upon request. Committee staff usually do not review FBI materials.

Almost all nominees are also asked by the Office of the Counsel to the President to complete an "Executive Personnel Financial Disclosure Report, SF-278," which is reviewed and certified by the relevant agency as well as the Director of the Office of Government Ethics. The documents are then forwarded to the relevant committee, along with opinion letters from ethics officers in the relevant agency and the director of the Office of Government Ethics. In contrast to FBI reports, financial disclosure forms are made public. All committees review financial disclosure reports and some make them available in committee offices to Members, staff, and the public.

To varying degrees, committees also conduct their own information-gathering exercises. Most committees have their own financial disclosure and personal background forms that a nominee must complete. Some committees, after reviewing responses to their standard questionnaire, might ask a nominee to complete a second questionnaire. Committees frequently require that written responses to these questionnaires be submitted before a hearing is scheduled. The Committee on the Judiciary sends form letters, sometimes called "blue slips," to Senators from a nominee's home state to determine whether they support the nomination. The Committee on the Judiciary also has its own investigative staff. The Committee on Rules and Administration handles relatively few nominations and conducts its own investigations, sometimes with the assistance of the FBI or the General Accountability Office (GAO).

It is not unusual for nominees to meet with committee staff prior to a hearing. High-level nominees may meet privately with Senators. Generally speaking, these meetings, sometimes initiated by the nominee, serve basically to acquaint the nominee with the Members and committee staff, and vice versa. They occasionally address substantive matters as well. A nominee also might meet with the committee's chief counsel to discuss the financial disclosure report and any potential conflict-of-interest issues.

## Hearings

Approximately half of all civilian appointees are confirmed without a hearing.11 All committees that receive nominations do hold hearings on some nominations, and the likelihood of hearings varies with the importance of the position and the workload of the committee. The Committee on the Judiciary, for example, which receives a large number of nominations, does not usually hold hearings for U.S. attorneys, U.S. marshals, or members of part-time commissions. The Committee on Agriculture, Nutrition, and Forestry and the Committee on Energy and Natural Resources, on the other hand, typically hold hearings on most nominations that are referred to them. Committees often combine related nominations into a single hearing.

The length and nature of hearings varies. One or both home-state Senators will often introduce a nominee. The nominee typically testifies at the hearing, and occasionally the committee will invite other witnesses, including Members of the House of Representatives, to testify as well. Some hearings function as routine welcomes, while others are directed at influencing the policy program of an appointee. In addition to policy views, hearings might address the nominee's qualifications and potential conflicts of interest. Senators also might take the opportunity to ask questions of particular concern to them or their constituents.

Committees sometimes send questions to nominees in advance of a hearing and ask for written responses. Nominees also might be asked to respond in writing to additional questions after a hearing. Especially for high-level positions, the nomination hearing may be only the first of many times an individual will be asked to testify before a committee. Therefore, the committee often gains a commitment from the nominee to be cooperative in future oversight activities of the committee [12].

Hearings, under Senate Rule XXVI, are open to the public unless closed by majority vote for one of the reasons specified in the rule. Witness testimony is sometimes made available online through the website of the relevant committee and also through several commercial services, including Congressional Quarterly and Lexis-Nexis. Most committees print the hearings, although no rule requires it. The number of Senators necessary to constitute a quorum for the purpose of taking testimony varies from committee to committee, but it is usually smaller than a majority of the membership [13].

## Reporting

A committee considering a nomination has four options. It may report the nomination to the Senate favorably, unfavorably, or without recommendation, or it may choose to take no action at all. It is more common for a committee to fail to take action on a nomination than to report unfavorably. Committees occasionally report a nomination favorably, subject to the commitment of the nominee to testify before a Senate committee. Sometimes, committees choose to report a nomination without recommendation. Even if a majority of Senators on a committee do not agree that a nomination should be reported favorably, a majority might agree to report a nomination without a recommendation in order to permit a vote by the whole Senate. It is rare for the full Senate to consider a nomination if a committee chooses not to report it and the committee is not discharged by unanimous consent. The practice of discharging a committee of the consideration of a nomination is discussed below.

The timing of a vote to report a nomination varies in accordance with committee rules and practice. Most committees do not vote to report a nomination on the same day that they hold a hearing, but instead wait until the next meeting of the committee. Senate Rule XXVI, clause 7(a)(1) requires that a quorum for making a recommendation on a nomination consist of a majority of the membership of the committee. In most cases, the number of Senators necessary to constitute a quorum for making a recommendation on a nomination to the Senate is the same that the committee requires for reporting a measure. Every committee reports a majority of nominations favorably.

Most of the time, committees do not formally present reports on nominations on the floor of the Senate. Instead, a Senator, typically the committee chair, informs the legislative clerk stationed at the desk of the committee's decision. The executive clerk then arranges for the nomination to be printed in the Congressional Record and placed on the Executive Calendar. If a report were presented on the floor, it would have to be done in executive session. Executive session and the Executive Calendar will be discussed in the next section. According to Senate Rule XXXI, the Senate cannot vote on a nomination the same day it is reported except by unanimous consent [14].

Although very few nominations proceed without the support of a committee, chamber rules make it possible for the full Senate to consider a nomination a committee does not report. Technically, Senate Rule XVII permits any Senator to submit a motion or resolution that a committee be discharged from the consideration of a subject referred to it. A motion to discharge a committee from the consideration of a nomination is, like all business concerning nominations, in order only in executive session [15]. If there is an objection to the motion to discharge, it must lie over until the next executive session on another day. It is fairly common for committees to be discharged from noncontroversial nominations by unanimous consent, often with the support of the committee, as a means of simplifying the process. It is far less common for Senators to attempt to discharge a committee from a nomination by motion or resolution [16].

# FLOOR PROCEDURES

The Senate handles executive business, which includes both nominations and treaties, separately from its legislative business. All nominations reported from committee, regardless of whether they were reported favorably, unfavorably, or without recommendation, are listed on the Executive Calendar, a separate document from the Calendar of Business, which lists pending bills and resolutions. Usually, the majority leader schedules the consideration of nominations on the calendar. Nominations are considered in executive session, a parliamentary form of the Senate in session that has its own journal and, to some extent, its own rules of procedure.

## Executive Calendar

After a committee reports a nomination or is discharged from considering it, the nomination is assigned a number by the executive clerk and placed on the Executive Calendar. The list of nominations in the Executive Calendar includes basic information such as the name and office of the nominee, the name of the previous holder of the office, and whether the committee reported the nomination favorably, unfavorably, or without recommendation. Long lists of routine nominations are printed in the Congressional Record and identified only by a short title in the Executive Calendar, such as "Foreign Service nominations (84) beginning John F. Aloia, and ending Paul G. Churchill." In addition to reported nominations and treaties, the Executive Calendar contains the text of any unanimous consent agreements concerning executive business.

The Executive Calendar is distributed to Senate personal offices and committee offices when there is business on it. It is also available to congressional personnel online by following the link to legislative and executive calendars on the website of the Legislative Information System of the U.S. Congress http://www.congress.gov/.

## Executive Session

Business on the Executive Calendar, which consists of nominations and treaties, is considered in executive session. In contrast, all measures and matters associated with lawmaking are considered in legislative session. Until 1929 executive sessions were also closed to the public, but now they are open unless ordered otherwise by the Senate.

The Senate usually begins the day in legislative session and enters executive session either by a non-debatable motion or, far more often, by unanimous consent. Only if the Senate adjourned or recessed while in executive session would the next meeting automatically open in executive session. The motion to go into executive session can be offered at any time, is not debatable, and cannot be laid upon the table.

All business concerning nominations, including seemingly routine matters such as requests for joint referral or motions to print hearings, must be done in executive session. In practice, Senators often make such motions or unanimous consent requests "as if in executive session." These usually brief proceedings during a legislative session do not constitute an official executive session. In addition, at the start of each Congress, the Senate adopts a standing order, by unanimous consent, that allows the Senate to receive nominations from the President and for them to be referred to committees even on days when the Senate does not meet in executive session.

## Taking up a Nomination

If the Senate simply resolves into executive session, the business immediately pending is the first item on the Executive Calendar. A motion to proceed to another matter on the calendar would be debatable and subject to a filibuster.

In practice, the Senate expedites the process by specifying the business to be considered as part of the motion or unanimous consent request to go into executive session. The majority leader, by custom, effectively determines when or whether a nomination will be called up for consideration. For example, the majority leader may move or ask unanimous consent to "immediately proceed to executive session to consider the following nomination on the executive calendar.... " By precedent, the motion to go into executive session to take up a specified nomination is not debatable [17]. The nomination itself, however, is debatable.

It is not in order for a Senator to move to consider a nomination that is not on the calendar, and, except by unanimous consent, a nomination on the calendar cannot be taken up until it has been on the calendar at least one day (Rule XXXI, clause 1). In other words, a nomination reported and placed on the calendar on a Monday can be considered on Tuesday, even if it is the same legislative day [18].

## Holds

A hold is a request by a Senator to his or her party leader to prevent or delay action on a nomination or a bill. Holds are not mentioned in the rules or precedents of the Senate, and they are enforced only through the agenda decisions of party leaders. A recent directive of the Senate aims to ensure that any Senator who places a hold on any matter (including a nomination) make public his or her objection to the matter [19].

The effectiveness of a hold ultimately is grounded in the power of the Senator placing the hold to filibuster the nomination and the difficulty of invoking cloture. The rules governing cloture in relation to nominations are discussed in a later section of this report. In another sense, however, holds are connected to the Senate traditions of mutual deference, since they may have originated as requests for more time to examine a pending nomination or bill.

Senators place holds on nominations for a number of reasons. One common purpose is to give a Senator more time to review a nomination or to consult with the nominee. Senators may also place holds because they disagree with the policy positions of the nominee. Senators have also admitted to using holds in order to gain concessions from the executive branch on matters not directly related to the nomination. Depending on the timing of the hold and the support for the nomination, a hold can kill a nomination by preventing it from ever coming to the Senate floor.

## Consideration and Disposition

The question before the Senate when a nomination is taken up is "will the Senate advise and consent to this nomination?" The Senate can approve, reject, or recommit a nomination.

Most nominations are brought up by unanimous consent and approved without objection; routine nominations often are called up and approved all together, or en bloc. A small proportion of nominations, generally to higher-level positions, can be controversial. When there is debate on a nomination, the chair of the committee usually makes an opening speech. For positions within a state, Senators from the state may wish to speak on the nominee, particularly if they were involved in the selection process. While floor debate is rarely lengthy, there are no time limits except when conducted under cloture or a unanimous consent agreement [20]

A majority of Senators present and voting, a quorum being present, is required to approve a nomination. Because nominations are vulnerable to filibusters, however, stronger support may be necessary in order to invoke cloture, as discussed further below. The majority leader is unlikely to bring a nomination to the floor unless it is expected to be approved.

After the Senate acts on a nomination, the secretary of the Senate attests to a resolution of confirmation or disapproval and transmits it to the White House.

### Recommital

In addition to approving and rejecting a nomination, the Senate has the option of sending a nomination back to a committee for further consideration. Although infrequently used, the motion to recommit is available and may allow a panel to reconsider its recommendation when information concerning a nominee comes to light after the committee has reported to the full Senate. The motion to recommit is debatable, and so may be subjected to a filibuster.

Nominations recommitted may be re-reported and have the same status as when originally reported. If not re-reported, however, the Senate will be unable to vote on recommitted nominations, unless the committee is discharged. The Senate may vote to recommit a nomination with instructions to re-report, perhaps by a set date or after gathering more information on the nomination.

A motion to recommit a nomination is not in order if a unanimous consent agreement to vote on the confirmation at a specified hour is in effect. Furthermore, groups of nominations cannot be recommitted without unanimous consent.

### *Reconsideration*

According to Senate Rule XXXI, any Senator who voted with the majority has the option of moving to reconsider a vote on the nomination. The motion to reconsider is in order on the day of the vote or the next two days the Senate meets in executive session. The motion is made in executive session or, by unanimous consent, "as in executive session." Only one motion to reconsider is in order on each nomination. Often, the motion to reconsider is laid upon the table, by unanimous consent, shortly after the vote on the nomination. This action prevents any subsequent attempt to reconsider.

Senate Rule XXXI requires that the secretary of the Senate wait until the time for moving to reconsider has expired before sending notice to the President; in practice, however, notice is usually sent immediately, permitted by unanimous consent. If a nomination has already been sent to the President, a motion to reconsider is accompanied by a request to the President to return the nomination. If the President does not comply with the request, the Senate cannot reconsider the nomination [21].

## Cloture

In most instances, the Senate imposes no limitation on floor debate on a nomination. As many Senators who are interested can speak on a nomination for as long as they want. If necessary, however, Senate Rule XXII provides a means to bring debate on a nomination to a close.

Rule XXII, known as the cloture rule, applies to any debatable question including bills, resolutions, amendments, conference reports, nominations, and various debatable motions. The rule operates the same way on nominations as it does on legislation and other debatable questions. Because the motion to go into executive session and take up a specific nomination is not debatable, however, it is not necessary, as it may be in the case of legislation, to file cloture both on a motion to take up a matter and on the matter itself.

Under the terms of Rule XXII, at least 16 Senators sign a cloture motion, also called a cloture petition, to end debate on a pending nomination. The motion proposed is "to bring to a close the debate upon [the pending nomination]." A Senator can interrupt a Senator who is speaking to present a cloture motion. Cloture may only be moved on a question that is pending before the Senate; therefore, absent unanimous consent, the Senate must be in executive session and considering the nomination when the motion is filed. After the clerk reads the motion, the Senate returns to the business it was considering before the presentation of the petition.

Unless a unanimous consent agreement provides otherwise, the Senate does not vote on the cloture motion until the second day after the day it is presented; if the motion was presented on a Monday, the Senate would act on it on Wednesday. One hour after the Senate has convened on the day the petition "ripened," the presiding officer can interrupt the proceedings during an executive session to present a cloture motion for a vote. If the Senate is in legislative session when the time arrives for voting on the cloture motion, it proceeds into executive session prior to taking action on the cloture petition.

According to Rule XXII, the presiding officer first directs the clerk to call the roll to ascertain that a quorum is present, although this requirement is often waived by unanimous consent. Senators then vote either yea or nay on the question: "Is it the sense of the Senate that the debate shall be brought to a close?" It takes three-fifths of the Senate, or 60 Senators if there are no vacancies, to invoke cloture on a nomination.

Once cloture is invoked, there can be a maximum of 30 hours of consideration, including debate and time consumed by quorum calls, parliamentary inquiries, and all other proceedings [22]

Although Senate rules have permitted cloture to be moved on nominations since 1949, cloture was not sought on a judicial nomination until 1968 or on an executive branch nomination until 1980 [23].

## NOMINATIONS RETURNED TO THE PRESIDENT

Nominations that are not confirmed or rejected are returned to the President at the end of a session or when the Senate adjourns or recesses for more than 30 days (Senate Rule XXXI, paragraph 6).

If the President still wants a nominee considered, he must submit a new nomination to the Senate. The Senate can, however, waive this rule by unanimous consent, and it often does to allow nominations to remain "in status quo" between the first and second sessions of a Congress. The majority leader or his designee also may exempt specific nominees by name from the unanimous consent agreement, allowing them to be returned during the recess or adjournment.

## RECESS APPOINTMENTS

The Constitution, in Article II, Section 2, grants the President the authority to fill temporarily vacancies that "may happen during the Recess of the Senate." These appointments do not require the advice and consent of the Senate; the appointees temporarily fill the vacancies without Senate confirmation. In most cases, recess appointees have also been nominated to the positions to which they were appointed. Furthermore, when a recess appointment is made, the President usually submits a new nomination to the Senate in order to comply with a provision of law affecting the pay of recess appointees (5 U.S.C. 5503(a)). Recess appointments have sometimes been controversial and have occasionally led to inter-branch conflict [24]

## RELATED CRS REPORTS

CRS Report RL32684, *Changing Senate Rules or Procedures: The "Constitutional" or "Nuclear" Option*, by Betsy Palmer.

CRS Report RL32102, *Constitutionality of a Senate Filibuster of a Judicial Nomination*, by Todd B. Tatelman.

CRS Report RL32878, *Cloture Attempts on Nominations*, by Richard S. Beth and Betsy Palmer.

CRS Report RL31948, *Evolution of the Senate's Role in the Nomination and Confirmation Process: A Brief History*, by Betsy Palmer.

CRS Report RL32843, *"Entrenchment" of Senate Procedure and the "Nuclear Option" for Change: Possible Proceedings and Their Implications*, by Richard S. Beth.

CRS Report RL33953, *Nominations to Article III Lower Courts by President George W. Bush During the 110th Congress*, by Denis Steven Rutkus, Susan Navarro Smelcer, and Maureen Bearden.

CRS Report 98-510, *Judicial Nominations by President Clinton During the 103rd-106th Congresses*, by Denis Steven Rutkus.

CRS Report RL30959, *Presidential Appointee Positions Requiring Senate Confirmation and Committees Handling Nominations*, by Henry B. Hogue, Maureen Bearden, and Terrence L. Lisbeth.

CRS Report RL33783, *Presidential Appointments to Full-time Positions in Executive Departments During the 108th Congress, 2003-2004*, by Henry B. Hogue, Maureen Bearden, and Dana Ely.

CRS Report RL32742, *Presidential Appointments to Full-Time Positions on Regulatory and Other Collegial Boards and Commissions, 108th Congress*, by Henry B. Hogue et al.

CRS Report RL3 2906, *Presidential Appointments to Full-Time Positions in Independent and Other Agencies During the 108th Congress*, by Henry B. Hogue, Maureen Bearden, and Dana Ely.

CRS Report RL33009, *Recess Appointments: A Legal Overview*, by T. J. Halstead.

CRS Report RL333 10, *Recess Appointments Made by President George W. Bush*, by Henry B. Hogue and Maureen Bearden.

CRS Report RS21308, *Recess Appointments: Frequently Asked Questions*, by Henry B. Hogue.

CRS Report RL33 118, *Speed of Presidential and Senate Actions on Supreme Court Nominations, 1900-2006*, by R. Sam Garrett, Denis Steven Rutkus, and Curtis W. Copeland.

CRS Report RL3 1989, *Supreme Court Appointment Process: Roles of the President, Judiciary Committee, and Senate*, by Denis Steven Rutkus.

CRS Report RL33225, *Supreme Court Nominations, 1789 - 2006: Actions by the Senate, the Judiciary Committee, and the President*, by Denis Steven Rutkus and Maureen Bearden.

CRS Report RL33247, *Supreme Court Nominations: Senate Floor Procedure and Practice, 1789- 2006*, by Richard S. Beth and Betsy Palmer.

CRS Report RL3 1171, *Supreme Court Nominations Not Confirmed*, 1789-2008, by Henry B. Hogue.

CRS Report RL3 1989, *Supreme Court Appointment Process: Roles of the President, Judiciary Committee, and Senate*, by Denis Steven Rutkus.

CRS Report RS2 1412, *Temporarily Filling Presidentially Appointed, Senate-Confirmed Positions*, by Henry B. Hogue.

CRS Report RL3 1868, *U.S. Circuit and District Court Nominations by President George W. Bush During the 107th-109th Congresses*, by Denis Steven Rutkus, Maureen Bearden, and Kevin M. Scott.

CRS Report R40470, *U.S. Circuit and District Court Nominations: Senate Rejections and Committee Votes Other Than to Report Favorably, 1939-2009*, by Denis Steven Rutkus and Susan Navarro Smelcer.

# REFERENCES

[1] A list of related CRS products is provided at the end of this report.

[2] For more information on the consideration of Supreme Court nominations, see CRS Report RL33225, *Supreme Court Nominations, 1789 - 2006: Actions by the Senate, the Judiciary Committee, and the President*, by Denis Steven Rutkus and Maureen Bearden; CRS Report RL33247, *Supreme Court Nominations: Senate Floor Procedure and Practice, 1789-2006*, by Richard S. Beth and Betsy Palmer; CRS Report RL3 1989, *Supreme Court Appointment Process: Roles of the President, Judiciary Committee, and Senate*, by Denis Steven Rutkus; and CRS Report RL33 118, *Speed of Presidential and Senate Actions on Supreme Court Nominations, 1900-2006*, by R. Sam Garrett, Denis Steven Rutkus, and Curtis W. Copeland.

[3] CRS Report 93-464, *Senate Action on Nominations to Policy Positions in the Executive Branch, 1981-1992*, by Rogelio Garcia. (For a copy of this archived CRS report, contact Elizabeth Rybicki).

[4] Joseph P. Harris, *The Advice and Consent of the Senate* (New York: Greenwood Press Publishers, 1968), p. 2; Richard Allan Baker, "Legislative Power Over Appointments and Confirmations," in Joel Silbey, ed., *Encyclopedia of the American Legislative System* (New York: C. Scribner's Sons, 1994), vol. 3, p. 1616.

[5] "Report of the Task Force on the Confirmation Process," *Congressional Record*, vol. 138 (February 4, 1992), pp. 1348-13 52.

[6] For more on senatorial courtesy and its history, see CRS Report RL3 1948, *Evolution of the Senate's Role in the Nomination and Confirmation Process: A Brief History*, by Betsy Palmer.

[7] For a list of appointee positions requiring Senate confirmation and the committees to which they are referred as of October 27, 2003, see CRS Report RL30959, *Presidential Appointee Positions Requiring Senate Confirmation and Committees Handling Nominations*, by Henry B. Hogue, Maureen Bearden, and Terrence L. Lisbeth.

[8] For example, nominations of two members of the Thrift Depositor Protection Oversight Board are referred to the Committee on Banking, Housing, and Urban Affairs (12 U.S. C. 1441a). Nominations of the United States trade representative and deputy United States trade representative are referred to the Committee on Finance (19 U.S.C. 2171).

[9] See, for example, "Joint Referral of Department of Energy Nominations," *Congressional Record*, vol. 136 (June 28, 1990), pp. 16573-16574.

[10] U.S. Congress, Senate Committee on Rules and Administration, *Authority and Rules of Senate Committees*, 2007- 2008, 110th Cong., 1st sess., S.Doc. 110-10 (Washington: GPO, 2007).

[11] The estimate excludes military appointees as well as civilian appointees usually submitted on lists to the Senate. Civilian nominations usually submitted on lists include appointments to, and promotions in, the Coast Guard, Foreign Service, National Oceanic and Atmospheric Administration, and Public Health Service.

[12] Roger H. Davidson and Walter J. Oleszek, *Congress and Its Members*, 9th ed. (Washington: CQ Press, 2004), p. 324.

[13] For more details concerning hearings, see CRS Report 98-3 37, *Senate Committee Hearings: Scheduling and Notification*, by Betsy Palmer, and CRS Report 98-3 92, *Senate Committee Hearings: Witness Testimony*, by Betsy Palmer.

[14] The reference in the rule to a "day" refers to a calendar day, not a legislative day. See Floyd M. Riddick and Alan S. Frumin, *Riddick's Senate Procedure: Precedents and Practices*, 101st Cong., 2nd sess., S.Doc. 101-28 (Washington: GPO, 1992), p. 943. A legislative day begins the first time the Senate meets after an adjournment and ends with the Senate adjourns again. A legislative day is not necessarily a calendar day because the Senate does not always adjourn prior to the end of a calendar day.

[15] Floyd M. Riddick and Alan S. Frumin, *Riddick's Senate Procedure: Precedents and Practices*, 101st Cong., 2nd sess., S. Doc. 101-28 (Washington: GPO, 1992), p. 944.

[16] For example, in 2003, then-Majority Leader Bill Frist submitted four resolutions to discharge the Judiciary Committee from further consideration of four U.S. Circuit Judge nominations. In each case, a Senator objected to immediate consideration of the resolution, and all four resolutions were placed on the Executive Calendar. No further action was taken the resolutions to discharge. See "Resolutions Placed on the Executive Calendar," *Congressional Record*, vol. 149 (July 7, 2003), pp. 16949-16950.

[17] Floyd M. Riddick and Alan S. Frumin, *Riddick's Senate Procedure,* 101st Cong., 2nd sess., S. Doc. 101-28 (Washington: GPO, 1992), p. 941.

[18] The reference in Senate Rule XXXI, clause 1 to a "day" refers to a calendar day, not a legislative day. See Floyd M. Riddick and Alan S. Frumin, *Riddick's Senate Procedure: Precedents and Practices*, 101st Cong., 2nd sess., S.Doc. 101- 28 (Washington: GPO, 1992), p. 943. A legislative day begins the first time the Senate meets after an adjournment and ends with the Senate adjourns again. A legislative day is not necessarily a calendar day because the Senate does not always adjourn prior to the end of a calendar day.

[19] For more information on the directive of the Senate concerning holds, see CRS Report RL34255, *Senate Policy on "Holds": Action in the 110th Congress*, coordinated by Walter J. Oleszek. For more information concerning the history, types, and potency of holds, see CRS Report RL3 1685, *Proposals to Reform "Holds" in the Senate*, by Walter J. Oleszek.

[20] In the 109th Congress, some Senators proposed changing Senate procedures for limiting debate on nominations. Procedures were not changed, but in response to the effort a bipartisan group of Senators entered into a "Memorandum of Understanding on Judicial Nominations" on May 23, 2005. The memorandum did not change the procedures of the Senate described in this report; it was a "commitment" that "nominees should only be filibustered under extraordinary circumstances" and an agreement "to oppose ... any amendment to or any interpretation of the Rules of the Senate that would force a vote on a judicial nomination by means other than unanimous consent or Rule XXII" [the cloture rule]. For more information on this bipartisan agreement, see CRS Report

RS22208, *The "Memorandum of Understanding": A Senate Compromise on Judicial Filibusters*, by Walter J. Oleszek. For more information on the proposed procedural change, see CRS Report RL32843, *"Entrenchment" of Senate Procedure and the "Nuclear Option" for Change: Possible Proceedings and Their Implications*, by Richard S. Beth.

[21] Floyd M. Riddick and Alan S. Frumin, *Riddick's Senate Procedure,* 101st Cong., 2nd sess., S. Doc. 10 1-28 (Washington: GPO, 1992), p. 948.

[22] For full details on the cloture process, see CRS Report RL3 03 60, *Filibusters and Cloture in the Senate*, by Richard S. Beth and Stanley Bach.

[23] For data on the nominations subjected to cloture attempts through 2008 , see CRS Report RL32878, *Cloture Attempts on Nominations*, by Richard S. Beth and Betsy Palmer.

[24] For more information on recess appointments, see CRS Report RS2 1308, *Recess Appointments: Frequently Asked Questions*, by Henry B. Hogue; CRS Report RL33009, *Recess Appointments: A Legal Overview*, by T. J. Halstead; and CRS Report RL333 10, *Recess Appointments Made by President George W. Bush*, by Henry B. Hogue and Maureen Bearden.

In: U.S. Political Programs: Functions and Assessments     ISBN: 978-1-61209-448-9
Editors: Julianna M. Moretti and Karen J. Chordstron   © 2011 Nova Science Publishers, Inc.

Chapter 2

# THE MANHATTAN PROJECT, THE APOLLO PROGRAM AND FEDERAL ENERGY TECHNOLOGY R&D PROGRAMS: A COMPARATIVE ANALYSIS[*]

*Deborah D. Stine*

## ABSTRACT

Some policymakers have concluded that the energy challenges facing the United States are so critical that a concentrated investment in energy research and development (R&D) should be undertaken. The Manhattan project, which produced the atomic bomb, and the Apollo program, which landed American men on the moon, have been cited as examples of the success such R&D investments can yield. Investment in federal energy technology R&D programs of the 1970s, in response to two energy crises, have generally been viewed as less successful than the earlier two efforts. This report compares and contrasts the three initiatives.

In 2008 dollars, the cumulative cost of the Manhattan project over 5 fiscal years was approximately $22 billion; of the Apollo program over 14 fiscal years, approximately $98 billion; of post-oil shock energy R&D efforts over 35 fiscal years, $118 billion. A measure of the nation's commitments to the programs is their relative shares of the federal outlays during the years of peak funding: for the Manhattan program, the peak year funding was 1% of federal outlays; for the Apollo program, 2.2%; and for energy technology R&D programs, 0.5%. Another measure of the commitment is their relative shares of the nation's gross domestic product (GDP) during the peak years of funding: for the Manhattan project and the Apollo program, the peak year funding reached 0.4% of GDP, and for the energy technology R&D programs, 0.1%.

Besides funding, several criteria might be used to compare these three initiatives including perception of the program or threat, goal clarity, and the customer of the technology being developed. By these criteria, while the Manhattan project and the Apollo program may provide some useful analogies for thinking about an energy

---

[*] This is an edited, reformatted and augmented edition of a United States Congressional Research Service publication, CRS Report RL34645, dated June 30, 2009.

technology R&D initiative, there are fundamental differences between the forces that drove these historical R&D success stories and the forces driving energy technology R&D today.

Critical differences include (1) the ability to transform the program or threat into a concrete goal, and (2) the use to which the technology would be put. On the issue of goal setting, for the Manhattan project, the response to the threat of enemy development of a nuclear bomb was the goal to construct a bomb; for the Apollo program, the threat of Soviet space dominance was translated into a specific goal of landing on the moon. For energy, the response to the problems of insecure oil sources and high prices has resulted in multiple, sometimes conflicting, goals. Regarding use, both the Manhattan project and the Apollo program goals pointed to technologies primarily for governmental use with little concern about their environmental impact; for energy, in contrast, the hoped-for outcome depends on commercial viability and mitigation of environmental impacts from energy use.

Although the Manhattan project and the Apollo program may provide some useful analogies for funding, these differences may limit their utility regarding energy policy. Rather, energy technology R&D has been driven by at least three not always commensurate goals—resource and technological diversity, commercial viability, and environmental protection—which were not goals of the historical programs.

Some policymakers have concluded that the energy challenges facing the United States are so critical that a concentrated investment in energy research and development (R&D) should be undertaken. The Manhattan project, which produced the atomic bomb, and the Apollo program, which landed American men on the moon, have been cited as examples of the success such R&D investments can yield.

Investment in federal energy technology R&D programs of the 1970s, in response to two energy crises, have generally been viewed as less successful than the earlier two efforts. This report compares and contrasts the goals of, and the investments in, the three initiatives, which may provide useful insights for Congress as it assesses and debates the nation's energy policy.

# THE MANHATTAN PROJECT

The Manhattan project took place from 1942 to 1946 [1]. Beginning in 1939, some key scientists expressed concern that Germany might be building an atomic weapon and proposed that the United States accelerate atomic research in response. Following the Pearl Harbor attack in December 1941, the United States entered World War II. In January 1942, President Franklin D. Roosevelt gave secret, tentative approval for the development of an atomic bomb. The Army Corps of Engineers was assigned the task and set up the Manhattan Engineer District to manage the project. A bomb research and design laboratory was built at Los Alamos, New Mexico. Due to uncertainties regarding production effectiveness, two possible fuels for the reactors were produced with uranium enrichment facilities at Oak Ridge, Tennessee, and plutonium production facilities at Hanford, Washington. In December 1942, Roosevelt gave final approval to construct a nuclear bomb. A bomb using plutonium as fuel was successfully tested south of Los Alamos in July 1945. In August 1945, President Truman decided to use the bomb against Japan at two locations. Japan surrendered a few days after the second bomb attack. At that point, the Manhattan project was deemed to have fulfilled its mission, although some additional nuclear weapons were still assembled. In 1946, the civilian

Atomic Energy Commission was established to manage the nation's future atomic activities, and the Manhattan project officially ended.

According to one estimate, the Manhattan project cost $2.2 billion from 1942 to 1946 ($22 billion in 2008 dollars), which is much greater than the original cost and time estimate of approximately $148 million for 1942 to 1 944 [2] General Leslie Groves, who managed the Manhattan project, has written that Members of Congress who inquired about the project were discouraged by the Secretary of War from asking questions or visiting sites [3] After the project was under way for over a year, in February 1944, War Department officials received essentially a "blank check" for the project from Congressional leadership who "remained completely in the dark" about the Manhattan project, according to Groves and other experts [4].

## THE APOLLO PROGRAM

The Apollo program, FY1960 to FY1973, encompassed 17 missions, including six lunar landings [5]. NASA was created in response to the Soviet launch of Sputnik in 1958 and began operation in 1959 [6]. Although preliminary discussions regarding the Apollo program began in 1960, Congress did not decide to fund it until 1961 after the Soviet Union became the first nation to launch a human into space. The goals of the Apollo program were

- To land Americans on the Moon and return them safely to Earth;
- To establish the technology to meet other national interests in space;
- To achieve preeminence in space for the United States;
- To carry out a program of scientific exploration of the Moon; and
- To develop man's capability to work in the lunar environment [7]

The program included a three-part spacecraft to take two astronauts to the Moon surface, support them while on the Moon, and return them to Earth [8]. Saturn rockets were used to launch this equipment. In July 1969, Apollo 11 achieved the goal of landing Americans on the Moon and returning them safely to Earth. The last lunar landing took place in December 1972.

The Apollo program was only one part of NASA's activities during this period. NASA's peak funding during the Apollo program occurred in FY1966 when its total funding was $4.5 billion (in current dollars), of which $3.0 billion went to the Apollo program [9]. According to NASA, the total cost of the Apollo program for FY1960-FY1973 was $19.4 billion ($97.9 billion in 2008 dollars) [10]. The activities with the greatest cost were the Saturn V rockets ($6.4 billion in current dollars) followed by the Command and Service Modules ($3.7 billion), the Lunar Modules ($2.2 billion), and Manned Space Flight Operations ($1.6 billion).

## ENERGY TECHNOLOGY RESEARCH AND DEVELOPMENT

The Arab oil embargo of 1973 (the "first" energy crisis) put energy policy on the national "agenda." At that time, Americans began to experience rapidly rising prices for fuel and related goods and services [11]. Until then, energy R&D had been focused on the development of nuclear power under the Atomic Energy Commission (AEC). After the Manhattan project ended, Congress had established the AEC to manage both civilian and military projects in the Atomic Energy Act of 1946 (P.L. 79-585) [12]. In response to the energy crisis, Congress subsumed the AEC, including the Manhattan project facilities, and other energy programs, into the Energy Research and Development Administration (ERDA), which became the focus for federal energy technology R&D, and the Nuclear Regulatory Commission (NRC) as part of the Energy Reorganization Act of 1974 (P.L. 93-438) [13]

In the Department of Energy Organization Act of 1977 (P.L. 95-91), Congress decided to combine the activities of ERDA with approximately 50 other energy offices and programs in a new Department of Energy (DOE), which began operations on October 1, 1977 [14]. In 1979, the Iranian Revolution precipitated the "second" energy crisis that took place from 1978-1981. High oil prices and inflation lasted for several years. An ensuing recession curbed demand and oil prices fell markedly by 1986. The scale of funding for most of DOE's energy R&D programs dropped steadily during the 1980s (see Figure 1).

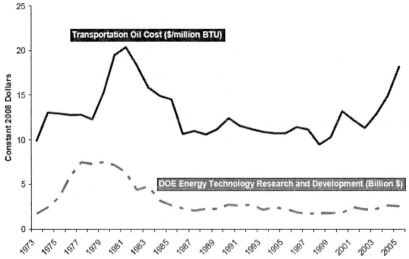

Source: Congressional Research Service. Transportation oil costs are from transportation/petroleum column of Table 3.4 Consumer Price Estimates for Energy by End-Use Sector, 1970-2005 in Energy Information Administration, Annual Energy Review 2007, Report No. DOE/EIA-0384(2007), Posted: June 23, 2008, at http://www.eia.doe.gov/aer/finan.html. DOE data is from CRS Report RS22858, Renewable Energy R&D Funding History: A Comparison with Funding for Nuclear Energy, Fossil Energy, and Energy Efficiency R&D, by Fred Sissine. Dollars for both transportation oil costs and DOE energy R&D were adjusted to 2008 dollars using the information from Bureau of Economic Analysis, Table 1.1.4. Price Indexes for Gross Domestic Product at http://www.bea.gov/
bea/dn/nipaweb/index.asp.

Figure 1. Comparison of Consumer Transportation Oil Cost and DOE Energy Technology R&D Funding, 1973-2005.

The large energy technology demonstration projects funded during the late 1970s and early 1980s were viewed by some as too elaborate and insufficiently linked to either existing energy research or the marketplace [15]. A well known example is the Synthetic Fuels Corporation (SFC) [16]. The goal of SFC was to support large-scale projects that industry was unwilling to support due to the technical, environmental, or financial uncertainties. The program ended in 1986 due to a combination of lower energy prices, environmental issues, lack of support by the Reagan Administration, and administrative challenges [17].

Oil prices rose substantially from 2004 to 2008, but funding for energy technology R&D has not so far increased as it did during the energy crisis of the late 1970s to early 1980s. However, the appropriations process for FY2009 and FY2010 has not yet been completed.

## COMPARATIVE ANALYSIS OF THE MANHATTAN PROJECT, THE APOLLO PROGRAM, AND FEDERAL ENERGY TECHNOLOGY R&D

A general understanding of driving forces of and funding histories for the Manhattan project and Apollo program, and a comparison of these two initiatives to Department of Energy (DOE) energy technology R&D programs, may provide useful insights for Congress as it assesses and determines the nation's energy R&D policy. Four criteria that might be used to compare these programs are funding, perception of threat, goal clarity, and technology customer. Each is discussed in more depth below.

### Funding

Table 1 provides a comparison of the total and annual average program costs for the Manhattan project, Apollo program, and federal energy technology R&D program since the first energy crisis. Annual average long-term (1974-2008) DOE energy technology R&D funding was approximately $3 billion (in 2008 constant dollars) as is the FY2008 budget and the FY2009 budget request.18 In comparison, the annual average funding (in 2008 constant dollars) for the Manhattan project was $4 billion and for the Apollo program and the DOE energy technology program at its peak (1975-1980) was $7 billion.

At the time of peak funding, the percentage of federal spending devoted to DOE energy technology R&D was half that of the Manhattan project, and one-fifth that of the Apollo program. From an overall economy standpoint, the percentage of the gross domestic product (GDP) spent on DOE energy technology R&D in the peak funding year was one-fourth that spent on either the Manhattan project or the Apollo program.

As shown in Figure 2, although cumulative funding for the DOE energy technology R&D program is greater than for the Manhattan project or the Apollo program, the annual funding for each of the historical programs was higher than that for energy technology R&D which occurred over a greater number of years.

This is an important distinction: the Manhattan project and the Apollo program were specific and distinct funding efforts whereas the national energy R&D effort has been ongoing over a longer period of time. In all three cases, a rapid increase in funding was followed by a rapid decline.

**Table 1. Cumulative and Annual Average Program Year Funding for the Manhattan Project, the Apollo Program, and DOE Energy Technology R&D Program**

| | Cumulative Funding (in billions of 2008 dollars) | No. of FY | Annual Average Funding Per Program Year (in billions of 2008 dollars) | Percent of Federal Outlays During Year of Peak Funding | Percent of GDP During Year of Peak Funding |
|---|---|---|---|---|---|
| The Manhattan Project (1942-1946) | $22 | 5 | $4 | 1.0 | 0.4 |
| The Apollo Program (1960-1973) | $98 | 14 | $7 | 2.2 | 0.4 |
| DOE Energy Technology Programs (1975-1980) | $40 | 6 | $7 | 0.5 | 0.1 |
| [Peak Funding] DOE Energy Technology Program (1974-2008) | $118 | 35 | $3 | 0.5 | 0.1 |
| [Long-Term Funding] | | | | | |

Source: Congressional Research Service. Manhattan Project data: Richard G. Hewlett and Oscar E. Anderson, Jr., A History of the United States Atomic Energy Commission: The New World,1939/1946,Volume I. Apollo program data: Richard Orloff, Apollo By The Numbers: A Statistical Reference, NASA SP-2000-4029, 2004 web update. DOE data: CRS Report RS22858, Renewable Energy R&D Funding History: A Comparison with Funding for Nuclear Energy, Fossil Energy, and Energy Efficiency R&D, by Fred Sissine. Federal Outlay and Gross Domestic Product (GDP) data: Office of Management and Budget, Historical Tables, Budget of the United States Government FY2009. Peak year of funding (in current dollars) for Manhattan project was 1946, for Apollo program, 1966, and for DOE Energy Technology R&D programs, 1980. The greatest annual funding (in constant dollars) for DOE energy technology programs took place from 1975-1980.

## Threat Perception

The Manhattan project and Apollo project were both responses to perceived threats, which compelled policymaker support for these initiatives. The Manhattan project took place during World War II. Although the public might have been unaware of the potential threat of Germany's use of nuclear weapons and the Manhattan project, the President and Members of Congress could feel confident about public support for the war effort of which the Manhattan project was a part. Similarly, the Apollo program took place during the Cold War with the Union of Soviet Socialist Republics (USSR). When the USSR launched the Sputnik satellite and first man into space, the U.S. public felt threatened by the potential that the USSR might take leadership in the development of space flight technology, and potentially greater control of outer space. President Jimmy Carter said that

> With the exception of preventing war, this [energy crisis] is the greatest challenge that our country will face during our lifetime ... our decision about energy will test the character of the American people and the ability of the President and the Congress to govern this Nation.
> This difficult effort will be the 'moral equivalent of war,' except that we will be uniting our efforts to build and not to destroy." [19]

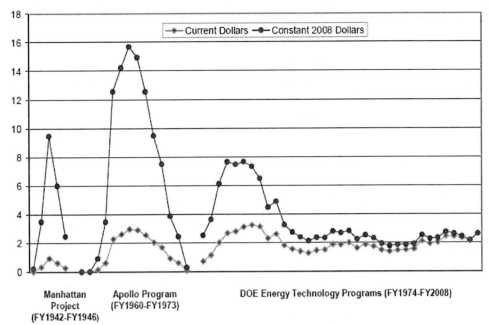

Source: Congressional Research Service. Manhattan Project data: Richard G. Hewlett and Oscar E. Anderson, Jr., A History of the United States Atomic Energy Commission: The New World, 1939/1946,Volume I. Apollo program data: Richard Orloff, Apollo By The Numbers: A Statistical Reference, NASA SP-2000-4029, 2004 web update. DOE data: CRS Report RS22858, Renewable Energy R&D Funding History: A Comparison with Funding for Nuclear Energy, Fossil Energy, and Energy Efficiency R&D, by Fred Sissine.

Figure 2. Annual Funding for Manhattan Project, Apollo Program, and DOE Energy Technology R&D Program.

The threat to which investment in energy technology R&D responds, however, is largely economic rather than military. In addition, the threat posed by climate change, which is related to energy consumption, will likely be gradual and long-term [20]

## Goal Clarity

Another issue is the degree to which there is clarity and consensus on the program goal. The Manhattan project had a clear and singular goal—the creation of a nuclear bomb. For the Apollo program, the goal was also clear and singular—land American astronauts on the moon and return them safely to Earth. In the case of energy technology R&D, however, the overall goal of clean, affordable, and reliable energy is multi-faceted. While "energy independence" has from time to time been a rallying cry, energy technology R&D has in fact, been driven by at least three not always commensurate goals: resource and technological diversity, commercial viability, and environmental protection. To help reduce the risk of dependence on a single energy source, diversity of resources and energy technologies have always been seen as a goal of the energy R&D program. Second, unlike the Manhattan project or the Apollo program, the DOE energy technology R&D program seeks ultimately to be commercially viable. Third, the energy R&D program must meet environmental goals, including reducing the impact of energy-related activities on land, water, air, and climate change.

## Technology Customer

Another comparison criterion is the customer for technologies that may result from the R&D. The government was the customer for both the Manhattan project and Apollo program. The private sector is the ultimate customer for any energy technology developed as a result of federal energy R&D programs. Therefore, the marketability of any technologies developed will be a key determinant of the degree to which the program is successful. Moreover, the inherent involvement of the private sector raises a number of issues related to the appropriateness of different government roles. Some believe that focusing R&D on one particular technology versus another may result in government, instead of the marketplace, picking "winners and losers." [21]. Some experts believe that the most important driver for private sector deployment or commercialization is not the need for new technologies, but regulation or economic incentives [22]/ Others, however, believe that without government support and intervention, the private sector is unlikely to conduct the R&D necessary to achieve the public goal of clean, affordable, and reliable energy, and that current technologies are insufficient to achieve this goal [23].

# IMPLICATIONS FOR CONGRESS

When the Manhattan project and the Apollo program are used as analogies for future DOE energy technology R&D, the following points may be important to consider:

- To be equivalent in annual average funding, DOE energy technology R&D funding would need to increase from approximately $3 billion in FY2008 to at least $4 billion per program year to match the Manhattan project funding, or $7 billion per program year to match Apollo program funding levels or DOE energy technology R&D funding at its peak. To be equivalent of peak year funding would require even greater increases. In terms of federal outlays, energy technology R&D funding would need to increase from 0.5% to 1% (Manhattan project) or 2.2 % (Apollo program) of federal outlays. As a percentage of GDP, this funding would need to increase from 0.1% to 0.4% of GDP (for both the Manhattan project and the Apollo program).
- Both the Manhattan project and the Apollo program had a singular and specific goal. For the Manhattan project, the response to the threat of enemy development of a nuclear bomb was the goal to construct a bomb; for the Apollo program, the threat of Soviet space dominance was translated into a specific goal of landing on the moon. For energy, however, the response to the problems of insecure oil sources and high prices has resulted in multiple, sometimes conflicting goals.
- Both the Manhattan project and the Apollo program goals pointed to technologies primarily for governmental use with little concern about their environmental impact;

for energy, in contrast, the hoped for outcome depends on commercial viability and mitigation of the environmental impacts of the energy technologies developed.

Although the Manhattan project and the Apollo program may provide some useful analogies for funding, these differences may limit their utility regarding energy policy. Rather, energy technology R&D has been driven by at least three not always commensurate goals—resource and technological diversity, commercial viability, and environmental protection—which were not goals of the historical programs.

## CONGRESSIONAL ACTIVITIES

The New Manhattan Project for Energy Independence (H.R. 513), a bill introduced in the House on January 14, 2009, would require the President to convene a summit to review the progress and promise of, the interrelationship of, and the additional funding needed to accelerate the progress of:

(a) developing alternative technology vehicles that are not more than 10% more expensive than comparable model year vehicles;

(b) developing and building energy efficient buildings that use no more than 50% of the energy of buildings of similar size and type;

(c) constructing a large scale solar thermal power plant or solar photovoltaic power plant capable of generating 300 megawatts or more at a cost of 10 cents or less per kilowatt-hour;

(d) developing and producing biofuel that does not exceed 105% of the cost for the energy equivalent of unleaded gasoline;

(e) developing and implementing a carbon capture and storage system for a large scale coal- burning power plant that does not increase operating costs more than 15% compared to a baseline design without carbon capture and storage while providing an estimated chance of carbon dioxide escape of no greater than 1% over 5,000 years;

(f) developing both a process to remediate radioactive waste so that it is not harmful for at least 5,000 years and a model that accounts for the effects of nuclear waste in that process; and

(g) developing a sustainable nuclear fusion reaction capable of providing a large-scale sustainable source of electricity for residential, commercial, or government entities.

The bill would also require the Secretary of Energy to implement a program to support such technologies; and competitively award cash prizes to advance the research, development, demonstration, and commercial application necessary to advance such technologies. In addition, the bill would establish a New Manhattan Project Commission on Energy Independence that would make recommendations to Congress as to the steps necessary to achieve 50% energy independence within 10 years and 100% energy independence within 20 years, as well as assessing the impact of foreign energy dependence on national security.

On June 26, 2009, a proposed amendment to replace the text of H.R. 2454 with this bill failed in the House 172-256.

# REFERENCES

[1]    U.S. Department of Energy, Office of History and Heritage Resources, "The Manhattan Project: An Interactive History," http://www.cfo.doe.gov/me70/manhattan/1939-1942.htm. F.G. Gosling, *The Manhattan Project: Making the Atomic Bomb*, January 1999 edition (Oak Ridge, TN: Department of Energy).

[2]    Richard G. Hewlett and Oscar E. Anderson, Jr., A *History of the United States Atomic Energy Commission: The New World, 1939/1946, Volume I,* (University Park, PA: The Pennsylvania State University Press, 1962). Appendix 2 provides the annual Manhattan project expenditures. These costs were adjusted to 2008 dollars using the price index for gross domestic product (GDP), available from the Bureau of Economic Affairs, National Income and Product Accounts Table webpage, Table 1.1.4, at http://www.bea.gov/bea/dn/nipaweb/.

[3]    Leslie R. Groves, *Now it Can be Told: The Story of the Manhattan Project* (New York: Harper & Brothers, 1962).

[4]    Ibid., Kevin O'Neil, "Building the Bomb," Chapter 1 in Stephen I. Schwartz (ed.), *Atomic Audit: The Costs and Consequences of U.S. Nuclear Weapons Since 1940* (Washington, DC: Brookings Institution Press, 1998), pp. 58-59.

[5]    Richard Orloff, National Aeronautics and Space Administration (NASA), *Apollo By The Numbers: A Statistical Reference*, NASA SP-2000-4029, 2004 web update at http://history.nasa.gov/SP-4029/
Apollo_00_Welcome.htm. There is some difference of opinion regarding what activities comprised the Apollo program, and thus when it began and ended. For example, two different cost figures are provided on NASA's website. This is probably because some analysts include the first studies for Apollo, Skylab, and the use of Apollo spacecraft in the Apollo-Soyuz Test Project. The Orloff analysis includes the first studies of Apollo, but not Skylab (1973-74) or Soyuz (1975) activities. Another NASA analysis provides the cost as $25.4 billion, but provides no details as to how the cost were determined. See Roger D. Launius, NASA, *The Legacy of Project Apollo* at http://history.nasa.gov/ap11-35ann/
legacy.html.

[6]    For more information, see CRS Report RL34263, *U.S. Civilian Space Policy Priorities: Reflections 50 Years After Sputnik*, by Deborah D. Stine.

[7]    NASA, Kennedy Space Center, "Project Apollo," webpage, at http://www-pao.ksc.nasa.gov/kscpao/history/apollo/ apollo.htm. A list of the top ten Apollo scientific discoveries as determined by the Smithsonian Institution is at http://www.nasm.si.edu/collections/imagery/apollo/apollotop10.htm.

[8]    NASA, Kennedy Space Center, "Project Apollo," webpage, at http://www-pao.ksc.nasa.gov/kscpao/history/apollo/ apollo.htm. The three parts were the command module (CM), the crew's quarters and flight control section; the service module (SM) for the propulsion and spacecraft support systems (when together, the two modules are called CSM); and the lunar module (LM).

[9]    The funding data is available at http://history.nasa.gov/SP-4214/app2.html#1965. It is based on information in NASA, The Apollo Spacecraft - A Chronology, NASA Special Publication-4009, at http://www.hq.nasa.gov/office/pao/History/ SP-4009/contents.htm. This data is from Volume 4, Appendix 7, at http://www.hq.nasa.gov/office/pao/History/SP4009/v4app7.htm.

[10]   Richard Orloff, *Apollo By The Numbers: A Statistical Reference*, NASA SP-2000-4029, 2004 web update, at http://history.nasa.gov/SP-4029/Apollo_00_Welcome.htm. The funding data is available at http://history.nasa.gov/SP4029/Apollo_18-16_A pollo_Program_Budget_Appropriations.htm. It is based on information in NASA, *The Apollo Spacecraft - A Chronology*, NASA Special Publication-4009, at http://www .hq.nasa.gov/office/pao/History/SP-4009/ contents.htm.

[11]   Energy Information Administration, "25th Anniversary of the 1973 Oil Embargo," at http://www.eia.doe.gov/emeu/ 25opec/anniversary.html.

[12]   U.S. Department of Energy, Office of History and Heritage Resources, "The Manhattan Project: An Interactive History," "Civilian Control of Atomic Energy" webpage at http://www.cfo.doe.gov/me70/manhattan/ civilian_control.htm.

[13]   Department of Energy, "Energy Research and Development Administration," webpage at http://www.ch.doe.gov/ html/site_info/energy_research.htm.

[14]   Although DOE did not begin operating until 1977, the term "DOE Energy Technology R&D Program" in this report is defined as encompassing DOE programs funded beginning in 1977 as well as energy R&D activities that occurred prior to 1977 that were managed by the organizations it subsumed.

[15]   See, for example, Bruce L.R. Smith, *American Science Policy Since World War II* (Washington, DC: Brookings Institution, 1990).

[16]   The Synthetic Fuels corporation was established by the United States Synthetic Fuels Corporation Act of 1980 (P.L. 96-294), and its operation was discontinued by the Synthetic Fuels Corporation Act of 1985 (P.L. 99-272).

[17]   National Academy of Sciences, *The Government Role in Civilian Technology: Building a New Alliance* (Washington, DC: National Academy Press 1992).

[18]   For information on the DOE energy technology R&D budget, see CRS Report RL34448, *Federal Research and Development Funding: FY2009*, coordinated by John F. Sargent Jr..

[19]   President Jimmy Carter, "Address to the Nation on Energy," speech, April 18, 1977. A video and text is at http://millercenter.org/scripps/archive/speeches/detail/3398.

[20]   CRS Report RL34513, *Climate Change: Current Issues and Policy Tools*, by Jane A. Leggett.

[21]   For more discussion of this issue, see CRS Report RL33528, *Industrial Competitiveness and Technological Advancement: Debate Over Government Policy*, by Wendy H. Schacht.

[22]   See for example, David Goldston, "Misspent Energy," Nature, 447:130, May 10, 2007 at http://www.nature.com/ nature/journal/v447/n7141/pdf/447130a.pdf.

[23]   See, for example, The National Academies, *Rising Above the Gathering Storm: Energizing and Employing America for a Brighter Economic Future* (Washington, DC: National Academy Press, 2007).

In: U.S. Political Programs: Functions and Assessments
Editors: Julianna M. Moretti and Karen J. Chordstron
ISBN: 978-1-61209-448-9
© 2011 Nova Science Publishers, Inc.

*Chapter 3*

# THE TECHNOLOGY INNOVATION PROGRAM[*]

## *Wendy H. Schacht*

## ABSTRACT

The Technology Innovation Program (TIP) at the National Institute of Standards and Technology (NIST) was established in 2007 to replace the Advanced Technology Program (ATP). This effort is designed " ... to support, promote, and accelerate innovation in the United States through high- risk, high-reward research in areas of critical national need," according to the authorizing legislation. Grants are provided to small and medium-sized firms for individual projects or joint ventures with other research organizations.

While similar to the Advanced Technology Program in the promotion of R&D that is expected to be of broad-based economic benefit to the Nation, TIP appears to have been structured to avoid what was seen as government funding of large firms that did not necessarily need federal support for research. The committee report to accompany H.R. 1868, part of which was incorporated into the final legislation, stated that TIP replaces ATP in consideration of a changing global innovation environment focusing on small and medium-sized companies. The design of the program also "acknowledges the important role universities play in the innovation cycle by allowing universities to fully participate in the program."

The elimination of ATP and the creation of TIP have renewed the debate over the role of the federal government in promoting commercial technology development. In arguing for less direct federal involvement, advocates believe that the market is superior to government in deciding technologies worthy of investment. Mechanisms that enhance the market's opportunities and abilities to make such choices are preferred. It is suggested that agency discretion in selecting one technology over another can lead to political intrusion and industry dependency. On the other hand, supporters of direct methods argue that it is important to focus on those technologies that have the greatest promise as determined by industry and supported by matching funds from the private sector. They assert that the government can serve as a catalyst for cooperation. As the 111th Congress makes budget decisions, the discussion may serve to redefine thinking about governmental efforts in facilitating technological advancement in the private sector.

---

[*] This is an edited, reformatted and augmented edition of a United States Congressional Research Service publication, CRS Report RS22815, dated June 29, 2009.

## INTRODUCTION

The Technology Innovation Program (TIP) at the National Institute of Standards and Technology (NIST) was created to "to support, promote, and accelerate innovation in the United States through high-risk, high-reward research in areas of critical national need," according to the authorizing legislation. The intent of the program is to provide grants to small and medium-sized firms for individual projects or joint ventures with other research organizations to undertake work that:

(a) has the potential for yielding transformational results with far-ranging or wide-ranging implications;

(b) addresses critical national needs within the National Institute of Standards and Technology's areas of technical competence; and

(c) is too novel or spans too diverse a range of disciplines to fare well in the traditional peer- review process [1]

NIST published the final rule prescribing the policies and procedures for the TIP activity on June 25, 2008 (15 C.F.R. Part 296). Small or medium-sized for-profit firms are eligible for individual project awards of up to $3 million over three years. Collaborative research ventures including small or medium-sized companies, national laboratories, universities, or other non-profit research institutions may be funded for a total of up to $9 million over five years. A competitive, merit- based process is to be used to make grants of up to 50% of total project costs. In January 2009, nine awards were announced for "new research projects to develop advanced sensing technologies that would enable timely and detailed monitoring and inspection of the structural health of bridges, roadways and water systems that comprise a significant component of the nation's public infrastructure." According to TIP, $42.5 million in federal money is expected to be matched by $45.7 in private sector support.

The Technology Innovation Program was authorized by the America COMPETES Act (P.L. 110- 69). The FY2008 Consolidated Appropriations Act, P.L. 110-161, provided the initiative $65.2 million (with an additional $5 million in unobligated balances from the FY2007 ATP appropriation). This was 17.6% less than FY2007 funding for the Advanced Technology Program which TIP replaced. According to NIST, the major portion of FY2008 support was to be used to meet previous ATP funding commitments. The President's FY2009 budget request did not contain any financial support for TIP. During the 110th Congress, the FY2009 appropriations bill reported from the House Committee on Appropriations provided $65.2 million for the program; the bill reported from the Senate Committee on Appropriations included $65 million for TIP.

No final FY2009 appropriations legislation was enacted for the program by the close of the 110th Congress; the Consolidated Security, Disaster Assistance, and Continuing Appropriations Act, 2009, P.L. 110-329, provided, in part, funding for TIP at FY2008 levels through March 6, 2009. P.L. 111-8, the FY2009 Omnibus Appropriations Act, provides $65.0 million for the program.

The President's FY2010 budget request and H.R. 2847, the Commerce, Justice, Science, and Related Agencies Appropriation Act, 2010, as passed by the House and reported from the

Senate Committee on Appropriations, include $69.9 million for TIP, an increase of 7.5% over the current fiscal year.

## BACKGROUND

The Advanced Technology Program, [2] which was replaced by the Technology Innovation Program, was established by Title V of the Omnibus Trade and Competitiveness Act (P.L. 100- 418). ATP was intended "to serve as a focal point for cooperation between the public and private sectors in the development of industrial technology" and to help solve "problems of concern to large segments of an industry," as noted in the Conference Report to accompany the bill. Placed within the National Institute of Standards and Technology (NIST), in recognition of the laboratory's ongoing relationship with industry, ATP provided seed funding to single companies or to industry-led consortia of universities, businesses, and/or government laboratories for development of generic (broad-based), pre-competitive technologies that had applications across industries. Awards, based on technical and business merit, were for high-risk work past the basic research stage but not yet ready for commercialization. Market potential was an important consideration in project selection.

Awards were for either product or process technology development. Individual firms were restricted to funding of $2 million over three years. Money was to be used only for direct R&D costs. Large firms provided at least 60% of total (direct and indirect) projects costs; small and medium-sized companies were not required to cost-share direct costs. Joint ventures could receive up to five years of financing for any amount, limited only by availability. In such cases, the private sector provided more than 50% of funding. While universities and federal laboratories could participate in collaborative work, the ATP grant was made solely to companies.

According to NIST, through the end of 2007 when ATP was terminated, 824 projects had been funded, of which about 28% were joint ventures. Approximately $1.6 billion in federal funds have been matched by $1.5 billion from the private sector. Small businesses or cooperative efforts led by such firms made up almost 68% of the awardees. (The legislation creating TIP required that the Director of NIST " ... continue to provide support originally awarded under the Advanced Technology Program, in accordance with the terms of the original award and consistent with the goals of the Technology Innovation Program.")

A major congressional funding issue was the continued support for the Advanced Technology Program. Opponents of the program cited it as a prime example of "corporate welfare," whereby the federal government invests in applied research activities that, they emphasize, should be conducted by the private sector. Others defended ATP, arguing that it assisted businesses (and small manufacturers) in developing technologies that, while crucial to industrial competitiveness, would not or could not be developed by the private sector alone.

The National Institute of Standards and Technology undertook numerous analyses of ATP; the General Accounting Office (GAO, now the Government Accountability Office) also studied the program. In its first evaluation (1994), NIST concluded the program had stimulated research that would not have been done without the federal support; that R&D cycles within companies have been abbreviated; and that "valuable business alliances" had been created [3]. However, in a May 1995 report, GAO argued that these conclusions can not be adequately substantiated by the information provided in the NIST study on which they were based [4]. Acknowledging that it was too early to determine the long-term impact of ATP, the GAO report stated that some of the indicators NIST utilized "may create false expectations of the program's economic success." NIST vigorously defended its methodology.

Additional studies funded by NIST found that ATP shortened R&D cycles by half and accelerated technological progress within the firm; stimulated productive collaborative activities among companies and between firms and universities; facilitated commercialization; and increased private sector investment in high risk technology development [5]. An April 2000 progress report reinforced these earlier findings [6]. This study indicated that "participants in 261 projects have identified more than 1,200 different applications (or uses) of the technologies under development," and that the majority of these are new solutions to market needs or improvements in existing products or processes. Product cycles were being reduced, and while 24% of respondents said that they would not have undertaken the project without ATP funding, most others noted that the R&D would have been significantly slower without such support. NIST found that "organizations are pursuing different R&D than they would have undertaken without ATP funding," and that this work is more technically advanced and risky. The ATP financing also stimulated additional private sector money in these technical areas than otherwise would be the case. Over half of the companies were able to make a new or improved product. In March 2000 testimony, Raymond Kammer, then director of NIST, stated that approximately 120 new technologies have been commercialized. According to NIST, more than 60% of ATP projects resulted in commercial products and processes available in the marketplace [7]

The concern over whether ATP supported projects that could reasonably attract private sector investment had been an issue throughout the life of the program. In a report examining award winners and "near winners" during the first four years of ATP, GAO found the program funded both projects that would not have progressed without this federal support and those that would have been financed by the private sector [8]. Half of the awardees stated that they would have continued without ATP financing. Of the "near winners," 50% pursued their efforts in the absence of federal money but took longer to achieve their goals. According to GAO, while 63% of the applicants did not look elsewhere for funds, about half of the applicants who did "were told by prospective funders that their projects were either too risky or 'precompetitive'—characteristics that fulfill the aims of ATP funding." Respondents also noted that the program facilitated development of joint ventures to pursue ATP activities.

A study undertaken by the American Enterprise Institute concluded that ATP "has had only limited success" in choosing projects that could not raise private sector funds. According to the authors, this occurred because companies are not interested in pursuing R&D that fails to complement work performed for profit. In addition, the ATP selection criteria focused on commercial sales and job creation, not on projects for which there are "broad social benefits" and insufficient private investment. An April 2000 report by GAO, reinforced by May 26, 2005 testimony, noted that "two inherent factors in ATP's current award selection process— the need to guard against conflicts of interest and the need to protect proprietary information—make it unlikely that ATP can avoid funding research already being pursued by the private sector in the same time period" [9]

## A DIFFERENT APPROACH

The Technology Innovation Program appears to have been designed to avoid what was seen as government funding of large firms that did not necessarily need federal support for R&D activities. The committee report to accompany H.R. 1868, part of which was incorporated into the final legislation, stated that TIP replaces ATP in consideration of a changing global innovation environment focusing on small and medium-sized companies. The structure of TIP also "acknowledges the important role universities play in the innovation cycle by allowing universities to fully participate in the program"[10].

While similar to ATP in the promotion of high-risk R&D that would be of broad-based economic benefit to the Nation, there are several differences in the expected operation of the new Technology Innovation Program primarily associated with the size of eligible companies. Financial support under TIP is limited to small and medium-sized businesses whereas grants under ATP were available to companies regardless of size. In addition, the Advanced Technology Program required that joint ventures include two separately owned for-profit firms and could include universities, government laboratories, and other research establishments as participants in the project but not as recipients of the grant. In the TIP initiative, a joint venture may involve two separately owned for-profit companies but may also be comprised of one small or medium-sized firm and a university (or other non-profit research institution). A single company could receive up to $2 million for up to three years under ATP; under TIP, the participating company (which must be a small or medium-sized business) may receive up to $3 million over three years. In ATP, small and medium-sized companies were not required to cost share (large firms provided 60% of the total cost of the project) while in TIP there is a 50% cost sharing requirement which, again, only applies to the small and medium-sized businesses that are eligible. There were no funding limits for the five-year funding available for joint ventures under ATP; the TIP limits joint venture funding to $9 million for up to five years. The Advisory Board that was created to assist in the Advanced Technology Program included industry representatives as well as federal government personnel and representatives from other research organizations. The Advisory Board for the Technology Innovation Program would be comprised of only private sector members.

## ISSUES AND OBSERVATIONS

The effort to terminate the Advanced Technology Program, along with additional attempts to withdraw government support for certain other technology development efforts, appeared to reflect a philosophy that eschewed direct federal financing of private sector R&D efforts aimed at the commercialization of new technologies and production processes. Such activities are seen by opponents as "industrial policy," the means by which government rather than the marketplace "picks winners and losers." Instead, measures that would occasion a better investment environment for industry to expand their innovation-related efforts would, proponents argue, be preferable to government funding.

The current approach, including the new Technology Innovation Program, involves varied mechanisms to facilitate technological advancement. Legislation has created a body of laws, programs, and policies that involve both indirect and direct measures to stimulate technology advancement in the private sector. Indirect incentives include a research and experimentation tax credit; changes to the antitrust laws to encourage collaborative R&D and cooperative manufacturing ventures; alterations of patent ownership policies to facilitate governmentindustry-university interaction; and practices to promote technology transfer. Direct measures involve, among other things, federal funding for TIP and the Small Business Innovation Research Program. These cost-shared programs have been supported, in part, because of what proponents argue is their potential contribution to the country's national or economic security.

The elimination of ATP and the creation of TIP have renewed the debate over the role of the federal government in promoting commercial technology development. In arguing for less direct federal involvement, advocates believe that the market is superior to government in deciding technologies worthy of investment. Mechanisms that enhance the market's opportunities and abilities to make such choices are preferred. It is suggested that agency discretion in selecting one technology over another can lead to political intrusion and industry dependency. On the other hand, supporters of direct methods argue that it is important to focus on those technologies that have the greatest promise as determined by industry and supported by matching funds from the private sector. They assert that the government can serve as a catalyst for cooperation.

Technological progress is important to the nation because of its contribution to economic growth and a high standard of living. How best to achieve this continues to be debated. Critics viewed ATP as a means for a federal agency to select commercial firms and/or technologies for support. They maintained that the absence of market-generated decisions will result in technologies that can not be utilized productively by participating companies. Such a program, they argue, encourages selection of well-written proposals rather than assistance for truly important technologies. However, proponents stressed that ATP was market driven and that the technical areas for investment had been developed in conjunction with industry. In addition, companies were required to put up significant amounts of funding and survive a rigorous business review; procedures that made the ATP different from other federal efforts. Replacing ATP with the Technology Innovation Program may be one response to criticisms that large firms should not be recipients of this form of federal research funding, support that should be reserved for small and medium-sized companies which do not have the financial resources available to major corporations.

# REFERENCES

[1]    P.L. 110-69.
[2]    For additional information on ATP see CRS Report 95-3 6, *The Advanced Technology Program*, by Wendy H. Schacht.
[3]    National Institute of Standards and Technology, *Setting Priorities and Measuring Results at the National Institute of Standards and Technology*, January 31, 1994.
[4]    General Accounting Office, *Performance Measurement, Efforts to Evaluate the Advanced Technology Program*, GAO/RCED-95-68, May 1995.

[5]   Silber and Associates, *Company Opinion about the ATP and Its Early Effects*, January 30, 1995; *Acceleration of Technology Development by the Advanced Technology Program: The Experience of 28 Projects Funded in 1991*, by Frances Jean Laidlaw, for the National Institute of Standards and Technology, Economic Assessment Office, October 23, 1997; National Institute of Standards and Technology, *Advanced Technology Program: Development, Commercialization, and Diffusion of Enabling Technologies*, by Jeanne W. Powell, December 1997; National Institute of Standards and Technology, *Advanced Technology Program Performance of Completed Projects, Status Report Number 1*, by William F. Long, March 1999.

[6]   National Institute of Standards and Technology, *Development, Commercialization, and Diffusion of Enabling Technologies: Progress Report*, by Jeanne W. Powell and Karen L. Lellock, April 2000.

[7]   National Institute of Standards and Technology, *ATP is Meeting Its Mission: Evidence From ATP Evaluation Studies*, available at http://www.atp.nist.gov/factsheets/1-a-1.htm.

[8]   General Accounting Office, *Measuring Performance: The Advanced Technology Program and Private-Sector Funding*, GAO/RCED-96-47, January 1996.

[9]   General Accounting Office, *Advanced Technology Program: Inherent Factors in Selection Process Could Limit Identification of Similar Research*, GAO/RCED-00-1 14, April 2000, 5.

[10]  U.S. Congress, House Committee on Science and Technology, *Technology Innovation and Manufacturing Stimulation Act of 2007*, Report to accompany H.R. 1868, H.Rept. 110-115, April 30, 2007, 21.

In: U.S. Political Programs: Functions and Assessments       ISBN: 978-1-61209-448-9
Editors: Julianna M. Moretti and Karen J. Chordstron    © 2011 Nova Science Publishers, Inc.

*Chapter 4*

# MILLENNIUM CHALLENGE CORPORATION*

## *Curt Tarnoff*

## ABSTRACT

In a speech on March 14, 2002, President Bush outlined a proposal for a major new U.S. foreign aid initiative. The Millennium Challenge Corporation (MCC) provides assistance through a competitive selection process to developing nations that are pursuing political and economic reforms in three areas: ruling justly, investing in people, and fostering economic freedom.

The MCC differs in several respects from past and current U.S. aid practices:

- the competitive process that rewards countries for past and current actions measured by 17 objective performance indicators;
- the pledge to segregate the funds from U.S. strategic foreign policy objectives that often strongly influence where U.S. aid is spent; and
- the requirement to solicit program proposals developed solely by qualifying countries with broad-based civil society involvement.

As announced by the President Bush in March 2002, the initial plan had been to fund the MCC annually at $5 billion by FY2006, but this figure has never been reached. The Administration has sought a combined $15.0 billion for the MCC program, FY2004-FY2009, while Congress appropriated $8.3 billion, or little more than half of the total sought (55%). Under the FY2009 Omnibus appropriations (P.L. 111-8), Congress provided $875 million to the MCC. On May 7, 2009, the Administration issued its FY20 10 budget request, providing $1 .425 billion for the MCC.

Congress authorized the MCC in P.L. 108-199 (January 23, 2004). Since that time, the MCC's Board of Directors has approved 18 Compacts: with Madagascar (April 2005), Honduras (June 2005), Cape Verde (July 2005), Nicaragua (July 2005), Georgia (September 2005), Benin (February 2006), Vanuatu (March 2006), Armenia (March 2006), Ghana (August 2006), Mali (November 2006), El Salvador (November 2006), Mozambique (July 2007), Lesotho (July 2007), Morocco (August 2007), Mongolia

---

* This is an edited, reformatted and augmented edition of a United States Congressional Research Service publication, CRS Report RL32427, dated June 26, 2009.

(September 2007), Tanzania (September 2007), Burkina Faso (June 2008), and Namibia (July 2008). In June 2009, the Madagascar Compact was terminated early, as were uncontracted components of the Nicaragua Compact. A suspension of the roads portion of the Armenia Compact has been continued.

MCC implementation matters continue to unfold, including the relationship of MCC and USAID, sectors chosen, and the impact of rising costs on country programs. A growing question raised by some Members of Congress concerns the level of funding to support MCC programs. Some fear that insufficient funds might force the MCC to reduce the number of recipients or the size of the grants. Others, however, support reductions in the MCC budget, disturbed by the slower-thananticipated pace of Compact agreements and lack of concrete results to date.

## MOST RECENT DEVELOPMENTS

On June 23, 2009, the House Appropriations Committee reported the FY2010 State, Foreign Operations Appropriations, providing $1.400 billion for the MCC, $25 million less than the request.

On June 10, 2009, the MCC Board of Directors partially terminated Nicaragua's Compact, ending assistance activities not already contracted, including a road and a property regularization project. These efforts had been suspended in December because of actions taken by the Nicaraguan government, contrary to the MCC requirement that countries promote political freedom and the rule of law. At the same time and for the same reasons, the Board decided to continue the suspension of funding of road construction and rehabilitation under the Compact with Armenia.

On May 19, 2009, the MCC Board of Directors authorized termination of the Madagascar Compact, which had been suspended since March 2009 because of the undemocratic change of government there.

On May 7, 2009, the Administration issued its FY2010 budget request, providing $1.425 billion for the MCC, a 63% increase over the FY2009 level.

On March 11, 2009, the President signed the FY2009 Omnibus appropriations (P.L. 111-8, H.R. 1105), providing $875 million to the MCC (in Division H of the legislation), $1.4 billion less than the Bush Administration request, and $611 million less than the FY2008 appropriation (after rescission). The explanatory report accompanying the act urges the MCC to limit Compact size to under $350 million and raises concerns regarding performance of threshold programs.

On December 11, 2008, the MCC Board of Directors announced countries eligible for Compacts in FY2009. New entries are Colombia, Indonesia, and Zambia. Countries not re-selected from the previous year are Bolivia, Ukraine, and Timor-Leste. Liberia was made eligible for a threshold agreement.

## OVERVIEW

In a speech on March 14, 2002, President Bush outlined a proposal for a new program that would represent a fundamental change in the way the United States invests and delivers economic assistance. The resulting Millennium Challenge Corporation (MCC) is based on the premise that economic development succeeds best where it is linked to free market economic and democratic principles and policies, and where governments are committed to implementing reform measures in order to achieve such goals. The MCC concept differs in several fundamental respects from past and current U.S. aid practices:

- the competitive process that rewards countries for past actions measured by 17 objective performance indicators;
- the pledge to segregate the funds from U.S. strategic foreign policy objectives that often strongly influence where U.S. aid is spent;
- the requirement to solicit program proposals developed solely by qualifying countries with broad-based civil society involvement; and
- the responsibility of recipient countries to implement their own MCC-funded programs.

The proposal also differed from previous aid efforts in the size of the original $5 billion commitment, an aim never even approximately met.

Congress authorized the new initiative in January 2004 (the Millennium Challenge Act of 2003, Division D of P.L. 108-199) and has closely followed its implementation [1]. As the program evolves, the 111th Congress will consider MCC funding issues and conduct oversight hearings on operations of the Corporation.

## MCC BACKGROUND

The Millennium Challenge Corporation (MCC) provides assistance through a competitive selection process to developing nations that are pursuing political and economic reforms in three areas:

- Ruling justly—promoting good governance, fighting corruption, respecting human rights, and adhering to the rule of law.
- Investing in people—providing adequate health care, education, and other opportunities promoting an educated and healthy population.
- Economic freedom—fostering enterprise and entrepreneurship and promoting open markets and sustainable budgets.

Country selection is based largely, but not exclusively, on a nation's record measured by 17 performance indicators related to the three categories, or "baskets." Countries that score above the median on half of the indicators in each of the three areas qualify. Emphasizing the importance of fighting corruption, the indicator for corruption is a "pass/fail" test: should a country fall below the median on the corruption indicator, it will be disqualified from consideration unless other, more recent trends suggest otherwise. (See Table 6 below for a complete list of the 17 performance indicators.) Administration officials, since announcing the MCC initiative in 2002, have said that the selection process would be guided by, but not necessarily bound to the outcomes of the performance indicators. Missing or old data, general trends, and recent steps taken by governments might also be taken into account when annual decisions are made.

Eligibility to receive MCC assistance, however, does not necessarily result in an aid grant. Once selected, countries are required to submit program proposals—referred to as MCC Compacts— that have been developed through a broad-based, national discussion that includes input from civil society. The focus of program submissions may vary among countries in size, purpose, and degree of specificity, and are evaluated by the Corporation for, among other things, how well the Compact supports a nation's economic growth and poverty reduction goals. Only those Compacts that meet the MCC criteria will be funded. It is expected that successful Compacts will support programs lasting three to five years, providing a level of resources roughly equivalent to the largest providers of assistance in the country. In most cases, this will likely result in a significant increase of U.S. economic assistance to MCC participant countries. In perhaps the most dramatic departure from previous U.S. assistance practices, MCC Compacts are implemented by the recipient country government.

To manage the new initiative, the Administration proposed and Congress authorized the creation of a Millennium Challenge Corporation (MCC), an independent government entity separate from the Departments of State and the Treasury and from the U.S. Agency for International Development (USAID). The MCC staff level is currently about 300. Until a new CEO is nominated by the Obama Administration and confirmed by the Senate, former deputy Rodney Bent is the acting CEO [2]. A Board of Directors oversees operations of the MCC and makes the country selections. It is chaired by the Secretary of State and composed of the Secretary of the Treasury, the USAID Administrator, the U.S. Trade Representative, the Corporation's CEO, and four individuals from the private sector drawn from lists of proposed nominees submitted by Congressional leaders [3]

The decision to house the initiative in a new organization was one of the most debated issues during early congressional deliberations. The Administration argued that because the initiative represents a new concept in aid delivery, it should have a "fresh" organizational structure, unencumbered by bureaucratic authorities and regulations that would interfere in effective management. Critics, however, contended that if the initiative was placed outside the formal U.S. government foreign aid structure, it would lead to further fragmentation of policy development and consistency. Some believed that USAID, the principal U.S. aid agency, should manage the program, while others said that it should reside in the State Department where more U.S. foreign policy entities have been integrated in recent years. At least, some argued, the USAID Administrator should be a member of the MCC Board, which had not been proposed in the initial Administration request.

The MCC's status remained unchanged under Secretary Rice's realignment of foreign aid authorities, announced on January 19, 2006. While gaining policy and budget authority over nearly all USAID and State Department foreign aid programs, the new Director of Foreign Assistance in the State Department has played a more limited role in other agency activities, by developing an overall U.S. government development strategy and providing "guidance" to foreign aid programs delivered through other agencies like the MCC.

# MCC IMPLEMENTATION

From the time the MCC Board of Directors held its initial meeting to establish the program and agree to Corporation by-laws on February 2, 2004, procedures and policies have continued to evolve. Program implementation moves chronologically through a number of steps: candidate countries are identified, criteria are formulated, Compact and threshold-eligible countries are selected, programs are developed and proposed, and those approved are funded and carried out. Elements in this process are discussed below.

## Selection of Candidate Countries

The selection of initial candidate countries is fairly straightforward and based on the authorizing statute. Countries must fall into specific economic categories determined by their per capita income status (as defined and ranked by the World Bank). During the first year of the program, in FY2004, MCC participation was limited to the poorest nations that were eligible to borrow from the World Bank's International Development Association; there were 74 of these. The list expanded in FY2005 to include all low-income countries (adding another 13 nations). Beginning in FY2006 and beyond, all low- and lower- middle-income countries (with per capita incomes between $1,785 and $3,705 in FY2009) compete for MCC resources (a total of 93 countries in FY2009). However, lower-middle-income countries may receive only a quarter of total MCC assistance in any year.

In addition to the income ceiling, countries may be candidates only if they are not statutorily prohibited from receiving U.S. economic assistance. In FY2009, 11 countries were excluded for this reason. Most had been barred in prior years as well [4].

One, Mauritania, excluded in FY2009 because of a military coup, had been selected as the one new threshold program-eligible country in FY2008 and will thereby lose its eligibility.

In August 2008, the MCC transmitted to Congress its annual notification of candidate countries, listing 64 low-income countries and 29 lower-middle-income countries (See Table 4 and Table 5). There was one new entry to the low-income candidates: Kosovo, now an independent state. Bosnia and Herzegovina is a new entry in the lower-middle-income group, and Thailand returns following democratic elections. Georgia and Vanuatu have moved from low-income to lowermiddle-income status. Three previously lower-middle-income countries are no longer candidates: Jamaica, Belarus, and Suriname have graduated to middle-income status.

## Country Selection Criteria and Methodology

The choice of criteria on which to base the eligibility of countries for threshold and Compact programs is one of the most important elements in MCC operations (See Table 6 for Performance Indicators). They are a key statement of MCC development priorities and ultimately determine which countries will receive U.S. assistance. Perhaps of equal significance, the current indicators themselves have become prominent objectives of some developing countries in what former Board CEO Danilovich has called the "MCC effect."5 Countries seeking eligibility are moving on their own to enact reforms and take measures that would enable them to meet MCC criteria. The criteria and the methodology for applying them have evolved over time.

Pursuant to reporting requirements set in the MCC legislation, each year the Corporation sends to Congress an overview of the criteria and methodology that would be used to determine the eligibility of the candidate countries in that fiscal year. The criteria have been altered and refined, sometimes dramatically, over time.

While the MCC legislative authorities broadly match criteria proposed by the Administration, lawmakers included four additional matters on which to evaluate a country's performance. These relate to the degree to which a country:

- recognizes the rights of people with disabilities;
- respects worker rights;
- supports a sustainable management of natural resources; and
- makes social investments, especially in women and girls.

For each of these, the MCC has sought to use supplemental data and qualitative information to inform its decisions on Compact eligibility. The latter two factors have led to the development of new indicators.

With regard to the requirement added by Congress regarding social investments in women and girls, at first the MCC reported it would draw on girls' primary enrollment rates to supplement the four social investment performance indicators. But in FY2005, an indicator measuring girls' primary education completion rates replaced a broader measure used in FY2004 that did not disaggregate primary education graduation by gender.

Beginning with the FY2005 selection process, the MCC lowered the inflation rate threshold from 20% to 15%, making it somewhat more difficult to pass this test (only 6 of the 63 candidate countries failed this test for FY2004). For FY2006, the Corporation added a new indicator—the Cost of Starting a Business—that replaced the Country Credit Rating, a measure that was used in the FY2004 and FY2005 evaluation process. The Corporation believed that not only did the new indicator have a strong correlation with economic growth, but that it was a measurement that might encourage governments to take action in order to improve their scores. Since the initial use of the indicator Days to Start a Business, MCC candidate countries had introduced many business start-up reforms, the results of which were reflected in a lowered median for this category. MCC officials hoped that adding an indicator for the Cost of Starting a Business would stimulate additional policy improvements. They believed that the Country Credit Rating indicator was not as well linked to policy reforms and that it had a greater income bias than other MCC indicators.

Efforts to develop a measurement to assess a country's commitment to policies that promote sustainable management of natural resources as required by Congress led to the adoption of two new indicators, first used as supplemental information in determining FY2007 MCC eligibility and then integrated with all the other indicators beginning with the FY2008 eligibility process. The Natural Resources Management index is a composite of indicators: whether the country is protecting at least 10% of its biomes, the percentage of population with access to sanitation and clean water, and child mortality levels. It has been placed in the Investing in People basket, raising the number of those indicators to five. The

Land Rights and Access index looks at whether land tenure is secure and access to land is equitable, and the number of days and cost of registering property. It has been placed in the Economic Freedom basket. That basket remains at six indicators, because, beginning in FY2008, the MCC collapsed the Days to Start a Business and Cost of Starting a Business indicators into one Business Start-Up indicator.

In addition to adding or refining indicators, the Corporation has also modified its principal that, in selected cases, countries must score above the median in order to pass a hurdle, with a rule that scores at the median will represent a passing grade. This comes into play especially for those indicators (civil liberties, political rights, and trade policy) where performance is measured on a relatively narrow scale of 1-5 or 1-7. A number of countries fall exactly on the median of these indicators and the methodology change allowed the MCC to make a more refined determination of whether a country passes or fails these hurdles.

In December 2006, the MCC began to apply gender analysis to all aspects of the MCC program, including country selection and Compact development and implementation.

In the explanatory statement accompanying the FY2009 Omnibus appropriations (), Congress urged the Board of Directors to consider establishment of an indicator that would take into consideration the votes and positions of countries in international institutions with regard to human rights issues.


## Selecting Eligible Countries

Shortly after release of the performance criteria, the MCC publishes a scorecard, showing where each candidate country's performance falls in relation to the other candidate countries in its peer group (i.e., lower income countries "compete" with other lower income countries and lower- middle income countries with other lower-middle income countries). Some time later, the MCC Board meets to select its list of countries eligible to apply for Compact assistance.

A review of the history of MCC selections suggests that the Board is guided by, but not entirely bound to, the outcome of the performance indicator review process; board members can apply discretion in their selection. Performance trends, missing or old data, and recent policy actions might come into play during selection deliberations.

For example, in its first year, FY2004, the MCC selected 16 countries. The selection reflected decisions that both strictly followed the performance indicator outcomes and applied Board discretion to take into account other factors. Ten of the countries complied with the stated criteria: performing above the median in relation to their peers on at least half of the indicators in each of the three policy "baskets" and performing above the median on corruption. The Board also examined whether a country performed substantially below average on any single indicator and whether their selection was supported by supplemental information. Each of the 10 countries also passed these additional tests.

For 10 other countries, however, some discretion was applied by the Board. In three cases, countries which met the criteria but fell significantly below average on one indicator were still selected by the Board due to recent policy changes or positive trend lines. Cape Verde, for example, scored poorly on the Trade Policy indicator, but the Board took into account the country's progress towards joining the World Trade Organization and implementing a value added tax that will reduce reliance on import tariffs. Lesotho did not score well on the measurement for Days to Start a Business. The MCC Board, however, took note of Lesotho's creation of a central office to facilitate new business formation and saw positive performance on other factors related to business start-ups. Sri Lanka scored far below the median on Fiscal Policy, but the most recent trends suggested that the government was making progress in reducing its budget deficit.

For three other countries—Bolivia, Georgia, and Mozambique—the Board deviated from a strict application of the selection criteria because of evidence that the governments were taking corrective actions in the deficient areas. Bolivia fell at the median (as opposed to above the median) on the corruption indicator, something that would eliminate it from consideration. The Board, however, noted that President Mesa, who took office in October 2003, had created a cabinet position to coordinate anti-corruption activities and an office to investigate police corruption. Georgia, with a newly elected government that had created an anti-corruption bureau and taken other steps to fight corruption, was also selected despite scoring below the median on corruption and three other "ruling justly" indicators. Mozambique, which failed on corruption and each of the four "investing in people" indicators, was chosen based on supplemental data that was more current than information available from the primary data sources. This evidence, the Board felt, demonstrated Mozambique's commitment to fighting corruption and improving its performance on health and education.

On the other hand, the MCC Board chose not to select four countries that technically met the performance criteria but fell substantially below the median on one or more indicator. In each of these cases, the Board did not believe that the government was taking any action to improve its performance. Although Bhutan, Mauritania, and Vietnam passed the corruption hurdle and half of the "ruling justly" indicators, they scored very low on the measurements for Political Rights and Civil Liberties, and in Vietnam's case, on the Voice and Accountability indicator. A fourth country—Guyana—was also not selected despite passing the necessary hurdles. It scored particularly low on the Fiscal Policy measurement [6]

As the candidate pool has expanded in succeeding years while funding levels failed to meet expectations, the Board has become increasingly more selective. Many outside the MCC support the approach of keeping the number of new participants to a few so that future Compacts can be larger and emphasize "transformational" development opportunities as the MCC program originally envisioned.

For FY2005, the Board did not select 10 countries that met the criteria, including Bhutan, Vietnam, Guyana, Burkina Faso, China, Djibouti, Egypt, Nepal, the Philippines, and Swaziland. The Corporation offered little explanation as to why these countries were not chosen [7]. It appeared, however, that scoring "substantially below"—perhaps in the lowest 25th percentile—on an indicator had become a de-facto criteria for exclusion. For example, the Corporation's then- CEO Paul Applegarth commented that the Philippines, a country that passed 13 of the 16 indicators, did not qualify because it scored "substantially below" the median on tests for health expenditures and fiscal policy, and that more recent trends indicated the fiscal policy situation was deteriorating further [8]. Each of the other nine nations that met the minimum qualifications but were not selected also had one score in the 25th percentile, although the Corporation has not commented on whether this was the reason for not choosing them.

Another Board departure in the FY2005 selection process was to avoid using its discretionary authority to qualify countries that did not meet the minimum performance indicators. For FY2004, the Board chose three nations—Bolivia, Georgia, and

Mozambique—that did not pass the so-called "hard-hurdle" of corruption. The latter two again qualified despite falling below the median on corruption, while Bolivia did not require an exemption after the median dropped below its score with the addition of new countries. For FY2005, five nations—Malawi, Moldova, Paraguay, Tanzania, and Ukraine—passed the required number of performance indicators, except corruption. Although Malawi, Paraguay, and Tanzania are Threshold Countries, none of the five were chosen for full MCC status.

In FY2006, the Board did not choose eight countries in the low-income group that qualified and did not use its discretionary powers to select any new nations that failed to meet the minimum requirements [9]. Bhutan, China, and Vietnam passed enough hurdles but did not qualify, as was the case the previous two years, based on very low scores on political rights and civil liberties. Kiribati, the Philippines, and India were not selected most likely because some of their scores were substantially below the median. India also presents a challenging case for the Board in that, despite qualifying, it is a country with a significantly large poor population which would require a sizable MCC Compact in order to produce a reasonable degree of impact on poverty reduction. It is also a nation with the means to attract capital and investment from other sources. Egypt, also not selected, falls into a somewhat different category as the second largest recipient of annual U.S. assistance based on a strategic rationale. The reason for not selecting Uganda, despite having passed 12 of the 16 indicators and not falling significantly below the median on the other 4, is less obvious.

In its first year of choosing among lower-middle-income countries, the Board's approach was less clear. A number of analysts had argued that especially given the less-than-anticipated budget available to the MCC, the Board should refrain from selecting any lower-middle-income countries (LMICs), at least in the FY2006 round [10]. Of the eight LMICs (out of 32 total) that passed sufficient performance hurdles, the Board chose two to participate in FY2006. In addition, the Board also selected Cape Verde, a country that passed only two of the six economic performance indicators and therefore, did not technically qualify [11]. It appears, however, that the Board could have decided to select none of the lower-middle-income nations by using criteria it had applied consistently in the two previous rounds. Moreover, it was not clear why the Board chose the two that did qualify and excluded others.

All eight LMICs that passed the performance indicator test fell significantly below the median on at least one of the indicators. El Salvador and Namibia, the two that were selected, both had low scores on fiscal policy. El Salvador also scored well below the median on the costs of starting a business, while Namibia also did poorly on days to start a business and immunization rates. The other six that were not chosen—Brazil, Bulgaria, Jordan, Samoa, Thailand, and Tunisia—also performed substantially below the median in at least one area, although Jordan was selected to participate in the Threshold program. What separated these latter six from El Salvador and Namibia, however, was not explained by the Board.

Although the Gambia was selected in FY2006, its eligibility for MCC assistance was suspended by the MCC Board on June 16, 2006, because of "a disturbing pattern of deteriorating conditions" in half of the 16 conditions that are used to determine candidate countries. Among the problems cited in this case were human rights abuses, restrictions on civil liberties and press freedom, and worsened anti-corruption efforts.

On November 8, 2006, the MCC Board added three new countries to the list of those eligible for FY2007 MCC grants—Moldova, Jordan, and Ukraine. Even prior to the selection, the possible choice of Jordan had come in for severe criticism. Freedom House, the organization whose annual Index of Freedom is drawn upon for two of the "Ruling Justly" indicators, had urged the MCC Board to bypass countries that had low scores on political rights and civil liberties. It argued that countries like Jordan that fall below 4 out of a possible 7 on its index should be automatically disqualified. Jordan, however, did well on three of the other indicators in this category. Several development analysts further argued that Jordan should not be selected, because the MCC is not an appropriate funding source. They assert that Jordan, already is one of the largest recipients of U.S. aid, has access to private sector capital, and is not a democracy [12]. In selecting Jordan, the MCC Board appears not to have been swayed by these arguments.

Another concern expressed by observers regarding the FY2007 selection process was that four of eleven current Compact countries—Ghana, Benin, Madagascar, and Cape Verde—would fail if measured under FY2007 indicators. While it was not expected that existing Compact funding would be withdrawn as it is based on eligibility in previous years, some had hoped the Board would send a signal of disapproval of such lapses. However, the MCC Board did not address this issue at the November 2006 candidate selection meeting.

For the 2008 selection process, the MCC Board added the Philippines and Malawi to the list of countries eligible to apply for a Compact. Two countries that had appeared in the past were absent in the 2008 list. Sri Lanka was left out because of the resurgent civil strife that would make a Compact problematic, and Cape Verde for more complicated reasons. Due to changes in the qualifying indicators, Cape Verde would not have been eligible for the third year in a row, and, as a lower-middle income country, would be more strictly judged. Nonetheless, according to the MCC, 12 of the 25 countries that made the cut did not meet the FY2008 criteria, five of them failing the control of corruption indicator. One reason that the MCC re-selected these countries was that they were viewed as maintaining or improving their performance rather than adopting policies contrary to the criteria. This approach was taken because countries following reasonable policies may fall behind the performance criteria when other countries are improving faster— thereby raising the bar. They may also fail when new criteria are introduced which countries have not had an opportunity to address and when institutions measuring performance refine or revise their indicators.

### Country Selection — FY2009

On December 11, 2008, the MCC Board added three new entries to the list of Compact-eligible countries—Indonesia, Zambia, and Colombia. The first two met the indicator criteria for the first time this year, both benefitting from threshold programs targeting corruption factors that had prevented them from eligibility in the past. The most striking aspect of this year's process was the decision not to re-select several countries that had been eligible in the previous year—Bolivia, Timor-Leste, and Ukraine. In FY2008 and FY2009, both Ukraine and Timor-Leste failed the corruption indicator. Timor-Leste, in addition, failed the "investing in people" basket in those years. Bolivia, however, has passed its indicator test in every year, including this one. The hold put on MCC consideration of its Compact proposal during the past year and its current exclusion from eligibility appears likely due to the political tensions currently existing between it and the United States rather than its performance in development-related matters. Countries previously selected that remain eligible in FY2009 and which continue to prepare Compact proposals are Jordan, Malawi, Moldova, Philippines, and Senegal. The Board, however, has noted that a Philippines Compact would not be signed until it passed the corruption indicator that it failed in FY2009.

### Table 1. Compact-Eligible Countries: FY2009

| | Low-Income Countries | |
|---|---|---|
| Benin | | Moldova |
| Burkina Faso | | Mongolia |
| Ghana | | Morocco |
| Honduras | | Mozambique |
| Indonesiaa | | Nicaragua |
| Lesotho | | Philippines |
| Madagascar | | Senegal |
| Malawi | | Tanzania |
| Mali | | Zambiaa |
| | Lower-Middle-Income Countries | |
| Armenia | | Georgia |
| Cape Verde | | Jordan |
| Colombiaa | | Namibia |
| El Salvador | | Vanuatu |

a. New for FY2009.

## MCC Compacts and Program Proposals

Once declared as eligible, countries may prepare and negotiate program proposals with the MCC. Only those Compact proposals that demonstrate a strong relationship between the program proposal and economic growth and poverty reduction will receive funding. Not all qualified MCC countries may submit successful Compact proposals.

While acknowledging that Compact proposal contents likely will vary, the Corporation expects each to discuss certain matters:

- a country's strategy for economic growth and poverty reduction, impediments to the strategy, how MCC aid will overcome the impediments, and the goals expected to be achieved during implementation of the Compact;
- why the proposed program is a high priority for economic development and poverty reduction and why it will succeed; the process through which a public/private dialogue took place in developing the proposal;
- how the program will be managed, monitored, and sustained after the Compact expires;
- the relationship of other donor activities in the priority area;
- examples of projects, where appropriate;
- a multi-year financial plan; and
- a country's commitment to future progress on MCC performance indicators.

The Corporation did not set hard deadlines for Compact submissions in order to allow countries adequate time to conduct a national dialogue over the contents of the program proposal. Proposals are developed by a country with the guidance of and in consultation with the MCC. Sometime during the proposal development process, the MCC may provide so-called pre-Compact development grants to assist the country's efforts. Among other things, grants may be used for design studies, baseline surveys, technical and feasibility studies, environmental and social assessments, ongoing consultations, fees for fiscal and/or procurement agents, and the like. For example, in June 2009, the MCC provided Jordan with a pre-Compact development grant of $13.34 million, not counted as part of the final Compact. It is being used for feasibility studies and other assessments for water and wastewater projects.

Once a proposal is submitted, the MCC conducts an initial assessment, then, on the basis of that assessment, launches a due diligence review that closely examines all aspects of the proposal, including costs and impacts. At the same time, MCC staff work with the country to refine program elements. Finally, the MCC negotiates a final Compact agreement prior to its approval by the MCC Board. The Compact is signed but does not enter into force until supplemental agreements on disbursements and procurement are reached [13].

The MCC signed its first Compact, with Madagascar, on April 18, 2005, an event that was followed by four other signings in 2005—with Honduras, Cape Verde, Nicaragua, and Georgia. In 2006, six more agreements were signed: Benin, Vanuatu, Armenia, Ghana, Mali and El Salvador. In 2007, four Compacts were signed—with Mozambique, Lesotho, Morocco, Mongolia. In 2008, three, with Tanzania, Burkina Faso, and Namibia were signed.

The case of Madagascar is a good example of how the Compact process is expected to take shape. Elements of the design, negotiation, and completion of the Madagascar Compact met several of the key criteria of the MCC process. Discussions regarding the scope and purpose of the MCC grant occurred at the regional and national level in Madagascar that included broad representation of civil society. Management and oversight of the Compact is handled by a new entity, MCA- Madagascar, whose Steering Committee includes government and non-government officials. Both of these steps underscore the "country-ownership" and broad participatory nature of MCC programs. The Compact also includes fiscal accountability requirements concerning audits, monitoring, and evaluation that support the transparency concept of the MCC. While the $110 million MCC grant was fully obligated when the Compact entered into force, resources were transferred periodically following a determination that performance continued satisfactorily. This funding plan emphasizes the MCC principles of accountability and results.

Madagascar is also a case of how things can go wrong. In June 2009, with little more than a year remaining in the Compact's five-year span and $88 million of the $110 project committed, the Compact was terminated because of the undemocratic change in government.

### Table 2. MCC Appropriations: FY2004-FY2010
### (in $ billions)

|               | FY2004 | FY2005 | FY2006 | FY2007 | FY2008 | FY2009 | FY2010 |
|---------------|--------|--------|--------|--------|--------|--------|--------|
| Request       | 1.300  | 2.500  | 3.000  | 3.000  | 3.000  | 2.225  | 1.425  |
| Appropriation | 0.994  | 1.488  | 1.752  | 1.752  | 1.486a | .875   |        |

a. Original appropriation was $1.544 million; $58 million was rescinded in P.L. 110-252.

## Compact Descriptions

The 18 Compacts agreed up to this point are described below (also see Table 3). In addition to individual Compact components noted in each description, Compact totals include administrative and monitoring costs.

## Madagascar

The Madagascar Compact was a five-year, $110 million program, focusing on rural agriculture development and poverty reduction. Specifically, the project had three objectives: (1) to increase land titling and land security ($36 million); (2) to expand the financial sector and increase competition ($36 million); and (3) to improve agricultural production technologies and market capacity in rural areas ($17 million). According to the MCC, the Compact was designed to assist Madagascar's rural poor, which account for 80% of the nation's impoverished population, and generate income by expanding opportunities to own land, to access credit, and to gain technical training in agriculture and market identification.

After restoring 149,000 land rights documents, digitizing another 128,000, and formalizing land rights for 12,800 families, constructing two new bank branches, and providing agriculture technical assistance to 34,450 farmers and 290 small businesses and farmers associations, the Madagascar Compact was terminated in June 2009 due to an undemocratic change in government.

## Honduras

The five-year, $215 million MCC Compact with Honduras focuses on two objectives—rural development and transportation. The rural development project, representing $72.2 million of the Compact, will assist small and medium-size farmers enhance their business skills and to transition from the production of basic grains to horticultural crops, such as cucumbers, peppers, and tomatoes. According to the MCC, these vegetable crops will generate about $2,000 to $4,000 in annual income per hectare, compared with roughly $500 for basic grains. The project intends to provide farmers with the appropriate infrastructure and necessary training for producing and marketing these different crops. The transportation project, totaling $125.7 million of the Compact, will improve the major highway linking Honduran Atlantic and Pacific ports, and major production centers in Honduras, El Salvador, and Nicaragua. Rural roads will also be upgraded, helping farmers transport their goods to markets at a lower cost. Specific results sought in the Compact are:

- double productivity in 15,000 hectares in rural areas
- expand access to credit for farmers by over 20%
- upgrade the major road that links Honduras with commercial centers
- upgrade about 1,500 kilometers of rural roads

## Cape Verde

The MCC and Cape Verde have a five-year, $110 million Compact focused largely on improving the country's investment climate, transportation networks, and agriculture productivity. The program's goal is to increase the annual income in Cape Verde by at least $10 million. The Compact evolves around three projects:

- Private Sector Development—with $7.2 million and additional participation with the International Finance Corporation, the project aims to remove constraints to private sector investment.
- Infrastructure—the project will invest $78.7 million in road and bridge construction to help link the nine inhabited islands and improve transportation links to social services, employment opportunities, local markets, and ports and airports.
- Watershed Management and Agriculture Support—by investing $10.8 million to increase the collection, storage, and distribution of rainfall water, the project hopes to increase agricultural production and double the household income of farmers.

In June 2009, the first road funded under the Cape Verde Compact was completed. The MCC expects that an estimated 12,500 farmers and families will benefit from use of the 10-kilometer road.

## Nicaragua

The five-year, $175 million Compact with Nicaragua focuses on promoting economic growth primarily in the northwestern region of the country where potential opportunities exist due to the area's fertile land and nearby markets in Honduras and El Salvador. The Compact has three components: (1) to strengthen property registration ($26.5 million); (2) to upgrade primary and secondary roads between Managua and Leon and to provide technical assistance to the Ministry of Transportation ($92.8 million); and (3) to promote higher-profit agriculture activities, especially for poor farmers, and to improve water supply in support of higher-value sustainable agriculture.

On June 10, 2009, the MCC Board voted to terminate assistance for activities not yet contracted under the Nicaragua Compact. These activities had been suspended since December 2008 because of the actions of the Nicaraguan government inconsistent with the MCC eligibility criteria, specifically in the area of good governance. In 2008, the credibility of Nicaragua's municipal elections was seriously questioned, and a fair resolution of the electoral issue has not been reached since that time. The termination, reducing about $62 million from the Compact total, affects a property regularization project and a major road.

## Georgia

The $295 million, five-year agreement with Georgia focuses on reducing poverty and promoting economic growth in areas outside of the capital where over half the population lives in poverty. The Compact is divided into two projects. The first and the largest component ($211.7 million) concentrates on infrastructure rehabilitation, including roads, the north-south gas pipeline, water supply networks, and solid waste facilities. The Enterprise Development Project ($47.5 million) will finance an investment fund aimed at providing risk capital and technical assistance to small and medium-sized businesses, and support farmers and agribusinesses that produce commodities for the domestic market. The program expects to:

- reduce in the incidence of poverty by 12% in the Samtskhi-Javakheti region;
- provide direct benefits to 500,000 people and indirectly benefit over 25% of Georgia's population;

- reduce the travel time by 43% to Tbilisi, the capital, from regional areas, thereby cutting transportation costs for farmers, businesses, and individuals needing health and other social services; and
- lower the risk of a major gas pipeline accident and improve the reliability of heat and electricity to over one million Georgians.

On September 4, 2008, the Bush Administration proposed a $1 billion aid initiative for Georgia, of which one component was adding $100 million to the existing $295 million MCC Compact. An amendment to the Compact was signed on November 20, 2008. The additional $100 million, complementing or completing projects begun in the original Compact, is directed at road projects, water and sanitation facilities, and a natural gas storage facility.

## Armenia

The five-year, $236 million Compact concentrates on the agricultural sector, investing in the rehabilitation of rural roads ($67 million) and improving irrigation ($146 million). The program anticipates that it will benefit about 750,000 people, 75% of Armenia's rural population, by improving 943 kilometers of rural roads and increasing the amount of land under irrigation by 40%.

Misgivings have been raised both prior to and during implementation of the Armenia Compact. In September 2005, the MCC expressed concerns with Armenian officials regarding slippage on two of the governance indicators and matters raised by international groups concerning political rights and freedoms in the country. Moreover, the MCC Board delayed final approval of the Compact following the November 27, 2005, constitutional referendum, after allegations of fraud, mismanagement, limited access by the press, and abuse of individuals were raised. In signing the Compact on March 27, 2006, the MCC issued a cautionary note, signaling that Armenia must maintain its commitment to the performance indicators or risk suspension or termination of the Compact. On March 11, 2008, the MCC issued a warning that assistance might be suspended or terminated in response to the government's actions, including the imposition of a state of emergency and restrictions on press freedoms [14]. In the autumn of 2008, the Armenian government used $17 million of its own funds to begin a road segment when there was some question of whether the MCC would continue its support. In December 2008, then-MCC CEO Danilovich noted that Armenia had since moved forward on a number of reforms addressing MCC concerns and he expected MCC support to resume in the spring of 2009 [15]. However, on March 11, 2009, the MCC Board of Directors decided to continue the suspension of assistance for the rural roads component of the Armenia Compact until an interim review session could be held prior to its normal June 2009 meeting in order to assess the status of democratic governance in Armenia. On June 10, 2009, the MCC Board decided to continue its hold on financial support for the roads project. At least one board member noted that the suspension was, in effect, a termination, as the work, if reapproved, could not be completed within the Compact lifespan [16]

## Vanuatu

The $65.7 million, five-year Compact targets improvements broadly in multiple types of infrastructure, including roads, wharfs, an airstrip, and warehouses. The objective is to increase the average per capita income by 15%, by helping rural agricultural producers and providers of tourism-related goods and services. The Compact further aims to help strengthen Vanuatu's Public Works Department in order to enhance capacity to maintain the country's entire transport network.

## Ghana

The five-year $547 million Compact focuses on agriculture and rural development. Poverty rates in the three targeted geographic areas are above 40%. The agriculture component ($241 million) will provide training for farmer-based organizations, improve irrigation, provide greater access to credit, and rehabilitate local roads. The transport component ($143 million) will seek to reduce transport costs to farmers by improving key roads, such as the one between the capital and the airport, and an important ferry service. Rural development programs ($101 million) will construct and rehabilitate education, water, and electric facilities, among other activities.

## Benin

Benin, one of the world's poorest countries with the lowest Human Development Index ranking of any MCC Compact nation, has been approved for a $307 million, five year program focused on four sectors:

- Land rights, reducing the time and cost of obtaining property title;
- Financial services, helping micro, small, and medium-sized businesses;
- Justice reform, assisting the judicial systems capacity to resolve business and investment claims; and
- Market access, improving the Port of Cotonou.

The Compact's goal is to benefit five million people, bringing 250,000 of the population out of poverty by 2015.

## Mali

The five-year $461 million Compact emphasizes an increase in agricultural production and expansion of trade. About half the funds ($234.6 million) will support a major irrigation project, including modernization of infrastructure and improvements in land tenure. Improvements in the airport ($89.6 million) will target both passenger and freight operations. An industrial park project located at the airport ($94.6 million) will assist agro-processing and other industry.

## El Salvador

The five-year $461 million Compact addresses economic growth and poverty reduction concerns in El Salvador's northern region where more than half the population lives below the poverty line. Education as well as water and sanitation, and electricity supply ($95.1 million); support for poor farmers and small and medium-sized business ($87.5 million); and transportation, including roads ($233.6 million) are the chief elements of program.

## Mozambique

The five-year $506.9 million Compact, like most other Compacts, targets specific districts, in this case the less prosperous North of the country. The Compact has four components. Water and sanitation services will be improved ($203.6 million), a major road will be rehabilitated ($176.3 million), land tenure services will be made more efficient ($39.1 million), and steps will be taken to protect existing coconut trees, improve coconut productivity, and support diversification to other cash crops ($17.4 million). The long-term objective is to reduce the projected poverty rate by more than 7%.

## Lesotho

The five-year $362.6 million Compact has three elements. A water sector project ($164 million) will focus on both industrial, supporting garment and textile operations, and domestic needs. It will also support a national watershed management and wetlands conservation plan. A health project ($122.4 million) will seek to strengthen the health care infrastructure, including renovation of up to 150 health centers, improved management of up to 14 hospital out-patient departments, construction and equipping of a central laboratory, and improved housing for medical staff and training for nurses. A private sector development project ($36.1 million) will address a wide range of legal and administrative obstacles to increased private sector activity, including development of land policy and administration authority, implementation of a new payments and settlement system, and improvement of case management of commercial courts.

## Morocco

The five-year, $697.5 million Compact has multiple components, all aimed at increasing private sector growth. These include efforts to increase fruit tree productivity ($300.9 million), modernize the small-scale fisheries industry ($116.2 million), and support artisan crafts ($111.9 million). In addition, the Compact will fund financial services to micro-enterprises ($46.2 million) and will provide business training and technical assistance aimed at young, unemployed graduates ($33.9 million).

## Mongolia

The most significant part of the five-year $285 million Compact intends to stimulate economic growth by refurbishing the rail system, including infrastructure and management ($188.38 million). In addition, the Compact will support improvements in the property registration and titling system ($23.06 million) and the vocational education system ($25.51 million). The Compact will also attempt to reform the health system to better address non-communicable diseases and injuries, which are rapidly increasing in the country ($17.03 million).

## Tanzania

The five-year, $698 million Compact focuses on three key economic infrastructure issues. A transport sector project ($373 million) will improve major trunk roads, select rural roads, general road maintenance capabilities, and upgrade an airport. An energy sector project ($206 million) will lay an electric transmission cable from the mainland to Zanzibar, will construct a small hydro-electric plant at Igamba Falls, and will rehabilitate the existing distribution system to unserved areas. A water sector project ($66 million) will expand a clean water treatment facility serving the capital, reduce water loss in the capital region, and improve the water supply in Morogoro, a growing city.

## Burkina Faso

The five-year, $480.9 million Compact has four elements. A rural land governance project ($59.9 million) will focus on improving legal and institutional approaches to rural land issues, including registration and land use management. An agriculture project ($141.9 million) will target water management and irrigation, diversified agriculture, and access to rural finance in specific regions of the country. A roads project ($194.1 million) will improve rural roads. The education effort ($28.8 million) will build on the country's MCC threshold program and construct additional classrooms and provide daily meals to children. The education project will be administered by USAID.

## Namibia

The five-year, $304.5 million Compact will focus on education, tourism, and agriculture. The education project ($145 million) will improve school infrastructure and training, vocational and skills training, and textbook acquisition. The tourism project ($67 million) will target management and infrastructure in Etosha National Park, the premier wildlife park in Namibia, and build ecotourism capacity in the country. The agriculture project ($47 million) will focus on land management, livestock support, and production of indigenous natural products.

## "Threshold" Countries and Programs

In order to encourage non-qualifying countries to improve in weak areas, the MCC will help governments that are committed to reform to strengthen performance so that they would be more competitive for MCC funding in future years. Congress provided in authorizing legislation that not more than 10% of MCC appropriations could be used for such purposes, stating that the funding could be made available through USAID. Subsequent foreign operations appropriations have made 10% of new MCC appropriations available for this Threshold assistance [17]

According to the Threshold Program Policy guidance issued by the Corporation,18 the program will assist countries make policy reforms and institutional changes in areas where they failed to meet the MCC performance criteria. Those countries deemed eligible for the program must submit concept papers identifying:

- where and why the country failed to pass specific indicators;
- proposals for policy, regulatory, or institutional reforms that would improve the country's performance on these indicators; and
- types of assistance, over a two-year maximum period, required to implement these reforms.

If the Corporation, in consultation with USAID, determines that the concept paper shows sufficient commitment to reform and a promise of success, the country will prepare a Threshold Country Plan that specifically establishes a program schedule, the means to measure progress, and financing requirements, among other considerations. USAID has been charged with overseeing the implementation of Threshold Country Plans, including working with countries to identify appropriate implementing partners such as local, U.S., and international firms; NGOs; U.S. government agencies; and international organizations. Like regular MCC Compacts, funding is not guaranteed for each country selected for the Threshold Program, but will be based on the quality of the Country Plan.

To date threshold programs worth a total of about $482 million have been awarded to 19 countries. Currently 13 countries are eligible for threshold assistance: Kenya, Liberia, Niger, Rwanda, Sao Tome and Principe, Uganda, Albania, Kyrgyz Republic, Timor-Leste, Ukraine, Guyana, Paraguay, and Peru. Of these, only Liberia, newly selected in the FY2009 round, and Timor-Leste have not yet been awarded threshold program support. Five other countries—Moldova, Philippines, Zambia, Jordan, and Indonesia—have ongoing threshold programs, but are also now Compact-eligible and in the process of developing their Compact programs. Three other countries—Burkina Faso, Malawi, and Tanzania—have completed threshold programs and either have Compacts or are Compact-eligible. Another, Yemen, had developed a program approved by the Board, but implementation was postponed on October 27, 2007, pending a review. It is no longer eligible for threshold assistance. Mauritania was made eligible in 2007, but could not be offered a program due to aid prohibitions on governments deposed by a coup.

In December 2007, the MCC Board invited three countries—Albania, Paraguay, and Zambia—to submit proposals for follow-on threshold programs (stage II) as their initial threshold programs were going to expire in 2008. In September 2008, the MCC Board approved a $16.4 million stage II program for Albania. In January 2009, the Board approved a $30.3 million stage II program for Paraguay, aimed at improving anti-corruption and rule of law indicators. Zambia will not require the stage II program as it now passes the corruption indicator the program was meant to address and was approved for Compact eligibility in December 2009.

Funding levels for threshold programs differ, most recently ranging from $8.7 million for Sao Tome and Principe to $35.6 million for Peru. Of the programs ongoing or completed, most have sought to improve country scores on the corruption indicator. Several countries have multiple objectives. Indonesia and Peru, for example, target both corruption and immunization indicators.

Albania's first program focused on corruption and improvements in its business environment. The Burkina Faso program was designed to improve girls' primary education, targeting areas of the country with the lowest primary completion rates.

Although eight of the 19 threshold country programs have been followed by Compact eligibility, Congress has raised concerns regarding the efficacy of threshold programs. In the explanatory statement accompanying the FY2009 Omnibus appropriations, appropriators suggested that an assessment of the programs be undertaken before more are approved. One analyst suggests that threshold programs should focus on better preparing countries to implement Compacts rather than on enabling them to qualify for eligibility. She argues that, by funding reform to improve an indicator, the threshold program undermines the principle that countries should themselves be responsible for reform and MCC eligibility [19]

# SELECT ISSUES

## Funding

In each year since the MCC was established, the MCC proposal was the largest increase sought by the Administration in the Foreign Operations appropriations bill and viewed by many observers as one of the most vulnerable items in an increasingly difficult budget environment. In each year as well, its enacted appropriation has been well below the President's request.

Supporters of the MCC are disturbed by this trend, reflected again in the congressional funding level for FY2009, well below the Bush Administration request. They argue that if fewer Compacts are offered annually, the incentive for countries to go through the whole process of seeking eligibility and designing and refining a proposal is diminished and the so-called MCC effect, which encourages countries to reform on their own in order to meet eligibility requirements, is likely to be lost.

### *MCC Request and Congressional Action for FY2009*

On February 4, 2008, the Administration requested $2.225 billion for the MCC in its FY2009 budget, a 44% increase over the FY2008 appropriation.

On July 16, 2008, the House State/Foreign Operations Subcommittee approved its version of the FY2009 appropriations, providing $1.5 billion for the MCC, a 33% cut from the Administration request and the same level as in FY2008.

On July 17, 2008, the Senate Appropriations Committee reported its version of the FY2009 State/Foreign Operations appropriations (S.Rept. 110-425), providing $254 million to the MCC, a cut of 86% from the Administration request, and $1.3 billion less than FY2008. The committee explained the cut as a "temporary pause" in signing of new Compacts to allow for an evaluation of MCC programs. It noted the small Compact disbursement rate (4% of total Compact funding at the time) and the lack of tangible results to date as factors in support of this step. The committee stated its intention to support future Compacts "if current country compacts are shown to be cost effective and achieving results." Its proposed funding level would allow for two threshold stage 2 agreements, continued due diligence and pre-compact support, and administrative costs to maintain the MCC. The MCC argued that the proposed cut would undermine Compact country faith in the MCC process and warned that several countries in the pipeline, including the Philippines, Jordan, Senegal, Malawi, Timor-Leste (since de-selected), and Moldova, would be negatively affected.

On September 18, 2008, 38 Members of Congress signed a letter addressed to House Appropriations Committee leadership supporting an FY2009 MCC funding level at least at the subcommittee-passed level of $1.54 billion.

On March 11, 2009, the President signed into law the FY2009 Omnibus appropriations (P.L. 111- 8, H.R. 1105, providing $875 million to the MCC (Division H of the legislation), $1.4 billion less than the Bush Administration request, and $611 million less than the FY2008 appropriation (after rescission). The MCC had earlier calculated that, of the projected six Compacts in the pipeline— Jordan, Moldova, Senegal, Malawi, Philippines, and Timor-Leste (since de-selected)—three could be funded with a $1.5 billion appropriation. It is not clear how many can be funded with the FY2009 amount available. The explanatory report accompanying the act urges the MCC to limit Compact size to under $350 million.

### *MCC Request and Congressional Action for FY2010*

On May 7, 2009, the Administration issued its FY20 10 budget request, providing $1 .425 billion for the MCC, a 63% increase over the FY2009 level. On June 23, 2009, the House Appropriations Committee reported the FY20 10 State, Foreign Operations Appropriations, providing $1 .400 billion for the MCC, $25 million less than the request.


## Authorizing Legislation and MCC Reform

Observers anticipate that an MCC reauthorization measure will be considered in the 111th Congress. A previous effort, in the 109th Congress (2006), was reported by the House International Relations Committee (H.R. 4014, H.Rept. 109-563), but received no further consideration. It would have made a number of policy modifications to the original legislation and would have authorized MCC appropriations ("such sums as may be necessary") for fiscal years 2007 through 2009. The requirement of an authorization of foreign aid programs has been routinely waived in annual Foreign Operations appropriations bills, as the FY2009 Omnibus appropriations measure did in the case of currently unauthorized foreign aid programs, including the MCC (section 7023).

A measure introduced in the 110th Congress, H.R. 7165 (Payne), addressed several existing restrictions in the authorizing statute. The bill would allow a Compact to exceed 5 years in length, but no more than 10, if the Board determines it cannot be completed in 5. It would allow concurrent Compacts (more than one at the same time), and permits follow-on (subsequent) Compacts, if the Board determines that a prior Compact has met its objectives. The bill would also allow regional Compacts, involving two or more countries.

The explanatory statement accompanying the FY2009 Omnibus appropriations (P.L. 111-8) suggested that the MCC notify the Appropriations Committee regarding Compacts not likely to be completed when their five-year term is over. It indicated that Congress might then consider an extension of the time limit.


## Compact Size

A closely examined characteristic of the early Compacts was the dollar size of the grants; or, more specifically, the lower-than-anticipated funding level for the first several Compacts. While Administration officials said repeatedly that Compacts would be funded at various levels depending on the nature and potential impact of the proposal, the presumption in its first years was that the MCC grant would represent a sizable increase in U.S. assistance to the eligible country. In order to realize its potential as a "transformational" aid program and to provide sufficient incentives to countries requesting "breakthrough" projects, the MCC said that the size of its grants must place MCC assistance among the top aid donors in a country [20]. Some had estimated that once the Corporation's budget reached $5 billion, each Compact would be supported with annual resources in the $150-$200 million range [21].

These levels could vary up or down depending on many factors, such as the number of people living in poverty, the size of the economy, and the scope of the proposed projects.

Most of the first several Compacts, however, did not meet the anticipated financial allocation thresholds. Madagascar's four-year, $110 million Compact roughly doubled U.S. assistance to the country, but did not place MCC assistance among the top donors. France was the largest bilateral donor, disbursing on average $189 million per year, 2001-2004. The European Commission's aid program, 2001-2004, averaged $82 million per year, while the World Bank's International Development Association was Madagascar's largest source of concessional assistance of about $209 million lent in each of 2001 through 2004 [22]. The $110 million Compact for Madagascar is also not very large relative to the country's population. Of the 16 qualified countries for FY2004, Madagascar had the fourth largest population (16.4 million), and might have been expected to receive one of the larger MCC grants given its population size and its per capita income.

For Honduras (a $215 million MCC program over five years), Georgia ($295 million over five years), and Armenia ($236 million over five years), the United States was the top bilateral donor without the MCC program, and will likely remain in that position as MCC grants are disbursed. But the MCC Compact for Honduras called for only a slightly higher annual amount ($43 million) than U.S. economic assistance provided ($34 million) at the time, while Georgia's Compact will average only about three-fourths and the Armenia Compact only about two-thirds of the annual level of recent American aid. While these are not insignificant amounts of new resources, they are far less than Administration officials had suggested previously [23]

In contrast, the early five-year Compacts with Cape Verde ($110 million), Benin ($307 million), and Vanuatu ($66 million) represented a substantial investment by the United States, relative to the size of recent American aid and the size of their economies. USAID, which last provided direct bilateral assistance to Cape Verde in the mid-1990s, does not maintain a mission presence, allocating small amounts of aid through regional programs. The Compact's $22 million annual average placed the United States second to Portugal, Cape Verde's former colonial power, as the leading donor, and represented more than a quarter of total bilateral development aid grants from all sources compared with figures for 2003 and 2004. Likewise, the United States does not maintain a bilateral program with Vanuatu, limiting direct aid through the Peace Corps. The $13 million annual average of the Vanuatu program places the United States as the country's top aid donor, along with Australia. In Benin, USAID manages an annual bilateral economic aid program of about $15 million, compared with the $61 million annual size of the MCC Compact. The Benin Compact likely places the MCC as the top aid donor, together with France [24]

This issue of Compact size was a priority of Ambassador Danilovich since his September 2005 confirmation hearing to be the MCC's new CEO. He noted that the MCC was "meant to create transformative programs," and to do so he said that "future Compacts will generally need to be larger than those signed thus far." Ambassador Danilovich cautioned, however, that with limited resources but larger Compacts, fewer countries would receive funding if MCC was to achieve its transformational goal [25]. After assuming the CEO position, he moved the MCC towards larger Compacts and placing the MCC as the largest donor in recipient countries. In 2005, the average amount of Compacts signed in that year was $181 million, in 2006, $364 million, in 2007, $463 million, and in 2008, $495 million.

Apparently, in the view of some in Congress, the move to larger Compacts went too far. In the explanatory statement accompanying the FY2009 Omnibus appropriations (P.L. 111-8), the MCC is urged to limit Compact size to under $350 million in order to "ensure that the MCC does not become overextended, that existing compacts are meeting their goals, and future compacts are of a manageable size."

## Speed of Implementation

A recurrent criticism of the MCC, especially in Congress, is the slow speed of implementation, reflected largely by the limited amount of disbursements made to date. As perhaps the leading cause of cuts in MCC funding from the Administration request and of threatened rescissions from amounts already appropriated during the past few years, this view has had severe consequences for the MCC (see below). As of the end of March 2009, of the $8.3 billion appropriated for the MCC, only $1.2 billion, or 14%, had been disbursed. About $6.6 billion, however, had been obligated by end-March 2009. There are some good reasons for this spending rate. The MCC is a new experiment, and it has taken considerable time to develop methods of operation, including settling on the rules of eligibility and the requirements of Compact proposals. Further, the countries themselves are responsible for developing proposals, and they have problems common to most developing countries in managing complex programs to meet donor requirements of accountability. The GAO found that for five signed Compacts in Africa—with Madagascar, Cape Verde, Benin, Ghana, and Mali—the process of going from eligibility to compact signature took between 12 and 31 months. Four of these compacts entered into force about five months after compact signature [26]

Once launched, Compacts may be slow to get underway. For example, Honduras and Cape Verde, both in their fourth year had disbursed only 29% and 40%, respectively, of their total grants by end of March 2009. Among the causes for these low rates are delays by Compact countries in filling managerial positions. The nature of many of the Compacts is also responsible for the delays. Typically, infrastructure projects are slow to disburse funds, the majority of activity in the first few years being the design and planning of projects rather than actual construction.

Whatever the causes, the MCC responded to the criticisms by shifting its organizational focus from the early emphasis on Compact development to Compact implementation. In October 2007, it announced a reorganization aimed at facilitating implementation. The MCC expects annual Compact disbursements to top $1 billion by 2010.

## Compact Sectors

One feature of the first series of Compacts drew particular attention. Most of the early Compacts included a similar sector concentration, focusing on agriculture and transportation infrastructure projects. While these activities are well justified, the similarity across Compacts surprised some observers. Given the wide diversity of conditions in each of the countries, plus the Corporation's willingness to support all types of programs, many had expected to see a greater degree of variation among the Compacts. Some believe that social sectors, including those in health and education, should be receiving greater attention in Compact design. Others had expected greater variety in aid delivery mechanisms, and are concerned that the MCC is reluctant to approve sector grants and other types of budget support assistance. While there can be greater accountability risks associated with budget support aid, countries that qualify for MCC support are selected because they have already demonstrated stronger performance in managing resources and fighting corruption [27]. As more Compacts are signed, some diversity in programs is creeping in—three of the more recent ones, in Lesotho, Mozambique, and Tanzania, feature a water and sanitation component. The Morocco Compact includes micro-credit and artisan crafts support among its projects. Burkina Faso and Namibia have education components.

## Compact Impact

The purpose of the MCC is to reduce poverty by supporting economic growth, but some observers have complained about the lack of measurable results to date. There are some possible reasons for this, most prominently the slow speed of Compact implementation noted above. As a result, it will likely be some time before a serious analysis of actual impacts can be undertaken. In the meantime, some reporting on outcomes has emerged. For instance, according to the MCC, the number of new registered businesses in Albania has grown by 20,000, and the time and cost of starting a business in Paraguay has fallen by nearly half. In March 2009, the MCC issued an independent impact analysis of the Burkina Faso Threshold Program, which constructed 132 primary schools and provided other assistance to increase girls' enrollment rates. It found that enrollment increased for both genders, by about 20%, and for girls over boys, by 5% [28]

A 2007 GAO report highlighted a concern, that, in the case of Vanuatu, projected impacts had been overstated. The GAO noted that the MCC estimated a rise from 2005 per capita income in Vanuatu of about 15% ($200) by 2015 when, in fact, the data suggest it would rise by 4.6%. Although the MCC states that the Compact would benefit 65,000 poor, rural inhabitants, the data, according to the GAO, do not establish the extent of benefit to the rural poor. Further, the MCC projections assume continued maintenance of projects following completion, whereas the experience of previous donors is that such maintenance has been poor [29]. The MCC response was that, although there may be varying views on the degree of benefit, both agencies agree that the underlying data show that the Compact will help Vanuatu address poverty reduction [30] In lieu of results from the Compacts, MCC officials have pointed to the impact made by the MCC process itself. Under the so-called MCC effect, many countries are said to be establishing reforms in an effort to qualify under the 17 indicators. Yemen has been cited in this regard, because, following its suspension from the threshold program in 2005, it approved a number of reforms to address indicators where its performance had lapsed (and subsequently was reinstated and then later suspended for different reasons). Both the House and Senate approved resolutions in 2007 (H.Res. 294 and S.Res. 103) noting the role the MCC played in encouraging Lesotho to adopt legislation improving the rights of married women.

Table 3. MCC Compacts

| Country | Compact Signed | GNI per capita | Population Living Below $2 p/day (%) | Human Development Index Ranking[a] | FY06 US Econ. Aid (millions)[b] | Compact Size (millions) | Compact Focus |
|---|---|---|---|---|---|---|---|
| Armenia | Mar. 27, 2006 | $2,640 | 31.1% | 83 | $58.0 | $236<br>5 years | -Agriculture/irrigation<br>-Rural roads |
| Benin | Feb. 22, 2006 | $570 | 73.7% | 163 | $14.2 | $307<br>5 years | -Land and property<br>-Financial services<br>-Judicial improvement<br>-Port rehabilitation |
| Burkina Faso | July 14, 2008 | $430 | 71.8% | 176 | $0.0 | $481<br>5 years | -Rural land governance<br>-Agriculture<br>-Roads<br>-Education |
| Cape Verde | July 4, 2005 | $2,430 | NA | 102 | $0.0 | $110<br>5 years | -Agriculture<br>-Transport/roads<br>-Private sector |
| El Salvador | November 29, 2006 | $2,850 | 40.5% | 103 | $24.0 | $461<br>5 years | -Education<br>-Transport/roads<br>-Small business/farm development |
| Georgia | Sept. 12, 2005 | $2,120 | 25.3% | 96 | $58.0 ($0.7) | $295<br>5 years | -Infrastructure/gas<br>-Transport/roads<br>-Agriculture/business |
| Ghana | August 1, 2006 | $590 | 78.5% | 135 | $41.1 ($0.3) | $547<br>5 years | -Agriculture<br>-Transport<br>-Rural Development |
| Honduras | June 13, 2005 | $1,600 | 44.0% | 115 | $27.7 ($0.8) | $215<br>5 years | -Agriculture<br>-Transport/roads |
| Lesotho | July 23, 2007 | $1,000 | 56.1% | 138 | $3.0 ($6.4) | $362.6<br>5 years | -Water sector<br>-Health sector<br>-Private sector |
| Madagascar | April 18, 2005 | $320 | 85.1% | 143 | $26.0 | $110<br>4 years | -Land titling/Agriculture<br>-Financial sector |
| Mali | November 13, 2006 | $500 | 90.6% | 173 | $38.1 | $460.8<br>5 years | -Irrigation<br>-Transport/airport |

# Table 3. MCC Compacts (Continued)

| Country | Compact Signed | GNI per capita | Population Living Below $2 p/day (%) | Human Development Index Ranking[a] | FY06 US Econ. Aid (millions)[b] | Compact Size (millions) | Compact Focus |
|---|---|---|---|---|---|---|---|
| Mongolia | October 22, 2007 | $1,290 | 74.9% | 114 | $6.6 | $285 5 years | -Industrial park<br>-Transport/rail<br>-Property Rights<br>-Voc Ed<br>-Health |
| Morocco | August 31, 2007 | $2,250 | 14.3% | 126 | $18.9 | $697.5 5 years | -Agriculture/Fisheries<br>-Artisan Crafts<br>-Financial Serv/ Enterprise Support |
| Mozambique | July 13, 2007 | $320 | 78.4% | 172 | $44.9 ($148.4) | $506.9 5 years | -Water and Sanitation<br>-Transportation<br>-Land Tenure/Agriculture |
| Namibia | July 28, 2008 | $3,360 | 55.8% | 125 | $7.1 ($51.5) | $305 5 years | - Education<br>- Tourism<br>- Agriculture |
| Nicaragua | July 14, 2005 | $980 | 79.9% | 110 | $24.1 ($0.1) | $175 5 years | - Land titling/Agriculture<br>- Transport/roads |
| Tanzania | February 17, 2008 | $400 | 89.9% | 159 | $57.3 ($176.5) | $698 5 years | -Transport/roads and airport<br>-Energy<br>-Water |
| Vanuatu | March 2, 2006 | $1,840 | NA | 120 | $0.0 | $66 5 years | -Transport rehab<br>-Public Works Dept. |

Sources: Population Living Below $2 Per Day—data from the World Bank, World Development Report, 2007; Gross National Income per capita—2007 data from the World Bank, World Development Indicators 2008. Human Development Index Rank—from UNDP, Human Development Report, 2007/08. MCC Information: Millennium Challenge Corporation. [a] The Human Development Index (HDI) is compiled by the U.N. Development Program and is published annually in the UNDP Human Development Report. It is a composite index that measures the average achievements in a country in three basic dimensions of human development: a long and healthy life, as measured by life expectancy at birth; knowledge, as measured by the adult literacy rate and the combined gross enrolment ratio for primary, secondary, and tertiary schools; and a decent standard of living, as measured by GDP per capita in purchasing power parity (PPP) U.S. dollars. The most recent report (2007/08) evaluates 177 countries, with number 1 having the best HDI and number 177 scoring the worst in the Index. [b] U.S. Economic Aid is defined here as Child Survival/Health, Development Assistance, Economic Support Fund, and FREEDOM Support Act. Figure in parenthesis is HIV/AIDS Initiative.

## Changing Costs

The majority of Compact projects support construction of economic infrastructure, primarily roads and water and sanitation systems. In 2007 and early 2008, costs for the machines and material necessary for these activities rose worldwide. At the same time, the U.S. dollar depreciated significantly. As a result, MCC projects were faced with having less funding than envisioned to meet the agreed-on objectives. The MCC reported that at least six projects were to be scaled-back from the original plans or supplemented by financing from other sources. It is not yet clear how the current worldwide economic crisis is affecting MCC program costs, but it is likely that projects planned for a five-year life span will continually require review and revision.

## Role of USAID and the Future of Agency Programs in MCC Countries

How USAID would participate in the MCC initiative has been a concern of Congress and various policy analysts. Legislation authorizing the MCC requires the Corporation's CEO to coordinate and consult with USAID and directs the Agency to ensure that its programs play a primary role in helping candidate countries prepare for MCC consideration. USAID maintains missions in most of the eligible countries and might be expected to support MCC programs, through contracting, procurement, and monitoring tasks. Although USAID is the chief implementor on behalf of the MCC of threshold programs, its role in other aspects of MCC activities is not clear. Although by way of criticism of the MCC, some in Congress recently have questioned USAID's threshold program role. The explanatory statement accompanying the FY2009 Omnibus expresses the concern that these programs are not meeting their objectives and suggests a review of their efficacy before any new ones are launched.

Another question is how USAID will adjust its own programs in MCC countries. Then-USAID Administrator Natsios told the House Appropriations Committee on May 13, 2004, that the Agency would not withdraw from or cut programs in MCC countries, but would not increase spending either. He said, however, that USAID would work to ensure that its programs operate in an integrated way with MCC-funded activities. Nonetheless, some critics continue to express concern that MCC funding is not always additive, as had been the pledge, but will substitute for portions of previous USAID bilateral development aid programs.

The FY2008 budget request offered a look at how funding levels might be affected by MCC Compacts. With the exceptions of new entries Lesotho, Mozambique, and Morocco, in Compact countries where there had been a bilateral economic assistance program, that assistance would be reduced under the FY2008 budget plan from FY2006 levels. In its FY2008 report on the State/Foreign Operations bill (H.Rept. 110-197), the House Appropriations Committee made note of this trend and expressed the view that MCC aid should be "a complement," not a substitute, to the current aid program.

## Table 4. MCC Low-Income Candidate Countries—FY2009

**Criteria:** Per capita income $1,785 and below, and not prohibited from receiving other U.S. economic assistance.

**Compact Eligible Countries (FY2009)** are in Bold

**Compact Countries** are followed with (C)

**Threshold Eligible Countries (FY2009)** are in Italics

**Threshold Program Countries** are followed with (TC)

### Africa

**Benin** (C)

**Burkina Faso** (TC) (C)

Burundi

Cameroon

Central African Rep

Chad

Comoros

Congo, Dem Rep of

Congo, Rep of

Djibouti

Eritrea

Ethiopia

Gambia

**Ghana** (C)

Guinea

Guinea-Bissau

*Kenya* (TC)

**Lesotho** (C)

*Liberia*

**Madagascar** (C)

**Malawi** (TC)

**Mali** (C)

**Mozambique** (C)

*Niger* (TC)

Nigeria

*Rwanda*

*Sao Tome & Principe* (TC)

Senegal

Sierra Leone

Somalia

Tanzania (C) (TC)

Togo

*Uganda* (TC)

**Zambia** (TC)

### South Asia

Afghanistan

Bangladesh

Bhutan

India

Nepal

Pakistan

Sri Lanka

### Eurasia

*Kyrgyz Rep.* (TC)

**Moldova** (TC)

Tajikistan

Turkmenistan

### East Asia/Pacific

Cambodia

*Timor-Leste*

**Indonesia** (TC)

Kiribati

Laos

**Mongolia** (C)

Papua New Guinea

**Philippines** (TC)

Solomon Islands

Vietnam

### Latin America

Bolivia

*Guyana* (TC)

Haiti

**Honduras** (C)

**Nicaragua** (C)

*Paraguay* (TC)

### Mid-East

Egypt

Yemen

**Morocco** (C)

### Europe

Kosovo

**Table 5. MCC Lower-Middle-Income Candidate Countries—FY2009**

*Criteria:* Per capita income between $1,786 and $3,705, and not prohibited from receiving other U.S. economic assistance.

*Compact Eligible Countries (FY2009)* are in Bold Compact Countries are followed with (C)

*Threshold Eligible Countries (FY2009)* are in Italics Threshold Program Countries are followed with (TC)

| Africa | East Asia/Pacific | Latin America |
|---|---|---|
| Angola | Marshall Islands | **Colombia** |
| **Cape Verde** (C) | Micronesia | Dominican Rep |
| **Namibia** (C) | Samoa | Ecuador |
| Swaziland | Thailand | **El Salvador**(C) |
| | Tonga | Guatemala |
| | Tuvalu | *Peru* (TC) |
| | **Vanuatu** (C) | |

| South Asia | Mid-East |
|---|---|
| Maldives | Algeria |
| | **Jordan** (TC) |
| | Tunisia |

| Eurasia | |
|---|---|
| **Armenia** (C) | **Europe** |
| Azerbaijan | *Albania* (TC) |
| **Georgia** (C) | Bosnia/Herzegovina |
| *Ukraine* (TC) | Macedonia |

# Table 6. MCC Performance Indicators for FY2009

| Ruling Justly | Investing in People | Economic Freedom |
|---|---|---|
| **Control of Corruption**<br>Source: World Bank Institute<br>http://www.worldbank.org/wbi/governance | **Public Primary Education Spending as % of GDP**<br>Sources: UNESCO and National governments | **Inflation**<br>Source: IMF World Economic Outlook |
| **Voice and Accountability**<br>Source: World Bank Institute<br>http://www.worldbank.org/wbi/governance | **Primary Girls' Education Completion Rate**<br>Source: UNESCO | **Fiscal Policy**<br>Source: National governments and IMF World Economic Outlook |
| **Government Effectiveness**<br>Source: World Bank Institute<br>http://www.worldbank.org/wbi/governance | **Public Expenditure on Health as % of GDP**<br>Source: World Health Organization (WHO) | **Trade Policy**<br>Source: The Heritage Foundation, Index of Economic Freedom<br>http://www.heritage.org/research/features/index/ |
| **Rule of Law**<br>Source: World Bank Institute<br>http://www.worldbank.org/wbi/governance | **Immunization Rates: DPT and Measles**<br>Source: World Health Organization (WHO) | **Regulatory Policy**<br>Source: World Bank Institute<br>http://www.worldbank.org/wbi/governance |
| **Civil Liberties**<br>Source: Freedom House<br>http://www.freedomhouse.org/template.cfm?page=15&year=2006 | **Natural Resource Management: Eco-Region Protection, Access to Clean Water and Sanitation, Child Mortality**<br>Sources: Columbia Center for Int'l Earth Science Info Network (CIESIN) and Yale Center for Env. Law and Policy (YCLEP) | **Business Start-Up: Days and Cost of Starting a Business**<br>Source: World Bank<br>http://www.doingbusiness.org |
| **Political Rights**<br>Source: Freedom House<br>http://www.freedomhouse.org/template.cfm?page=15&year=2006 | | **Land Rights and Access**<br>Source: Int'l Fund for Agricultural Development (IFAD) and Int'l Finance Corporation |

# REFERENCES

[1]   When first proposed and in its early years, the initiative was known as the Millennium Challenge Account. Today, both the program and the funding account in the foreign operations budget are more commonly known by the name of the managing entity, the MCC. For a more in-depth discussion of the original MCC proposal and issues debated by Congress in 2003, see CRS Report RL31687, *The Millennium Challenge Account: Congressional Consideration of a New Foreign Aid Initiative*, by Larry Nowels.

[2]   CEO Ambassador John Danilovich stepped down on January 20, 2009.

[3]   The private sector board members are Alan Patricof, co-founder of a venture capital corporation; Lorne Craner, President of the International Republican Institute; former Senate Majority Leader William Frist; and Kenneth Hackett, President and CEO of Catholic Relief Services. The latter is a reappointment, permitted a two-year term; the others are serving their first three-year terms.

[4]   Various types of aid restrictions applied to these countries. For several—Mauritania, Sudan, Cote d'Ivoire,—U.S. aid was blocked because an elected head of government had been deposed by a military coup. For Uzbekistan, legislation banned assistance to the central government. Aid restrictions imposed on nations not cooperating in counter-narcotics efforts (Burma), that are on the terrorist list (Sudan, Syria, North Korea, Iran), or in arrears on debt owed the United States (Syria, Sudan, Zimbabwe) also applied. Notwithstanding these restrictions, each country remained eligible for humanitarian assistance from the United States.

[5]   MCC Public Outreach Meeting, February 15, 2007.

[6]   For a complete statement regarding the Board's rationale, see *Report on the Selection of MCA Eligible Countries for* FY2004, found at http://www.mcc.gov, "Congressional Reports."

[7]   The MCC's authorizing legislation (section 608(d)) requires the Corporation's CEO to provide justification to Congress regarding only those countries declared as eligible for MCC assistance and for those selected for Compact negotiation. Otherwise, there is no statutory requirement for the MCC to comment on its decision-making process, including the rationale for not selecting specific countries.

[8]   Comments by Paul Applegarth at a State Department Foreign Press Center Briefing, November 9, 2004.

[9]   Georgia and Senegal were selected despite not passing the necessary hurdles, but both had been chosen in FY2004 and FY2005.

[10]  See, for example, Steve Radelet, Kaysie Brown, and Bilal Siddiqi, "Round Three of the MCA: Which Countries are Most Likely to Qualify in FY 2006?" Center for Global Development, October 27, 2005.

[11]  Cape Verde had been classified as an eligible low-income country in FY2004 and signed a Compact in July 2005. The Cape Verde case, however, also points out a limitation in using the system of 16 performance indicators. For two of the economic categories, no data are available for Cape Verde, resulting in a failing score on those hurdles.

[12]  Freedom House, "Millennium Challenge Corporation Should Hold Countries to Higher Standards of Democratic Governance," November 2, 2006, http://www.freedomho

use.org; Sheila Herrling, Steve Radelet, and Sarah Rose, "Will Politics Encroach in the MCA FY2007 Selection Round? The Cases of Jordan and Indonesia," Center for Global Development, October 30, 2006, http://www.cgdev.org

[13] Details on each of the negotiated Compacts can be found at the MCC website: http://www.mcc.gov

[14] See letters of John Danilovich to Armenia President Robert Kocharyan on December 16, 2005 and March 11, 2008 on MCC website.

[15] MCC, Public Outreach Meeting Transcript, December 12, 2008, p. 12.

[16] Lorne Craner at Public Outreach Meeting, June 11, 2009.

[17] Initially, assistance for Threshold countries was authorized only for FY2004.

[18] Found at http://www.MCC.gov

[19] Sheila Herrling, "Precedent-Setting Board Meeting for Team Obama," *MCA Monitor Blog*, June 9, 2009, Center for Global Development website http://blogs.cgdev.org/mca-monitor.

[20] See, for example, Millennium Challenge Corporation FY2005 Budget Justification, p. 7. Found at http://www.mcc.gov/about/reports/congressional/budgetjustifications/budget_justification_fy05.pdf.

[21] Prepared statement of Steve Radelet, Senior Fellow at the Center for Global Development, before a hearing of the House International Relations Committee, April 27, 2005.

[22] Organization for Economic Cooperation and Development (OECD), Geographical Distribution of Financial Flows to Aid Recipients, 2000/2004: 2006 edition.

[23] For example, USAID Administrator Natsios remarked in an October 22, 2002 speech at the American Embassy in London that "we estimate in most countries the MCA will provide funding 5 to 10 times higher than existing levels" of U.S. assistance.

[24] Geographical Distribution of Financial Flows to Aid Recipients, 2000/2004: 2006 edition.

[25] Prepared statement of John J. Danilovich, before the Senate Committee on Foreign Relations, September 27, 2005.

[26] Government Accountability Office, *Millennium Challenge Corporation: Progress and Challenges with Compact in Africa*, Testimony, June 28, 2007, GAO-07-1049T.

[27] James Fox and Lex Rieffel, *The Millennium Challenge Account: Moving Toward Smarter Aid*. The Brookings Institution, July 14, 2005, p. 24.

[28] MCC Public Board Meeting, June 11, 2009. Mathematica Policy Research, Inc., *Impact Evaluation of Burkina Faso's BRIGHT Program*, March 2009.

[29] Government Accountability Office, *Millennium Challenge Corporation: Vanuatu Compact Overstates Projected Program Impact*, July 2007, GAO-07-909.

[30] Testimony of Rodney Bent before the House Committee on Foreign Affairs, Subcommittee on Asia, the Pacific, and the Global Environment, July 26, 2007.

In: U.S. Political Programs: Functions and Assessments        ISBN: 978-1-61209-448-9
Editors: Julianna M. Moretti and Karen J. Chordstron    © 2011 Nova Science Publishers, Inc.

*Chapter 5*

# PEACEKEEPING/STABILIZATION AND CONFLICT TRANSITIONS: BACKGROUND AND CONGRESSIONAL ACTION ON THE CIVILIAN RESPONSE/RESERVE CORPS AND OTHER CIVILIAN STABILIZATION AND RECONSTRUCTION CAPABILITIES[*]

## *Nina M. Serafino*

## ABSTRACT

The 111th Congress will face a number of issues regarding the development of civilian capabilities to carry out stabilization and reconstruction activities. In September 2008, Congress passed the Reconstruction and Stabilization Civilian Management Act, 2008, as Title XVI of the Duncan Hunter National Defense Authorization Act for Fiscal Year 2009 (S. 3001, P.L. 110-417, signed into law October 14, 2008). This legislation codified the existence and functions of the State Department Office of the Coordinator for Reconstruction and Stabilization (S/CRS) and authorized new operational capabilities within the State Department, a Civilian Response Corps of government employees with an active and a standby component, and a Civilian Reserve Corps.

S/CRS was established in 2004 to address longstanding concerns, both within Congress and the broader foreign policy community, over the perceived lack of the appropriate capabilities and processes to deal with transitions from conflict to stability. These capabilities and procedures include adequate planning mechanisms for stabilization and reconstruction operations, efficient interagency coordination structures and procedures in carrying out such tasks, and appropriate civilian personnel for many of the non-military tasks required. Effectively distributing resources among the various executive branch actors, maintaining clear lines of authority and jurisdiction, and balancing short- and long-term objectives are major challenges for designing, planning, and conducting post-conflict operations, as is fielding the appropriate civilian personnel.

---

[*] This is an edited, reformatted and augmented edition of a United States Congressional Research Service publication, CRS Report RL32862, dated June 16, 2009.

Since July 2004, S/CRS has worked to establish the basic concepts, mechanisms, and capabilities necessary to carry out such operations. Working with a staff that has slowly grown from a few dozen to 112 individuals from the State Department, other executive branch agencies, and on contract as of January 30, 2009, S/CRS has taken steps to monitor and plan for potential conflicts, to develop a rapid-response crisis management "surge" capability, to improve interagency and international coordination, to develop interagency training exercises, and to help State Department regional bureaus develop concepts and proposals for preventive action.

In June 2008, Congress specifically provided $65 million for S/CRS and USAID S&R activities, including the establishment and implementation of civilian response capabilities, in the Supplemental Appropriations Act, 2008 (P.L. 110-252). Congress provided another $75 million in FY2009 appropriations in the Omnibus Appropriations Act, 2009 (P.L. 111-8).

On March 7, 2009, the Obama Administration requested $323.3 million in FY20 10 funds to continue the development of the Civilian Response Corps (CRC) active and standby components, formally launched in July 2008, and the establishment of a 2,000-member civilian reserve component. In addition, the Administration requested a $40 million Stabilization Bridge Fund under the Economic Support Fund (ESF) to fund activities of deployed CRC members responding to urgent needs until other funds are reprogrammed, transferred, appropriated, or otherwise made available for that purpose. Among the issues that Congress will face regarding the development of civilian capabilities are the means to support, maintain, and deploy the civilian response and reserve corps.

In action on the Foreign Relations Authorization Act, Fiscal Years 2010 and 2011 (H.R. 2410), the House authorized the Administration's CSI FY2010 funding request of $323.3 million and "such sums as may be necessary for fiscal year 2011." In floor action, the House incorporated an amendment to expand the categories of persons who would be permitted to participate in the CRC.

## INTRODUCTION

In its FY2010 budget request, submitted to Congress on May 7, 2009, the Obama Administration requested $323 million in the State Department budget for the Civilian Stabilization Initiative (CSI), the effort begun by the George W. Bush Administration to develop a three-component "ready response" civilian force of 4,250 members. In addition, the May 7 budget request included a $40 million Stabilization Bridge Fund to deploy members of this force. If approved by Congress, these funds would enable the Administration to complete the recruitment, hiring, and training of force members. This "surge capacity" would enable the U.S. government to deploy rapidly civilians to address emergency stabilization needs.

For well over a decade, there has been widespread concern that the U.S. government lacks appropriate civilian "tools" to carry out state-building tasks in post-conflict situations. This concern grew from U.S. military operations in Haiti, Somalia, Bosnia, and elsewhere, where military forces were tasked with a variety of state-building tasks, such as creating justice systems, assisting police, and promoting governance. With the wars in Afghanistan and Iraq, consensus increased that the United States must develop adequate civilian organizational structures, procedures, and personnel to response effectively to post-conflict and other "stabilization and reconstruction" (S&R) situations.

The George W. Bush Administration launched several initiatives to do just that. The centerpiece of its efforts was the establishment of the Office of the Coordinator for Reconstruction and Stabilization (S/CRS) in the Office of the Secretary of State. Created in mid-2004, S/CRS was tasked with designing, and in some cases establishing, the new structures within the State Department and elsewhere that would allow civilian agencies to develop effective policies, processes, and personnel to build stable and democratic states. Among other tasks, S/CRS developed plans for the creation of a civilian "surge" capability that could respond rapidly to S&R emergencies.

In the early months of the Obama Administration, Administration officials signaled their support for civilian S&R capabilities. In her January 2009 confirmation hearings before the Senate Foreign Relations Committee, Secretary of State Hillary R. Clinton mentioned the State Department's new S&R responsibilities, citing a Department need to demonstrate competence and secure funding to carry them out. Secretary of Defense Robert Gates, while serving in that position under former President George Bush, urged the development of civilian capabilities in major speeches [1].

As Senator, Vice President Joseph Biden was the co-sponsor, with Senator Lugar, of legislation, first introduced in 2004, to create an office within the State Department that would coordinate U.S. government S&R operations and deploy civilian government employees and private citizens to carry out state-building activities in crises abroad.

In its second session, the 110$^{th}$ Congress enacted legislation that "operationalizes" certain groups of personnel within the Department of State and other federal agencies for S&R efforts by authorizing the creation of federal civilian "response" units, as well as the creation of a volunteer S&R civilian reserve force, akin to the military reserve force. This legislation advances the work of previous Congresses regarding Bush Administration initiatives to improve the conduct of (S&R) efforts. With the passage in September 2008 of Title XVI of the Duncan Hunter National Defense Authorization Act for Fiscal Year 2009 (S. 3001/P.L. 110-417), signed into law October 14, 2008, Congress took two important steps:

- It established S/CRS as part of permanent law.
- It formally "operationalized" certain units in civilian federal agencies, most particularly the State Department, transforming it from an institution devoted solely to diplomacy to one that also has a role in effecting change through "onthe-ground" personnel and programs dedicated to promoting security and stability in transitions from conflict and post-conflict situations. This was accomplished by authorizing the creation of a two component "readiness response" corps consisting of a small active unit of federal employees drawn from several agencies and a federal standby unit, and a large civilian reserve corps, analogous to the military reserve.

The 111$^{th}$ Congress is faced with several remaining tasks. One is whether to create a mechanism, such as envisioned in early legislation, to create a flexible, no-year, discretionary Conflict Response Fund to be drawn upon by civilian agencies for S&R efforts. The other is the appropriate level of staffing and funding for S/CRS, and the means to develop, maintain, support and deploy the Civilian Response Corps and Civilian Reserve Corps.

This report provides background on these issues. It also discusses proposals and tracks related legislative action.

# BACKGROUND

Former President George W. Bush's pledge, articulated in his February 2, 2005, State of the Union address, "to build and preserve a community of free and independent nations, with governments that answer to their citizens, and reflect their own cultures" cast the once-discredited concept of building or rebuilding government institutions, economies, and civic cultures in a new light. During the 1990s, many policymakers considered the establishment of new institutions in troubled countries to be an overly expensive, if not futile exercise. The use of U.S. military forces for such activities, particularly in the first half of the decade, was troubling to many Members. In the past few years, however, the Bush Administration, in response to concerns about the threats posed by weak and fragile states, reframed both U.S. security and international development policy and initiated dramatic corresponding changes in U.S. governmental structures and practices. These changes, the Bush Administration argued, would enable the United States to perform such tasks more efficiently and at a lesser cost, particularly in transitions from conflict and in post-conflict situations.

A key component of these changes was the establishment and reinforcement of new civilian structures and forces, in particular S/CRS and the civilian response/reserve corps. The Bush Administration made these new civilian entities a prominent feature in two initiatives: the National Security Presidential Directive 44 (NSPD-44) of December 2005 on the management of interagency reconstruction and stabilization operations and the "transformational diplomacy" reorganization of State Department personnel and practices announced in January 2006.

These initiatives were intended to enhance the United States' ability to function effectively on the world scene in the environment. created by the terrorist attacks on the United States of September 11, 2001 (9/11). In that environment, many analysts perceive that the greatest threats to U.S. security often will emerge within states that are either too weak to police their territory or lack the political will or capacity to do so. To deal with that environment, in 2006 former Secretary of State Condeleezza Rice outlined a new U.S. foreign policy strategy focusing on the "intersections of diplomacy, democracy promotion, economic reconstruction and military security" and involving extensive changes in government to carry that strategy out.2 State-building (or nation- building as it is often called) was at the center of this strategy. Both initiatives reinforced the important role that the Bush Administration gave S/CRS in policymaking and implementation dealing with conflict transitions and weak and fragile states.

## Evolving Perceptions of Post-Conflict Needs [3]

The creation of S/CRS in July 2004 responded to increasing calls for the improvement of U.S. civilian capabilities to plan and carry out post-conflict state-building operations. Several factors combined after 9/11 to lead many analysts to conclude that such operations are vital to U.S. security and that the United States must reorganize itself to conduct them effectively, in particular by creating new and improving existing civilian institutions to carry them out. Foremost among these factors, for many analysts, was the widespread perception since 9/11 that global instability directly threatens U.S. security and that it is a vital U.S. interest to transform weak and failing states into stable, democratic ones. Related to this was the expectation that responding to the threat of instability will require the United States and the international community to intervene periodically in foreign conflicts with "peacekeeping" [4] and "stabilization" forces at about the same intensive pace as it had done since the early 1990s. Because that pace stressed the U.S. military, many policymakers believed that the United States must create and enhance civilian capabilities to carry out the peacebuilding tasks that are widely viewed as necessary for stability and reconstruction in fragile, conflict-prone, and post-conflict states. Finally, numerous analyses distilling the past decade and a half of experience with multifaceted peacekeeeping and peacebuilding operations raised hopes that rapid, comprehensive, and improved peacebuilding efforts could significantly raise the possibilities of achieving sustainable peace.

Post-conflict operations are complex undertakings, usually involving the participation of several United Nations departments and U.N. system agencies, the international financial institutions and a plethora of non-governmental humanitarian and development organizations, as well as the military and other departments or ministries of the United States and other nations [5]. The United States developed its contributions to the earliest international "peacekeeping" operations of the 1990s on an ad hoc basis, with little interagency planning and coordination, and often with the U.S. military in the lead. The military was called upon to perform such missions not only for its extensive resources but also because no other U.S. government agency could match the military's superior planning and organizational capabilities. In addition, because of its manpower, the military carried out most of the U.S. humanitarian and nation-building contribution, even though some believed that civilians might be better suited to carry out such tasks, especially those tasks involving cooperation with humanitarian NGOs.

During the 1990s, many analysts began to perceive the need to improve and increase civilian contributions to peacekeeping operations, especially for those activities related to planning and conducting operations and to establishing a secure environment. An important Clinton Administration initiative was the May 1997 Presidential Decision Directive (PDD) 56, entitled The Clinton Administration's Policy on Managing Complex Contingency Operations. According to the white paper explaining it, PDD 56 sought to address interagency planning and coordination problems through new planning and implementing mechanisms [6]. Due to what some analysts describe as internal bureaucratic resistance, PDD 56's provisions were never formally implemented, although some of its practices were informally adopted. (In December 2005, President Bush issued National Security Presidential Directive (NSPD) 44, which replaced PDD56. For more information, see below.) The Clinton Administration also attempted to remedy the shortage of one critical nation-building tool, international civilian police forces, through PDD 71, which a white paper describes as outlining policy guidelines for strengthening criminal justice systems in support of peace operations [7]. While never implemented by the Clinton Administration, PDD 71 has been partially put into force by the Bush Administration [8]

Improvements in the provision of social and economic assistance were also viewed as crucial to successful outcomes. Post-conflict populations need "safety net" and poverty alleviation programs, as well as technical assistance and advice on monetary and fiscal policy and debt management in order to create an environment conducive to democratization and economic growth [9] While the popular image of U.S. post-conflict assistance is the post-World War II Marshall Plan, through which the United States provided the foreign assistance needed for Europe's post-conflict reconstruction, the United States is no longer the sole, and often not the dominant, donor in post-conflict situations. Multilateral institutions became increasingly important during the 1990s, when small, regional conflicts proliferated following the collapse of the Soviet Union.

International organizations such as the World Bank and the International Monetary Fund now play crucial roles, working with the U.S. government to provide economic assistance and technical advice on rebuilding post-conflict economies. (Nevertheless, although the United States has provided some funding for economic reconstruction multilaterally for the recent Afghanistan and Iraq operations, most U.S. funding for post-conflict operations is provided bilaterally.) Many analysts now judge that multilateral assistance is more effective for the recipient country than bilateral aid for two reasons [10]. First, disbursing funds multilaterally through U.N. agencies or international organizations gives greater assurance that it will reach recipients than providing aid bilaterally with direct payments to individual governments or non-governmental organizations (NGOs). In addition, analysts find that bilateral aid is more likely to be apportioned according to the donor's foreign policy priorities rather than the economic needs of the recipient country [11].

For many analysts and policymakers, the ongoing Iraq operation has illustrated a U.S. government need for new planning and coordination arrangements that would provide a leadership role for civilians in post-conflict phases of military operations and new civilian capabilities to augment and relieve the military as soon as possible, and greater international coordination. The perception of a continued need for such operations, and the perceived inefficiencies of the still largely ad hoc U.S. responses have reinvigorated calls for planning and coordination reform. The extreme stresses placed on the U.S. military by combat roles in Iraq and Afghanistan have pushed those calls in a new direction, to the development of adequate civilian capabilities to perform those tasks.

## Calls for Change

The perception that international terrorism can exploit weak, unstable states convinced many policymakers and analysts of the need to strengthen U.S. and international capabilities to foster security, good governance and economic development, especially in post-conflict situations. The 9/11 Commission and the Commission on Weak States and U.S. National Security found that weak states, as well as unsuccessful post-conflict transitions, pose a threat to U.S. security [12]. These groups argued that such states often experience economic strife and political instability that make them vulnerable to drug trafficking, human trafficking and other criminal enterprises, and to linkage with non-state terrorist groups (such as the links between the previous Taliban government in Afghanistan and the Al Qaeda terrorist network). Weak states also are unprepared to handle major public health issues, such as HIV/AIDS, that can generate political and economic instability [13]. These commissions, and other analysts, argued for assistance to the governments of weak states and of post-conflict transitions regimes to help them control their territories, meet their citizens' basic needs, and create legitimate governments based on effective, transparent institutions.

These and other studies recognized a need to enhance U.S. government structures and capabilities for conducting post-conflict operations [14]. Although differing in several respects, the studies largely agreed on five points: (1) the ad hoc system needs to be replaced with a permanent mechanism for developing contingency plans and procedures for joint civil-military operations led by civilians; (2) mechanisms to rapidly deploy U.S. civilian government and government- contracted personnel need to be put in place; (3) preventive action needs to be considered; (4) the U.S. government needs to enhance multinational capabilities to carry out post-conflict security tasks and to better coordinate international aid; and (5) flexible funding arrangements are needed to deal with such situations. In addition, some urged substantial amounts of funding for flexible U.S. and international accounts [15]

### *Proposals for New Civilian Forces*

A prominent feature of several of the reports on stabilization and reconstruction operations was a recommendation to develop rapidly-deployable civilian forces to undertake state-building functions, particularly those related to rule of law, even before hostilities had ceased. Many analysts view the early deployment of rule of law personnel as essential to providing security from the outset of an operation, which they argue will enhance the possibilities for long-term stability and democracy in an intervened or post-conflict country. Many view the development of civilian groups to do so as permitting the earlier withdrawal of military personnel than would otherwise be possible.

The concept of a cohesive, rapidly deployable unit of civilian experts for stabilization and reconstruction operations dates back at least to the Clinton Administration. In PDD-71, which dealt with strengthening criminal justice systems in peace operations, the Clinton Administration identified such an initiative as a high priority, according to the PDD-71 White Paper [16]. Six studies between 2003 and 2005 endorsed the creation of cohesive, rapidly deployable units of civilian experts for stabilization and reconstruction operations. These include a 2003 report of the National Defense University (NDU; [17] a March 2004 report of the Center for Strategic and International Studies (CSIS); [18] an April 2004 report of the U.S. Institute of Peace (USIP); [19] a book by a USIP analyst; [20] and the Defense Science Board 2004 Summer Study on transitions from hostilities [21]. The establishment and deployment of such a corps, now in its initial stages (see below), marks a substantial change from past practices.

## Critics Respond

Some analysts have questioned the utility of S/CRS and of the rationale that underlines its creation and the adoption of the transformational diplomacy strategy more broadly. Two think- tank studies published in January 2006 dispute the concept that weak and failed states are per se among the most significant threats to the United States. They point out that weak states are not the only locations where terrorists have found recruits or sought safe-haven as they have exploited discontent and operated in developed countries as well. A report of the Center for Global Development states that many factors beyond the weakness or lack of government institutions—demographic, political, religious, cultural, and geographic—contribute to the development of terrorism [22]. As a result, an emphasis on weak and failed states can lead the United States to give short shrift to more tangible threats and to areas of greater U.S. interest. The CATO Institute study worries that former Secretary Rice's focus on promoting "responsible sovereignty" as an underpinning of transformational diplomacy may provide potential justification for eroding the current international norm of respect for national sovereignty, leading the United States into fruitless interventions [23]

In addition, some analysts are skeptical that the problems of weak and failed states can be most dealt with through military and political interventions aimed at creating viable government institutions. The effectiveness of past efforts is a subject of debate, with differing views on the criteria for and the number of successes, draws, and failures, as is the best means to achieve success.

There is some skepticism that state-building efforts will result in success in most instances. In the words of one scholar, "barring exceptional circumstances (the war against the Taliban after 9/11), we had best steer clear of missions that deploy forces (of whatever kind) into countries to remake them anew.... The success stories (Germany, Japan) are the exceptions and were possible because of several helpful conditions that will not be replicated elsewhere." [24]. Others, however, point to cases such as Mozambique and El Salvador as examples that state building efforts can promote peace after civil strife.

## Creating Civilian Reconstruction and Stabilization Capabilities: Congressional and Executive Actions, 2004-2007

### The "Lugar-Biden" Legislation

On February 25, 2004, Senators Lugar and Biden introduced the Stabilization and Reconstruction Civilian Management Act of 2004 "to build operational readiness in civilian agencies...." (At the time, these senators were respectively the Chairman and Ranking Member of the Senate Foreign Relations Committee [SFRC].) The bill provided concrete proposals for establishing and funding the two new "operational" entities that had been recommended in think tank reports. This legislation contained three main proposals: (1) establish in law and fund a State Department Office for Stabilization and Reconstruction, (2) create an Emergency Response Readiness Force, and (3) create and fund an annually replenishable emergency response fund similar to that used for refugee and migration funds [25]. The SFRC reported S. 2127 on March 18, 2004, but it was not considered by the full Senate; its companion bill (H.R. 3996, 108th Congress, introduced by Representative Schiff) was not considered by the House International Relations Committee. In subsequent years, similar legislation was introduced, [26] but until 2008 the only bill to pass either chamber was a subsequent Lugar-Biden measure, the Reconstruction and Stabilization Civilian Management Act of 2006 (S. 3322/109th Congress). S.3322 was introduced in the Senate May 26, 2006, and approved without amendment by unanimous consent the same day. It was received by the House on June 6, 2006, and referred to the House International Relations Committee. No further action occurred until the 110th Congress until the House passage of on March 5, 2008, of a House bill with almost the same title, *the Reconstruction and Stabilization Civilian Management Act of 2008* (H.R. 1084) , and the incorporation of a version of that bill into the conference version of the FY2009 NDAA, (S. 3001, P.L. 110-417, see below.)

## *S/CRS Start-Up and Early Congressional Mandate*

S/CRS began operations in July 2004 on a somewhat more tentative status than that envisioned by the Lugar-Biden bill. The office was created by then Secretary of State Colin Powell without statutory authority and the Coordinator, appointed by the Secretary, was not given the rank of "Ambassador-at-Large." By the beginning of 2005, S/CRS had a staff of 37 individuals from the State Department, USAID, and several other U.S. government agencies, including the Departments of Defense, Commerce, and the Treasury.

The U.S. military supported S/CRS' creation and its mission. In prepared statement for testimony before the Armed Services committees in February 2005, General Richard B. Myers, Chairman of the Joint Chiefs of Staff, cited the creation of S/CRS as "an important step" in helping "post- conflict nations achieve peace, democracy, and a sustainable market economy." "In the future, provided this office is given appropriate resources, it will synchronize military and civilian efforts and ensure an integrated national approach is applied to post-combat peacekeeping, reconstruction and stability operations," according to General Myers [27]. S/CRS also received an endorsement from a task force headed by two former Members. The June 2005 report of the Congressionally-mandated Task Force on the United Nations, chaired by former Speaker of the House of Representatives Newt Gingrich and former Senate Majority Leader George Mitchell, recommended that the United States strengthen S/CRS and that Congress provide it with the necessary resources to coordinate with the United Nations [28]

## *2004 Congressional Mandate*

Congress first endorsed the creation of S/CRS in 2004 as part of the Consolidated Appropriations Act for FY2005 (H.R. 4818, P.L. 108-447), signed into law December 8, 2004. Section 408, Division D, defined six responsibilities for the office, the first five of which respond to the first need—to create a readily deployable crisis response mechanism—stated above. As legislated by P.L. 108-447, S/CRS' functions are (1) to catalogue and monitor the non-military resources and capabilities of executive branch agencies, state and local governments, and private and non-profit organizations "that are available to address crises in countries or regions that are in, or are in transition from, conflict or civil strife"; (2) to determine the appropriate non-military U.S. response to those crises, "including but not limited to demobilization, policy, human rights monitoring, and public information efforts"; (3) to plan that response; (4) to coordinate the development of interagency contingency plans for that response; (5) to coordinate the training of civilian personnel to perform stabilization and reconstruction activities in response to crises in such countries or regions"; and (6) to monitor political and economic instability worldwide to anticipate the need for U.S. and international assistance. In subsequent legislation (S. 3001, P.L. 110-417, the Duncan Hunter National Defense Authorization Act for Fiscal Year 2009), Congress expanded this list of functions. (See below.)

Congress funds S/CRS under the State Department's Diplomatic and Consular Affairs budget. S/CRS has received funding through annual appropriations and supplemental appropriations.

### S/CRS Role in Interagency Coordination

The S/CRS role in interagency coordination was formalized under NSPD-44, issued by former President Bush on December 7, 2005, to improve conflict-response coordination among executive branch agencies. NSPD-44 assigns the Secretary of State the lead responsibility for developing the civilian response for conflict situations and related S&R activities; the Secretary may direct the Coordinator for Reconstruction and Stabilization to assist with those tasks. Under NSPD-44, the Secretary of State is also responsible for, and may delegate to the Coordinator, coordination of the interagency processes to identify states at risk, the leadership of interagency planning to prevent or mitigate conflict, and the development of detailed contingency plans for stabilization and reconstruction operations, as well as for identifying appropriate issues for resolution or action through the National Security Council (NSC) interagency process as outlined in President Bush's first National Security Policy Directive (NSPD- 1, "Organization of the National Security Council System," signed February 1, 200129). NSPD-44,, entitled "Management of Interagency Efforts Concerning Reconstruction and Stabilization," expanded S/CRS activities beyond those conferred by the Congressional mandate (see above). (NSPD-44 supersedes PDD-56, referred to above.)

S/CRS developed the mechanism for interagency cooperation in actual operations, drafting the January 22, 2007, Interagency Management System (IMS) for Reconstruction and Stabilization, which was approved by a National Security Council (NSC) deputies meeting. This document lays out a plan for interagency coordination in responding to highly complex reconstruction and stabilization crises. Under the IMS, the Coordinator for Reconstruction and Stabilization is one of three co-chairs of the central coordinating body for the U.S. government response to a crisis. (The others are the appropriate regional Assistant Secretary of State and the relevant NSC Director.) Under the plan, S/CRS is charged with providing support to a civilian planning cell integrated with relevant military entities (a geographic combatant command or an equivalent multinational headquarters).

## CODIFYING CIVILIAN RECONSTRUCTION AND STABILIZATION ASSISTANCE AND STATE DEPARTMENT

## Capabilities: Title XVI, P.L. 110-417, October 14, 2008

The effort to expand civilian capabilities to perform stabilization and reconstruction tasks reached an important benchmark in October 2008. Through Title XVI of the Duncan Hunter National Defense Authorization Act for Fiscal Year 2009 (P.L. 110-417), Congress amended the basic foreign assistance and State Department statutes to (1) authorize the President to provide assistance for a reconstruction and stabilization crisis, (2) formally establish S/CRS and assign it specific functions, and (3) authorize a Response Readiness Corps (RRC) and a Civilian Reserve Corps (CRC). The authority to provide assistance for a reconstruction and stabilization crisis was created by amending chapter 1 of part III of the Foreign Assistance Act of 1961, as amended (FAA, 22 U.S.C. 2351 et. seq.) by inserting a new section. This authority is, however, subject to a time limitation: it may be exercised only during FY2009-FY20 11. The new authority for S/CRS, the RRC and the CRC was created by amending Title

I of the State Department Basic Authorities Act of 1956 (22 U.S.C..2651a et. seq.). These authorities are permanent.

Authorizes Assistance for Reconstruction and Stabilization Crises Under the heading Authority to Provide Assistance for Reconstruction and Stabilization Crises, Section 1604 of P.L. 110-417 adds a new section to the FAA. Section 681 provides authority for the President to use U.S. civilian agencies or non-Federal employees to furnish assistance for reconstruction and stabilization in order to prevent conflict and to secure peace. The specific authority permits the President to "to assist in reconstructing and stabilizing a country or region that is at risk of, in, or is in transition from, conflict or civil strife... ." As passed in P.L. 110-417, this authority may be exercised for three fiscal years (FY2009-FY201 1).

To provide such assistance, the President must determine that U.S. national security interests are served by using such personnel. The President may use funds made available under any other provision of the FAA that are transferred or reprogrammed for the purposes of this section, subject to the 1 5-day prior notification to congress required by section 634A, FAA. The President must also consult with and provide a written policy justification to Congress' foreign affairs and appropriations committees (under Section 614(a)(3), FAA) prior to its use. The assistance may be provided notwithstanding any other provision of law, and on such terms and conditions as the President may determine. The section does not provided authority "to transfer funds between accounts or between Federal departments or agencies."

### Makes S/CRS a Permanent State Department Office and Assigns Specific Functions

A major objective of proponents of improving the civilian capacity to perform stabilization and reconstruction operations was to provide S/CRS with a permanent authorization and specified functions mandated by law. Such an authorization was a key feature of the initial and subsequent versions of the Lugar-Biden legislation. P.L. 110-417, Section 1605, codifies the existence of S/CRS by amending Title 1 of the State Department Basic Authorities Act of 1956 (22 U.S.C. 2651 et seq.), which, among other functions, provides for the establishment of the higher level positions within the Department of State. This codification prevents the dismantling of the office without the legislative consent of Congress.

It also assigns nine specific functions to S/CRS, largely mirroring the functions assigned by Congress in its original legislation on S/CRS, as cited above. In general, these functions convey on the Coordinator for Reconstruction and Stabilization an overall responsibility for monitoring and assessing political and economic instability, and planning an appropriate U.S. response. Some of these functions are to be undertaken in coordination or conjunction with USAID and other relevant executive branch agencies [30]

### Authorizes a Civilian Response Readiness Corps and a Civilian Reserve Corps

Civilian personnel available through the U.S. government to perform S&R activities are scarce, decentralized in organization, and difficult to call up. Many analysts viewed the remedy to this situation as the creation of a corps of "on-the-ground" civilian personnel which could develop and implement state-building activities and interact with U.S. military personnel at all levels in order to foster security and stability in troubled situations.

From the beginning, Luger\Biden legislation sought to authorize the establishment of such a corps. The Bush Administration began creating a small response cadre of government employees in its FY2006 and FY2007 budget submissions, and proposed a full-scale corps in its February 2008 Civilian Stabilization Initiative [31].

P.L. 110-417 establishes the Response Readiness Corps and the Civilian Reserve Corps "to provide assistance in support of stabilization and reconstruction activities in foreign countries or regions that are at risk of, in, or are in transition from, conflict or civil strife."

[*Note that the terminology for this "surge" capability differs in the legislation from that used by the Bush and Obama Administration in naming its components. The Obama Administration combines the Civilian Response Readiness Corps and the Civilian Reserve Corps into one "Civilian Response Corps" (CRC) with three components. The Obama Administration's CRC active and standby units (CRC-A and CRC-S) correspond to this legislation's Civilian Response Readiness Corps, and the reserve component (CRC-R) corresponds to this legislation's Civilian Reserve Corps.*]

This civilian capability consists of two components:

- The Response Readiness Corps (RRC) of federal employees composed of active and standby components consisting of U.S. government personnel, including employees of the Department of State, USAID, and other agencies who are recruited and trained to provide reconstruction and stabilization assistance when deployed to do so by the Secretary of State. No specific number is provided for members of these components. The legislation notes that members of the active component would be specifically employed to serve in the Corps. The Secretary of State is authorized to establish and maintain the SRC, in consultation with the Administrator of USAID and the heads of other appropriate U.S. government agencies. The Secretary of State alone is authorized to deploy its members.

- The Civilian Reserve Corps (CRC) of individuals with "the skills necessary for carrying out reconstruction and stabilization activities, and who have volunteered for that purpose." The Secretary is authorized to establish the Corps in consultation with the Administrator of USAID, and is authorized to employ and train its members, as well as to deploy them subject to a presidential determination under the proposed Section 618 of the Foreign Assistance Act of 1961, as amended. No size was specified for the Civilian Reserve Corp. For the Corps to deploy, the President must issue a determination that U.S. national security interests would be served by providing assistance for a reconstruction and stabilization crisis (see above).

## DEVELOPMENT OF THE S/CRS OFFICE, RESPONSIBILITIES, AND CAPABILITIES

Since 2004, S/CRS has worked to develop the knowledge, capacity, procedures to ably respond to the needs of countries at risk of conflict, in transitions from conflict, and in the early stages of recovery from conflict. S/CRS has grown from a few dozen to a staff of 112, as of January 30, 2009. Of that staff, a little over half were State Department personnel: 36 Foreign Service officers on one-year tours, 22 State Department permanent civil service employees, and an additional three State Department personnel on detail.

Another nine are on detail from other executive branch agencies: Commerce (1); Justice (1); Office of the Director of National Intelligence (1); USAID (2); and DOD (4). (Of the four from DOD, one is from the Joint Staff, one from the Office of the Secretary of Defense, one from the Army Corps of Engineers, and one from the Air Force.)

In addition, 36 contractors work for S/CRS, as do six fellows and interns. S/CRS carries out a range of activities: monitoring potential conflict, planning for U.S. responses to conflict, and evaluating and initiating programs to prevent conflict or the spread of conflict, among others.

## Monitoring and Planning for Potential Conflicts

To monitor potential crises, S/CRS asked the National Intelligence Council (NIC) to provide it twice a year with a list of weak states most susceptible to crisis, from which S/CRS chooses one or more as test cases to prepare contingency plans for possible interventions.

S/CRS also has worked with the USAID Office of Conflict Management and Mitigation, which develops techniques for preparing highly detailed assessments of current and impending conflicts.

In addition, S/CRS has worked with the U.S. military's Joint Forces Command (JFCOM) to develop a common civilian-military planning model for stabilization and reconstruction operations. S/CRS also assists U.S. embassies abroad in assessing the potential for conflict in individual countries.

## Developing and Carrying Out Conflict Response Activities

S/CRS takes a lead in planning, developing, and implementing most of the small conflict response programs that are carried out with funds and other assistance provided under DOD's "Section 1207" authority [32]. Since FY2006, "Section 1207" authority has been used to carry out conflict prevention and response efforts in 11 individual countries and two regions [33]. These targeted programs to address specific problems range from $4 million to help provide basic health, education and infrastructure in areas recently reclaimed from insurgents in Colombia, to a $5 million to improve the Lebanese Internal Security Force comm.-unications capacity, to $30 million to assist internally displaced persons in Georgia.

## The Response Corps Pilot Project

Well before Congress authorized the creation of a Civilian Response Corps (see above), S/CRS took the first steps in the lengthy process of creating integrated and coherent groups of crisis- response personnel from executive branch agencies. In 2006, S/CRS created, as a pilot project, a small nucleus of active and retired government employees to deploy to operations. S/CRS began deploying members of the active response component during the last half of 2006. In 2006, ARC members were deployed to Darfur, Lebanon, Chad, and Nepal. About ten other deployments followed, some with standby component members and other members of the S/CRS staff [34]

## Other Activities

To address the need for greater interagency, particularly civil-military, planning and coordination, S/CRS worked with the military entities to develop civilian-military training exercises for stabilization and reconstruction operations. It has entered into an agreement with the U.S. Army to train civilian planners. And, among other activities, it has developed ties with other international participants to coordinate and enhance civilian capabilities for stabilization and reconstruction activities.

# CURRENT DEVELOPMENT OF THE CIVILIAN RESPONSE CORPS (CRC)

On July 16, 2008, then Secretary of State Rice formally launched the Civilian Response Corps active and standby components with a speech thanking Congress for the passage of funding in the Supplemental Appropriations Act, 2008, to establish the CRC. Under plans developed by the Bush Administration (and continued by the Obama Administration) the three-component corps would consist of a 250-member active component (CRC-A) of U.S. government employees who could deploy within 48 hours, a 2,000-member standby component (CRC-S) of U.S. government employees who could deploy within 30 days, and a 2,000 member reserve component (CRC-R) of experts from other public institutions and the private sectors who would be available for deployment in 45-60 days.

Under the leadership of S/CRS, two other State Department offices and eight other contributing departments and agencies are now recruiting the first 100 members of the CRC-A, and 500 members of the stand-by component. Besides the State Department, contributors are USAID and the Departments of Agriculture, Commerce, Justice, Health and Human Services, Homeland Security, Treasury, and Transportation.

## Initial CRC Funding: FY2008 and FY2009

As of May 7, 2009, the date the Obama Administration presented its detailed FY20 10 budget request, Congress had appropriated $140 million for the establishment and deployment of the active and standby civilian response components. These FY2008 and FY2009 funds together provided for the establishment of a 250-member active component and a 500-member standby component.

In June 2008, Congress specifically provided $65 million for S/CRS and USAID S&R activities in supplemental appropriations through the Supplemental Appropriations Act, 2008, P.L. 110-252, signed into law June 30, 2008.35 Of that amount, up to $30 million was appropriated as FY2008 funds (under the State Department Diplomatic and Consular Programs account) for the State Department "to establish and implement a coordinated civilian response capacity" and up to $25 million was appropriated to USAID as FY2008 supplemental funds for that agency to do the same (122 Stat.2328-2329). The remaining $10 million was part of FY2009 supplemental bridge fund appropriations for the State Department. (This appropriations was less than the $248.6 million that the Bush

Administration requested in February 2008, for its "Civilian Stabilization Initiative" [CSI], which rolled into one its request for funds for continued operations of S/CRS, funds for a 250-member interagency CRC Active Response component and a 2,000-member Standby Response component, and a 2,000-member Civilian Reserve component, and money for deployment of experts.) The P.L. 110-252 funding expires on September 30, 2009.

In March 2009, Congress provided $75 million in FY2009 appropriations to the newly created Civilian Stabilization Initiative account in order to establish and support the CRC active and standby components (Omnibus Appropriations Act, 2009, P.L. 111-8, signed into law March 11, 2009). This included $45 million in State Department funds and $30 million in USAID funds.

## FY2010 Budget Request

The Obama Administration's May 7, 2009, FY2010 budget request of $323.272 million for the Civilian Stabilization Initiative (CSI) continues the Bush Administration plans for the establishment of a 4,250 member, three-component civilian response corps. According to the State Department request for these funds, the CSI will provide "trained, equipped, and mission- ready civilian experts and institutionalized systems to meet national security imperatives, including in partnership with the U.S. Armed Forces.... " This corps will enable the President and Secretary of State "to react to unanticipated conflict in foreign countries" while reducing or eliminating "the need for large military deployments in such crises," according to the State Department request.

The requested FY2010 CSI funding would support the continued development of the CRC, including the establishment of a reserve component, which has yet to receive funds, and would provide for the institutional structure to coordinate interagency conflict response efforts. CRC development requires not only recruitment and hiring, but the training and pre-positioning of equipment for U.S. government response personnel. The State Department breaks down the uses of the requested $323 million as follows:

- $136.9 million to build and support an active component of 250 members and a standby component of 2,000 members, to fund up to 1,000 members of the active and standby component to deploy to S&R missions in FY2010;
- $63.6 million to establish a trained and equipped 2,000 member reserve component that will draw other public and private sector experts into U.S. S&R responses;
- $12.5 million to fund the deployment of other experts during the first three months of an operation, "ensuring that critical staff such as police trainers and advisors can be deployed when.... most needed";
- $51.3 million to sustain deployed personnel and provide logistics for up to 130 responders for three months, including $7.1 million to operate and maintain a civilian deployment center;
- $34.3 million to provide security for up to 130 civilian responders (in up to three deployed field teams) in a semi-permissive environment for three months; and

- $24.7 million to augment Washington-area leadership, including 10 new positions for S/CRS operations and staff.

The Obama Administration requested an additional $40 million in the Economic Support Fund (ESF) account for Stabilization Bridge Funds (SBF) to provide for urgent on-the-ground needs during the initial stages of a crisis. These funds could be used while other funds are reprogrammed, transferred, or appropriated for the crisis. Under its "General Provisions" request, the Obama Administration asks authority to transfer SBF funds into the CSI account.

## Establishing the Civilian Response Corps Active Response Component (CRC-A)

As of May 27, 2009, the CRC-A totaled about 39 active component members. By the end of FY2009, the CRC-A will total 100 members. All participating agencies are currently hiring. USAID will contribute 37, the largest number. The State Department will contribute 30 members from three offices (12 will be from S/CRS, 9 from International Narcotics and Law Enforcement [INL]; and 9 from Diplomatic Security).

By the end of Calendar Year (CY) 2009, the CRC-A is expected to reach its full complement of 250 members. Plans call for all to be trained and ready for deployment by the end of FY2010.

The Civilian Response Corps will be composed of personnel filling over 100 specific job specialties. The first 100 active component members will be hired for roughly half of those specialties. These include 29 rule of law personnel dealing with police, the judicial system, corrections, and human rights.

Other personnel will be skilled in commerce, finance, revenue and budgets; civil works and infrastructure; demobilization, disarmament, and reintegration; security sector reform; agriculture; strategic communications; health; drug enforcement; environment; urban and rural planning and management; and disarming explosives. According to S/CRS, the State Department and the other participating agencies have not completed work on the distribution of specialties for the full active component of 250. Tentative plans, however, appear to call for a little under half that number to be rule of law specialists.

## Establishing the Civilian Response Corps Standby Component (CRC-S)

As of April 29, the CRC-S had 311 members: 177 are from State, 81 from USAID, 50 from Justice, and 3 from USDA.

### Table 1. CRC-A Contributions: First 100 Members

| State | USAID | Justice | USDA | HHS | Commerce | DHS | Treasury |
|-------|-------|---------|------|-----|----------|-----|----------|
| 30    | 37    | 24      | 3    | 2   | 2        | 1   | 1        |

By May 27, 2009, there will be 366 Standby members.

By the end of CY2009, plans call for the CRC-S to number 500. The distribution of these positions among departments and agencies, below, is not firm and subject to change.

### Table 2. CRC-A Contributions: Full 250-Member Component (Tentative)

| State | USAID | Justice | USDA | HHS | Commerce | DHS | Treasury |
|-------|-------|---------|------|-----|----------|-----|----------|
| 72    | 93    | 62      | 8    | 5   | 5        | 3   | 2        |

Current plans call for a CRC-S of 2,000 members. The tentative agency/department contributions call for the largest component from USAID, the second largest from State, and the third largest from Justice. Together these three agencies would provide about 90% of the CRC-S members. USDA, DHS, HHS, Commerce, and Treasury would provide the rest.

### Table 3. CRC-S Contributions: First 500

| State | USAID | Justice | USDA | HHS | Commerce | DHS | Treasury |
|-------|-------|---------|------|-----|----------|-----|----------|
| 196   | 186   | 72      | 16   | 10  | 10       | 6   | 4        |

According to S/CRS, plans for the standby component specialties have not been completed.


## Establishing a Civilian Reserve Capability

The Obama Administration's FY2010 budget request calls for $63.3 million (as noted above) to establish a 2,000-member CRC reserve component (CRC-R), whose members would be deployable within 45-60 days.

S/CRS has developed a general concept for a reserve component of retired government personnel, personnel from state and local governments, private for-profit companies, and non-profit NGOs to carry out rule of law, civil administration, and reconstruction activities [36]

In his January 23, 2007, State of the Union address, former President Bush pointed to the need for a civilian reserve corps as a tool in the generational struggle against terrorism. "Such a corps would function much like our military reserve," he said. "It would ease the burden on the armed forces by allowing us to hire civilians with critical skills to serve on missions abroad when America needs them. It would give people across America who do not wear the uniform a chance to serve in the defining struggle of our time."

The Bush Administration's 2008 CSI called for the establishment of a reserve component of 2,000, but Congress did not provide any FY2008 or FY2009 funding for that purpose.

# CONGRESSIONAL ACTION FOR FY2010

## Foreign Relations Authorization Act, FY2010-FY2011 (H.R.2410)

The 111th Congress's first action on the Civilian Stabilization Initiative occurred during House consideration of the Foreign Relations Authorization Act, Fiscal Years 2010 and 2011 (H.R. 2410), which passed the House on June 10, 2009. In action on that bill, the House authorized the Obama Administration's full CSI FY20 10 funding request of $323.272 million and "such sums as may be necessary for fiscal year 2011." In addition, in floor action, the House incorporated as Section 305 an amendment offered by Representative Berman (as part of en bloc amendment 181) to expand the definition of "personnel" in the Reconstruction and Stabilization Civilian Management Act of 2008 (Title XVI, P.L. 110-417, see above). The new definition would include not only personnel from all executive branch appointive positions per the current definition, but also individuals employed by personal services contracts [37] and appointed by the Secretary of State [38]. The practical effect of Section 305, according to an S/CRS official, would be to permit individuals employed under personal services contracts and foreign service nationals to participate in the CRC.

# ISSUES FOR CONGRESS

## S/CRS Capacity and Status

Some observers have argued that the magnitude of the S/CRS mission requires improved capabilities within the office and enhanced status, if it is to provide adequate direction and personnel for an interagency response to stabilization and reconstruction crises. "It is not clear that S/CRS is large enough, well enough funded, or sufficiently high in rank to pull an interagency effort together," according to a 2008 MIT Security Studies Program report [39].

Such reservations persist about the office's ability and capacity to carry out its mission, despite widespread support for S/CRS. Especially in the early years, some observers argued that S/CRS had not moved expeditiously in carrying out its functions. This perceived lack of initiative has often been blamed on an "anti-operational" social culture of the State Department and a lack of support from top State Department leadership. Given that perspective, some observers question whether all of the functions assigned S/CRS are appropriate for that office. For instance, some contend that an office with the mission of mobilizing civilian personnel for stabilization and reconstruction missions would be better placed in USAID, [40] which fields disaster response units (the Disaster Assistance Response Teams) and has an Office of Transition Initiatives that has worked in post-conflict settings. Others, however, fault a lack of adequate resources for any S/CRS shortcomings.

Some urge firm support for S/CRS [41]. With the passage of the Civilian Stabilization and Reconstruction Assistance Management Act of 2008, see above, Congress appears to have mooted the debate on which agency is best suited to accomplish the S/CRS mission, although the issue may resurface within the context of a larger debate on interagency reform.

For the moment, the most salient question seems how best to enhance S/CRS capabilities to carry out assigned functions. One improvement suggested would be to extend the period of

Foreign Service officer (FSOs) tours with S/CRS. FSOs now serve on one-year rotations with S/CRS, rather than the two to three year rotations standard for other assignments.

To provide the head of S/CRS with greater clout within the State Department and in dealing with other departments and agencies, some suggest that rank of that official or the Status of the Office itself, be upgraded. Some suggest that the Coordinator's functions be assigned to an Under Secretary, or that S/CRS become a State Department bureau headed by an Assistant Secretary. (The "Coordinator" position is the equivalent of an Assistant Secretary, according to an S/CRS official.)

## Appropriate Size for the Civilian Response Corps

Some policymakers and analysts question whether the CRC active, standby, and reserve components are large enough to perform effectively their intended functions. One study, prepared by the National Defense University (NDU) Center for Technology and National Security Policy, argues that the CRC should be considerably larger, with 5,000 total in the active and standby components and 10,000 in the reserve component. An active/standby component of that size "would provide a fairly large pool of trained experts in each category" if personnel were "properly distributed," according to the study. "This sizable, diverse pool, in turn, would help provide the flexibility, adaptability, and modularity to tailor complex operations to the missions and tasks at hand in each case, without worrying that the act of responding effectively to one contingency would drain the force or expertise in key areas needed to handle additional contingencies." [42]. This study also states that a combined active and standby force numbering 2,500 (compared to the 2,250 now planned) "should be backed by a reserve force of 4,500 personnel, not 2,000" [43].

Another study envisions the possibility of a larger corps than currently contemplated by the Obama Administration, but somewhat smaller than that proposed in the NDU study. Co-sponsored by the American Academy of Diplomacy and the Stimson Center, this study finds that the "magnitude of growth beyond FY2010 will depend largely on the experience gained based on deployments in that year. For the purposes of projection, we propose that the active response team would grow to 500 by FY2014, the standby response corps would remain at 2,000, and the civilian reserve would grow to 4,000." [44]

## Flexible Funding for CRC Operations

For many years, proponents of "operational" civilian capabilities for S&R operations have urged Congress to provide the State Department with a flexible conflict or crisis response fund that would allow U.S. government civilian agencies to respond rapidly to S&R emergencies. The Bush Administration repeatedly requested such a fund, and proposals for a flexible, replenishable fund were including in early versions of the Lugar-Biden legislation and subsequent related legislation [45]. But Congress, which has long resisted the provision of "blank check" pots of money as an abdication of constitutional appropriation and oversight powers, turned down several Administration requests for more flexible S&R funding mechanisms in the State Department budget [46].

Proponents of flexible funding argue that it is needed because many crises that demand a U.S. rapid response cannot be foreseen and thus planned for in annual budget submissions. In addition, they argue, the existing mechanisms for transferring funds to an emergency situation are too time- consuming to provide an immediate response. Some proponents have argued for a mechanism like the automatically replenishable Emergency Refugee and Migration Assistance (ERMA) emergency relief account, funded through foreign operations appropriations. Many proponents suggest that ERMA provides a model for a response fund to be used for conflicts or related crisis situations. Several bills were introduced that would, among other provisions, permanently establish a conflict response fund, but none passed Congress.

(In December 2007, the HELP Commission recommended the establishment of two rapid- response crisis funds. One would be a permanent humanitarian crisis response fund to meet the needs of natural disasters. The other would be a foreign crisis fund to meet security challenges. No recommendation was made regarding the agency responsible for these funds [47]) Since 2006, the funding that Congress has made available through the DOD budget for conflict response has served as a de facto response fund for small S&R projects. Section 1207 of the conference version of the National Defense Authorization Act for Fiscal Year 2006 (P.L. 109-163, H.R. 1815/S. 1042; signed into law January 6, 2006 and subsequently amended) authorizes the Secretary of Defense to provide the Secretary of State with up to $100 million in services, defense articles and funding for reconstruction, security, or stabilization assistance to a foreign country per fiscal year. This authority expires in FY2009.

## Further Authority and Funding for the Reserve Component

The 2008 authorization of a Civilian Reserve Corps (P.L. 110-417, see above) may provide impetus for the development of a reserve that could substitute for military troops in a wide variety of state-building activities. Although S/CRS developed plans for a reserve (and the Bush Administration's CSI plan contemplated a size of 2,000 members) no steps implementing those plans have been taken, according to S/CRS. The Obama Administration has requested funding to establish a 2,000-member reserve.

Proponents of the creation of a civilian reserve corps foresee a variety of advantages from the creation of such a corps. DOD promoted the concept on the grounds that it would free military personnel from state-building tasks during military operations, thus increasing the personnel available for combat and other more strictly military tasks [48]. Proponents also view such a corps as a means to enhance prospects for success in S&R operations as the personnel who would be sent to perform such tasks would in general have a much higher level of expertise and depth of experience than soldiers and could, unlike many military personnel assigned to such tasks, perform at peak efficiency from the outset. Many view this as particularly true at the national level, where extensive experience with developing national-level structures is desirable over the long run. (Although military Civil Affairs officers are largely reservists whose civilian jobs are relevant to state-building tasks, many analysts state that there are too few civil affairs personnel to provide the depth needed to deploy the appropriate person in most circumstances.) Many argue that civilian personnel are also preferable for symbolic reasons, as they may signal a greater commitment to the construction of a democratic state.

Skeptics look at the concept of a civilian reserve as untested and potentially unfeasible. Some wonder whether qualified experts would sign up in sufficient quantities to make the corps an effective replacement for military troops in S&R operations [49]. Some question whether the existence of such a corps would provide an incentive to interventions of various types that the United States otherwise would not have undertaken.

Cost is likely to be a major issue. In 2008, the Congressional Budget Office (CBO) assembled a cost estimate for the Bush Administration's CSI. Its estimate for the recruiting, screening, enrolling, training, and equipping the 2,000 members contemplated by the CSI was $87 million in FY2009 and $47 million in 2010 [50]. (The CBO estimate of first-year costs is considerably higher than the Obama Administration's $63.6 million FY2010 request to establish the reserve.) Although some may view the potential cost of the civilian corps as high, some proponents argue that the costs of deploying civilian personnel would result in a net savings to the military. (It is likely, however, that any possible savings would depend on the circumstances in which such civilian personnel were deployed and the effect of their deployment on the number of military personnel needed.) Proponents also maintain that even if high, the monetary cost to maintain and deploy civilian reservists would still be relatively inexpensive when compared to the multiple costs, both tangible (such as money and lives) and intangible (such as domestic and international political support and loss of strategic leverage) of prolonged or failed military interventions.

## REFERENCES

[1] U.S. Department of Defense. Speech by Secretary of Defense Robert M. Gates delivered at Kansas State University, Manhattan, KA (the "Landon Lecture"), November 26, 2007, and U.S. Department of Defense, Speech by Secretary of Defense Robert M. Gates, at the AFRICOM Activation Ceremony, Washington, D.C., October 1, 2008. Accessed through http://www.defenselink.mil/speeches/secdef.aspx; last accessed February 3, 2009.

[2] Taken from a speech delivered by then-Secretary of State Condeleeza Rice. Remarks at Georgetown School of Foreign Service, January 18, 2006. Available at http://www.state.gov/secretary/rm/2006/59306.htm. This theme was reiterated by Stephen Krasner, director of Policy Planning at the State Department. Remarks at the Center for Global Development, January 20, 2006. Available at http://www.cgdev.org/doc/even t%20docs/Krasner%20Transcript.pdf.

[3] Parts of this Background section and the following section on S/CRS are drawn from a now archived CRS Report RS22031, *Peacekeeping and Post-Conflict Capabilities: The State Department's Office for Reconstruction and Stabilization*, by Nina M. Serafino and Martin A. Weiss.

[4] "Peacekeeping" is a broad, generic, and often imprecise term to describe the many activities that the United Nations and other international organizations, and sometimes ad hoc coalitions of nations or individual nations, undertake to promote, maintain, enforce, or enhance the possibilities for peace. These activities range from providing election observers, recreating police or civil defense forces for the new governments of those countries, organizing and providing security for humanitarian relief efforts, and

monitoring and enforcing cease-fires and other arrangements designed to separate parties recently in conflict. (Many of these activities are often also referred to as "nation-building"; a better term, some analysts suggest, is "state-building.") As used here, the term encompasses both "peace enforcement" operations, sent to enforce an international mandate to establish peace, and "peacebuilding" activities. Peacebuilding activities, usually undertaken in a post-conflict environment, are designed to strengthen peace and prevent the resumption or spread of conflict, including disarmament and demobilization of warring parties, repatriation of refugees, reform and strengthening of government institutions, election-monitoring, and promotion of political participation and human rights.

[5]   The term "post-conflict stabilization and reconstruction" is broad but is usually understood to encompass tasks and missions to promote security and encourage stable, democratic governance and economic growth following major hostilities. In the past, many of the "stabilization" activities were loosely labeled "peacekeeping." Reconstruction involves repairing (in some cases creating) the infrastructure necessary to support long-term economic growth and development. This infrastructure can be physical (e.g., roads and schools), or institutional (e.g., legal and tax systems) For additional background on various aspects of post-conflict reconstruction and assistance, see CRS Report RL33557, *Peacekeeping and Related Stability Operations: Issues of U.S. Military Involvement*, by Nina M. Serafino; and CRS Report RL33700, *United Nations Peacekeeping: Issues for Congress*, by Marjorie Ann Browne.

[6]   *The Clinton Administration's Policy on Managing Complex Contingency Operations: Presidential Decision Directive.* May 1997. http://www.fas.org/irp/offdocs/pdd56.htm.

[7]   U.S. *Text: The Clinton Administration White Paper on Peace Operations.* February 24, 2000 http://www.fas.org/irp/ offdocs/pdd/pdd-71-4.htm, hereafter referred to as PDD-71 White Paper; and U.S. *Text: Summary of Presidential Decision Directive 71*, http://www.fas.org/ irp/offdocs/pdd/pdd-71-1.htm.

[8]   See CRS Report RL32321, Policing *in Peacekeeping and Related Stability Operations: Problems and Proposed Solutions*, by Nina M. Serafino.

[9]   Collier, Paul and Hoeffler, Anke "Aid, Policy and Growth in Post-Conflict Societies," *World Bank Working Paper*, October 2002.

[10]  Milner, Helen, "Why Multilateralism? Foreign Aid and Domestic Principal Agent Problems," available at http://www.wcfia.harvard.edu/seminars/pegroup/milner.pdf, and Schiavo-Campo, S., "Financing and Aid Arrangements In Post-Conflict Situations," *World Bank Working Paper,* May 2003.

[11]  Alesina, Alberto and Dollar, David, "Who Gives Foreign Aid to Whom and Why?" *NBER Working Paper No. w6612*, June 1998.

[12]  The 9/11 Commission Report: Final Report of the National Commission on Terrorist Attacks upon the United States, New York: W.W. Norton and Company, 2004, and On the Brink: A Report of the Commission on Weak States and US National Security, sponsored by the Center for Global Development, May 2004. Also see CRS Report RL34253, *Weak and Failing States: Evolving Security Threats and U.S. Policy*, by Liana Sun Wyler.

[13]  Prins, Gwyn, "AIDS and Global Security," *International Affairs*, vol. 80, Issue 5, 2004.

[14] The reports are (1) *Play to Win: The Final Report of the Bi-partisan Commission on Post-Conflict Reconstruction,* Center for Strategic and International Studies (CSIS) and the Association of the U.S. Army (AUSA), 2003 (a book- length version was published in mid-2004, *Winning the Peace: An American Strategy for Post-Conflict Reconstruction,* Robert C. Orr, ed.); (2) Clark A. Murdock, Michèle A. Flournoy, Christopher A. Williams, and Kurt M. Campbell, principal authors. *Beyond Goldwater-Nichols: Defense Reform for a New Strategic Era Phase I Report,* CSIS, March 2004; (3) Hans Binnendijk and Stuart Johnson, eds. *Transforming for Stabilization and Reconstruction Operations,* National Defense University Center for Technology and National Security Policy, April 2004, (4) *On the Brink: Weak States and US National Security,* Center for Global Development, May 2004; Office of the Under Secretary of Defense for Acquisition, Technology, and Logistics. *Defense Science Board 2004 Summer Study on Transition to and From Hostilities,* December 2004; and *In the Wake of War: Improving U.S. Post-Conflict Capabilities,* Washington, D.C.: Council on Foreign Relations, Report of an Independent Task Force, July 2005.

[15] The July 2005 Council on Foreign Relations report recommends the establishment of a conflict response fund of $500 million, a five-fold increase over the amount requested by the Bush Administration for FY2006. In addition, the report recommends establishing a new $1 billion standing multilateral reconstruction trust fund under the auspices of the Group of Eight industrialized nations. This trust fund would be modeled on existing post-conflict trust funds located at the United Nations and the World Bank.

[16] That white paper states that PDD 71 instructed that "programs must be developed that enable the U.S. to respond quickly to help establish rudimentary judicial and penal capacity during peace operations and complex contingencies." *PDD-71 White Paper,* op.cit., p. 6.

[17] Transforming for Stabilization and Reconstruction Operations, op.cit.

[18] Beyond Goldwater-Nichols: Defense Reform for a New Strategic Era, Phase 1 Report, op.cit. See pp. 64-65.

[19] Robert M. Perito, Michael Dziedzic and Beth C. DeGrasse, *Building Civilian Capacity for U.S. Stability Operations.* Washington, DC: United States Institute of Peace, Special Report 118, April 2004.

[20] Robert M. Perito, *Where is the Lone Ranger When We Need Him? America's Search for a Postconflict Stability Force.* Washington, DC: United States Institute of Peace Press, 2004. See pp 323-337 for an extensive discussion of this proposal.

[21] Transition to and From Hostilities, op.cit., p 58.

[22] Patrick Stewart. *Weak States and Global Threats: Assessing Evidence of "Spillovers."* Working Paper No. 73, Center for Global Development, January 2006.

[23] Justin Logan and Christopher Preble. *Failed States and Flawed Logic: The Case against a Standing Nation-Building Office.* CATO Policy Analysis Paper No. 560, Cato Institute, January 11, 2006. The authors make substantial reference to a Fall 2004 paper by Stephen Krasner, State Department Director of Policy Planning, that challenged the conventional sovereignty norms. Krasner argues that these norms are outmoded and an obstacle to dealing with the international threats caused by weak and unstable states. He argues for granting international acceptance to new norms of shared-sovereignty (more than one country) or international trusteeships following successful

interventions, Stephen Krasner, "Sharing Sovereignty," International Security, Vol. 28, No. 4, Spring 2004, pp. 5-43.

[24] Rajan Menon, "Low Intensity Conflict in the Emerging Strategic Environment," as reproduced in U.S. Army Peacekeeping and Stability Operations Institute. *Strategic Requirements for Stability Operations and Reconstruction: Final Report.* pp. 80-8 1. This report summarizes the result of a conference held April 19-20, 2006, and three preceding workshops, conducted under the aegis of the Dwight D. Eisenhower National Security Series. It also reproduces several papers presented at one workshop. The final report was distributed by e-mail in late 2006, but as of January 18, 2007, does not appear on either the PKSOI or Eisenhower Series website.

[25] The emergency response fund would have been subject to limited conditions, but requiring extensive consultation with Congress, similar to spending authority provisions of Section 614 of the Foreign Assistance Act of 1961, as amended. FAA Section 614(a)(3) requires the President to consult with and provide a written policy justification to the House Committee on Foreign Affairs (now International Relations), the Senate Committee on Foreign Relations, and the Appropriations committee of each chamber. CBO estimated that implementing the bill would cost some $50 million in 2005 and $550 million from 2005 through 2009.

[26] These include two similar versions of the original Lugar-Biden bill with same name: the Stabilization and Reconstruction Civilian Management Act of 2005 (S. 209/109th Congress, by Senators Lugar, Biden, and Hagel), and of 2006 (S. 3322/109th Congress by Senators Lugar, Biden, Hagel, Alexander and Warner, and H.R. 6104/109th Congress by Representatives Farr, Blumenauer and Saxton). Similar provisions were included in Title VII of the Senate version of the Foreign Relations Authorization Act for FY2006 and FY2007 (S. 600/109th Congress). A related bill was the International Security Enhancement Act of 2005 (H.R. 1361/109th Congress, introduced by Representative Dreier), which also would provide authority for preventive action not included in the other bills. (H.R. 1361 would have allowed the president, acting through S/CRS, to authorize the deployment to a country likely to enter into conflict or civil strife in addition to countries emerging from conflict.) Related bills were: The Winning the Peace Act of 2003 (H.R. 2616/108th Congress, introduced by Representative Farr); the International Security Enhancement Act of 2004 (H.R. 41 85/108th Congress, introduced by Representative Dreier); and the United States Assistance for Civilians Affected by Conflict Act of 2004 (H.R. 4058/108th Congress, introduced by Representative Hyde).

[27] Posture Statement of General Richard B. Myers, USAF, Chairman of the Joint Chiefs of Staff, before the 109th Congress. Senate Armed Services Committee, February 17, 2005, p. 31, as posted on the Senate Armed Services Committee website.

[28] American Interests and U.N. Reform: Report of the Task Force on the United Nations. Washington, DC: United States Institute of Peace, June 2005, p. 25.

[29] NSPD-1 established 17 NSC/PPCs to "be the main day-to-day fora for interagency coordination of national security policy," providing policy analysis for more senior committees (the NSC Principals Committee and the NSC Deputies Committee) and ensuring timely responses to presidential decisions. Membership on the NSC/PCC is to consist of representatives from the departments of State, Defense, Justice and the Treasury, and the Office of Management and Budget, the offices of the President and

Vice President, the Central Intelligence Agency, the Joint Chiefs of Staff, and the NSC. Representatives from the Departments of Agriculture and Commerce, and the Office of the U.S. Trade Representative, are to participate when issues pertain to their responsibilities.

[30] The specific functions, as detailed in P.L. 110-417, Section 1605, are (1) "Monitoring, in coordination with relevant bureaus within the Department of State and the United States Agency for International Development (USAID), political and economic instability worldwide to anticipate the need for mobilizing United States and international assistance for the stabilization and reconstruction of a country or region that is at risk of, in, or ... in transition from, conflict or civil strife"; (2) "Assessing the various types of stabilization and reconstruction crises that could occur and cataloging and monitoring the non-military resources and capabilities of agencies ... that are available to address such crises"; (3) "Planning, in conjunction with USAID, to address requirements, such as demobilization, rebuilding of civil society, policing, human rights monitoring, and public information, that commonly arise in stabilization and reconstruction crises"; (4) "Coordinating with relevant agencies to develop interagency contingency plans to mobilize and deploy civilian personnel to address the various types of such crises"; (5) "Entering into appropriate arrangements with agencies to carry out activities under this section and the Reconstruction and Stabilization Civilian Management Act of 2008"; (6) "Identifying personnel in State and local governments and in the private sector who are available to participate in the Civilian Reserve Corps ... or to otherwise participate in or contribute to reconstruction and stabilization activities"; (7) "Taking steps to ensure that training of civilian personnel to perform such reconstruction and stabilization activities is adequate and, is carried out, as appropriate, with other agencies involved with stabilization operations"; (8) "Taking steps to ensure that plans for United States reconstruction and stabilization operations are coordinated with and complementary to reconstruction and stabilization activities of other governments and international and nongovernmental organizations, to improve effectiveness and avoid duplication"; and (9) "Maintaining the capacity to field on short notice an evaluation team to undertake on-site needs assessment."

[31] In its FY2006 and FY2007 budget requests, the Bush Administration's budget proposed funding for S/CRS to establish a 100-person ready-response cadre of government employees. Congress has not yet provided funds for establishing such a cadre or a civilian reserve corps: although in 2007, Congress approved $50 million in supplemental funds (available through FY2008) to establish and maintain a civilian reserve corps, the release of these funds was made contingent on a subsequent authorization of the corps. (Section 3810, [U.S. Troop Readiness, Veterans' Care, Katrina Recovery, and Iraq Accountability Appropriations Act, 2007, H.R. 2206, P.L. 110-28, signed into law May 25, 2007.)

[32] For more on this program, see CRS Report RS22871, *Department of Defense "Section 1207" Security and Stabilization Assistance: Background and Congressional Concerns*, by Nina M. Serafino.

[33] Afghanistan, Colombia, Democratic Republic of Congo, Georgia, Haiti, Lebanon, Nepal, Somalia, Sri Lanka, Tajikistan, Yemen, Southeast Asia region and Trans-Sahara region.

[34] The first active response component member was deployed to Lebanon, to assist with efforts to train and equip additional Lebanese Internal Security (LIS) forces. (The purpose of this effort was to enhance LIS ability to replace the Lebanese Army Forces which had been maintaining law and order in conflictive areas such as the Bekaa Valley before being deployed to southern Lebanon.) Several standby response component members also deployed to post-conflict situations in 2006. The first person from this group was deployed to Eastern Chad and two more began working in Nepal on demobilizing and reintegrating Maoist rebels. In the course of early 2007, several active component members deployed to Kosovo to help prepare for the status settlement process, one deployed to Beirut to help coordinate reconstruction assistance, and one to Chad to monitor activities on the Chad side of the border with Sudan. Other response corps deployments were to Afghanistan, Bangladesh, Cuba, the Democratic Republic of Congo, Georgia, Haiti, Iraq, Liberia, and Sri Lanka, as well as to work with the U.S. Africa Command (AFRICOM). Original plans had called for the ARC to number 30 by the end of 2006. U.S. Department of State. *Fact Sheet: State Department Stands Up Active Response Corps.* August 23, 2006. http://www.state.gov/s/crs/rls/71038.htm.

[35] The $10 million in FY2009 bridge fund supplemental appropriations for the State Department was provided as part of a lump sum for State Department diplomatic and consular programs.

[36] Two outside studies forming the basis for planning for the reserve were completed in 2006. BearingPoint, Inc. *Management Study for Establishing and Managing a Civilian Reserve.* Prepared for the U.S. Department of State, Office of the Coordinator for Reconstruction and Stabilization. May 30, 2006.

[37] Individuals employed by personal services contract, including those employed pursuant to section 2(c) of the State Department Basic Authorities Act of 1956 (22 U.S.C. 2669(c)) and section 636(a)(3) of the Foreign Assistance Act of 1961 (22 U.S.C. 2396 (a)(3).

[38] Individuals appointed by the Secretary of State under section 303 of the Foreign Service Act of 1980 (22 U.S.C. 3943); this group includes foreign national employees.

[39] Cindy Williams and Gordon Adams. Strengthening Statecraft and Security: Reforming U.S. Planning and Resource Allocation. MIT Security Studies Program Occasional Paper, June 2008, p. 89.

[40] Gordon Adams, Obama's test: Bringing order to the national security process. Bulletin of the Atomic Scientists, web version, posted January 26, 2009. Accessed through http://www.thebulletin.org. Last accessed February 4, 2009.

[41] The HELP Commission, established by Congress in January 2004 (Consolidated Appropriations Act, 2004, P.L. 108- 199, Section 637) to study U.S. foreign assistance programs, recommended in its report of December 2007 that Congress "strengthen and fund the capacities of the State Department Office S/CRS and assign it responsibility for coordinating Sate and Defense Department programs for security-related aspects of addressing crises and weak and failing states." Recommendation 2.2.2., at http://www.helpcommission.gov/portals/
0/recommendations_final.pdf; last accessed February 3, 2009.

[42] Christel Fonzo-Eberhard and Richard L. Kugler. "Sizing the Civilian Response Capacity for Complex Operations" in *Civilian Surge: Key to Complex Operations,*

edited by Hans Binnendijk and Patrick M. Cronin. Center for Technology and National Security Policy, National Defense University. December 2008. p. 7.

[43] Ibid., p. 9.

[44] Ambassador Thomas Boyatt, et.al., *A Foreign Affairs Budget for the Future: Fixing the Crisis in Diplomatic Readiness*, American Academy of Diplomacy and the Henry L. Stimson Center, October 2008, p. 45. Accessed through http://www.stimson.org. Last accessed May 22, 2009.

[45] A provision for a flexible, replenishable fund was included in early versions of the Lugar-Biden legislation. Most recently, some legislation in the 110th Congress contained provisions for a $75 million replenishable fund that could be used by the President to respond to crises in countries or regions at risk of, in, or in transition from conflict or civil strife. Of that, some $25 million could be used for expenses related to the development, training, and operations of the Response Readiness Corps.

[46] These requests were contained in both annual and supplemental appropriations measures) for no-year funds to be used for conflict emergencies in foreign countries or regions, and proposals in previous iterations of the Lugar/Biden legislation to establish a replenishable fund for conflict response.

[47] http://www.helpcommission.gov/portals/0/recommendations_final.pdf. Recommendation 3.5. Last accessed February 3, 2009.

[48] However, DOD Directive 3000.05, *Military Support for Stability, Security, Transition and Reconstruction (SSR) Operations*, issued November 28, 2005, states that many stability operations tasks "are best performed by indigenous, foreign, or U.S. civilian professionals," but nonetheless "U.S. military forces shall be prepared to perform all tasks necessary to establish or maintain order when civilians cannot do so." Among the tasks listed are the rebuilding of various types of security forces, correctional facilities, and judicial systems, the revival or building of the private sector, and the development of representative governmental institutions. (Points 4.3, 4.3.1-4.3.3. Access through http://www.dtic.mil/whs/directives/corres/html/300005.htm.)
Some military analysts argue that at the beginning of an operation or in extremely volatile situations the use of U.S. troops to perform nation-building efforts may be considered highly desirable as they can "multi-task," performing combat missions in one area while switching quickly to state-building efforts in another. In addition, some believe that it will always be desirable to have trained military civil affairs officers who can deal with civilian leaders and populations involved in state-building efforts at the local level, as a means of demonstrating goodwill toward such populations and enhancing the image of soldiers, especially in counterinsurgency operations.

[49] For information on the experiences of the Germany, Canada, and the United Nations in recruiting personnel for state- building rosters and deployments to other countries see CRS Report RL33647, *A Civilian Reserve for Stabilization and Reconstruction Abroad: Summary of a Workshop on U.S. Proposals and International Experiences and Related Issues for Congress*, by Nina M. Serafino.

[50] The Congressional Budget Office estimated the cost of implementing the Civilian Reconstruction and Stabilization Management Act, H.R. 1084 (110th Congress), if "employed in a manner consistent with the [President's] Civilian Stabilization Initiative." (The estimate is included in H.Rept. 110-537, 110th Congress.)

In: U.S. Political Programs: Functions and Assessments    ISBN: 978-1-61209-448-9
Editors: Julianna M. Moretti and Karen J. Chordstron    © 2011 Nova Science Publishers, Inc.

*Chapter 6*

# AMERICA COMPETES ACT AND THE FY2010 BUDGET*

*Deborah D. Stine*

## ABSTRACT

The America COMPETES Act (P.L. 110-69) became law on August 9, 2007. The act is intended to increase the nation's investment in research and development (R&D), and in science, technology, engineering, and mathematics (STEM) education. It is designed to focus on two perceived concerns believed to influence future U.S. competitiveness: inadequate R&D funding to generate sufficient technological progress, and inadequate numbers of American students proficient in STEM or interested in STEM careers relative to other countries.

The act authorizes funding increases for the National Science Foundation (NSF), National Institute of Standards and Technology (NIST) laboratories, and the Department of Energy Office of Science (DOE SC) over FY2008-FY2010. If maintained, the increases would double the budgets of those entities over seven years. The act establishes the Advanced Research Projects Agency – Energy (ARPA-E) within DOE, designed to support transformational energy technology research projects with the goal of enhancing U.S. economic and energy security. A new program, Discovery Science and Engineering Innovation Institutes, would establish multidisciplinary institutes at DOE National Laboratories to "apply fundamental science and engineering discoveries to technological innovations," according to the act.

Among the act's education activities, many of which are focused on high-need school districts, are programs to recruit new K-12 STEM teachers, enhance existing STEM teacher skills, and provide more STEM education opportunities for students. The new Department of Education (ED) Teachers for a Competitive Tomorrow and existing NSF Robert Noyce Teacher Scholarship (Noyce) programs provide opportunities, through institutional grants, for students pursuing STEM degrees and STEM professionals to gain teaching skills and teacher certification, and for current STEM teachers to enhance their teaching skills and understanding of STEM content. The act also authorizes a new program at NSF that would provide grants to create or improve

---

* This is an edited, reformatted and augmented edition of a United States Congressional Research Service publication, CRS Report R40519, dated June 15, 2009.

professional science master's degree (PSM) programs that emphasize practical training and preparation for the workforce in high-need fields.

The America COMPETES Act is an authorization act. New programs established by the act will not be initiated and authorized increases in appropriations for existing programs will not occur unless funded through subsequent appropriation acts. The 110th Congress provided FY2008 appropriations to establish ED's Teachers for a Competitive Tomorrow program, and NIST's Technology Improvement Program (TIP), which replaced the existing Advanced Technology Program. The 111th Congress provided FY2009 appropriations, supplemented by the American Recovery and Reinvestment Act (ARRA), to establish DOE's ARPA-E and NSF's PSM program. Although some America COMPETES Act research and STEM education programs received appropriations at authorized levels in FY2009, others did not.

As Congress deliberates the FY2010 budget, an issue for Congress is what level, if any, it will appropriate funds for America COMPETES Act programs. Although the Obama Administration requested FY2010 funding for most America COMPETES Act R&D programs at levels below that authorized, it contends that FY2009 (due to ARRA funding), and if approved as requested, FY20 10 appropriations would fund federal R&D programs at the highest levels in U.S. history. Several programs newly authorized in the act have never been appropriated funds and the Obama Administration has not proposed funding them. An issue for these programs is whether or not they will receive the funding necessary to establish them. The America COMPETES Act provides authorization levels only through FY2010.

Congress passed the America Creating Opportunities to Meaningfully Promote Excellence in Technology, Education, and Science Act (P.L. 110-69), known as the America COMPETES Act, in August 2007. In response to concerns about U.S. competitiveness, the act provides for investments in science and engineering research and science, technology, engineering, and mathematics (STEM) education in the present so that the United States can enhance its potential to be more competitive with other nations in the future. The purpose of this report is to provide information on the President's FY2010 budget request and the status of Congressional budget and appropriation activities regarding that budget relative to the America COMPETES Act. For more general information on the America COMPETES Act, see CRS Report RL34328, *America COMPETES Act: Programs, Funding, and Selected Issues,* by Deborah D. Stine, and for information on the FY2009 budget, see CRS Report RL34396, *The America COMPETES Act and the FY2009 Budget,* by Deborah D. Stine.

## OVERVIEW OF THE AMERICA COMPETES ACT

The America COMPETES Act was a response to concerns that the United States may not be able to compete economically with other nations in the future. Many believe that investments in science and engineering research; science, technology, engineering, and mathematics (STEM) education; and STEM workforce development will enhance U.S. competitiveness. As a result, the act mainly addresses concerns about insufficient investment in those areas.

The America COMPETES Act authorizes an increase in federal science and engineering research funding and support for kindergarten through postdoctoral education. The act authorizes funding increases through FY2010 for the National Science Foundation (NSF), the

National Institute of Standards and Technology (NIST) laboratories, and the Department of Energy (DOE) Office of Science (DOESC). The act also authorizes within DOE the establishment of the Advanced Research Projects Agency-Energy (ARPA-E) [1] and Discovery Science and Engineering Innovation Institutes. In addition, the act authorizes new STEM education programs at DOE, the Department of Education (ED), and NSF, and increases the authorization level for several existing NSF STEM education programs. The America COMPETES Act is an authorization act. New programs established by the act will not be initiated unless funded through subsequent federal appropriations. Similarly, increases in the authorization level of existing programs may or may not translate into increased federal funding.

## OVERVIEW OF **FY2008** AND **FY2009** APPROPRIATIONS

The America COMPETES Act was passed after much of the FY2008 appropriations process had already taken place during the 110th Congress. Although America COMPETES Act programs were not funded at authorized levels, the 110th Congress did provide FY2008 appropriations to establish ED's Teachers for a Competitive Tomorrow program, and NIST's Technology Improvement Program (TIP), which replaced the existing Advanced Technology Program.

The 111th Congress passed the Omnibus Appropriations Act, 2009 (P.L. 111-8) and the American Recovery and Reinvestment Act (P.L. 111-5) to supplement FY2009 funds. Although some America COMPETES Act programs were funded at authorized levels, others were not. The following activities were funded at or above authorized levels: NIST Scientific & Technical Research and Services (STRS); NIST Construction and Maintenance; DOESC; NSF and its Research and Related Activities; Major Research Instrumentation; Major Research Equipment and Facilities Construction; Professional Science Master's; Robert Noyce Teacher Scholarship; and Graduate Research Fellowship programs. Other programs were funded either below authorized levels or not funded. The acts provided funding to establish DOE's ARPA-E and NSF's PSM program. In addition, portions of the P-16 Alignment of Secondary School Graduate Requirements with the Demands of 21st Century Postsecondary Endeavors and Support for P-16 Education Data Systems were funded through the ARRA.

As was the case for the Bush Administration, the Obama Administration contends that the following America COMPETES Act programs correspond to existing DOE programs:

- Summer Institutes (§5003) to the pre-existing DOE Academies Creating Teacher Scientists program (DOE ACTS);
- Early Career Awards for Science, Engineering, and Mathematics Researchers (§5006) to pre-existing High Energy Physics Outstanding Junior Investigator, Nuclear Physics Outstanding Junior Investigator, Fusion Energy Sciences Plasma Physics Junior Faculty Development; Advanced Scientific Computing Research Early Career Principle Investigator; and the Office of Science Early Career Scientist and Engineer Award programs;

- Discovery Science and Engineering Innovation Institutes (§5008) with preexisting Bioenergy Research Centers, SciDAC Institutes, and the Energy Frontier Research Centers; and
- Protecting America's Competitive Edge (PACE) Graduate Fellowship Program (§5009) to pre-existing Computer Science Graduate Fellowships; Graduate Research Environmental Fellowships; American Meteorological Society/Industry/Government Graduate Fellowships; Spallation Neutron Source Instrumentation Fellowships, and the Fusion Energy Sciences Graduate Fellowships [2]

If members of Congress agree with this contention, these America COMPETES Act programs were funded as well.

## OBAMA ADMINISTRATION BUDGET REQUEST

This section provides an overview of the Obama Administration's FY20 10 budget request for research and STEM education activities. Table 1 (located at the end of this report) provides a program-specific comparison of the Obama Administration's FY20 10 budget request to America COMPETES Act authorization levels.

## Research

In its budget request to Congress, the Administration states that it plans to double the budget for the NSF, NIST laboratories, and DOE SC between 2006 and 2016 (see Figure 1). The Obama Administration's proposed plan would continue the efforts of the Bush Administration's American Competitiveness Initiative (ACI) [3] which had the goal of doubling these agency's budgets over ten years. This differs from the doubling path of the America COMPETES Act which placed these same agencies on a track to double their budgets over seven years.

As a result, the funding requested for these agencies by the Obama Administration are below that authorized in the America COMPETES Act in FY2010. When the total funds authorized and appropriated in FY2008 and FY2009 or requested for FY2010 by the President are compared, however, the funding appropriated/requested for FY2008-FY20 10 exceeds that authorized for NSF and NIST STRS. For DOE SC, the funding appropriated/requested is slightly below that authorized. As shown in Figure 2, the total authorized for NSF during this time period is $22,058 million, while the total appropriated/requested is $22,665 million—resulting in funding that, if appropriated at this level in FY20 10, would be $607 million above the authorized level.

For NIST STRS, the total authorized is $1,629 million, the funding appropriated/requested is $1,667 million, so the appropriated/requested funding exceeds that authorized by $38 million For DOESC, the total authorized is $15,500 million, while the total appropriated/requested is $15,335 million, resulting in $165 million below or 99% of the authorized level.

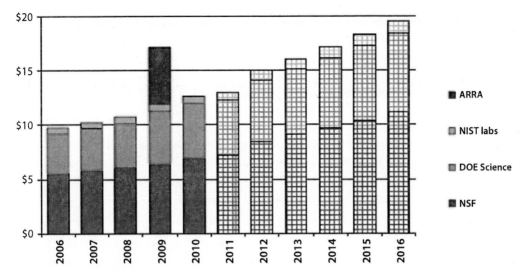

Source: Office of Science and Technology Policy, A Renewed Commitment to Science and Technology: Federal R&D, Technology, and STEM Education in the 2010 Budget, May 2009 at http://www.ostp.gov/galleries/budget/FY2010RD.pdf.

Notes: 2006-2009 figures are enacted budget authority; 2011-2016 figures are projections in the 2010 budget.

Figure 1. Obama Administration Plan for Science and Innovation, FY2006-2016 Budget Authority in Billions of Current Dollars.

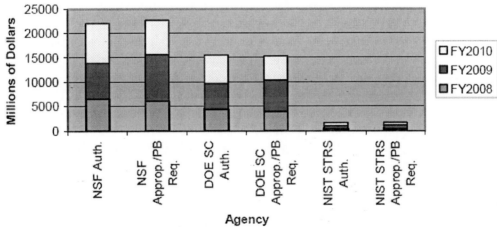

Source: Congressional Research Service.

Notes: Auth. = Authorized; Approp. = Appropriated. PB Req. = President's Budget Request. NSF = National Science Foundation. DOE SC = Department of Energy Office of Science. NIST = National Institute of Standards and Technology. STRS = Scientific and Technical Research and Services. FY2008 and FY2009 are as appropriated by Congress. FY2010 is as requested by the President. This analysis does not take into account inflation.

Figure 2. Comparison of America COMPETES Act Authorized and Appropriated/ Requested funding for NSF, DOE Office of Science (SC), and NIST Scientific and Technical Research and Services (STRS).

At NIST, funding of $69.9 million is requested for the TIP program, slightly above that received in FY2009 of $65.0 million and half that authorized at $140.5 million. MEP funding is requested at $124.7 million, slightly below that authorized ($131.89 million), and above that appropriated in FY2009 ($110.0 million). Funding for NIST's construction and maintenance account is requested at $116.9 million more than double the authorized level of $49.7 million.

The Obama Administration is requesting $10 million of FY20 10 funding for DOE's ARPA-E, which received $415 million in funding in FY2009 ($15 million as part of the regular FY2009 appropriation, $400 million in the ARRA). The Obama Administration is proposing to focus $280 million of its FY2010 funds on new Energy Innovation Hubs. As stated by Secretary of Energy Chu in congressional testimony:

> Specifically, this budget request includes three initiatives designed to cover the spectrum of basic to applied science to maximize our chances of energy breakthroughs. The FY 2010 budget will launch eight Energy Innovation Hubs, while the Energy Frontier Research Centers (EFRCs) and ARPA-E were launched last month. Let me briefly explain the differences and why I believe launching these Hubs is so important.
>
> EFRCs are small-scale collaborations (predominantly at universities) that focus on overcoming known hurdles in basic science that block energy breakthroughs – not on developing energy technologies themselves.
>
> ARPA-E is a highly entrepreneurial funding model that explores potentially revolutionary technologies that are too risky for industry to fund.
>
> The proposed Energy Innovation Hubs will take a very different approach – they will be multi-disciplinary, highly collaborative teams ideally working under one roof to solve priority technology challenges, such as artificial photosynthesis (creating fuels from sunlight) [4]

At NSF, the Obama Administration is requesting funding at the authorized level of $203.8 million for the Faculty Early Career Development (CAREER) program. Funding for the Experimental Programs to Stimulate Competitive Research (EPSCoR) program is proposed for $147.2 million, similar to the authorized level of $147.8 million. The Research and Related Activities (R&RA) Directorate portion of NSF's Graduate Research Fellowship (GRF) program is proposed for 19.4 million above the authorized level of $15.0 million; however, the Education and Human Resources (EHR) Directorate portion of GRF proposed funding of $102.6 million is below the authorized level of $119.0 million. No FY20 10 funding is requested for NSF 's Professional Science Master's (PSM) program, newly established in FY2009 through ARRA funding.

## Science, Technology, Engineering, and Mathematics (STEM) Education

The Obama Administration is not requesting funding to establish the new STEM education programs authorized in the America COMPETES Act. As shown in Figure 3, however, the administration does indicate it is funding other STEM education initiatives. For example, at DOE, the Obama Administration is proposing to establish a new DOE-NSF initiative called "REgaining our ENERGY Science and Engineering Edge" (RE-ENERGYSE) to encourage American students to pursue STEM careers, particularly in clean energy, with DOE funding of $115 million. As a point of comparison, the total FY2010 authorization level for all the DOE STEM education programs authorized in the America COMPETES Act is $117.5 million. As stated by Secretary of Energy Chu during congressional testimony:

> As part of this initiative, the Department will launch a comprehensive K-20+ science and engineering initiative, funded at $115 million in FY 2010, to educate thousands of students at all levels in the fields contributing to the fundamental understanding of energy science and engineering systems. This initiative, which complements the Department's other education efforts, will provide graduate research fellowships in scientific and technical fields that advance the Department's energy mission; provide training grants to universities that establish multidisciplinary research and education programs related to clean energy; support universities that dramatically expand energy-related research opportunities for undergraduates; build partnerships between community colleges and different segments of the clean tech industry to develop customized curriculum for "green collar" jobs; and increase public awareness, particularly among young people, about the role that science and technology can play in responsible environmental stewardship [5]

| | FY 2008 Enacted | FY 2009 Enacted | FY 2009 ARRA 1/ | FY 2010 Budget | Change FY 09-10 2/ | |
| --- | --- | --- | --- | --- | --- | --- |
| | | | | | Amount | Percent |
| Corporation for Nat'l & Community Service | 3 | 7 | 0 | 7 | 0 | 0.0% |
| Agriculture | 44 | 47 | 0 | 88 | 41 | 87.2% |
| Commerce | 47 | 50 | 43 | 36 | -14 | -28.0% |
| Defense | 209 | 218 | 0 | 229 | 11 | 5.0% |
| Education | 708 | 850 | 0 | 763 | -87 | -10.2% |
| Energy | 20 | 24 | 13 | 148 | 124 | 516.7% |
| Health and Human Services | 837 | 845 | 0 | 853 | 8 | 0.9% |
| Homeland Security | 93 | 99 | 0 | 106 | 7 | 7.1% |
| Labor | 0 | 10 | 0 | 0 | -10 | -100.0% |
| Interior | 23 | 24 | 0 | 26 | 2 | 8.3% |
| Transportation | 158 | 159 | 0 | 174 | 15 | 9.4% |
| Environmental Protection Agency | 10 | 10 | 0 | 11 | 1 | 10.0% |
| NASA | 147 | 169 | 0 | 126 | -43 | -25.4% |
| National Science Foundation | 1,013 | 1,066 | 220 | 1,109 | 43 | 4.0% |
| **Total STEM Education** | 3,312 | 3,578 | 276 | 3,676 | 98 | 2.7% |

Source: Office of Science and Technology Policy, A Renewed Commitment to Science and Technology: Federal R&D, Technology, and STEM Education in the 2010 Budget, May 2009 at http://www.ostp.gov/galleries/budget/FY2010RD.pdf.

Notes: 1/ Based on preliminary allocations of Recovery Act (P.L. 111-5) appropriations. These figures may change. 2/ Excludes Recovery Act appropriations. Change is regular FY2009 appropriations to FY2010 request.

Figure 3. Obama Administration FY2010 Budget Request for STEM Education Programs Budget Authority in Millions.

As discussed earlier, the Obama Administration is maintaining the Bush Administration's decision that several existing DOE STEM education programs serve the same purpose as those newly authorized in the America COMPETES Act. No new funding is requested for America COMPETES Act STEM education programs at ED, although the Obama Administration does request the same funding as that appropriated in FY2009 for ED's Teachers for a Competitive Tomorrow program of $2 million. At NSF, funding at the authorized level of $64.0 million is requested for its Advanced Technological Education

(ATE) program. All other requested funding is below authorized FY20 10 levels. No funding is requested for the Laboratory Science Pilot program, newly authorized in the act, which has never received funding.

# CONGRESSIONAL ACTIVITIES

Following the Obama Administration's release of its FY2010 budget outline, Congress developed a budget resolution that sets the budgetary spending amounts for each functional category of the budget [6]. The budget resolution does not allocate funds among specific programs or accounts. Major program assumptions underlying the functional amounts, however, are often discussed in the reports accompanying the resolution. These program assumptions and budget functions are not binding, although congressional action has been taken [7]

## Budget Resolution

In April 2009, the House and Senate agreed to the concurrent budget resolution (S.Con.Res. 13), which states the following:

SEC. 603. SENSE OF THE CONGRESS ON PROMOTING AMERICAN INNOVATION AND ECONOMIC COMPETITIVENESS.
It is the sense of the Congress that—
(1) the Congress should provide sufficient investments to enable our Nation to continue to be the world leader in education ,innovation, and economic growth as envisioned in the goals of the America COMPETES Act;
(2) this resolution builds on significant funding provided in the American Recovery and Reinvestment Act for scientific research and education in Function 250 (General Science, Space and Technology), Function 270 (Energy), Function 300 (Natural Resources and Environment), Function 500 (Education, Training, Employment, and Social Services), and Function 550(Health);
(3) the Congress also should pursue policies designed to ensure that American students, teachers, businesses, and workers are prepared to continue leading the world in innovation, research, and technology well into the future; and
(4) this resolution recognizes the importance of the extension of investments and tax policies that promote research and development and encourage innovation and future technologies that will ensure American economic competitiveness.

## Appropriations Committee

Following the budget resolution, the House Committee on Appropriations and the Senate Committee on Appropriations subdivides the budget allocations among the appropriations committees' 12 subcommittees. The committee's jurisdictions [8] for the federal agencies that have programs authorized by the America COMPETES Act programs are divided among at least three Appropriations subcommittees:

- Commerce, Justice, Science, and Related Agencies (CJS): NSF, NIST, NASA, and OSTP;
- Energy and Water Development (Energy-Water): DOE;
- Labor, Health and Human Services, Education, and Related Agencies (LaborHHS-Education): ED.

Typically, these subcommittees will review the President's budget request and provide their recommendations to the House and Senate Committees on Appropriations [9].

### Commerce, Justice, Science, and Related Agencies

On June 9, 2009, the House Committee on Appropriations approved the CJS bill (H.R. 2847) and report (H.Rept. 111-149) for consideration by the House. Table 1 provides the committee's funding recommendations for NSF and NIST.

At NIST, the House committee recommended funding for STRS and construction at a level less than that requested by the Administration, and funding for MEP and TIP was at the same level as requested. According to the committee, the reduction in the STRS activities funding was in order to support higher priority activities, and those in the construction program were due to the availability of funding from prior years [10]

The House committee proposed overall NSF funding of $6.9 billion, $108 million less that that requested by the Administration. Funding is less than that requested in the Research and Related Activities (R&RA) directorate, although it is more than that requested in the Education and Human Resources (EHR) directorate. Within R&RA, reductions were made in proposed funding for Major Research Instrumentation due to the availability of prior year funds such that it would receive no new funding in FY2010 [11].

EPSCoR funding was specified for the same level as that requested by the Administration. An increase in funding of $14.0 million greater than the request was recommended for the Graduate Research Fellowship (GRF) program to enable support for an additional 2,000 new fellows in FY2010 so that, overall, the agency would be able to fund approximately 3,654 fellows and reach its overall goal of funding 3,000 fellows by FY2013 at a faster pace.

The House Committee on Appropriations CJS subcommittee report also supported the proposal in NSF's budget request to set aside a minimum of $2 million in each reach division to explore methodologies that support transformative research.

In NSF's EHR directorate, funding was $10 million higher than that requested for the Robert Noyce program, $2.6 million higher for the STEM talent expansion program, and $2.78 higher for the MSP program. The ATE program funding recommendation was $42 million less that that requested due to the availability of prior year funds [12]. In addition, the committee recommended that future requests for the ATE program be made in a more appropriate department or agency such as ED. Funding for MREFC was reduced in response to the availability of prior year funds, and funding for agency operations and award management was reduced to support higher priority programs [13].

Table 1. America COMPETES Act Programs and Appropriations Status

| Programs with Specific Authorized Budgets in the America COMPETES Act | FY2008 Consolidated Appropriations Act, 2008 (P.L. 110-161); Supplemental Appropriations Act, 2008 (P.L. 110-252) | FY2009 Omnibus Appropriations Act, 2009 (P.L. 111-8); American Recovery and Reinvestment Act (ARRA; P.L. 111-5) | FY2010 America COMPETES Act (P.L. 110-69) Authorization of Appropriation | FY2010 President's Budget Request | FY2010 House Committee on Appropriations (NIST and NSF only) | FY2010 Senate Committee on Appropriations |
|---|---|---|---|---|---|---|
| Department of Commerce | | | | | | |
| National Institute of Standards and Technology (Sec. 3001) | | | | | | |
| —Scientific & Technical Research and Services (STRS) (Sec. 3001) | $440.5 | $692.0 (472.0 omnibus + 220.0 ARRA) | $584.8 | $534.6 | $510.0 | |
| —Construction & Maintenance (Sec. 3001) | 160.5 | 532.0 (172.0 omnibus +360.0 ARRA) | 49.7 | 116.9 | 76.5 | |
| —Technology Innovation Program (TIP) (Sec. 3001/3012) [NEW] | 65.2a | 65.0 | 140.5 | 69.9 | 69.9 | |
| —Manufacturing Extension Partnership (MEP) (Sec. 3001/3003) | 89.6 | 110.0 | 131.8 | 124.7 | $124.7 | |

Table 1 (Continued).

| Programs with Specific Authorized Budgets in the America COMPETES Act | FY2008 Consolidated Appropriations Act, 2008 (P.L. 110-161); Supplemental Appropriations Act, 2008 (P.L. 110-252)) | FY2009 Omnibus Appropriations Act, 2009 (P.L. 111-8); American Recovery and Reinvestment Act (ARRA; P.L. 111-5) | FY2010 America COMPETES Act (P.L. 110-69) Authorization of Appropriation | FY2010 President's Budget Request | FY2010 House Committee on Appropriations (NIST and NSF only) | FY2010 Senate Committee on Appropriations |
|---|---|---|---|---|---|---|
| Department of Energy | | | | | | |
| DOE Science, Engineering and Mathematics Programs (Sec. 5003) | | | | | | |
| —Pilot Program of Grants to Specialty Schools for Science and Mathematics (Sec. 5003) [NEW] | Not Included | Not Included | 30.0 | Not Included | | |
| —Experiential Based Learning Opportunities (Sec. 5003) [NEW] | Not Included | Not Included | 7.5 | Not Included | | |
| —Summer Institutes (Sec. 5003) [NEW] | Not Included | Not Included | 25.0 | Not Included[b] | | |

Table 1 (Continued).

| Programs with Specific Authorized Budgets in the America COMPETES Act | FY2008 Consolidated Appropriations Act, 2008 (P.L. 110-161); Supplemental Appropriations Act, 2008 (P.L. 110-252) | FY2009 Omnibus Appropriations Act, 2009 (P.L. 111-8); American Recovery and Reinvestment Act (ARRA; P.L. 111-5) | FY2010 America COMPETES Act (P.L. 110-69) Authorization of Appropriation | FY2010 President's Budget Request | FY2010 House Committee on Appropriations (NIST and NSF only) | FY2010 Senate Committee on Appropriations |
|---|---|---|---|---|---|---|
| —National Energy Education Development (Sec. 5003) [NEW] | Not Included | Not Included | Such sums as necessary | Not Included | | |
| Nuclear Science Talent Expansion Program (Sec. 5004) | | | | | | |
| —Nuclear Science Program Expansion Grants for Institutions of Higher Education (Sec. 5004) [NEW] | Not Included | Not Included | 9.5 | Not Included | | |
| —Nuclear Science Competitiveness Grants for Institutions of Higher Education (Sec. 5004) [NEW] | Not Included | Not Included | 8.0 | Not Included | | |
| Hydrocarbon Systems Science Talent Expansion Program (Sec. 5005) | | | | | | |

Table 1 (Continued).

| Programs with Specific Authorized Budgets in the America COMPETES Act | FY2008 Consolidated Appropriations Act, 2008 (P.L. 110-161); Supplemental Appropriations Act, 2008 (P.L. 110-252) | FY2009 Omnibus Appropriations Act, 2009 (P.L. 111-8); American Recovery and Reinvestment Act (ARRA; P.L. 111-5) | FY2010 America COMPETES Act (P.L. 110-69) Authorization of Appropriation | FY2010 President's Budget Request | FY2010 House Committee on Appropriations (NIST and NSF only) | FY2010 Senate Committee on Appropriations |
|---|---|---|---|---|---|---|
| —Hydrocarbon Systems Science Program Expansion Grants for Institutions of Higher Education (Sec. 5005) [NEW] | Not Included | Not Included | 9.5 | Not Included | | |
| —Hydrocarbon Systems Science Competitiveness Grants for Institutions of Higher Education (Sec. 5005) [NEW] | Not Included | Not Included | 8.0 | Not Included | | |
| Office of Science (Sec. 5007) (as act amends the Energy Policy Act of 2005 for FY2010) | 4,035.6 (3,973.1 consolidated +62.5 supplemental) | 6,357.6 4,757.6 omnibus +1,600.0 ARRA | 5,814.0 | 4,941.7 | | |

Table 1 (Continued).

| Programs with Specific Authorized Budgets in the America COMPETES Act | FY2008 Consolidated Appropriations Act, 2008 (P.L. 110-161); Supplemental Appropriations Act, 2008 (P.L. 110-252) | FY2009 Omnibus Appropriations Act, 2009 (P.L. 111-8); American Recovery and Reinvestment Act (ARRA; P.L. 111-5) | FY2010 America COMPETES Act (P.L. 110-69) Authorization of Appropriation | FY2010 President's Budget Request | FY2010 House Committee on Appropriations (NIST and NSF only) | FY2010 Senate Committee on Appropriations |
|---|---|---|---|---|---|---|
| —Early Career Awards for Science, Engineering, and Mathematics Researchers (Sec. 5006)[NEW] | Not Included | Not Included | 25.0 | Not Included[d] | | |
| Discovery Science and Engineering Innovation Institutes (Sec. 5008) [NEW] | Not Included | Not Included | 10.0-30.0[e] | Not Included[f] | | |
| Protecting America's Competitive Edge (PACE) Graduate Fellowship Program (Sec. 5009)[NEW] | Not Included | Not Included | 20.0 | Not Included[g] | | |
| Distinguished Scientist Program (Sec. 5011) [NEW] | Not Included | Not Included | 30.0 | Not Included | | |
| Advanced Research Projects Agency—Energy [ARPA-E] (Sec. 5012) [NEW] | Not Included | *415.0 (15.0 Omnibus + 400.0 ARRA) | Such sums as are necessary | 10.0 | | |

Table 1 (Continued).

| Programs with Specific Authorized Budgets in the America COMPETES Act | FY2008 Consolidated Appropriations Act, 2008 (P.L. 110-161); Supplemental Appropriations Act, 2008 (P.L. 110-252)) | FY2009 Omnibus Appropriations Act, 2009 (P.L. 111-8); American Recovery and Reinvestment Act (ARRA; P.L. 111-5) | FY2010 America COMPETES Act (P.L. 110-69) Authorization of Appropriation | FY2010 President's Budget Request | FY2010 House Committee on Appropriations (NIST and NSF only) | FY2010 Senate Committee on Appropriations |
|---|---|---|---|---|---|---|
| **Department of Education** | | | | | | |
| Teachers for a Competitive Tomorrow: Baccalaureate Degrees (Sec. 6113, 6115, 6116) [NEW] | *0.98 | *1.1 | 151.2 | 1.1 | | |
| Teachers for a Competitive Tomorrow: Master's Degrees (Sec. 6114-6116) [NEW] | *0.98 | *1.1 | 125.0 | 1.1 | | |
| Advanced Placement and International Baccalaureate Programs (Sec. 6121-6123) [NEW] | Not Included | *0.0 | Such sums as may be necessary | 0.0 | | |
| Math Now (Sec. 6201) [NEW] | *0.0 | *0.0 | Such sums as may be necessary | Not Included | | |
| Summer Term Education Programs (Sec. 6202) [NEW] | Not Included | Not Included | Such sums as may be necessary | Not Included | | |
| Math Skills for Secondary School Students (Sec. 6203) [NEW] | Not Included | Not Included | 95.0 | Not Included | | |

# Table 1 (Continued).

| Programs with Specific Authorized Budgets in the America COMPETES Act | FY2008 Consolidated Appropriations Act, 2008 (P.L. 110-161); Supplemental Appropriations Act, 2008 (P.L. 110-252)) | FY2009 Omnibus Appropriations Act, 2009 (P.L. 111-8); American Recovery and Reinvestment Act (ARRA; P.L. 111-5)) | FY2010 America COMPETES Act (P.L. 110-69) Authorization of Appropriation | FY2010 President's Budget Request | FY2010 House Committee on Appropriations (NIST and NSF only) | FY2010 Senate Committee on Appropriations |
|---|---|---|---|---|---|---|
| Advancing America Through Foreign Language Partnership Program[b] (Sec. 6301-6304) [NEW] | Not Included | *0.0 | Such sums as may be necessary | Not Included | | |
| P-16 Alignment of Secondary School Graduate Requirements with the Demands of 21st Century Postsecondary Endeavors and Support for P-16 Education Data Systems (Sec. 6401) [NEW] | Not Included | Not Included[i] | Such sums as may be necessary | Not Included | | |
| Mathematics and Science Partnership Bonus Grants (Sec. 6501) [NEW] | Not Included | Not Included | Such sums as may be necessary | Not Included | | |
| National Science Foundation (Sec. 7002) | 6,127.5 (6,065.0 consolidated +62.5 supplemental) | 9,492.4 (6,490.4 omnibus +3,002.0 ARRA) | 8,132.0 | 7,045.0 | 6936.5 | |
| Research and Related Activities (R&RA) | 4,844.0 (4,821.5 consolidated +22.5 supplemental) | 7,683.1 (5,183.1 omnibus +2,500.0 ARRA) | 6,401.0 | 5,733.2 | 5642.1 | |

Table 1 (Continued).

| Programs with Specific Authorized Budgets in the America COMPETES Act | FY2008 Consolidated Appropriations Act, 2008 (P.L. 110-161); Supplemental Appropriations Act, 2008 (P.L. 110-252) | FY2009 Omnibus Appropriations Act, 2009 (P.L. 111-8); American Recovery and Reinvestment Act (ARRA; P.L. 111-5) | FY2010 America COMPETES Act (P.L. 110-69) Authorization of Appropriation | FY2010 President's Budget Request | FY2010 House Committee on Appropriations (NIST and NSF only) | FY2010 Senate Committee on Appropriations |
|---|---|---|---|---|---|---|
| —Major Research Instrumentation (MRI) (Sec. 7002/Sec. 7036) | Not Included | *300.0 (Not Included omnibus +300.0 ARRA) | 131.7 | 100.0 | 0.0 | |
| —Faculty Early Career Development (CAREER) (Sec.7002) | Not Included | Not Included | 203.8 | 203.8 | Not Included | |
| —Research Experiences for Undergraduates (REU) (Sec.7002) | Not Included | Not Included | 75.9 | 67.7 | Not Included | |
| —Experimental Programs to Stimulate Competitive Research (EPSCoR) (Sec.7002) | *120.0 (115.0 consolidated +5.0k supplemental) | 133.0 | 147.8 | 147.1 | 147.1 | |
| —Integrative Graduate Education and Research Traineeship/R&RA (IGERT) (Sec.7002)[m] | Not Included | Not Included | 58.3 | 39.0 | Not Included | |

Table 1 (Continued).

| Programs with Specific Authorized Budgets in the America COMPETES Act | FY2008 Consolidated Appropriations Act, 2008 (P.L. 110-161); Supplemental Appropriations Act, 2008 (P.L. 110-252) | FY2009 Omnibus Appropriations Act, 2009 (P.L. 111-8); American Recovery and Reinvestment Act (ARRA; P.L. 111-5) | FY2010 America COMPETES Act (P.L. 110-69) Authorization of Appropriation | FY2010 President's Budget Request | FY2010 House Committee on Appropriations (NIST and NSF only) | FY2010 Senate Committee on Appropriations |
|---|---|---|---|---|---|---|
| —Graduate Research Fellowship/R&RA (GRF) (Sec.7002) | Not Included | Not Included | 11.1 | 19.4 | *33.4 | |
| —Professional Science Master's Degree Program (Sec. 7002/7034) [NEW] | Not Included | 15.0n (Not Included omnibus +15.0 ARRA) | 15.0 | 0.0 | Not Included | |
| Education and Human Resources (EHR) | 765.6 (725.6 consolidated +40.0 supplemental) | 945.3 (845.3 omnibus +100.0 ARRA) | 1,104.0 | 857.8 | 862.9 | |
| —Mathematics and Science Education Partnership (MSP) (Sec.7002/7028) | Not Included | 86.0 (*61.0 omnibus +25.0 ARRA) | 123.2 | 58.2 | *61.0 | |
| —Robert Noyce Teacher Scholarship Program (Sec.7002/7030) | *55.0 (15.0 consolidated +40.0 supplemental) | 115.0 (55.0l omnibus +*60.0 ARRA) | 140.5 | 55.0 | 65.0 | |
| —Science, Mathematics, Engineering, and Technology Talent Expansion (Sec.7002/7025) | Not Included | Not Included | 55.0 | 31.5p | *34.1 | |
| —Advanced Technological Education (ATE) (Sec.7002) | Not Included | Not Included | 64.0 | 64.0 | 22.4 | |

Table 1 (Continued).

| Programs with Specific Authorized Budgets in the America COMPETES Act | FY2008 Consolidated Appropriations Act, 2008 (P.L. 110-161); Supplemental Appropriations Act, 2008 (P.L. 110-252)) | FY2009 Omnibus Appropriations Act, 2009 (P.L. 111-8); American Recovery and Reinvestment Act (ARRA; P.L. 111-5)) | FY2010 America COMPETES Act (P.L. 110-69) Authorization of Appropriation | FY2010 President's Budget Request | FY2010 House Committee on Appropriations (NIST and NSF only) | FY2010 Senate Committee on Appropriations |
|---|---|---|---|---|---|---|
| —Integrative Graduate Education and Research Traineeship/EHR (IGERT) (Sec.7002)$^{m}$ | Not Included | Not Included | 33.4 | 29.9 | Not Included | |
| —Graduate Research Fellowship/EHR (GRF) (Sec.7002) | Not Included | *107.0 | 119.0 | 102.6 | Not Included | |
| Major Research Equipment and Facilities Construction (Sec.7002) | 220.7 | 552.0 (152.0 omnibus +400.0 ARRA) | 280.0 | 117.3 | 114.3 | |
| Agency Operations and Award Management (Sec.7002) | 281.8 | 294.0 | 329.5 | 318.4 | 299.9 | |
| National Science Board (Sec.7002) | 4.0 | 4.0 | 4.3 | 4.3 | 4.3 | |
| Inspector General (Sec.7002) | 11.4 | 14.0 (12.0 omnibus +2.0 ARRA) | 13.2 | 14.0 | 13.0 | |
| Laboratory Science Pilot Program (Sec. 7026) [NEW] | Not Included | Not Included | Such sums as may be necessary | Not Included | Not Included | |

Source: America COMPETES Act (P.L. 110-69); Omnibus Appropriations Act, 2009 (P.L. 111-8) and explanatory statement; American Recovery and Reinvestment Act of 2009 (P.L. 111-5); H.Rept. 111-16 and joint explanatory statement. For FY2008, information is from the Consolidated Appropriations Act, 2008 (P.L. 110-161) and joint explanatory statement; Congressional Record, December 17, 2007; Supplemental Appropriations Act, 2008 (P.L. 110-252); H.Rept. 110-240; S.Rept. 110-124; H.Rept. 110-231; and S.Rept. 110-107. FY2010 budget documents for the following agencies: NIST budget summary at http://www.nist.gov/public_affairs/releases/approps-summary2008-2010.htm; ED budget justification at http://www.ed.gov/about/overview/budget/budget10/justifications/index.html; DOE detailed budget justification (Volume 3 – ARPA-E;Volume 4-Science) at http://www.cfo.doe.gov/budget/10budget/Start.htm#Detailed%20Budget%20Justifications; and NSF budget request at http://www.nsf.gov/about/budget/fy2010/toc.jsp. Information in FY2010 House Committee on Appropriations column is from H.R. 2847 and H.Rept. 111-149.

Notes: Section numbers refer to the America COMPETES Act. "[NEW]" means a program that was not authorized prior to the America COMPETES Act. "Not Included" means that these programs were not specifically identified in the budget request, bill, act, or report, but it does not necessarily mean no funding is being provided for those programs. * = as recommended in the committee's report associated with that bill. All other appropriations are numbers from bill language.

a. The following statement is in the Consolidated Appropriations Act joint explanatory statement: "Of the amounts provided to ITS [Industrial Technology Services], $65,200,000 is for the Technology Innovation Program as authorized by P.L. 110-69 [the America COMPETES Act]. TIP is structured to fund high-risk, high reward research focused on broad national needs such as advanced automotive batteries, aquaculture, novel lightweight materials, and other emerging technologies. The funding provided for TIP will address mortgage obligations relating to projects created under the Advanced Technology Program (ATP). The amended bill also includes language to allow the TIP immediate access to an additional $5,000,000 from deobligations and prior-year recoveries from ATP."

b. According to a personal communication between CRS and OSTP, the Obama Administration contends that Summer Institutes correspond to the pre-existing DOE Academies Creating Teacher Scientists program (DOE ACTS).

c. The P.L. 111-8 explanatory statement provides $4,772.6 million for science at DOE with $15.0 million of that total for the organizationally separate Advanced Research Projects Agency – Energy (ARPA-E) and the remainder for DOE Office of Science Activities.

d. According to a personal communication between CRS and OSTP, the Obama Administration contends that Early Career Awards for Science, Engineering, and Mathematics Researchers correspond to pre-existing High Energy Physics Outstanding Junior Investigator, Nuclear Physics Outstanding Junior Investigator, Fusion Energy Sciences Plasma Physics Junior Faculty Development; Advanced Scientific Computing Research Early Career Principle Investigator; and the Office of Science Early Career Scientist and Engineer Award programs.

e. The Secretary of Energy can decide to establish up to three institutes per fiscal year. Each institute could receive $10 million per year for three fiscal years.

f. According to a personal communication between CRS and OSTP, the Obama Administration contends that Discovery Science and Engineering Innovation Institutes correspond with pre-existing Bioenergy Research Centers, SciDAC Institutes, and Energy Frontier Research Centers.

g. According to a personal communication between CRS and OSTP, the Obama Administration contends that the Protecting America's Competitive Edge (PACE) Graduate Fellowship Program corresponds to pre-existing Computer Science Graduate Fellowships; Graduate Research Environmental Fellowships; American Meteorological Society/Industry/Government Graduate Fellowships; Spallation Neutron Source Instrumentation Fellowships, and the Fusion Energy Sciences Graduate Fellowships.

h. The title for this program in the America COMPETES Act is the Foreign Language Partnership Program. The table uses the title for this program from the ED FY2009 congressional budget justification to help distinguish it from other ED foreign language programs such as the existing Foreign Language Assistance program.

i. P.L. 111-5 indicates that part of the funding provided to States for Institutions of Higher Education as part of the State Fiscal Stabilization Fund (Title XIV) should be used for "IMPROVING COLLECTION AND USE OF DATA.—The State will establish a longitudinal data system that includes the elements described in section 6401(e)(2)(D) of the America COMPETES Act (20 U.S.C. 9871)." In addition, the State "will take steps to improve State academic content standards and student academic achievement standards consistent with 6401(e)(1)(A)(ii) of the America COMPETES Act." No specific appropriation is noted for either purpose. Section 6401 of the America COMPETES Act addresses the "Alignment of secondary school graduate requirements with the demands of 21st century postsecondary endeavors and support for P-16 education systems." With that Section, subsection (e)(2)(D) provides required elements of a statewide P-16 education data system such as demographic information, yearly test records, teacher identification information, and student-level transcripts and college readiness test scores. Section (e)(1)(A)(ii) discusses the use of grant funds for "identifying and making changes that need to be made to the State's secondary school graduation from secondary school in order to align requirements, standards, and assessments with the knowledge standards, and assessments preceding graduation from secondary school in order to align requirements, standards, and assessments with the knowledge and skills necessary for success in academic credit-bearing coursework in postsecondary education, in the 21st century workforce, and in the Armed Forces without the need for remediation."

j. The following statement is in the Consolidated Appropriations Act joint explanatory statement: "The Appropriations Committees strongly support increases for the math and physical sciences, computer sciences, and engineering directorates in fiscal year 2008 for research and related activities (R&RA). However, the Committees also believe the Foundation should maintain comparable growth in fiscal year 2008, to the extent possible, for the biological sciences and social, behavioral and economic sciences directorates. Each of the science disciplines is valuable in maintaining U.S. competitiveness. The Committees urge NSF to provide each directorate with funding levels that are consistent with the goals of the America COMPETES Act and look forward to the Foundation's operating plan in addressing these concerns."

k. Although included in the FY2008 supplemental appropriation, the act specifies a section in the America COMPETES Act authorizing funding for the FY2009 EPSCoR program.

l. The explanatory statement indicates that "The increase provided in the bill for the Noyce Program is for the purpose of expanding participation in the grants program established in section10 and section 10A of the National Science Foundation Authorization Act of 2002 (42 U.S.C. 1862n-1) as amended by the America COMPETES Act."

m. Two directorates of the NSF manage the Integrative Graduate Education and Research Traineeship (IGERT) program—the Education and Human Resources Directorate (EHR) and the Research and Related Activities (R&RA) directorate. The America COMPETES Act and the NSF budget request both identify the allocations for each directorate.

n. The America COMPETES Act provides the authorization amount within R&RA; however, the explanatory language for P.L. 111-5 places the program within EHR.

o. Of this $40 million, $20 million is for the general Robert Noyce Teacher Scholarship Program, and $20 million is for the NSF Teaching Fellowships and Master Teaching Fellowships that are part of the Noyce program.

p. An additional $1 million is proposed for the R&RA portion of the program. According to NSF's budget request, "The STEP Program seeks to increase the number of students receiving degrees in established or emerging fields within science, technology, engineering, and mathematics. Awards are made both to provide for implementation efforts at academic institutions and to support research degree attainment in STEM. The America Competes Act authorized the establishment of centers within this program, to be jointly funded with one or more disciplinary directorates, to explore fundamental changes in undergraduate practice that promise to significantly improve recruitment and retention of students, and lead to improvement in their learning. The $1.83 million increase will permit the establishment of two additional centers in FY 2010 in collaboration with the R&RA Directorates."

In addition, the House Committee on Appropriations CJS subcommittee notes in its report that missing from the America COMPETES Act investment plan for science and technology are "critical elements of the National Aeronautics and Space Administration (NASA) and the National Oceanic and Atmospheric Administration (NOAA), which equally support the science enterprise of our Nation" and which are "not markedly different or less important than other science disciplines funded by the NSF and NIST," leading the subcommittee to provide "appropriate increases for NSF, and NIST, while also providing appropriate and necessary increases for critical science activities of NASA and NOAA."

### *Future Activities*

A tentative schedule [14] available from the House Committee on Appropriations states that the Energy and Water Development bill may be considered by the relevant subcommittee on June 25, 2009, and voted upon by the House on July 7, 2009. The Labor, Health and Human Services, Education, and Related Agencies bill may be considered by the subcommittee on July 8, 2009, and by the House on July 14, 2009. A schedule of Senate Committee on Appropriations activities is not available.

## Issues for Congress

As Congress deliberates the FY2010 budget, an issue for Congress is what level, if any, will it appropriate funding for America COMPETES Act programs. Several programs newly authorized in the act have never been appropriated funds. An issue for these programs is whether or not they will receive the funding necessary to establish them. The America COMPETES Act provides authorization levels only through FY2010.

## REFERENCES

[1]    For more information on ARPA-E, see CRS Report RL34497, Advanced Research Projects Agency - Energy (ARPAE): Background, Status, and Selected Issues for Congress, by Deborah D. Stine.

[2]    According to an email communication between CRS and the Bush Administration OMB and OSTP received on October 14, 2008, and between CRS and the Obama Administration OSTP on May 19, 2009

[3]    U.S. President (G.W. Bush), American Competitiveness Initiative, Domestic Policy Council/Office of Science and Technology Policy, February 2006, p. 19, at http://www.ostp.gov/pdf/acibooklet.pdf.

[4]    Testimony of Secretary of Energy Steven Chu, FY 2010 Appropriations Hearing, Senate Committee on Appropriations Subcommittee on Energy and Water Development, and Related Agencies, May 19, 2009 at http://appropria tions.senate.gov/Hearings/2009_05_19_-Energy-_Testimony_of_Secretary_Chu_at_May_19_Energy_and_Water_Subcommittee_Heari ng.pdf?CFID=3770527& CFTOKEN=27868417.

[5] Testimony of Secretary of Energy Steven Chu, FY 2010 Appropriations Hearing, Senate Committee on Appropriations Subcommittee on Energy and Water Development, and Related Agencies, May 19, 2009 at http://appropriat ions.senate.gov/Hearings/2009_05_19_-Energy- _Testimony_of_Secretary_Chu_at_May_19_Energy_and_Water_Subcommittee_Heari ng.pdf?CFID=3770527& CFTOKEN=27868417.

[6] CRS Report 97-684, The Congressional Appropriations Process: An Introduction, by Sandy Streeter.

[7] CRS Report 98-721, *Introduction to the Federal Budget Process*, by Robert Keith. This process is set forth in the Congressional Budget Act, Titles I-IX of the Congressional Budget and Impoundment Control Act of 1974 (P.L. 93- 344; July 12, 1974; 88 Stat. 297-339), as amended and codified at 2 U.S.C. 621-692.

[8] It is important to note that the House and Senate Parliamentarians are the sole definitive authorities on questions relating to the jurisdiction of congressional committees and should be consulted for a formal opinion on any specific jurisdictional question.

[9] For additional information on the appropriations process, see CRS Report 97-684, *The Congressional Appropriations Process: An Introduction,* by Sandy Streeter.

[10] House Committee on Appropriations, "Fiscal Year 2010: Commerce, Justice, Science Appropriations Bill, Terminations & Reductions," at http://appropriations.ho use.gov/pdf/CJS_Cuts_Table_FC2010-06-09-2009.pdf.

[11] Ibid.

[12] Ibid

[13] Ibid.

[14] For more information, see http://appropriations.house.gov/pdf/Tentative_ 2010_Schedule-06-09-2009.pdf.

In: U.S. Political Programs: Functions and Assessments  ISBN: 978-1-61209-448-9
Editors: Julianna M. Moretti and Karen J. Chordstron © 2011 Nova Science Publishers, Inc.

*Chapter 7*

# EMPLOYMENT-BASED HEALTH COVERAGE AND HEALTH REFORM: SELECTED LEGAL CONSIDERATIONS[*]

## *Jennifer Staman and Edward C. Liu*

### ABSTRACT

It is estimated that nearly 170 million individuals have employer-based health coverage. As part of a comprehensive health care reform effort, there has been support (including from the Obama Administration) in enacting comprehensive health insurance reform that retains the employer- based system. This report presents selected legal considerations inherent in amending two of the primary federal laws governing employer-sponsored health care: the Employee Retirement Income Security Act (ERISA) and the Internal Revenue Code (IRC).

ERISA may be a key part of the health reform discussion in two main ways. The first way is if Congress desires to amend the employer-based system, for example, to require financing or benefits for group health plans as provided by employers. If a national proposal were to require employers to provide or contribute to the payment of health benefits or to provide specific benefits as part of group health plans, ERISA could be a vehicle for this type of proposal. Second, if Congress were to amend the role of states in regulating employment-based health benefits, ERISA's express preemption provision, § 514, would likely be implicated. Section 514 of ERISA is commonly seen as a barrier for states in enacting health reform that affects the employer-based system. This report provides an overview of ERISA preemption and analyzes some of the current issues dealing with the extent to which ERISA can preempt state health reform efforts, as well as issues that may be considered in a national health reform effort.

While the current tax treatment of employer-provided health insurance is not technically an obstacle to health reform, various health reform proposals have included amendments to these tax provisions. The value of employer-provided health insurance is generally not subject to income or payroll taxes. This effectively results in the subsidization of employer-provided health insurance by the federal government. Some

---

[*] This is an edited, reformatted and augmented edition of a United States Congressional Research Service publication, CRS Report R40635, dated June 12, 2009.

have argued that this subsidization is partly responsible for increasing costs of health insurance, as it gives participants an inaccurate sense of the true cost of their health care and leads to increased utilization of health care resources. Therefore, some have proposed reducing or eliminating this exclusion in order to provide individuals with a more accurate economic picture of their health care choices, while simultaneously raising federal revenue to pay for other aspects of health care reform. This report discusses the legal framework underlying the current tax treatment of employer-provided health care.

It has been estimated that nearly 170 million individuals, or approximately 64% of the non- elderly population, have employer-based health coverage in the United States [1]. While under federal law, employers are not required to provide coverage to employees, many do so voluntarily [2]. Employment-based insurance has several strengths, including risk pools that are not formed on the basis of health status, ease of acquisition by workers, and tax subsidies that exceed those for individual market insurance [3]. In addition, employers may have greater negotiating power with an insurance company than does an individual consumer [4].

On the other hand, plans chosen by employers may not meet individual workers' needs, and changing jobs may require obtaining both new insurance and new doctors. Nevertheless, given that employers are a large source of financing for health coverage in the United States, whether employment-based insurance should be strengthened, weakened, or kept the same is likely to be evaluated by Congress. If Congress chooses to amend the employer-based system as part of a federal health reform effort, it is possible that two primary federal laws governing employer-based coverage, Employee Retirement Income Security Act and the Internal Revenue Code, may be the vehicle for making changes [5]. This report provides an analysis of selected legal considerations in amending these two federal laws [6]

## THE EMPLOYEE RETIREMENT INCOME SECURITY ACT (ERISA)

The Employee Retirement Income Security Act (ERISA) [7] provides a comprehensive federal scheme for the regulation of private sector employee benefit plans [8] While ERISA does not require an employer to provide employee benefits, it does mandate compliance with its provisions if such benefits are offered. Enacted in 1974, the act sought to eliminate the conflicting and inconsistent regulation of employee benefit plans by various state laws [9]. Such laws were believed by some to be inadequate in protecting the interests of plan participants and beneficiaries [10]

While ERISA was enacted primarily to regulate pension plans, ERISA also regulates welfare benefit plans [11] offered by an employer to provide medical, surgical, and other health benefits [12]. ERISA applies to health benefit coverage offered through health insurance or other arrangements (e.g., self-funded plans) [13]. Health plans, like other welfare benefit plans governed by ERISA, must comply with certain standards, including plan fiduciary standards and reporting and disclosure requirements. However, while ERISA provides extensive regulation of pension plans, its regulation of health and other welfare benefit plans is less detailed. For example, unlike its regulation of pension plans, ERISA does not include vesting requirements for welfare benefit plans, under which a benefit becomes non-forfeitable [14]. In addition, ERISA requires pension plans to meet extensive funding requirements, but these requirements do not apply to health and other welfare benefit plans.

Thus, if an employer with a self-funded plan were to go bankrupt, there is little federal protection for employee medical claims.

Since the enactment of ERISA, Congress has taken certain steps to regulate the nature and content of group health plans more comprehensively [15]. These requirements, found in Part 6 and Part 7 of Title I of ERISA, only apply to group health plans and health insurance issuers offering group health coverage [16]. For example, the *Consolidated Omnibus Budget Reconciliation Act of 1985* (COBRA) amended ERISA and the IRC to require the sponsor of a group health plan to provide an option of temporarily continuing health care coverage for plan participants and beneficiaries under certain circumstances [17]. *The Health Insurance Portability and Accountability Act* of 1996 (HIPAA) created additional health plan coverage requirements under ERISA and other federal laws, including limitations on an exclusion period for an individual's preexisting condition [18]. HIPAA also prohibits a health plan from requiring an individual to pay a higher premium or contribution than another "similarly situated" participant, based on certain health- related factors, such as medical history or disability [19].

Further, ERISA also contains provisions that do not require employers to provide specific benefits, but regulates these benefits if such coverage is offered. For example, health plans that choose to provide mental health benefits must provide a certain amount of parity between medical/surgical benefits and mental health benefits offered, and plans that provide hospital coverage in connection with the birth of a child must allow for certain minimum hospital stay requirements for these mothers following childbirth [20]. In addition, ERISA requires group health plans providing mastectomy coverage to cover prosthetic devices and reconstructive surgery [21]. Congress also recently enacted Michelle's Law, [22] which amended ERISA and other laws to require group health plans and health insurance issuers that provide coverage for dependents to retain as dependents on the health plan, college-age students who are required to take a medically necessary leave of absence from school [23].

While some commentators may argue that ERISA's regulation of health plans is sufficient in scope and should not be expanded (so that employers are not discouraged from providing health benefits to employees), others have pointed to a lack of regulation in this area [24].

ERISA may be a key part of the health reform discussion in two main ways. The first way is if Congress desires to amend the employer-based system, for example, to require financing or benefits for group health plans as provided by employers [25]. If a national proposal were to require employers to provide or contribute to the payment of health benefits or to provide specific benefits as part of group health plans, ERISA could be a vehicle for this type of proposal.

Second, if Congress were to amend the role of states in regulating employment-based health benefits, ERISA's express preemption provision, § 514, would likely be implicated. Section 514 of ERISA is commonly seen as a barrier for states in enacting health reform that affects the employer-based system [26].

This report will provide an overview of ERISA preemption and analyze some of the current issues dealing with the extent to which ERISA can preempt state health reform efforts, as well as issues that may considered in a national health reform effort.

## Overview of ERISA Preemption

In an effort to protect employee benefit plans and participants, Congress, through ERISA, federalized regulation of plan administration "to minimize the administrative and financial burden of complying with conflicting directives among States or between States and the Federal Government" [27] This goal is carried out through a critical feature of ERISA: its preemption of state laws [28]. According to the Supreme Court, Congress provided for ERISA preemption in order to "avoid a multiplicity of regulation in order to permit the nationally uniform administration of employee benefit plans" [29]. The question of whether ERISA preempts state law has, at times, been complex and controversial. The provisions at issue in the preemption debate are (1) § 514, ERISA's express preemption section, under which ERISA may supersede state law, and (2) §502(a), which limits claims that may be brought and remedies a plaintiff may recover under ERISA, and may preempt a state law cause of action [30]. Section 514 will be the focus of this report.

ERISA § 514 preempts "any and all State laws insofar as they may now or hereafter relate to any employee benefit plan.... " [31]. The U.S. Supreme Court has interpreted this language as applying to any state law that "has a connection with or reference to such a plan." [32]. In conjunction with these two factors articulated by the Supreme Court, a court's preemption analysis typically examines whether a state law interferes with the ERISA's goal of uniform national standards [33] The Supreme Court has explained that to determine whether a state law has a "connection with" an ERISA plan, a court must consider the objectives of ERISA as a guide to the scope of the statute that Congress understood would survive, as well as the nature of the effect of the state law on ERISA plans [34]. State laws that attempt to regulate plan benefits or the administration, operation, or structure of the plan may be seen as having an improper connection with an ERISA plan. For example, in Shaw v. Delta Airlines, [35] a New York law which required plans to provide pregnancy-related benefits was found preempted because it burdened the administration of employee benefit plans [36]. Similarly, in Egelhoff v. Egelhoff, the Washington law at issue provided that the designation of a spouse as the beneficiary of a non-probate asset (e.g., a pension plan) would be revoked automatically upon divorce. In determining that the Washington law had an impermissible connection with ERISA plans because it interfered with nationally uniform plan administration, the Court explained that one of the principal goals of ERISA is to enable employers to establish a uniform administrative scheme that provides standard procedures for the processing of claims and disbursement of benefits. The Court maintained that uniformity is impossible if plans are subject to different legal obligations in different states.

A state law has a "reference to" an ERISA plan if it acts "immediately and exclusively" on ERISA plans or if the existence of such a plan is essential to the law's operations [37]. For example, in Mackey v. Lanier Collection Agency & Service, [38] the Court evaluated Georgia statutes which addressed the garnishment of funds from ERISA employee welfare benefit plans. The Court held that ERISA preempted the state statute that specifically exempted ERISA plans under state garnishment procedures. The Court declared that "any state law which singles out ERISA plans, by express reference, for special treatment is pre-empted." [39]

Despite §514's wide scope, ERISA does not preempt every state action that affects an employee benefit plan [40]. As the Supreme Court has articulated, "[s]ome state actions may affect employee benefit plans in too tenuous, remote, or peripheral a manner to warrant a finding that the law 'relates to' the plan." [41]. While the Court's early ERISA preemption decisions suggested that the application of ERISA's explicit preemption clause was virtually limitless, its decision in New York State Conference of Blue Cross & Blue Shield Plans v. Travelers Insurance Co. signaled a change in the Court's interpretation of §514(a) [42]. In Travelers, several commercial insurers challenged a state law that required them, but not Blue Cross and Blue Shield, to pay hospital surcharges. The commercial insurers argued that the law was preempted by ERISA because it "relate[d] to" employer-sponsored health insurance plans. In addressing the issue of ERISA's preemption clause, the Court first noted that there is a "presumption that Congress does not intend to supplant state law" [43]. The Court then turned to whether Congress intended to preempt state law by looking to "the structure and purpose of the act." [44]. The Court concluded that "nothing in the language of the act or the context of its passage indicates that Congress chose to displace general health care regulation, which historically has been a matter of local concern." [45]. In other cases, the Court has similarly recognized the states' ability to regulate matters of health and safety, and has concluded that state laws of general applicability are not necessarily preempted by ERISA [46]. However, in spite of an arguable narrowing in the scope of § 514(a), this section still is considered to broadly preempt state law [47]. Under §514(b)(2)(A), a state law that relates to an ERISA plan may avoid preemption if it regulates insurance within the meaning of ERISA's "saving clause." This section "saves" from preemption "any law of any State which regulates insurance, banking, or securities" [48]. Thus, the savings clause permits states to regulate health insurance without running afoul of ERISA's preemptive scheme, and states may therefore impose requirements on health insurers that are more comprehensive than the requirements set forth under ERISA [49]. However, under §514(b)(2)(B) of ERISA, commonly referred to as the "deemer clause," a state law that "purport[s] to regulate insurance" cannot deem an employee benefit plan to be an insurance company for purposes of regulation [50]. In interpreting this provision, the Supreme Court has found that a self-insured health plan cannot be "deemed" an insured plan for the purpose of state regulation [51].

Accordingly, a plan that provides health benefits through an insurance company can, in effect, be regulated by state insurance law, as well as by ERISA. On the other hand, a plan that is self- insured is only subject to ERISA's requirements, and is immune from state law. It is estimated that approximately 55% of workers with employment-based health coverage participate in self- insured plans [52]. Thus, by self-insuring an employer can avoid compliance with state requirements that may be more onerous or costly, and may be able to provide the same coverage to all employees, regardless of the state where the employee works or resides, which may have administrative advantages. However, it has been noted that leaving self-insured plans out of state regulation can lead to greater costs for states [53]

## ERISA PREEMPTION AND HEALTH REFORM

ERISA's preemptive scheme is important in examining possible roles that states might plan in regulating employment-based health benefits. ERISA preemption arises in the health reform debate in two primary contexts. *First,* in the absence of federal legislation, states and localities have undertaken certain efforts to improve health coverage for their residents, and questions have been raised about whether ERISA preempts these state laws. *Second,* if a federal health reform effort includes a larger role for the states in terms of employee benefit regulation, then ERISA's preemption provisions may need to be reviewed.

## ERISA and Current State Health Reform Efforts

As discussed above, ERISA preemption may limit the types of health reform initiatives states may enact. For example, based on judicial precedent interpreting ERISA §514, states cannot require employers to provide a minimum level of coverage or specific health benefits [54]. While states may regulate health insurance, they cannot impose regulation on self-insured plans. In addition, while states may have some flexibility to pass laws of general applicability in order to generate revenue to pay for health insurance for their constituents (e.g., a tax on all employers), it has been pointed out that there may be some downsides to this type of approach [55]. Despite these obstacles, and in response to an increasing number of uninsured individuals, the declining number of employers offering insurance to their employees, and the absence of federal action, states and localities have experimented with certain measures to address the problems of health care financing and access, and have sought ways to make employers pay for health coverage of their employees. One leading approach that states and localities have taken is "fair share laws" (also referred to as "pay or play" statutes), which generally require employers to choose between paying a certain amount toward health expenditures or coverage for their employees, or contributing to a state or locality to offset the cost of medical expenses for uninsured residents. Recently, questions have been raised as to whether §514 of ERISA prevents the application of fair share laws.

Legal challenges to fair share laws enacted in Maryland and San Francisco have yielded varying conclusions. In 2006, Maryland enacted the Fair Share Health Care Fund Act, which would have required for-profit employers with 10,000 or more employees in the state to either spend at least 8% of their total payroll costs on employee health insurance costs, or pay to the state the amount their spending fell short of that percentage [56]. Shortly after the Fair Share Act was enacted, a retail trade association that includes Wal-Mart as a member, challenged the measure on the grounds that it was preempted by ERISA. In Retail Industry Leaders Association v. Fielder, [57] the Fourth Circuit found the Maryland Fair Share Act was preempted because it effectively forced employers to restructure their employee health plans, and as such, interfered with ERISA's goal of providing uniform nationwide administration of these plans [58]. The Fielder court opined that just because an employer had the option not to spend money on health care for their employees, this option was not a "meaningful alternative" and did not protect the law from preemption [59]

The City of San Francisco passed the *San Francisco Health Care Security Ordinance,* which requires covered employers to make minimum health care expenditures on behalf of covered employees [60]. The San Francisco Ordinance identifies various qualifying health care expenditures, including contributions to health savings accounts and payments to a third party for the purpose of providing health care services for covered employees. Covered employers may also satisfy the Ordinance's spending requirement by making payments directly to the city. Regulations that implement the Ordinance confirm that a covered employer has discretion with regard to the type of health care expenditure it chooses to make for its covered employees. In a case challenging the Ordinance, Golden Gate Restaurant Ass 'n v. City and County of San Francisco, the Ninth Circuit upheld San Francisco's Act as not preempted by ERISA [61]. In its opinion, the Ninth Circuit refuted the argument that the Ordinance established an ERISA plan (and therefore, "related to" and ERISA plan) because of the administrative obligations imposed on employers by the Ordinance. The court found that the Ordinance only places minimal duties on employers, and does not bind plan administrators to a particular choice of rules for determining plan eligibility or entitlement to particular benefits [62]. The court further explained that the Ordinance does not require employers to structure their employee benefit plans in a particular manner or to provide specific benefits. The Ninth Circuit also distinguished *Fielder,* emphasizing that the Ordinance does not require employers to structure their employee health care plans to provide a certain level of benefits. In contrast, the court maintained, the Maryland Fair Share Act did not provide meaningful alternatives to comply with the law. It is expected that the Golden Gate Restaurant Association will petition the Supreme Court for review of the case [63]

The state of Massachusetts, which has received a great deal of attention for enacting comprehensive health care reform, maintains a fair share requirement as part of its health care reform package. Under the Massachusetts Act, [64] employers with more than 11 full-time equivalent employees that do not make a "fair and reasonable" contribution to a group health plan for their employees' health coverage must pay a "fair-share contribution" into a state trust fund in order to help cover costs of health care provided to uninsured Massachusetts residents "fair and reasonable" contribution to a group health plan for their employees' health coverage [65]. The Massachusetts law has not been challenged on preemption grounds, but if the Supreme Court were to review Golden Gate Restaurant Association, there could be implications for the Massachusetts law. For a more detailed discussion of fair share laws, ERISA preemption and an analysis of the Massachusetts statute, see CRS Report RL34637, *Legal Issues Relating to State Health Care Regulation: ERISA Preemption and Fair Share Laws,* by Jon O. Shimabukuro and Jennifer Staman.

## ERISA and National Health Reform Efforts

ERISA may come into play in a national health reform effort in two primary ways. First, as mentioned above, Congress may choose to supplement the current federal regulation of health plans under ERISA. If Congress were to require employers to establish a health plan, provide specific health benefits, or provide financing of health benefits, ERISA may be a vehicle for carrying out these types of proposals. For example, Congress may choose to create additional requirements for group health plans under Parts 6 and 7 of Title I of ERISA (which includes include rules on health care continuation coverage (COBRA), limitations on exclusions from health care coverage based on preexisting conditions, and parity between medical/surgical benefits and mental health benefits.) [66] While some may be in favor of using ERISA as a tool for requiring employers to play a potentially larger role in the financing of health coverage for employees, others may argue that adding requirements may cause employers to cease to provide benefits (assuming a proposal retains the voluntary nature of these benefits) or impose burdensome costs on employers. It is also possible that Congress could legislate in this area without amending ERISA. Congress could repeal ERISA's provisions as they relate to group health plans and create a new federal law with entirely new requirements. However, if national health reform includes an expansion or contraction of private-sector employment-based health coverage, ERISA's current regulation of health benefits may need to be amended or repealed.

Second, ERISA preemption may be implicated in any federal health reform proposal that involves greater state regulation of employment-related health benefits. As discussed above, there are impediments to states' involvement in the regulation of employment-based health coverage. Thus, any federal proposal that may involve a role for the states in regulating employment-based health coverage, may need to take ERISA preemption into account. For example, there has been interest in implementing some type of health insurance exchange, [67] either on a national, state, or local level [68]. Among the other federal laws that may be amended in this type of proposal, ERISA could come into play in the insurance exchange context with respect to state laws that seek some way to compel an employer or employee benefit plan to participate in an exchange [69]

Another area where ERISA preemption may need to be evaluated is under a federal proposal that allows for states to have some flexibility to enact their own reforms. If Congress, as part of a large scale health reform effort, desires to preserve Massachusetts' fair share requirements, or wants to clarify that fair share legislation such as the San Francisco Ordinance are acceptable under ERISA, or to allow states to enact other types of legislation that could, at least in theory, "relate to" employee benefit plans, amending ERISA's preemption provision may be considered. While some may argue that states should be allowed to be laboratories of experimentation [70] in figuring out what practices work and what practices do not in controlling costs and assuring access to health care, others may argue that, as was desired by many when ERISA was enacted, [71] there is a need for national uniformity in regulating health plans and that a patchwork of state regulation could be burdensome on employers.

Some commentators have suggested that a waiver of ERISA preemption may be an avenue to pursue for allowing states to enact health reform legislation while keeping national standards in place [72]. Congress has granted one waiver to the state of Hawaii. Under the Hawaii Prepaid Health Care Act of 1974, employers are required to provide health insurance to employees who work more than 20 hours per week, but may require employees to contribute up to 50% of the costs of premiums or 1.5% of their salaries to health insurance, whichever is lower [73]. This mandate was challenged Standard Oil Co. v. Agsalud, [74] in which the Ninth Circuit found that the statute was preempted by ERISA [75]. After the Supreme Court affirmed the decision, in 1983 Congress exempted Hawaii's Act from ERISA preemption [76]. This type of waiver has been sought for other states, however, Congress has not granted them [77]. Case-by-case waivers may offer some state flexibility while maintaining some national uniformity. However, unless Congress articulates standards for acceptable state legislation and delegates the review process to an appropriate entity, Congress may have to umpire up to 50 separate disputes between employers and insurance companies arguing cost and uniformity against states arguing for local flexibility.

# FEDERAL TAX TREATMENT FOR EMPLOYER-PROVIDED HEALTH CARE INSURANCE

In some ways, the cost of employer-provided health insurance is subsidized by the tax code. The tax burden of both employers and employees may be reduced when an employer provides health benefits to an employee. For example, the Joint Committee on Taxation recently estimated that limiting the size of this benefit to "the 75th percentile of health insurance premiums paid by or through employers" would increase federal revenues by $108.1 billion over the 2009-2013 period and by $452 billion over the 2009-2018 period [78]

Although the preferential tax treatment of employer-provided health insurance does not technically provide a legal obstacle to legislative changes in health insurance coverage or delivery, some reform proposals have suggested repeal or modification of these provisions [79]. This section of this report is intended to provide an overview of the operation of these provisions as they currently exist, as well as a general description of the effects they can have on one's income tax liability.

## Employer Paid Health Insurance Premiums

Under § 106 of the IRC, gross income does not include amounts paid by an employer to provide health insurance for an employee [80]. As an example, consider an employee who earns a salary of $30,000, but also participates in a group health insurance plan offered through his employer that covers the medical expenses of himself and his family. The plan has annual premiums of $6,000, two-thirds of which are paid by the employer. The other third of the premiums is paid for through deductions from the employee's salary. In the absence of §106, and assuming the employee has no other income, the employee would have $34,000 of gross income during a taxable year: the $30,000 he receives as salary plus the $4,000 contributed by his employer towards health insurance premiums. However, §106 excludes the employer-provided premiums from gross income, leaving the employee with only the $30,000 in salary as gross income during the taxable year.

A similar tax benefit is provided for self-employed individuals under §162(l) of the IRC [81]. Self- employed individuals cannot take advantage of §106 to exclude the costs of health insurance because self-employed individuals do not qualify as "employees" as that term is generally used under the IRC. Therefore, §162(l) permits a deduction equal to the cost of health insurance coverage for a self employed individual and her family. This deduction is not permitted if the self- employed individual is eligible for coverage offered by an employer of the individual or her spouse [82].

Any amounts that are paid to individuals under a health insurance plan to reimburse the individual for medical costs [83] are also excluded from gross income [84]. For example, if an individual receives $1,000 worth of care through his employer-provided health insurance plan, the value of that care is not includable in his gross income [85].

## Premium Conversion

Section 106 only excludes amounts contributed by an employer. In contrast, amounts deducted from an employee's paycheck to pay for that employee's portion of employer-provided health insurance do not receive favorable tax treatment under §106. However, many employers have established "premium conversion" programs in which an employee's contributions to health insurance premiums are converted into employer paid premiums that may be excluded under §106.

For example, if an employee and his employer pay $100 and $200, respectively, toward health insurance for that employee, § 106 would only exclude the $200 provided by the employer from the employee's gross income. The employee would still be taxed on the $100 he contributes, as it constitutes part of his wages, even though it is likely deducted from his paycheck automatically. Under a premium conversion program, the employee's wages would be reduced by $100, but the employer would assume the $100 payment formerly contributed by the employee. For the employee, there is no difference in take home pay, but his overall tax liability decreases because the entire $300 premium is now paid by the employer, and is consequently excludable under §106. Premium conversion is made possible in part by §125 of the IRC [86]. Under the doctrine of constructive receipt, if a taxpayer has a choice between a taxable benefit and a non-taxable benefit, he must include the value of the taxable benefit in gross income, even if he chooses the non-taxable benefit [87] However, §125 permits employees to choose between taxable and non-taxable benefits in a "cafeteria plan" without being forced to recognize the constructive receipt of income. Therefore, §125 allows employees to participate in a premium conversion program, essentially choosing between higher wages or employer paid premiums, without including the value of those premiums in gross income [88].

## Employment and Unemployment Taxes

Employer paid health insurance premiums similarly are not subject to employment tax liability [89]. Employees and employers both pay employment taxes on wages as defined under the Federal Insurance Contributions Act (FICA) [90]. However, the statutory definition of wages excludes:

> the amount of any payment (including any amount paid by an employer for insurance or annuities, or into a fund, to provide for any such payment) made to, or on behalf of, an employee or any of his dependents under a plan or system established by an employer which makes provision for his employees generally (or for his employees generally and their dependents) or for a class or classes of his employees (or for a class or classes of his employees and their dependents), on account of ... medical or hospitalization expenses in connection with sickness or accident disability [91].

Therefore, amounts paid by an employer to provide health insurance on behalf of an employee are not considered wages when calculating either employment tax liability of either employers or employees.

Employers are also required to pay unemployment taxes on all wages under the *Federal Unemployment Tax Act (FUTA)* [92]. As with FICA, the act's definition of wages excludes employer paid health insurance premiums [93].

## Incentives for Employees to Elect Employer-provided Health Insurance

The exclusion of health insurance premiums for employer-provided plans has a number of beneficial tax consequences for an employee's perspective. First, the taxpayer may benefit through a reduction in both his income and FICA tax liability [94]. Although a taxpayer who did not receive health benefits from his employer, but purchased health insurance independently, could deduct the cost of that insurance as an unreimbursed medical expense under §213, that deduction would only be permitted to the extent that the taxpayers' total unreimbursed medical expenses exceeded 7.5% of his adjusted gross income. Taxpayers would also have to itemize their deductions in order to take advantage of §213 [95].

Additionally, the operation of a number of other tax provisions may be affected by the reduction of a taxpayer's adjusted gross income (AGI). For example, a taxpayer that chooses to itemize her deductions is only permitted to take certain deductions to the extent that the aggregate amount of those deductions exceed 2% of her AGI [96]. Therefore, a reduction in AGI represents not only a reduction in taxable income directly, but also a reduction in the initial barrier to taking certain deductions. Other provisions also limit or reduce tax benefits to taxpayers above a certain AGI [97]. For individuals with AGI that is approaching that limit, whether employer paid health insurance premiums are included or excluded can affect whether these deductions or benefits can be claimed.

Excluding employer paid health insurance premiums from gross income also reduces an individual's earned income. Earned income is used primarily for determining the size of a taxpayer's earned income tax credit, if any. The statutory definition of earned income includes "wages, salaries, tips, and other employee compensation, but only if such amounts are includible in gross income for the taxable year." Therefore, because employer paid health insurance premiums are not includible in gross income, those amounts are similarly not includible in earned income. The effect of a reduction in earned income varies. The size of the earned income tax credit is directly proportional to earned income, up to a certain point. But, after earned income exceeds a statutorily defined "phaseout amount," the size of the credit gradually decreases. For individuals with earned income above the phaseout amount, reducing earned income can have the effect of increasing the size of the earned income credit.

## Incentives for Employers to Offer Health Insurance

The exclusion of employer paid health insurance premiums also creates incentives for an employer to offer health benefits to its employees. Some of these are unrelated to an employer's income tax liability. For example, providing health benefits as compensation directly to employees results in lower tax liability for those employees than if the employer had simply raised their wages by the same amount. When comparing two jobs, an employee may find that a job with a lower salary plus health benefits results in a lower tax burden than a job with the same total compensation value paid entirely as salary. Therefore, an employer who provides health benefits may have a hiring advantage over other employers who offer higher nominal wages without health benefits.

Employers may also enjoy payroll tax deductions as a result of providing health benefits to employees. From an employer's perspective, the principal tax implication of providing health care to employees, instead of the comparable value in cash, is a reduction in the wage base of their employees. The reduction in wages means employer's tax burden, under FICA and FUTA, can be reduced by offering health insurance instead of increasing actual wages.

## REFERENCES

[1]   See CRS Report 96-891, *Health Insurance Coverage: Characteristics of the Insured and Uninsured Populations in 2007*, by Chris L. Peterson and April Grady.

[2]   It should be noted that employers may provide health benefits pursuant to a collective bargaining agreement. This report does not discuss possible implications that the presence of an agreement may have on amending employer-based health coverage.

[3]   For more information on the advantages or disadvantages of an employer-based system, see CRS Report R40517, *Health Care Reform: An Introduction*, by Bob Lyke.

[4]   Joint Committee on Taxation, Background Materials for Senate Committee on Finance Roundtable on Health Care Financing, JCX-27-09 (May 8, 2009).

[5]   It is important to note that ERISA is not the only federal law that governs health coverage. In general, while ERISA covers private-sector employee benefit plans and health insurance issuers providing group health coverage, it does not cover governmental plans, church plans, or plans with less than 2 participants. The Public Health Service Act covers both group health plans, health insurance issuers providing group health coverage, and coverage in the individual market, including some governmental plans. The Internal Revenue Code covers group health plans, including church plans, but does not cover health insurers. The requirements of the PHSA may apply to church plans if the plan provides coverage through a health insurer.

[6]   One predominant concern that Congress will likely address in enacting major health reform legislation is how to improve health care quality. While employers may play a role in attempting to improve health care quality for employees and beneficiaries (e.g., by creating a wellness program), issues of health care quality will not be discussed in this report.

[7]   P.L. 93-406, 88 Stat. 829 (Sept. 2, 1974).

[8]   For a general discussion of ERISA's requirements, see CRS Report RL34443, Summary of the Employee Retirement Income Security Act (ERISA), by Patrick Purcell and Jennifer Staman.

[9]   According to a statement made by one of ERISA's sponsors, Representative Dent, "I wish to make note of what is to many the crowning achievement of this legislation, the reservation to Federal authority the sole power to regulate the field of employee benefit plans. ...[W]e round out the protection afforded participants by eliminating the threat of conflicting and inconsistent State and local regulation." 120 Cong. Rec. 29197 (1974).

[10] See, e.g., id. See also generally, James A. Wooten, A Legislative and Political History of ERISA Preemption, Parts 1- 3, Journal of Pension Benefits, Vols. 14-15, (2006-2008).

[11] ERISA considers a number of non-pension benefit programs offered by an employer to be "employee welfare benefit plans." For example, health plans, life insurance plans, and plans that provide dependent care assistance, educational assistance, or legal assistance can all be deemed welfare benefit plans. See 29 U.S.C. § 1002(1).

[12] See Phyllis C. Borzi, Symposium: On the Cusp: Insight and Perspectives on health Reform: Part II: Private and Public health Coverage: How Should They Change?: There's Private and then There's "Private": ERISA, Its Impact, and Options for Reform, 36 J.L. Med. & Ethics, 660 (Winter 2008), for a discussion of the reasoning behind the disparity between regulation of pension and welfare benefit plans under ERISA.

[13] Under self-funded (or self-insured) plans, instead of using health insurance (i.e., where an employer pays a premium to an insurer to cover the claims of plan participants) an employer acts as the insurer itself and pays the health care claims of the plan participants. While self-insured plans may use an insurance company or other third party to administer the plan, the employer bears the risk associated with offering health benefits. See Employee Benefits Research Institute, Capping the Tax Exclusion for Employment-Based Health Coverage: Implications for Employers and Workers, January 2009, available at http://www.ebri.org/publications/ib/index. cfm?fa=i bDisp&content_id=4159.

[14] However, it should be noted that in the context of retiree health benefits, some courts have found that under certain circumstances, when an employer has made a promise to provide health benefits for an employee's lifetime or other length of time, the health benefits have been found to vest. For a discussion of this issue, see James P. Baker, Andy Kramer, Evan Miller, and Steve Sacher, Retiree Medical Litigation's Dirty Little Secret-"Location, Location, Location!" 22 Benefits Law Journal 26 (2009).

[15] For additional information on the regulation of health benefits under ERISA, see CRS Report RS22643, Regulation of Health Benefits Under ERISA: An Outline, by Jennifer Staman.

[16] It should be noted that insurance matters are primarily regulated at the state, rather than the federal, level. Congress explicitly recognized the role of the states in the regulation of insurance with the passage of the McCarran-Ferguson Act of 1945. This law was passed in response to the Supreme Court's ruling in United States v. South-Eastern Underwriters, 322 U.S. 533 (1944), in which the Court affirmed the federal government's right to regulate the competitive practices of insurers under the Commerce Clause of the United States Constitution. The intent of the McCarran-Ferguson Act was to grant states the explicit authority to regulate insurance in light of the South- Eastern Underwriters decision. Section 2(a) of the act states: The business of insurance, and every person engaged therein, shall be subject to the laws of the several States which relate to the regulation or taxation of such business. 15 U.S.C. § 1012(a). However, under the act, Congress also reserved to itself the right to enact federal statutes that "specifically" relate to "the business of insurance." 15 U.S.C. § 1012(b). Parts 6 and 7 of ERISA are examples of where Congress has exercised this right.

[17] P.L. 99-272, tit. X, 100 Stat. 327 (1985). For additional information on COBRA, see CRS Report R40142, Health Insurance Continuation Coverage Under COBRA, by Janet Kinzer. It also should be noted that COBRA amended the Public Health Service Act to that requires coverage for certain state and local government employees (if the state receives funds under the act). See 42 U.S.C. § 300bb-1 et. seq.

[18] P.L. 104-191, 110 Stat. 1936 (1996).

[19] 29 U.S.C. § 11 82(a)(1)(A)-(H).

[20] 29 U.S.C. § 1185a; 29 U.S.C. § 1185.

[21] 29 U.S.C. § 1185b.

[22] P.L. 110-381, §2(a)(1), 122 Stat. 4081 (Oct. 9, 2008).

[23] 29 U.S.C. § 1185c.

[24] See, e.g., The ERISA Industry Committee Health Policy Issue Brief, Successful Employer-Provided Health Plans Depend On Nationally Uniform Standards (Oct. 15, 2007), cf. Rebecca A.D. O'Reilly, Is ERISA Ready for a New Generation of State Health Care Reform? Preemption, Innovation, and Expanding Access to Health Care Coverage, 8 U. Pa. J. Lab. & Emp. L. 387 (Winter 2006) ("The scope of ERISA preemption in the context of health and welfare plans is particularly significant because ... unlike ERISA's expansive regulation of pension plans, it provides relatively little substantive regulation of health plans. The result is that health plans governed by ERISA can be structured to go largely unregulated." citations omitted.)

[25] Id.

[26] See generally, e.g., Peter D. Jacobson, The Role of ERISA Preemption in Health Reform: Opportunities and Limits, Legal Solutions in Health Reform, available at http://www.rwjf.org/pr/product.jsp?id=39410; Wendy Parmet, Regulation and Federalism: Legal Impediments to State Health Care Reform, 19 Am. J. L. and Med. 121(1993).

[27] Ingersoll-R& Co. v. McClendon, 498 U.S. 133, 142 (1990).

[28] The preemption doctrine derives from the Supremacy Clause of the Constitution, which establishes that the laws of the United States "shall be the supreme Law of the Land; and the Judges in every State shall be bound thereby, any Thing in the Constitution or Laws of any State to the Contrary notwithstanding." U.S. Const., art. VI, cl. 2. In general, federal preemption occurs when a validly enacted federal law supersedes an inconsistent state law. For a discussion of preemption doctrine, see Constitution of the United States of America, Analysis and Interpretation, Congressional Research Service, pp. 257-278.

[29] Travelers, 514 U.S. at 657.

[30] Section 502(a) of ERISA (29 U.S.C. § 1132) creates a civil enforcement scheme that allows a participant or beneficiary of a plan to bring a civil action for various reasons, including "to recover benefits due to him under the terms of the plan, to enforce his rights under the terms of the plan, or to clarify his rights to future benefits under the terms of the plan." If a plaintiff seeks to bring a state law claim is "within the scope" of § 502(a), the state law claim can be preempted. While the remedial provisions of ERISA may come into play in a federal health reform effort, this report will only address preemption under § 514. For more information on preemption under § 502 of ERISA, see CRS Report 98-286, ERISA 's Impact on Medical Malpractice and Negligence Claims Against Managed Care Plans, by Jon O. Shimabukuro.

[31] 29 U.S.C. § 1144(a). "State law" includes "[a]ll laws, decisions, rules, regulations, or other State actions have the effect of law of any State. A law of the United States, applicable only to the District of Columbia, shall be treated as a State law rather than a law of the United States." 29 U.S.C. § 1 144(c)(1).

[32] See Shaw v. Delta Air Lines, Inc., 463 U.S. 85, 97 (1982).

[33] As the Supreme Court has stated with regard to ERISA preemption, "[t]he purpose of Congress is the ultimate touchstone." Ingersoll-Rand Co. v. McClendon, 498 U.S. 133, 138 (1990), quoting Allis-Chalmers Corp. v. Lueck, 471 U.S. 202, 208, (1985).

[34] See California Div. of Lab. Standards Enforcement v. Dillingham Construction, 519 U.S. 316 (1997).

[35] 463 U.S. 85 (1983).

[36] In Shaw, which first articulated this test, the Court found that the law had both an impermissible connection and related to a plan.

[37] *Id.* at 325.

[38] 486 U.S. 825 (1988).

[39] Id. at 838, n. 12.

[40] Marram v. Kobrick Offshore Fund, Ltd, 2009 Mass. Super. LEXIS 85, (Jan. 30, 2009).

[41] Shaw, 463 U.S. at 100 n. 21.

[42] 514 U.S. 645 (1995).

[43] *Id.* at 654.

[44] *Id.* at 655.

[45] *Id.* at 661.

[46] De Buono v. NYSA-ILSA Medical and Clinical Services Fund, 520 U.S. 806 (1997) (state tax on gross receipts of health care facilities not preempted by ERISA); California Div. of Labor Standards Enforcement v. Dillingham Constr., 519 U.S. 316 (1997) (California's prevailing wage law not preempted by ERISA).

[47] See Constitution of the United States of America, Analysis and Interpretation, Congressional Research Service, p. 262, stating that ERISA's preemption provision is "[p]erhaps the broadest preemption section ever enacted."

[48] 29 U.S.C. § 1 144(b)(2)(A).

[49] Every state has adopted various standards for health insurance, including requirements for the prompt payment of claims, access to health insurance (e.g., a requirement to cover dependants under a policy up to a certain age), rating requirements that affect insurance premiums, and mandated benefit requirements (i.e., requirements for health insurers cover services provided by certain medical specialties or cover treatments for specific diseases). See Mila Kaufman and Karen Pollitz, Health Insurance Regulation by States and the Federal Government: A Review of Current Approaches and Proposals for Change, April 2006.

[50] 29 U.S.C. § 1 144(b)(2)(B). See Metropolitan Life Ins. Co. v. Massachusetts, 471 U.S. 724, 733 (1984) (discussing ERISA's "saving clause" and "deemer clause").

[51] FMC v. Holliday, 498 U.S. 52 (1990).

[52] Kaiser Family Foundation and Health Research & Educational Trust, Employee Health Benefits, 2008 Annual Survey, Exhibit 10.1, http://ehbs.kff.org/pdf/7790.pdf.

[53] See Mila Kofman, "Health Care Reform: Recommendations to Improve Coordination of Federal and State Initiatives," Testimony before the U.S. House of Representatives, Committee on Education and Labor Subcommittee on Health, Employment, Labor and

Pensions, May 22, 2007 (discussing, among other things, that [w]hen small businesses with healthy workers self-insure, their claims are not pooled with others and coverage is more expensive in state-regulated products as fewer healthy people help pay for the sicker ones.") See also generally Russell Korobkin, The Battle over Self-Insured Health Plans, or "One Good Loophole Deserves Another," 5 Yale J. Health Pol'y L. & Ethics 89 (2005).

[54]  See e.g., Shaw, footnote 32 supra; Standard Oil v. Agsalud, 633 F.2d 760 (9th Cir. 1980), aff'd. mem., 454 U.S. 801 (1981).

[55]  See Borzi, footnote 12 supra (explaining that a proposal to tax all employers in a state in order to pay for health coverage could be inequitable, as it would affect both employers who offer coverage, as well as those who do not).

[56]  2006 Md. Laws 1.

[57]  475 F.3d 180 (4th Cir. 2007).

[58]  The Department of Labor, in an Amicus brief, had argued for this result. It was argued that "[b]y setting an aggregate amount (by percentage of payroll) affected employers must spend on employee health benefits, Maryland is taking away employers' fundamental authority over whether, and on what terms, to sponsor a plan, and potentially subjecting employers to the competing demands of a multiplicity of state and local regulatory schemes." Brief of the Secretary of Labor as Amicus Curiae, Supporting Plaintiff-Appellee and Requesting Affirmance, RILA v. Fielder, 475 F.3d 180 (4th Cir. 2007) (No. 06-1840, 06-1901).

[59]  See also RILA v. Suffolk County, 497 F.Supp.2d 403, 407 (E.D.N.Y. 2007) (Suffolk County Act, which enacted fair share legislation, found to be preempted by ERISA under similar reasoning as Fielder).

[60]  "Covered employers" are defined by the Ordinance as employers engaged in business within the city that have an average of at least 20 employees performing work for compensation during a quarter. The term also applies to nonprofit corporations with an average of at least 50 employees performing work for compensation during a quarter. A "covered employee" under the Ordinance is defined as any individual who works in the city and county of San Francisco, works at least 10 hours per week, has worked for his employer for at least 90 days, and is not excluded from coverage by other provisions of the Ordinance.

[61]  546 F.3d 639 (9th Cir. 2008).

[62]  Id. at 643-47.

[63]  After the Ninth Circuit decision, Golden Gate Restaurant Association petitioned for a rehearing, which was denied. Golden Gate Rest. Ass'n v. City & County of San Francisco, 558 F.3d 1000 (9th Cir. 2009). Following the rehearing, Golden Gate Restaurant Association filed an emergency stay application with the Supreme Court, which was also denied. The association's petition to the Supreme Court for review is due on June 8, 2009.

[64]  An Act Providing Access to Affordable, Quality, Accountable Health Care, Ch. 58 of the Acts of 2006, available at http://www.mass.gov/legis/laws/seslaw06/sl060058.htm.

[65]  MASS. GEN. LAWS ch. 149, § 188 (2008).

[66]  See footnotes 15 through 23 and accompanying text.

[67]  A health insurance exchange generally entails a public or private entity that facilitates the purchase of health insurance by private individuals or small employers and consists

of a range of plans. See Timothy Stolzfus Jost, Health Insurance Exchanges: Legal Issues, Legal Solutions in Health Reform, available at http://www.rwjf.org/coverage/product.

jsp?id=38 109&c=OTC-RSS&attr=PA.

[68] See, e.g., Description of Policy Options, Expanding Health Care Coverage: Proposals to Provide Affordable Coverage to All Americans, Senate Finance Committee (May 14, 2009), available at http://finance. senate.gov/sitepages/leg/LEG%202009/051109%20Health%20Care%20Description%20of%20Policy%20Options.pdf. For additional legal issues regarding a Health Insurance Exchange, see Stolzfus, footnote 66 at 11.

[69] *Id.*

[70] As constitutional expert Erwin Chemerensky has explained, the Supreme Court has often recognized the idea that there is a need to protect states rights so that states can serve as "laboratories for experimentation." Justice Brandeis first articulated this idea:

To stay experimentation in things social and economic is a grave responsibility. Denial of the right to experiment might be fraught with serious consequences to the Nation. It is one of the happy incidents of the federal system that a single courageous State may, if its citizens choose, serve as a laboratory; and try novel social and economic experiments without risk to the rest of the country.

See Erwin Chemerinsky, David G. Trager Public Policy Symposium: Our New Federalism? National Authority And Local Autonomy In The War On Terror: Empowering States When It Matters: A Different Approach to Preemption*quoting New State Ice Co. v. Liebmann, 285 U.S. 262, 311 (1932) (Brandeis, J., dissenting).

[71] Indeed, legislative history indicates that a number of Members of Congress influential the passage of ERISA expressed the desire to preempt state regulation of employer-provided health care. See, e.g., remarks of Senator Javits, "the emergence of a comprehensive and pervasive Federal interest and the interests of uniformity with respect to interstate plans required ... the displacement of State action in the field of private employee benefits programs." 129 Cong. Rec. 29942 (Aug. 22, 1974).

[72] See, e.g., Jacobson, footnote 26 supra.

[73] See Haw. Rev. Stat. Ann. 393-13. Excluded from this list are emergency state employees, workers covered by collective bargaining agreements, independent contractors and part-time workers.

[74] 633 F.2d 760 (9th Cir. 1980), aff'd. mem., 454 U.S. 801 (1981).

[75] As the Supreme Court explained in Fort Halifax Packing Co. v. Coyne, 482 U.S. 1 (1987), the Hawaii law was struck down because of the obstacles it placed on the administration of ERISA health plans. As the Court explained:

The Hawaii law was struck down, for it posed two types of problems. First, the employer in that case already had in place a health care plan governed by ERISA, which did not comply in all respects with the Hawaii Act. If the employer sought to achieve administrative efficiencies by integrating the Hawaii plan into its existing plan, different components of its single plan would be subject to different requirements. If it established a separate plan to administer the program directed by Hawaii, it would lose the benefits of maintaining a single administrative scheme. Second, if Hawaii could demand the operation of a particular benefit plan, so could other States, which would require that the employer coordinate perhaps dozens of programs. Agsalud thus illustrates that whether a State requires an existing plan to pay certain benefits, or whether it requires the establishment of a separate plan where none existed before, the problem is the same. Faced with the difficulty or impossibility of structuring administrative practices according to a set of uniform guidelines, an employer may decide to reduce benefits or simply not to pay them at all. Id. at 12-13 (citations omitted).

[76]  29 U.S.C. § 1144(b)(5).

[77]  See, e.g., H.R. 3618, Universal Health Care for Oregonians Act of 1993, 103rd Congress, 1st Sess. (1993). See also 139 Cong. Rec. E3 126 (daily ed. Nov. 24, 1993) (statement of Rep. Wyden) (explaining the necessity of obtaining an ERISA waiver for Oregon's health care reform legislation).

[78]  CONGRESSIONAL BUDGET OFFICE, Budget Option, Volume I: Health Care, at 24 (Dec. 2008).

[79]  For an analysis of the policy arguments surrounding the repeal or modification of these provisions, see CRS Report RL34767, The Tax Exclusion for Employer-Provided Health Insurance: Policy Issues Regarding the Repeal Debate, by Bob Lyke.

[80]  26 U.S.C. § 106.

[81]  26 U.S.C. § 162(l). For more information, see CRS Report RL333 11, Federal Tax Treatment of Health Insurance Expenditures by the Self-Employed: Current Law and Issues for Congress, by Gary Guenther.

[82]  26 U.S.C. § 162(l)(2)(B).

[83]  Eligible medical costs are limited to those that also fall under 26 U.S.C. § 213 (providing a deduction for unreimbursed medical expenses).

[84]  26 U.S.C. § 105.

[85]  This exclusion also applies to benefits paid from health insurance plans that are not provided by an employer.

[86]  26 U.S.C. § 125.

[87]  Treas. Reg. § 1.451-2(a).

[88]  Whether a premium conversion plan is offered to employees is subject to that employer's discretion. See, Rev. Rul. 2002-3.

[89]  26 U.S.C. § 3121(a)(2).

[90]  26 U.S.C. §§ 3101, 3111. The amounts collected from these taxes partially fund Medicare and Social Security.

[91]  26 U.S.C. § 3121(a)(2).

[92]  26 U.S.C. § 3301.

[93]  26 U.S.C. § 3306(b)(2).

[94]  The amount of the reduction in tax liability is governed by the taxpayer's marginal tax rate.

[95]  26 U.S.C. § 213(a).

[96]  26 U.S.C. § 67(a).

[97]  See, e.g., 26 U.S.C. § 24(b)(1) (phase out of child tax credit based on AGI); 26 U.S.C. § 25A(d) (phase out of Lifetime Learning Credit based on AGI); 26 U.S.C. § 213(a) (restricts deduction for unreimbursed medical expenses to aggregate amount in excess of 7.5% of AGI); 26 U.S.C. § 221(b)(2) (limiting deduction for interest on education loans based on AGI); 26 U.S.C. § 222(b) (amount of deduction for qualified tuition and related expenses dependant upon AGI).

In: U.S. Political Programs: Functions and Assessments     ISBN: 978-1-61209-448-9
Editors: Julianna M. Moretti and Karen J. Chordstron   © 2011 Nova Science Publishers, Inc.

*Chapter 8*

# SCIENCE, TECHNOLOGY, AND AMERICAN DIPLOMACY: BACKGROUND AND ISSUES FOR CONGRESS[*]

*Deborah D. Stine*

## ABSTRACT

Science and engineering activities have always been international. Scientists, engineers, and health professionals frequently communicate and cooperate with one another without regard to national boundaries. This report discusses international science and technology (S&T) diplomacy, instances when American leadership in S&T is used as a diplomatic tool to enhance another country's development and to improve understanding by other nations of U.S. values and ways of doing business. According to the National Research Council, five developmental challenges where S&T could play a role include child health and child survival, safe water, agricultural research to reduce hunger and poverty, micro-economic reform, and mitigation of natural disasters.

Title V of the Foreign Relations Authorization Act, FY1 979 (P.L. 9 5-426) provides the current legislative guidance for U.S. international S&T policy. This act states that Department of State (DOS) is the lead federal agency in developing S&T agreements. The National Science and Technology Policy, Organization, and Priorities Act of 1976 (P.L. 94-282) states that the director of the White House Office of Science and Technology Policy (OSTP) is to advise the President on international S&T cooperation policies and the role of S&T considerations in foreign relations. DOS sets the overall policy direction for U.S. international S&T diplomacy, and works with other federal agencies as needed. OSTP acts as a interagency liaison. A number of federal agencies that both sponsor research and use S&T in developing policy are involved in international S&T policy.

A fundamental question is why the United States should invest in international S&T diplomacy instead of domestic research and development (R&D) and science, technology, engineering, and mathematics education (STEM) activities, which are facing budget constraints. If Congress should decide that funding international S&T activities is

---

[*] This is an edited, reformatted and augmented edition of a United States Congressional Research Service publication, CRS Report RL34503, dated June 29, 2009.

important, agreeing on a policy goal beyond enhancing the country's development, such as improving U.S. relations with other countries, or enhancing popular opinion of the United States may help set priorities.

Policy options identified for Congress by expert committees who have assessed U.S. international S&T diplomacy efforts include ensuring a baseline of science, engineering, and technical (SET) literacy among all appropriate DOS personnel, increasing the presence overseas of personnel with significant SET expertise, and expanding the Department's engagement within global SET networks through exchanges, assistance, and joint research activities addressing key global issues. Other proposed actions include increasing USAID support that builds S&T capacity in developing countries, and orienting other departments and agencies S&T developing country programs to support the development priorities of the host countries. Another proposal would establish a new U.S. government organization called the "Development Applications Research Institute" (DARI) to develop and apply innovative technologies to development problems. In all of these efforts, Congress might wish to consider enhancing the prominence of the STAS, and coordination among S&T leaders at OES, STAS, and OSTP.

On June 4, 2009, President Obama announced several international S&T diplomacy programs in Muslim-majority countries including a new fund for technological development in these countries, establishing centers of scientific excellence, and appointing new science envoys. On June 8, 2009, the House passed the International Science and Technology Cooperation Act of 2009 (H.R. 1736), which would require the OSTP Director to establish an interagency committee to identify and coordinate international science and technology cooperation.

## INTRODUCTION

Scientists, engineers, and health professionals frequently communicate and cooperate with one another without regard to national boundaries. Dating back to the 1700s, Benjamin Franklin and Thomas Jefferson are thought of as the nation's first scientific diplomats [1]. Scientists and inventors themselves, they corresponded with colleagues and brought knowledge back from their visits to Europe to enhance the development and policies of the very young United States. Today, the United States serves the same role for other countries that are in the early stages of development or at a major point of transition. Congress is currently discussing how to maximize the effectiveness of these international science and technology (S&T) policy activities [2]

This report provides an overview of current U.S. international S&T policy; describes the role of the Department of State (DOS), the White House Office of Science and Technology Policy (OSTP), the U.S. Agency for International Development (USAID), and other federal agencies; and discusses possible policy options for Congress. It focuses on international science and technology diplomacy, where American leadership in science and technology is used as a diplomatic tool to enhance another country's development and to improve understanding by other nations of U.S. values and ways of doing business. These efforts could focus on both enhancing a nation's science and technology (S&T) resources, as well as addressing developmental challenges where S&T could play a role. According to the National Research Council, five potential challenges include child health and child survival, safe water, agricultural research to reduce hunger and poverty, micro-economic reform, and mitigation of natural disasters [3]

# OVERVIEW OF U.S. INTERNATIONAL SCIENCE AND TECHNOLOGY (S&T) POLICY ORGANIZATIONS

Title V of the Foreign Relations Authorization Act, Fiscal Year 1979 (P.L. 95-426, 22 U.S.C. 2656a - 22 U.S.C. 2656d, as amended) provides the current legislative guidance for U.S. international S&T policy, and made DOS the lead federal agency in developing S&T agreements [4]. In that act, Congress found that the consequences of modern S&T advances are of major significance in U.S. foreign policy—providing many problems and opportunities— meaning that its diplomacy workforce should have an appropriate level of knowledge of these topics. Further, it indicated that this workforce should conduct long-range planning to make effective use of S&T in international relations, and seek out and consult with public and private industrial, academic, and research institutions in the formulation, implementation, and evaluation of U.S. foreign policy.

The National Science and Technology Policy, Organization, and Priorities Act of 1976 (P.L. 94-282) states that the OSTP director is to advise the President on S&T considerations in foreign relations. Further, the OSTP director is to "assess and advise [the President] on policies for international cooperation in S&T which will advance the national and international objectives of the United States." The following sections discuss the international S&T activities of DOS, OSTP, USAID, and other federal agencies.

## Department of State (DOS)

DOS sets the overall policy direction for U.S. international S&T diplomacy, and works with other federal agencies, as needed. In its May 2007 strategic plan, DOS and USAID identify the following key S&T diplomatic strategies:

- encourage science and technology cooperation to advance knowledge in areas related to water management;
- promote sharing of knowledge in the international scientific community that will enhance the efficiency and hasten the fruition of U.S. research efforts, and promote international scientific collaboration;
- strengthen major international collaborations on cutting-edge energy technology research and development in carbon sequestration, biofuels, clean coal power generation, as well as hydrogen, methane, and wind power;
- apply research including promotion of technological improvements to foster more sustainable natural resource use, conservation of biodiversity, and resilience to climate change impacts;
- support scientific and technological applications, including biotechnology, that harness new technology to raise agricultural productivity and provide a more stable, nutritious, and affordable food supply; and
- enhance outreach to key communities in the private sector [5]
- DOS uses a variety of tools to implement this strategy, such as formal bilateral S&T cooperation agreements that facilitate international collaboration by federal agencies; promotion and support of S&T entrepreneurs and innovators; [6] scientist and

student exchanges; workshops, conferences, and meetings; public-private partnerships; seed funding for scientific programs and innovation activities; and production of educational materials, including films, websites, posters, and cards [7]

Within the State Department, the Bureau of Oceans and International Environmental and Scientific Affairs (OES) coordinates international S&T activities, and the Science and Technology Advisor (STAS) provides S&T advice to the Secretary of State, DOS staff, and the director of USAID. USAID is an independent federal government agency that, with guidance from DOS, supports developmental and U.S. strategic interests, among other duties.

### Bureau of Oceans and International Environmental and Scientific Affairs (OES)

OES coordinates international S&T cooperative activities throughout the federal government.8 Within OES is the Health, Space, and Science Directorate, which works with federal agencies on S&T policy issues.9 In addition, some U.S. embassies have bilateral Environment, Science, Technology, and Health foreign service officers. Embassies may host their own country-specific activities such as joint research grants, junior scientist visit grants, events, and workshops. Some have a joint board that includes both scientists from the host country as well as government scientists to oversee these activities [10]. There are also "hubs" that focus on environmental issues on a regional basis.

### Science and Technology Advisor to the Secretary of State (STAS)

Within the State Department, but distinct from the OES, is the Science and Technology Advisor to the Secretary of State (STAS) [11]. The STAS acts as an advisor for both DOS and USAID. The goals of this office are to enhance the S&T literacy and capacity of DOS; build partnerships with the outside S&T community, within the U.S. government, with S&T partners abroad, and with foreign embassies in the United States; provide accurate S&T advice to DOS; and shape a global perspective on the emerging and "at the horizon" S&T developments anticipated to affect current and future U.S. foreign policy [12].

### U.S. Agency for International Development (USAID)

USAID is an independent federal government agency with the goal of supporting transformational development, strengthening fragile states, supporting U.S. geostrategic interests, addressing transnational problems, and providing humanitarian relief [13]. Although independent, USAID's overall foreign policy guidance comes from the Secretary of State. At one time S&T had a major role at USAID. Today, however, S&T capacity, staffing, and funding, particularly in overseas missions, are far less than in the past [14].

## White House Office of Science and Technology Policy (OSTP) and the National Science and Technology Council (NSTC)

OSTP, a staff office within the Executive Office of the President (EOP), does not fund domestic or international programs. Rather, the Assistant to the Director for International Relations acts as a liaison: within the EOP, to organizations such as the National Security Council; with federal agencies, including DOS and the international offices of federal agencies such as the National Science Foundation; and with the science liaisons of foreign country embassies in the United States [15]. Within OSTP, the National Science and Technology Council (NSTC), currently established by Executive Order 12881, coordinates S&T policy across the federal government [16].

Management of international S&T policy issues at OSTP and NSTC has varied among Presidential administrations [17]. During the Clinton Administration, OSTP had a Presidentially- appointed associate director whose primary focus was on international policy. This presidential appointee, along with a DOS presidential appointee, co-chaired a NSTC Committee on International Science, Engineering, and Technology (CISET) that addressed "international science cooperation as it related to foreign policy and the Nation's research and development (R&D) agenda" [18]. In the George W. Bush Administration, rather than an OSTP political appointee focused on international issues, there was a staff member who serves as an assistant to the director for international affairs [19]. Another difference is that rather than focusing an NSTC committee on overall international S&T policy, the Bush Administration OSTP coordinated federal international S&T activities through NSTC committees that focus on a particular topic, like nanotechnology, or a specific country, like Brazil [20].

The Obama Administration has stated that it will return to the Clinton Administration practice, and nominate an Associate Director for National Security and International Affairs, who will hold a joint appointment on the National Security Council [21]. The individual who would take that post has not yet been nominated. The Assistant Director to the Director for International Director position has been maintained [22]. There is currently no NSTC committee focused on international issues as was the case during the Clinton Administration [23]. This situation may change once an Associate Director is nominated and confirmed.

## Role of Other Federal Agencies and Nongovernmental Organizations

A number of federal agencies that both sponsor research and use S&T in developing policy are involved in international S&T policy. These include National Science Foundation (NSF), National Institutes of Health, Department of Energy, National Aeronautics and Space Administration (NASA), Department of Agriculture, Environmental Protection Agency, Department of Interior, and others [24]. Federal programs may be formal "top-down" activities focused on the agencies' mission and identified by agency leadership, or "bottom-up" activities identified by scientists and engineers. Examples of "Top-down" activities include the National Oceanic and Atmospheric Administration (NOAA) 's National Environmental Satellite, Data, and Information Service focused on Earth observation data exchange, or the National Institute for Science and Technology (NIST)'s development of uniform measurement standards for ethanol and biodiesel. "Bottom-up" activities often arise from proposals submitted in response to a specific solicitation or as part of a general solicitation for research in their field [25].

# OBAMA ADMINISTRATION ACTIONS

In a June 4, 2009 speech in Cairo, the President stated the Administration will take the following actions regarding international science and technology cooperation:

> On science and technology, we will launch a new fund to support technological development in Muslim-majority countries, and to help transfer ideas to the marketplace so they can create more jobs. We'll open centers of scientific excellence in Africa, the Middle East and Southeast Asia, and appoint new science envoys to collaborate on programs that develop new sources of energy, create green jobs, digitize records, clean water, grow new crops. Today I'm announcing a new global effort with the Organization of the Islamic Conference to eradicate polio. And we will also expand partnerships with Muslim communities to promote child and maternal health [26]

# ROLE OF CONGRESS

An April 2008 House Committee on Science and Technology Subcommittee on Research and Science Education hearing examined global and domestic benefits from cooperation in science and technology [27]. One fundamental question asked during the hearing was why the United States should support international science diplomacy rather than invest in domestic R&D. Table 1 provides a summary of the Bush Administration's response.

For the United States to be competitive, according to Bush Administration witnesses, it needs to know where the frontier of science is occurring. As other countries increase their investment in higher education and R&D, the top science and engineering research and facilities may not be in the United States, but in other countries.

This increases the importance of U.S. investment in international S&T diplomatic activities, said Bush Administration witnesses, including federal programs that support U.S. scientists' collaborations with foreign scientists, and access to the best research facilities in the world, as well as enhancing the international connections of U.S. science and engineering students and leaders. In addition, U.S. science and engineering higher education and research helps developing countries by enhancing their human resource capacity, and as a result, their ability to achieve long-term development.

These international connections can be important, said Bush Administration witnesses, not just for those countries, but in helping the U.S. respond to global challenges such as infectious diseases such as avian flu. Further, according to a Bush Administration witness, international cooperative activities at their agency in almost all instances are conducted on a "no exchange of funds" basis with U.S. funding supporting U.S. scientists and engineers, not those in the cooperating country [28]. The degree to which the Obama Administration agrees with this position is not known at this time.

**Table 1. U.S. Objectives in International Research and Development Programs**

| | |
|---|---|
| 1. | To maintain and continually improve the quality of U.S. science by applying global standards of excellence. (Performing science to the highest standards) |
| 2. | To provide access by U.S. scientists to the frontiers of science without regard to national borders. (Access to the frontiers of science) |
| 3. | To increase the productivity of U.S. science through collaborations between U.S. scientists and the world's leading scientists, regardless of national origin. (Access to scientific talent) |
| 4. | To strengthen U.S. science through visits, exchanges, and immigration by outstanding scientists from other nations. (Augmentation of scientific human capital) |
| 5. | To increase U.S. national security and economic prosperity by fostering the improvement of conditions in other countries through increased technical capability. (Security through technology-based equity) |
| 6. | To accelerate the progress of science across a broader front than the U.S. may choose to pursue with its own resources. (Leveraging on foreign science capabilities) |
| 7. | To improve understanding by other nations of U.S. values and ways of doing business. (Science diplomacy) |
| 8. | To address U.S. interests of such global nature that the U.S. alone cannot satisfy them. (Global support for global scientific issues) |
| 9. | To discharge obligations negotiated in connection with treaties. (Science as a tradable asset) |
| 10. | To increase U.S. prestige and influence with other nations. (Science for glory) |

Source: John Marburger, Director, Office of Science and Technology Policy, Bush Administration, "National Science Board Hearing on International Science Partnerships," speech, May 11, 2006. John H. Marburger, Director, OSTP, Bush Administration, Response to questions at House Committee on Science and Technology, Subcommittee on Research and Science Education, International Science and Technology Cooperation, 110th Cong. 2nd sess., April 2, 2008, at http://science.house.gov/publications/hearings_markups_details.aspx?NewsID=2134.


Some believe, however, that the United States should enhance its international science and technology activities. They believe that such investments are sometimes viewed by policymakers as either "giving away knowledge" or a "humanitarian luxury," when they actually could help all countries to reach common goals such as developing safe and reliable nuclear power, or enhancing all countries' economic development [29]. Others express concerns that although the United States has many programs to promote science and technology in the developing world, such programs have limited due to insufficient financial and human resources at DOS, AID, and OSTP that limit the ability of these agencies to achieve their mission [30].

If Congress should decide that funding international S&T activities is important, agreeing on a policy goal beyond enhancing the country's development, such as improving U.S. relations with other countries, or enhancing popular opinion of the United States may help set priorities. Activities funded might differ depending on those priorities. For example, two possible goals might be (1) improving U.S. relations with the government of a country or in a region, or (2) raising popular opinion of the United States in that country or region. In the case of the first goal, activities might focus on enhancing the foreign government(s) decision-making based on science and engineering information or providing financial or technical aid to a country's science and engineering efforts. In the case of the second goal, activities might focus on a challenge more visible to the public, such as increasing access to water, enhancing agricultural productivity, or obtaining high quality STEM education.

Although the effectiveness of different S&T diplomatic initiatives has not been studied, the State Department contends that some key elements for success are finding areas or programs that (1) break new ground, sometimes in a neglected area of science or development; (2) are educationally and developmentally transformative; (3) address core developmental issues of poverty and human development; (4) promote sustainable uses of natural resources; (5) stimulate job creation and private sector investment; and (6) are collaborative projects with tangible results [31].

Six broad categories of international S&T cooperative activities include (1) agreements; (2) research; (3) facilities and equipment; (4) academic opportunities from primary through postsecondary education; (5) meetings, dialogues, and visits; and (6) private sector activities (see Table 2). International S&T cooperative activities can be multinational, regional, or bilateral. A related question is who might best lead such efforts relative to the desired goal. Options include scientists, engineers, and health professionals at academic institutions, business and industry, and non-governmental organizations; scientists, engineers, and health professionals who work for the federal government; and S&T federal government leaders.

Expert committees which have assessed U.S. international S&T diplomacy efforts express concerns about (1) the lack of S&T expertise, presence, and global engagement at DOS, (2) a decline in support for S&T capacity at USAID, (3) a lack of coherent and integrated international S&T policy direction and federal coordination role at OSTP, and (4) insufficient technological research to respond to development challenges. The following sections discuss proposed recommendations to respond to these concerns.

## S&T Expertise, Presence, and Global Engagement at DOS

The report of the State Department Advisory Committee on Transformational Diplomacy, State Department in 2025 Working Group [32] recommends that the State Department expand its investment in Science, Engineering, and Technology (SET) expertise, presence, and global engagement. The report's specific recommendations include ensuring a baseline of SET literacy among all appropriate Department personnel, increasing the presence overseas of personnel with significant SET expertise, and expanding the Department's engagement within global SET networks through exchanges, assistance, and joint research activities addressing key global issues. In addition, the report recommends creating a closer connection between the roles of the Assistant Secretary for OES and the STAS to bring senior attention to the full range of SET challenges and opportunities facing the Department. For example, if the Assistant Secretary for OES is a scientist, that person could serve simultaneously as the Science and Technology Advisor to the Secretary of State. Otherwise, the STAS could become the Principal Deputy Assistant Secretary of State (PDAS) in OES [33].

## S&T Capacity at USAID

A National Research Council (NRC) report recommends Congress and others take action to reverse what they state is the decline in USAID support for building S&T capacity, and strengthen the capabilities of its leadership and program managers in Washington, DC, and in foreign countries on S&T issues. In addition, the report recommends that Congress encourage other departments and agencies to orient their S&T developing country programs to support the development priorities of the host countries, and that USAID take actions to enhance interagency coordination [34].

### Table 2. International Science and Technology Policy Mechanisms

*Agreements*
- Formal multinational, regional, and bilateral agreements between the U.S. government and the government of another country.
- Government-level bilateral agreements between a U.S. agency and a research agency of a foreign country that are related to a government-level agreement and provide additional details that define how each agency will cooperate.
- Agency-level bilateral agreements between a U.S. agency and a research agency of a foreign country that are not related to a government-level agreement.
- Agency-level multilateral agreements between a U.S. agency and research agencies of international organization and/or of two or more foreign countries.

*Research*
- Joint research sponsorship where a U.S. and foreign researcher, group of researchers, or institutions work together.
- Visiting foreign researchers who come to the United States, or U.S. researchers who visit the foreign country.
- Sponsorship of foreign researchers in early stage of their careers.
- Sponsorship of research conducted by a U.S. researcher in a foreign country or a researcher in the foreign country.

*Education*
- Fellowships, research assistantships, and traineeships.
- Undergraduate and graduate student exchange programs.
- Visiting foreign lecturers who come to the United States, or U.S. researchers who visit the foreign country.
- K- 12 science, technology, engineering, and mathematics (STEM) curriculum development and teacher training, methods, and certification.
- Educational materials including films, websites, posters, and cards.

*Meetings, Dialogues, and Guidance*
- Meetings to exchange ideas.
- Workshops to learn about a science and technology topic.
- Guidance on the application of research and technology.
- Dialogues on how best to harmonize S&T regulatory activities.

**Table 2. (Continued).**

*Facility, Equipment, Data, and Information*
- Facility utilization.
- Equipment provision and lending.
- Data and information measurement, provision, and exchange.

*Private Sector*
- Promotion and support of S&T entrepreneurs and innovators.
- Public-private partnerships.

Source: Congressional Research Service. Agreements section is based on General Accounting Office, Federal Research: Information on Science and Technology International Agreements, Report Number RCED-99-108, April 1999 at http://www.gao.gov/archive/1999/rc99108.pdf.

## International S&T Policy Direction and Federal Coordination at OSTP and NSTC

A National Science Board (NSB) report [35] recommends that the United States create a coherent and integrated international science and engineering strategy, balance U.S. foreign and R&D policy, and promote intellectual exchange. In addition, it recommends reestablishing the NSTC Committee on International Science, Engineering, and Technology, and appointing a high-level international S&T policy official in OSTP. Congress, according to NSB, should amend the Government Performance and Results Act to require Federal agencies to address international S&T partnerships. Further, Congress should direct the Department of Commerce, OSTP, DOS, and the Department of Homeland Security to balance U.S. security policies with international science and engineering (S&E) needs.

The report also contends it is important to facilitate "brain circulation" as opposed to "brain drain," by supporting study abroad opportunities for American students, streamlining the visa process for foreign scientists, engineers and students, and identifying and increasing the use of U.S. and international facilities for collaborative research [36].

## New Institute to Support Technology Research

The United States Commission on Helping to Enhance the Livelihood of People Around the Globe (HELP Commission) was charged in Section 637 of P.L. 108-199 (Consolidated Appropriations Act, 2004) to study, develop, and deliver to the President, Congress, and the Secretary of State actionable proposals to enhance and leverage the efficiency and effectiveness of U.S. foreign assistance to reduce poverty through sustained economic growth and selfsufficiency [37]. One study by several commissioners found the following characteristics of successful efforts:

- Ownership and initiative must be local;
- Partnership is the premise;

- Technology adaptation and adoption matter;
- Leaders and policy must drive toward self-reliance; and
- Continual information loops contribute to learning and adjustments [38].

The study found that some of the most widely acknowledged foreign assistance successes have incorporated the application of technologies including the Green Revolution of the mid-20th century, which they state doubled food production in developing countries, and the presence today of Consultative Group on International Agricultural Research (CGIAR), a partnership of government, nongovernmental organizations, and businesses that support 15 international research centers to provide technical support. Other examples include bednets to reduce malaria, smallpox and polio vaccines, and "smart cards" that provide loans to businesses located in poor areas where no bank is available. The study also indicates that the scientific and technological capacity of developing countries is growing, such as the African Laser Center.

In its report, the Commission proposed the establishment of a new U.S. government organization, modeled on the Defense Advanced Research Projects Agency (DARPA) known for its risk-taking and innovation, [39] called the "Development Applications Research Institute" [40] (DARI). According to the Commission, DARI could "develop and apply innovative technologies to development problems in order to jumpstart research and development aimed at reducing global poverty," and its head could serve as the science advisor to the lead U.S. government official in charge of development policy. The Commission proposed that DARI focus on all relevant development areas including agriculture, health, and education; carry out its work in partnership with development countries to spur the development of local R&D capabilities; and carefully structured to ensure accountability and performance. The cost of DARI, according to the Commission would be $50-100 million per year.

## Additional Considerations

If Congress should decide to address the trends described above, additional financial resources and personnel with expertise in S&T may be necessary. If Congress is concerned about a lack of overall international S&T policy direction at OSTP or coordination among the White House and federal agencies as described by the reports above, possible actions include enhancing the prominence of the STAS, and coordination among, S&T leaders at OES, STAS, and OSTP.

One option that takes into account all three reports is for the STAS to play a greater role in coordination by appointment to a high-level position within OES as well as chairing a revived CISET. If Congress decides to establish DARI, the STAS might also play a leadership role there as well.

# CONGRESSIONAL ACTIVITIES

On June 8, 2009, the House passed the International Science and Technology Cooperation Act of 2009 (H.R. 1736). This bill would require the OSTP Director to establish an NSTC committee, co-chaired by senior-level officials from the OSTP and DOS, with the responsibility to identify and coordinate international science and technology cooperation that can strengthen the United States science and technology enterprise, improve economic and national security, and support United States foreign policy goals. Specifically, the committee is to

(1) plan and coordinate interagency international science and technology cooperative research and training activities and partnerships supported or managed by Federal agencies and work with other National Science and Technology Council committees to help plan and coordinate the international component of national science and technology priorities;

(2) establish Federal priorities and policies for aligning, as appropriate, international science and technology cooperative research and training activities and partnerships supported or managed by Federal agencies with the foreign policy goals of the United States;

(3) identify opportunities for new international science and technology cooperative research and training partnerships that advance both the science and technology and the foreign policy priorities of the United States;

(4) in carrying out paragraph (3), solicit input and recommendations from non-Federal science and technology stakeholders, including universities, scientific and professional societies, industry, and relevant organizations and institutions, through workshops and other appropriate venues;

(5) work with international science and technology counterparts, both non-governmental and governmental (in coordination with the Department of State), to establish and maintain international science and technology cooperative research and training partnerships, as identified under paragraph (3); and

(6) address broad issues that influence the ability of United States scientists and engineers to collaborate with foreign counterparts, including barriers to collaboration and access to scientific information.

OSTP is to provide an annual report to Congress with a description of activities carried out in the previous fiscal year and of how stakeholder input was received. In its report (H.Rept. 111-128), the House Committee on Science and Technology states

> The Committee intends that the NSTC committee, in setting priorities and carrying out its charge, will take into account not just Federal offices and programs that support international S&T partnerships, but also the role that non-governmental organizations with expertise in developing and maintaining international S&T partnerships, including the American Association for the Advancement of Science, the National Academies of Science, the Civilian Research and Development Foundation, and the U.S. Israel Science and Technology Foundation, might play in helping the agencies achieve their goals. The Committee also intends for the NSTC committee to take full advantage of the wealth of S&T expertise at U.S. universities and other non-governmental research institutions rather than relying solely on Federal agencies.

# REFERENCES

[1]    Silvio A. Bedini, Thomas Jefferson: Statesman of Science (New York: Macmillian, 1990). I. Bernard Cohen, Benjamin Franklin's Science (Cambridge: Harvard University Press, 1996). Joyce E. Chaplin, *The First Scientific American: Benjamin Franklin and the Pursuit of Genius* (New York: Basic Books, 2007).

[2]    See, for example, U.S. Congress, House Committee on Science and Technology, Subcommittee on Research and Science Education, International Science and Technology Cooperation, hearing, 110th Cong., 2nd sess., April 2, 2008, at http:// science.house.gov/publications/ hearings_markups_details.aspx?NewsID=2134.

[3]    National Research Council, *The Fundamental Role of Science and Technology in International Development: An Imperative for the U.S. Agency for International Development* (Washington, DC: National Academy Press, 2006), at http://www .nap.edu/catalog.php?record_id=11583.

[4]    According to DOS, science and technology agreements "establish frameworks to facilitate the exchange of scientific results, provide for protection and allocation of intellectual property rights and benefit sharing, facilitate access for researchers, address taxation issues, and respond to the complex set of issues associated with economic development, domestic security and regional stability." See State Department, "List of Umbrella S&T Agreements," at http://www.state.gov/g/oes/rls/fs/2006/77212.htm for more information

[5]    U.S. Department of State/U.S. Agency for International Development Strategic Plan, Fiscal Years 2007-20 12: Transformational Democracy, May 7, 2007, available at http://www.usaid.gov/policy/coordination/stratplan_fy07- 12.pdf.

[6]    This report does not discuss issues related to the promotion and support of technological innovation such as export controls or technology, trade, and security issues. For more information on these issues, see CRS Report RL31832, *The Export Administration Act: Evolution, Provisions, and Debate*, by Ian F. Fergusson, and CRS Report RL32591, *U.S. Terms of Trade: Significance, Trends, and Policy*, by Craig K. Elwell.

[7]    Jeff Miotke, Deputy Assistant Secretary for Science, Space, and Health, OES, DOS, Testimony before the House Committee on Science and Technology, Subcommittee on Research and Science Education, *International Science and Technology Cooperation*,110th Cong. 2nd sess., April 2, 2008, at http://democrats.scien ce.house.gov/Media/File/ Commdocs/hearings/2008/Research /2apr/Miotke_Testi mony.pdf.

[8]    For more information, see http://www.state.gov/g/oes/c20049.htm. The FY2008 budget estimate for OES is $31 million. See State Department FY2009 budget justification, available at http://www.state.gov/s/d/rm/rls/statecbj/2009/.

[9]    According to the FY2009 State Department budget justification, the FY2008 budget estimate for this directorate is $4 million and includes 24 staff members.

[10]   For an illustration, see http://egypt.usembassy.gov/usegypt/contacts.htm.

[11]   For more information, see Nina Fedoroff, Science and Technology Adviser to the Secretary of State and the Administrator of USAID, Testimony before the House

Committee on Science and Technology, Subcommittee on Research and Science Education, International Science and Technology Cooperation, 110th Cong. 2nd sess., April 2, 2008, at http://democrats.science.house.gov/Media/File/Commdocs/hearings /2008/Research/2apr/ Fedoroff_Testimony.pdf.

[12] For more information, see http://www.state.gov/g/stas/c6063.htm.

[13] U.S. Agency for International Development, *USAID Primer: What We Do and How We Do It, January 2006*, at http://www.usaid.gov/about_usaid/PDACG100.pdf.

[14] National Research Council, The Fundamental Role of Science and Technology in International Development: An Imperative for the U.S. Agency for International Development (Washington, DC: National Academy Press, 2006) at http://www.n ap.edu/catalog.php?record_id=11583. Nina Fedoroff, Science and Technology Adviser to the Secretary of State and the Administrator of USAID, Testimony before the House Committee on Science and Technology, Subcommittee on Research and Science Education, International Science and Technology Cooperation,110th Cong. 2nd sess., April 2, 2008, at http://democrats.science.house.gov/Media/File/Commdocs/hearings/20 08/Research/ 2apr/ Fedoroff_Testimony.pdf.

[15] John H. Marburger, Director, OSTP, Bush Administration, Testimony before the House Committee on Science and Technology, Subcommittee on Research and Science Education, *International Science and Technology Cooperation*, 110th Cong. 2nd sess., April 2, 2008, at http://democrats.science.house.gov/Media/File /Commdocs/hearings/2 008/ Research/2apr/Marburger_Testimony.pdf.

[16] National Science and Technology Council, at http://www.ostp.gov/cs/nstc.

[17] A Woodrow Wilson Center report identifies what they consider to be the best practices regarding OSTP and international S&T policy. For more information, see Jennifer Sue Bond, Mark Schaefer, David Rejeski, Rodney W. Nichols, *OSTP 2.0: Critical Upgrade: Enhancing Capacity for White House Science and Technology Policymaking: Recommendations for the Next President* (Washington, DC: Woodrow Wilson International Center for Scholars, June 2008) at http://wilsoncenter.org/news/docs/O STP%20Paper1.pdf.

[18] National Science and Technology Council, 2000 Annual Report, at http://www.ostp.gov/pdf/nstc_ar.pdf.

[19] John H. Marburger, Director, OSTP, Bush Administration ,Testimony before the House Committee on Science and Technology, Subcommittee on Research and Science Education, *International Science and Technology Cooperation*, 110th Cong. 2nd sess., April 2, 2008, at http://democrats.science.house.gov/Media/File/ Commdocs/hearings/2 008/ Research/2apr/Marburger_Testimony.pdf.

[20] Ibid.

[21] Testimony of Dr. John P. Holdren, Director-designate, Office of Science and Technology Policy, Executive Office of the President, "Nominations Hearing," Senate Committee on Commerce, Science, and Transportation, hearing, 111th Congress, 1st sess., February 12, 2009 at http://commerce.senate.gov/public/_files/ JohnHoldren Senatetestimony_21009.pdf. Jeffrey Mervis, "John Holdren Brings More than Energy to His Role as Science Adviser," *Science*, vol. 324 (April 17, 2009), pp. 324-325 at http://www.sciencemag.org/cgi/reprint/324/5925/ 324.pdf.

[22] For more information, see http://www.ostp.gov/cs/about_ostp/leadership_staff.

[23] For more information, see http://www.ostp.gov/cs/nstc/committees.

[24] A description of federal agency international S&T activities is provided in Jeff Miotke, Deputy Assistant Secretary for Science, Space, and Health, OES, DOS, Testimony before the House Committee on Science and Technology, Subcommittee on Research and Science Education, *International Science and Technology Cooperation*, 110th Cong. 2nd sess., April 2, 2008, at http://democrats.science.house.gov/Media/File/Comm docs/hearings/2008/Research/2apr/ Miotke_Testimony.pdf.

[25] Ibid.

[26] U.S. President (Obama), "Remarks By The President On A New Beginning," Cairo University, Cairo, Egypt White House press release, June 4, 2009, at http://www.whitehouse.gov/the_press_office/Remarks-by-the-President-at-Cairo-University-6-04-09/.

[27] U.S. Congress, House Committee on Science and Technology, Subcommittee on Research and Science Education, International Science and Technology Cooperation, hearing, 110th Cong., 2nd sess., April 2, 2008, at http://science.house.go v/publications/hearings_markups_details. aspx?NewsID=2134.

[28] Testimony and response to questions by John H. Marburger (OSTP), Arden Bement (NSF), Nina Fedoroff (STAS), Jeff Mitoke (DOS), and Michael O'Brien (NASA) at U.S. Congress, House Committee on Science and Technology, Subcommittee on Research and Science Education, International Science and Technology Cooperation, hearing, 110th Cong., 2nd sess., April 2, 2008, at http://science. house.gov/pub lications/hearings_markups_details.aspx?NewsID=2134. A transcript of the hearing is available from Congressional Quarterly.

[29] See, for example, Rodney W. Nichols, *US Science Office Must Promote Global Collaboration*, Science and Development Network, October 31, 2008 at http://www.scidev.net/en/opinions/us-science-office-must-promote-global-collaboratio.html?utm_source=link&utm _medium=rss&utm_campaign=en_opinions.

[30] David Dickson, *The World's Poor Deserve Better U.S. Leadership*, Science and Development Network, October 31, 2008, at http://www.scidev.net/en/editorials/the-world-s-poor-deserve-better-us-leadership.html.

[31] Jeff Miotke, Deputy Assistant Secretary for Science, Space, and Health, OES, DOS, Testimony before the House Committee on Science and Technology, Subcommittee on Research and Science Education, International Science and Technology Cooperation,1 10th Cong. 2nd sess., April 2, 2008, at http://democrats.science.house.gov/Media/File/ Commdocs/hearings/2008/Research/2apr/Miotke_Testimony.pdf

[32] State Department, Advisory Committee on Transformational Diplomacy: Final report of the State Department in 2025 Working Group, at http://www.state.gov/secre tary/diplomacy/99774.htm.

[33] Ibid.

[34] National Research Council, *The Fundamental Role of Science and Technology in International Development: An Imperative for the U.S. Agency for International Development* (Washington, DC: National Academy Press, 2006), at http://www.n ap.edu/catalog.php?record_id=11583.

[35] National Science Board, *International Science and Engineering Partnerships: A Priority for U.S. Foreign Policy and Our Nation's Innovation Enterprise*, NSB08-4

(Arlington, VA: National Science Foundation, 2008), at http://www.nsf.gov/nsb /publications/2008/nsb084.pdf.

[36]  Ibid.

[37]  The HELP Comission, "Mission," webpage at http://www.helpcommissi on.gov/Mission/tabid/53/Default.aspx.

[38]  Carol Adelman, Nicholas Eberstadt, Susan Raymond, and Melissa Griswold, *Foreign Assistance: What Works and What Doesn't with Recommendations for Future Improvements*, December 14, 2007 at http://www.helpcommission.gov/ portals/ 0/HELP_WWWD.pdf.

[39]  For more information on DARPA and other similar models, see CRS Report RL34497, *Advanced Research Projects Agency - Energy (ARPA-E): Background, Status, and Selected Issues for Congress*, by Deborah D. Stine.

[40]  HELP Commission, *Beyond Assistance: The HELP Commission Report on Foreign Assistance Reform*, December 7, 2007 at http://www.helpcommission.gov/portals/0/ Beyond%20Assistance_HELP_Commission_Report.pdf.

In: U.S. Political Programs: Functions and Assessments ISBN: 978-1-61209-448-9
Editors: Julianna M. Moretti and Karen J. Chordstron © 2011 Nova Science Publishers, Inc.

*Chapter 9*

# THE NATIONAL SECURITY COUNCIL:
# AN ORGANIZATIONAL ASSESSMENT*

*Richard A. Best Jr.*

## ABSTRACT

The National Security Council (NSC) was established by statute in 1947 to create an interdepartmental body to advise the President with respect to the integration of domestic, foreign, and military policies relating to the national security so as to enable the military services and the other departments and agencies of the Government to cooperate more effectively in matters involving the national security. Currently, statutory members of the Council are the President, Vice President, the Secretary of State, and the Secretary of Defense; but, at the President's request, other senior officials participate in NSC deliberations. The Chairman of the Joint Chiefs of Staff and the Director of National Intelligence are statutory advisers. In 2007 the Secretary of Energy was added to the NSC membership.

The President clearly holds final decision-making authority in the executive branch. Over the years, however, the NSC staff has emerged as a major factor in the formulation (and at times in the implementation) of national security policy. Similarly, the head of the NSC staff, the National Security Adviser, has played important, and occasionally highly public, roles in policymaking. This report traces the evolution of the NSC from its creation to the present.

The organization and influence of the NSC have varied significantly from one Administration to another, from a highly structured and formal system to loose-knit teams of experts. It is universally acknowledged that the NSC staff should be organized to meet the particular goals and work habits of an incumbent President. The history of the NSC provides ample evidence of the advantages and disadvantages of different types of policymaking structures.

Congress enacted the statute creating the NSC and has altered the character of its membership over the years. Congress annually appropriates funds for its activities, but does not, routinely, receive testimony on substantive matters from the National Security

---

* This is an edited, reformatted and augmented edition of a United States Congressional Research Service publication, CRS Report RL30840, dated June 8, 2009.

Adviser or from NSC staff. Proposals to require Senate confirmation of the Security Adviser have been discussed but not adopted.

The post-Cold War world has posed new challenges to NSC policymaking. Some argue that the NSC should be broadened to reflect an expanding role of economic, environmental, and demographic issues in national security policymaking. The Clinton Administration created a National Economic Council tasked with cooperating closely with the NSC on international economic matters. In the wake of the 9/11 attacks, the George W. Bush Administration established a Homeland Security Council. The Obama Administration has combined the staffs of the Homeland Security Council and the National Security Council, while retaining the two positions of National Security Adviser and Homeland Security Adviser. Although the latter has direct access to the President, the incumbent is to organizationally report to the National Security Adviser.

## INTRODUCTION

The National Security Council (NSC) has been an integral part of U.S. national security policymaking since 1947. Of the various organizations in the Executive Office of the President that have been concerned with national security matters, the NSC is the most important and the only one established by statute. The NSC lies at the heart of the national security apparatus, being the highest coordinative and advisory body within the Government in this area aside from the President's Cabinet. The Cabinet has no statutory role, but the NSC does.

This study reviews the organizational history of the NSC and other related components of the Executive Office and their changing role in the national security policy process. It is intended to provide information on the NSC's development as well as subsequent usage. This study is not intended to be a comprehensive organizational history of all components of the national security policy process nor of the process itself as a whole. Moreover, the high sensitivity and security classification of the NSC's work and organization limit available sources. It is also important to keep in mind the distinction between the NSC's statutory membership (i.e., the President, Vice President, Secretary of State, Secretary of Defense, and Secretary of Energy) and its staff (i.e., the National Security Adviser and his assistants). These two groups have very different roles and levels of influence.

## PRE-NSC COORDINATION METHODS

### The Need for Interdepartmental Coordination

Successful national security policymaking is based on careful analysis of the international situation, including diplomatic, economic, intelligence, military, and morale factors. Based on a comprehensive assessment, effective government leaders attempt to attain their goals by selecting the most appropriate instrument of policy, whether it is military, diplomatic, economic, based on the intelligence services, or a combination of more than one. Although this approach has been an ideal throughout the history of international relations, prior to World War II, U.S. Presidents, focused primarily on domestic matters, and lacked organizational support to integrate national security policies. They relied instead on ad hoc arrangements and informal groups of advisers. However, in the early 1940s, the complexities of global war and the need to work together with allies led to more structured processes of national security decisionmaking to ensure that the efforts of the State, War, and Navy Departments were focused on the same objectives. There was an increasingly apparent need for an organizational entity to support the President in looking at the multiplicity of factors, military and diplomatic, that had to be faced during wartime and in the early postwar months when crucial decisions had to be made regarding the future of Germany and Japan and a large number of other countries.

Given continuing worldwide responsibilities in the postwar years that involved active diplomacy, sizable military forces, sophisticated intelligence agencies, in addition to economic assistance in various forms, the United States established organizational mechanisms to analyze the international environment, identify priorities, and recommend appropriate policy options. Four decades later, the end of the Cold War saw the emergence of new international concerns, including transnational threats such as international terrorism and drug trafficking, that have continued to require the coordination of various departments and agencies concerned with national security policies.

## Past Modes of Policy Coordination

Coordinative mechanisms to implement policy are largely creations of the Executive Branch, but they directly influence choices that Congress may be called upon to support and fund. Congress thus takes interest in the processes by which policies and the roles of various participants are determined. Poor coordination of national security policy can result in calls for Congress to take actions that have major costs, both international and domestic, without the likelihood of a successful outcome. Effective coordination, on the other hand, can mean the achievement of policy goals with minimal losses of human lives while providing the opportunity to devote material resources to other needs.

Throughout most of the history of the United States, until the twentieth century, policy coordination centered on the President, who was virtually the sole means of such coordination. The Constitution designates the President as Commander-in-Chief of the armed forces (Article II, Section 2) and grants him broad powers in the areas of foreign affairs (Article II, Section 2), powers that have expanded considerably in the twentieth century through usage. Given limited U.S. foreign involvements for the first hundred or so years under the Constitution, the small size of the armed forces, the relative geographic isolation of the Nation, and the absence of any proximate threat, the President, or his executive agents in the Cabinet, provided a sufficient coordinative base.

However, the advent of World War I, which represented a modern, complex military effort involving broad domestic and international coordination, forced new demands on the system that the President alone could not meet. In 1916, the Council of National Defense was established by statute (Army Appropriation Act of 1916). It reflected proposals that went back to 1911 and consisted of the Secretaries of War, Navy, Interior, Agriculture, Commerce and Labor. The statute also allowed the President to appoint an advisory commission of outside specialists to aid the Council [1]. The Council of National Defense was intended as an economic mobilization coordinating group, as reflected by its membership—which excluded the Secretary of State. His inclusion would have given the Council a much wider coordinative scope. Furthermore, the authorizing statute itself limited the role of the Council basically to economic mobilization issues. The Council of National Defense was disbanded in 1921, but it set a precedent for coordinative efforts that would be needed in World War II.

The President remained the sole national security coordinator until 1938, when the prewar crisis began to build in intensity, presenting numerous and wide-ranging threats to the inadequately armed United States. The State Department, in reaction to reports of Axis activities in Latin America, proposed that interdepartmental conferences be held with War and Navy Department representatives. In April 1938, Secretary of State Cordell Hull, in a letter to President Franklin Roosevelt, formally proposed the creation of a standing committee made up of the second ranking officers of the three departments, for purposes of liaison and coordination. The President approved this idea, and the Standing Liaison Committee, or Liaison Committee as it was also called, was established, the members being the Under Secretary of State, the Chief of Staff of the Army, and the Chief of Naval Operations. The Standing Liaison Committee was the first significant effort toward interdepartmental liaison and coordination, although its work in the area was limited and uneven. The Liaison Committee largely concentrated its efforts on Latin American problems, and it met irregularly. Although it did foster some worthwhile studies during the crisis following the fall of France, it was soon superseded by other coordinative modes. It was more a forum for exchanging information than a new coordinative and directing body [2].

An informal coordinating mechanism, which complemented the Standing Liaison Committee, evolved during the weekly meetings established by Secretary of War Henry L. Stimson, who took office in June 1940. Stimson arranged for weekly luncheons with his Navy counterpart, Frank Knox, and Cordell Hull, but these meetings also did not fully meet the growing coordinative needs of the wartime government.

In May 1940 President Roosevelt used the precedent of the 1916 statute and established the National Defense Advisory Council (NDAC), composed of private citizens with expertise in specific economic sectors [3]. As with the earlier Council of National Defense, NDAC was organized to handle problems of economic mobilization; and by the end of the year it had given way to another organization in a succession of such groups.

During the war, there were a number of interdepartmental committees formed to handle various issues, and, while these did help achieve coordination, they suffered from two problems. First, their very multiplicity was to some degree counter-productive to coordination, and they still represented a piecemeal approach to these issues. Second, and more important, these committees in many cases were not advising the President directly, but were advising his advisers. Although their multiplicity and possible overlapping fit Roosevelt's preferred working methods, they did not represent coordination at the top. Roosevelt ran the war largely through the Joint Chiefs of Staff (JCS), who were then an ad hoc and de facto group, and through key advisers such as Harry Hopkins and James F. Byrnes, and via his own personal link with British Prime Minister Winston Churchill.

The weekly meetings arranged by Stimson evolved, however, into a significant coordinative body by 1945, with the formal creation of the State, War, Navy Coordinating Committee (SWNCC). SWNCC had its own secretariat and a number of regional and topical subcommittees; its members were assistant secretaries in each pertinent department. The role of SWNCC members was to aid their superiors "on politico-military matters and [in] coordinating the views of the three departments on matters in which all have a common interest, particularly those involving foreign policy and relations with foreign nations...." SWNCC was a significant improvement in civilian-military liaison, and meshed well with the

JCS system; it did not, however, concern itself with fundamental questions of national policy during the early months of the Cold War [4]. SWNCC operated through the end of the war and beyond, becoming SANACC (State, Army, Navy, Air Force Coordinating Committee) after the National Security Act of 1947. It was dissolved in 1949, by which time it had been superseded by the NSC.

The creation of SWNCC, virtually at the end of the war, and its continued existence after the surrender of Germany and Japan reflected the growing awareness within the Federal Government that better means of coordination were necessary. The World War II system had largely reflected the preferred working methods of President Roosevelt, who relied on informal consultations with various advisers in addition to the JCS structure. However, the complex demands of global war and the post-war world rendered this system inadequate, and it was generally recognized that a return to the simple and limited prewar system would not be possible if the United States was to take on the responsibilities thrust upon it by the war and its aftermath.

# THE CREATION OF THE NSC [5]

## Introduction

The NSC was not created independently, but rather as one part of a complete restructuring of the entire national security apparatus, civilian and military, including intelligence efforts, as accomplished in the National Security Act of 1947. Thus, it is difficult to isolate the creation of the NSC from the larger reorganization, especially as the NSC was much less controversial than the unification of the military and so attracted less attention.

## Proposals

As early as 1943, General George C. Marshall, Army Chief of Staff, had proposed that the prospect of a unified military establishment be assessed. Congress first began to consider this idea in 1944, with the Army showing interest while the Navy was opposed. At the request of the Navy these investigations were put off until 1945, although by then it was clear to Secretary of the Navy James Forrestal that President Truman, who had come to the White House upon the death of President Roosevelt in April 1945, favored some sort of reorganization. Forrestal believed that outright opposition would not be a satisfactory Navy stance. He also realized that the State Department had to be included in any new national security apparatus. Therefore, he had Ferdinand Eberstadt, a leading New York attorney and banker who had served in several high- level Executive Branch positions, investigate the problem [6].

With respect to the formation of the NSC, the most significant of the three questions posed by Forrestal to Eberstadt, was:

> What form of postwar organization should be established and maintained to enable the military services and other governmental departments and agencies most effectively to provide for and protect our national security?

Eberstadt's response to this question covered the military establishment, where he favored three separate departments and the continuation of the JCS, as well as the civilian sphere, where he suggested the formation of two new major bodies "to coordinate all these [civilian and military] elements." These two bodies he called the National Security Council (NSC), composed of the President, the Secretaries of State and of the three military departments, the JCS "in attendance," and the chairman of the other new body, the National Security Resources Board (NSRB). Eberstadt also favored the creation of a Central Intelligence Agency (CIA) under the NSC [7].

Eberstadt's recommendations clearly presaged the eventual national security apparatus, with the exception of a unified Department of Defense. Furthermore, it was a central point in Forrestal's plans for holding the proposed reorganization to Navy desires, bringing in the State Department, as he desired, and hopefully obviating the need for some coalescence of the military services. The NSC was also a useful negotiating point for Forrestal with the Army, as Eberstadt had described one of its functions as being the "building up [of] public support for clear-cut, consistent, and effective foreign and military policies." This would appeal to all the service factions as they thought back on the lean and insecure prewar years.8

War-Navy negotiations over the shape of the reorganization continued throughout 1946 and into 1947. However, some form of central coordination, for a while called the Council of Common Defense, was not one of the contentious issues. By the end of May 1946, agreement had been reached on this and several other points, and by the end of the year the two sides had agreed on the composition of the new coordinative body [9].

## Congressional Consideration

The creation of the NSC was one of the least controversial sections of the National Security Act and so drew little attention in comparison with the basic concept of a single military department, around which most of the congressional debate centered.

The concept of a regular and permanent organization for the coordination of national security policy was as widely accepted in Congress as in the Executive. When the NSC was considered in debate, the major issues were the mechanics of the new organization, its membership, assurances that it would be a civilian organization and would not be dominated by the new Secretary of the National Military Establishment, and whether future positions on the NSC would be subject to approval by the Senate [10].

## The NSC as Created in 1947

The NSC was created by the National Security Act, which was signed by the President on July 26, 1947. The NSC appears in Section 101 of Title I, Coordination for National Security, and its purpose is stated as follows:

(a)  ... The function of the Council shall be to advise the President with respect to the integration of domestic, foreign, and military policies relating to the national security so as to enable the military services and the other departments and agencies of the Government to cooperate more effectively in matters involving the national security.

(b) In addition to performing such other functions as the President may direct, for the purpose of more effectively coordinating the policies and functions of the departments and agencies of the Government relating to the national security, it shall, subject to the direction of the President, be the duty of the Council

(1) to assess and appraise the objectives, commitments, and risks of the United States in relation to our actual and potential military power, in the interest of national security, for the purpose of making recommendations to the President in connection there with; and

(2) to consider policies on matters of common interest to the departments and agencies of the Government concerned with the national security, and to make recommendations to the President in connection therewith. . . .

(d) The Council shall, from time to time, make such recommendations, and such other reports to the President as it deems appropriate or as the President may require [11].

The following officers were designated as members of the NSC: the President; the Secretaries of State, Defense, Army, Navy, and Air Force; and the Chairman of the National Security Resources Board. The President could also designate the following officers as members "from time to time:" secretaries of other executive departments and the Chairmen of the Munitions Board and the Research and Development Board. Any further expansion required Senate approval. The NSC was provided with a staff headed by a civilian executive secretary, appointed by the President.

The National Security Act also established the Central Intelligence Agency under the NSC, but the Director of Central Intelligence (DCI) was not designated as an NSC member. The act also created a National Military Establishment, with three executive departments (Army, Navy, and Air Force) under a Secretary of Defense.

Implicit in the provisions of the National Security Act was an assumption that the NSC would have a role in ensuring that the U.S. industrial base would be capable of supporting national security strategies. The Chairman of the National Security Resources Board, set up by the same act to deal directly with industrial base and civilian mobilization issues, was provided a seat on the NSC. Over the years, however, these arrangements proved unsatisfactory and questions of defense mobilization and civil defense were transferred to other federal agencies and the membership of the NSC was limited to the President, Vice President, the Secretary of State and the Secretary of Defense [12]. Thus, the need for a coordinative entity that had initially been perceived to center on economic mobilization issues during World War I had evolved to one that engaged the more permanent themes of what had come to be known as national security policy.

The creation of the NSC was a definite improvement over past coordinative methods and organization, bringing together as it did the top diplomatic, military, and resource personnel with the President. The addition of the CIA, subordinate to the NSC, also provided the necessary intelligence and analyses for the Council so that it could keep pace with events and trends. The changeable nature of its organization and its designation as an advisory body to the President also meant that the NSC was a malleable organization, to be used as each President saw fit. Thus, its use, internal substructure, and ultimate effect would be directly dependent on the style and wishes of the President.

# THE NATIONAL SECURITY COUNCIL, 1947-2009

## The Truman NSC, 1947-1953

*Early Use.* The NSC first met on September 26, 1947. President Truman attended the first session, but did not attend regularly thereafter, thus emphasizing the NSC's advisory role. In his place, the President designated the Secretary of State as chairman, which also was in accord with the President's view of the major role that the State Department should play. Truman viewed the NSC as a forum for studying and appraising problems and making recommendations, but not one for setting policy or serving as a centralized office to coordinate implementation.

The NSC met irregularly for the first 10 months. In May 1948, meetings twice a month were scheduled, although some were canceled, and special sessions were convened as needed.

*The Hoover Commission.* The first review of NSC operations came in January 1949 with the report of the Hoover Commission (the Commission on Organization of the Executive Branch of the Government), which found that the NSC was not fully meeting coordination needs, especially in the area of comprehensive statements of current and long-range policies [13].

The Hoover Commission recommended that better working-level liaison between the NSC and JCS be developed, that the Secretary of Defense become an NSC member, replacing the service secretaries, and that various other steps be taken to clarify and tighten roles and liaison.

*1949 Amendments.* In January 1949, President Truman directed the Secretary of the Treasury to attend all NSC meetings. In August 1949, amendments to the National Security Act were passed (P.L. 81-216), changing the membership of the NSC to consist of the following officers: the President, Vice President, Secretaries of State and Defense, and Chairman of the National Security Resources Board. This act also designated the JCS as "the principal military advisers to the President," thus opening the way for their attendance, beginning in 1950, even though the Service Secretaries were excluded. In August 1949, by Reorganization Plan No. 4, the NSC also became part of the Executive Office of the President, formalizing a de facto situation.

*Subsequent Usage and Evaluation.* The outbreak of the Korean War in June 1950 brought greater reliance on the NSC system. The President ordered weekly meetings and specified that all major national security recommendations be coordinated through the NSC and its staff. Truman began presiding regularly, chairing 62 of the 71 meetings between June 1950 and January 1953. The NSC became to a much larger extent the focus of national security decisionmaking. Still, the NSC's role remained limited. Truman continued to use alternate sources of information and advice [14]. As one scholar has concluded:

> Throughout his administration Truman's use of the NSC process remained entirely consistent with his views of its purpose and value. The president and his secretary of state remained completely responsible for foreign policy. Once policy decisions were made, the NSC was there to advise the president on matters requiring specific diplomatic, military, and intelligence coordination [15].

## The Eisenhower NSC, 1953-1961

President Dwight Eisenhower, whose experience with a well-ordered staff was extensive, gave new life to the NSC. Under his Administration, the NSC staff was institutionalized and expanded, with clear lines of responsibility and authority, and it came to closely resemble Eberstadt's original conception as the President's principal arm for formulating and coordinating military, international, and internal security affairs. Meetings were held weekly and, in addition to Eisenhower himself and the other statutory members, participants often included the Secretary of the Treasury, the Budget Director, the Chairman of the JCS, and the Director of Central Intelligence.

*Organizational Changes.* In his role as chairman of the NSC, Eisenhower created the position of Special Assistant for National Security Affairs, [16] who became the supervisory officer of the NSC, including the Executive Secretary. The Special Assistant—initially Robert Cutler, a banker who had served under Stimson during World War II—was intended to be the President's agent on the NSC, not an independent policymaker in his own right, and to be a source of advice [17].

Eisenhower established two important subordinate bodies: the NSC Planning Board, which prepared studies, policy recommendations, and basic drafts for NSC coordination, and the Operations Coordinating Board, which was the coordinating and integrating arm of the NSC for all aspects of the implementation of national security policy.

By the end of the Eisenhower Administration, the NSC membership had changed slightly. The National Security Resources Board had been abolished by Reorganization Plan No. 3 in June 1953, and this vacancy was then filled by the Director of the Office of Civil and Defense Mobilization.

In 1956, President Eisenhower, partly in response to recommendations of the second Hoover Commission on the Organization of the Executive Branch of Government, also established the Board of Consultants on Foreign Intelligence Activities in the Executive Office. This board was established by Executive Order 10656 and was tasked to provide the President with independent evaluations of the U.S. foreign intelligence effort. The Board of Consultants lapsed at the end of the Eisenhower Administration, but a similar body, the President's Foreign Intelligence Advisory Board (PFIAB), was created by President Kennedy after the Bay of Pigs failure. PFIAB was itself abolished in 1977, but was resurrected during the Reagan Administration in 1981. Members are selected by the President and serve at his discretion.

Evaluation. The formal structure of the NSC under Eisenhower allowed it to handle an increasing volume of matters. Its work included comprehensive assessments of the country's basic national security strategy, which were designed to serve as the basis for military planning and foreign policymaking. The complexity of NSC procedures under Eisenhower and its lengthy papers led to charges that quantity was achieved at the expense of quality and that the NSC was too large and inflexible in its operations. Critics alleged that it was unable to focus sufficiently on major issue areas [18]. Some observers also held that NSC recommendations were often compromises based on the broadest mutually acceptable grounds from all the agencies involved, leading to a noticeable lack of innovative national security ideas. The Eisenhower NSC did, nonetheless, establish national security policies that were accepted and implemented throughout the Government and that laid the basis for sustained competition with the Soviet Union for several decades.

It may be that the NSC process became overly bureaucratic towards the end of the Eisenhower Administration, perhaps affected by the President's declining health. Hearings by the Senate Government Operations Committee in 1960-61, led by Senator Henry Jackson, produced proposals for a substantial reorientation of this "over-institutionalized" structure, and its replacement by a smaller, less formal NSC that would offer the President a clear choice of alternatives on a limited number of major problems [19].

Some scholars have noted that Eisenhower himself found the lengthy NSC procedures burdensome and argue that many key decisions were made in the Oval Office in the presence of only a few advisers. Nonetheless, Eisenhower saw the NSC process as one which produced a consensus within the Administration which would lead to effective policy implementation. According to this view, the process was largely one of education and clarification [20]. A recent analysis has concluded, that NSC meetings

> brought Eisenhower's thinking into sharper focus by forcing him to weigh it against a range of alternatives that were presented and defended by individuals whose opinions the president took seriously and whose exposure to requisite information and expertise he assured. These individuals, in turn, were educated about the problems in the same way as Eisenhower [21]

## The Kennedy NSC, 1961-1963

President John Kennedy, who did not share Eisenhower's preference for formal staff procedures, accepted many of the recommendations of the Jackson Committee and proceeded to dismantle much of the NSC structure, reducing it to its statutory base. Staff work was carried out mainly by the various departments and agencies, and personal contacts and ad hoc task forces became the main vehicles for policy discussion and formulation. The NSC was now one among many sources of advice.

Kennedy's National Security Adviser, McGeorge Bundy, played an important policy role directly under the President. The nature of this position was no longer that of a "neutral keeper of the machinery"; for the first time, the Adviser emerged in an active policymaking role, in part because of the absence of any definite NSC process that might preoccupy him [22].

Kennedy met regularly with the statutory NSC members and the DCI, but not in formal NSC sessions. Studies and coordination were assigned to specific Cabinet officers or subordinates in a system that placed great emphasis on individual responsibility, initiative and action. The Secretary of State, Dean Rusk, was initially seen as the second most important national security official in the President's plans, and Kennedy indicated that he did not want any other organizations interposed between him and Rusk. However, Kennedy came to be disappointed by the State Department's inability or unwillingness to fill this role as the leading agency in national security policy [23].

At the beginning of the Kennedy Administration, the NSC was reportedly cut from seventy-one to forty-eight and "in place of weighty policy papers, produced at regular intervals, Bundy's staff would produce crisp and timely National Security Action Memoranda (NSAMs). The new name signified the premium that would be placed on 'action' over 'planning.'"24 With an emphasis on current operations and crisis management, special ad hoc bodies came into use. The outstanding example of this was the Executive Committee (ExCom), formed in October 1962 during the Cuban Missile Crisis, which orchestrated the U.S. response to Soviet moves to introduce missiles in Cuba.

*Organizational Changes.* Kennedy added the Director of the Office of Emergency Planning to the NSC, replacing the Director of the Office of Civil and Defense Mobilization. It was planned that the new appointee would fill the role originally envisioned for the National Security Resources Board in coordinating emergency management of resources.

The Planning Board and the Operations Control Board were both abolished (by Executive Order 10920) in order to avoid the Eisenhower Administration's distinction between planning and operations. The NSC staff was reduced, and outside policy experts were brought in. Bundy noted that they were all staff officers:

> Their job is to help the President, not to supersede or supplement any of the high officials who hold line responsibilities in the executive departments and agencies. Their task is that of all staff officers: to extend the range and enlarge the direct effectiveness of the man they serve. Heavy responsibilities for operation, for coordination, and for diplomatic relations can be and are delegated to the Department of State. Full use of all the powers of leadership can be and is expected in other departments and agencies. There remains a crushing burden of responsibility, and of sheer work, on the President himself; there remains also the steady flow of questions, of ideas, of executive energy which a strong President will give off like sparks. If his Cabinet officers are to be free to do their own work, the President's work must be done—to the extent that he cannot do its himself—by staff officers under his direct oversight. But this is, I repeat, something entirely different from the interposition of such a staff between the President and his Cabinet officers [25].

*Evaluation.* Some critics attacked the informality of the system under Kennedy, arguing that it lacked form and direction, as well as coordination and control, and that it emphasized current developments at the expense of planning. As noted, Kennedy himself was disappointed by the State Department, on which he had hoped to rely. In retrospect, Kennedy's system was designed to serve his approach to the presidency and depended upon the President's active interest and continuous involvement. Some critics, both at the time and subsequently, have suggested that the informal methods that the Kennedy Administration adopted contributed to the Bay of Pigs debacle and the confusion that surrounded U.S. policy in the coup against President Diem of South Vietnam in 1963.

## The Johnson NSC, 1963-1969

President Lyndon Johnson's sudden accession to power, the need for a show of continuity, and pressures from the upcoming Presidential election all forced Johnson, at least until 1965, to rely heavily on Kennedy's system and personnel, especially as Johnson was less familiar with national security than domestic affairs.

*Organizational Changes.* Johnson, like Truman, sought out advice from a number of sources other than the NSC and its member departments, although he relied heavily on the Secretaries of State and Defense, Dean Rusk and Robert McNamara.

The institutional system that evolved under Johnson depended heavily on the ability of the State Department to handle the planning and coordination process. This system came about from a study headed by General Maxwell Taylor in 1966 that led to National Security Action Memorandum (NSAM) 341 which concluded that it was necessary to enhance the State Department's role in the policy process and to improve "country team expertise" in Washington, which was felt to be far below that in the various embassies. NSAM 341 led to a new system of interagency committees. The most important of these was the Senior Interdepartmental Group (SIG), whose members were: the Under Secretary of State, Deputy Secretary of Defense, Administrator of the Agency for International Development, DCI, JCS Chairman, Director of the U.S. Information Agency, and the National Security Adviser. In support of the SIG were a number of Interdepartmental Regional Groups (IRGs), each headed by the appropriate Assistant Secretary of State.

Within the NSC itself, structure and membership remained what they had been under Kennedy (with the Office of Emergency Planning changing title to the Office of Emergency Preparedness in 1968), although the title Special Assistant to the President for National Security Affairs was shortened to Special Assistant when Walt W. Rostow replaced Bundy in 1966. This reflected the frequent diversion of the occupant of this position away from NSC affairs to more general concerns.

*Evaluation.* Johnson's NSC system barely existed as such. The role of the NSC staff was more restricted, and budget and personnel both declined. Key decisions, those especially regarding the war in Vietnam, were made during Tuesday lunches attended by the President, the Secretaries of State and Defense, and a few other invited officials.

Johnson's informal system was not a wholly successful replacement for the highly structured system developed in the Eisenhower Administration. The SIG/IRG system fulfilled neither old functions nor the objectives set forth in NSAM341. Although this new structure was dominated by the State Department, there was little enthusiasm for the system as a whole on the part of the department's leadership. The State Department did not provide decisive leadership and settled for a system of consensus opinions. Vagueness as to authority in the SIG/IRG system reduced its effect on the bureaucracies. Moreover, there was an insufficient allocation of resources for staff support for the new organization. By 1969, the NSC existed largely in name. Johnson conferred constantly with a wide number of advisers within and outside government; while he respected institutional responsibilities, his own decisionmaking was an intensely personal process.

## The Nixon NSC, 1969-1974

Experience in the Eisenhower Administration clearly had a formative effect on President Richard Nixon's approach to national security organization. Wanting to switch White House priorities from current operations and crisis management to long-range planning, Nixon revived the NSC. Nixon's NSC staff structure resembled Eisenhower's, with an emphasis on examining policy choices and alternatives, aiming for a number of clear options reaching the highest level, where they would be treated systematically and then effectively implemented. Nixon made it clear that he wanted distinct options presented to him from which he could choose, rather than consensus opinions requiring only acceptance or rejection. Nixon used an NSC framework similar to that set in place by Eisenhower but intended, as much as Kennedy, to give the NSC staff a powerful policy role.

*Organizational Changes.* While adopting the basic form of the Eisenhower NSC, Nixon streamlined its procedures [26]. The position of Assistant for National Security Affairs was revived, and Henry Kissinger, a Harvard professor and occasional government adviser, was named to fill it. NSC meetings were limited to the statutory members, with Kissinger and the JCS Chairman also sitting in and the DCI attending for intelligence matters. In January 1973, the Office of Emergency Preparedness was abolished along with the NSC seat that originally had belonged to the Chairman of the National Security Resources Board.

Six interdepartmental groups, similar to Johnson's IRGs, formed the NSC's support network, preparing basic studies and developing policy options. However, the influence of the State Department was reduced, and Kissinger's influence soon predominated. Four major new bodies were created:

- *Washington Special Action Group (WASAG):* headed by Kissinger and designed to handle contingency planning and crises.
- *NSC Intelligence Committee*: chaired by Kissinger and responsible for providing guidance for national intelligence needs and continuing evaluations of intelligence products.
- *Defense Program Review Committee*: chaired by Kissinger and designed to achieve greater integration of defense and domestic considerations in the allocation of natural resources. This committee was intended to allow the President, through the NSC, to gain greater control over the defense budget and its implications and policy requirements. As a result of opposition by Defense Secretary Melvin Laird, its role was, however, significantly circumscribed.
- *Senior Policy Review Group:* chaired by Kissinger, this group directed and reviewed policy studies and also served as a top level deliberative body.

This system had two principal objectives: the retention of control at the top, and the development of clear alternative choices for decisionmakers.

*Evaluation.* Most of the criticism of the Nixon NSC centered on the role played by Kissinger. His position in a number of the key committees gave him control over virtually the entire NSC apparatus, leading to charges that the system, for all its efficiency, now suffered from over- centralization, and later from domination by one man.

During Nixon's first term, Kissinger competed with the State Department for control of foreign policy, and soon overshadowed Secretary of State William Rogers. Critics felt that Kissinger stifled dissent within the NSC and the rest of the national security apparatus. Kissinger's venture into "shuttle diplomacy" and the unique circumstances of the Watergate scandal further emphasized his key role. Kissinger's accession to Rogers' position in September 1973, while retaining his National Security Council post, brought renewed criticism of his role. The direct involvement of the NSC Adviser in diplomatic negotiations set a precedent that some observers have criticized as undercutting the established responsibilities of the State Department and as an attempt to orchestrate national security policy beyond the reach of congressional oversight.

Kissinger's predominance derived from his unique intellectual abilities, skill at bureaucratic maneuvering, and the support of a President determined to act boldly in international affairs without being restrained by bureaucratic or congressional inhibitions. It was achieved at a time of profound political differences over foreign policy in which

Administration and congressional goals were, on occasion, diametrically opposed. However, under President Nixon, the NSC was restored to a central role in the policy process, acting as the major vehicle and conduit for the formation of national security policy.

## The Ford NSC, 1974-1977

President Gerald Ford, who inherited his predecessor's NSC, took no major steps to change the system per se, although Kissinger was replaced as National Security Adviser by Air Force Lt. General Brent Scowcroft in November 1975. The national security policy process continued to be dominated by Kissinger, who retained his position as Secretary of State, an indication of the preeminence he had achieved, as well as a reflection of Ford's limited experience in the conduct of foreign policy prior to his sudden accession.

In June 1975, the Commission on the Organization of the Government for the Conduct of Foreign Policy, also known as the Murphy Commission, issued a report on ways to more effectively formulate and implement foreign policy. Its recommendations dealt in part with the Executive Office of the President and the NSC structure [27].

Implicitly criticizing the expansive role of the NSC staff under Kissinger, the Commission recommended that only the President should have line responsibility in the White House; that staff officials should not themselves issue directives to departmental officials; that, in the future, the National Security Adviser have no other official responsibilities; that the Secretary of the Treasury be made a statutory member of the NSC and that the NSC's scope be expanded to include major international economic policy issues; and that senior officials concerned with domestic policy be invited to NSC meetings when issues with domestic implications were discussed.

The Commission also considered general alternative structures and pointed out their basic advantages and disadvantages. It also noted that,

> Policymaking is not a branch of mechanics; however wisely designed or carefully utilized, no machinery is adequate to assure its results. The selective use of various mechanisms and forums in ways which fit the particular issues, positions, and personalities involved is as much a part of the President's responsibility as is the necessity, finally, to decide the substantive issues [28].

There were no immediate steps taken to implement the Report's recommendations.

*Organizational Changes.* In February 1976, President Ford issued Executive Order 11905 reorganizing the intelligence community, in response to ongoing investigations in that area. This order, among other things, reaffirmed the NSC's overall policy control over the foreign intelligence community. Some changes were made in the NSC sub-structure, including the abolition of the NSC Intelligence Committee. The so-called 40 Committee of the NSC, which was responsible for covert operations and certain sensitive foreign intelligence operations, was replaced by the Operations Advisory Group. This Executive Order also created the Intelligence Oversight Board in the Executive Office (subsequently disbanded in 1993). It was composed of three civilians and was tasked with reviewing the propriety and legality of the intelligence agencies' operations. In December 1975, Ford vetoed a bill that would have made the Secretary of the Treasury a statutory member of the NSC, saying that the Treasury

Secretary is invited to participate in NSC affairs having significant economic and monetary implications, but that there is no need to involve him in all NSC activities [29].

*Evaluation.* These changes did not detract from the central role that the NSC had achieved under President Nixon. Kissinger's loss of his dual position did not seem to lessen his influence over the policy process, leading critics to charge that this change was largely cosmetic. The new National Security Adviser, Brent Scowcroft, had previously served as Kissinger's deputy on the NSC staff, and was unlikely to challenge Kissinger's pre-eminence. The Ford NSC reflected the close relationship between the President and the Secretary of State, a relationship that itself became a source of controversy both in the Republican primaries of 1976 as well as the ensuing general election. Critics continued to maintain that the Ford Administration decisionmaking was secretive, impervious to congressional input, and out of touch with public opinion.

## The Carter NSC, 1977-1981 [30]

Under President Jimmy Carter, steps were taken to end the dominant role of the NSC staff and make it a more coequal and cooperating partner with the Departments of State and Defense. The NSC underwent a major reorganization in the new Administration.

*Organizational Changes.* Upon taking office in January 1977, President Carter issued a directive (PD-2) reorganizing the NSC staff. The avowed purpose of the reorganization was "to place more responsibility in the departments and agencies while insuring that the NSC, with my Assistant for National Security Affairs, continues to integrate and facilitate foreign and defense policy decisions." [31].

The number of NSC staff committees was reduced from seven to two, the Policy Review Committee (PRC) and the Special Coordination Committee (SCC). The functions of these two committees were as follows:

- *Policy Review Committee*: the PRC had responsibility for subjects which "fall primarily within a given department but where the subject also has important implications for other departments and agencies." Examples were "foreign policy issues that contain significant military or other interagency aspects; defense policy issues having international implications and the coordination of the annual Defense budget with foreign policy objectives; the preparation of a consolidated national intelligence budget and resource allocation for the Intelligence Community...; and those international economic issues pertinent to the U.S. foreign policy and security...." [32] Executive Order 12036 of January 24, 1978, added responsibility for the establishment of national foreign intelligence requirements and priorities, and periodic reviews and evaluations of national foreign intelligence products [33]. The Vice President, the Secretaries of State and Defense, and the Assistant for National Security Affairs were members of the PRC; the DCI and the Chairman of the JCS also attended. The Secretary of the Treasury, the Chairman of the Council of Economic Advisers, and other officials attended when pertinent topics were being considered. Appropriate Cabinet officers chaired the PRC in accordance with matters being considered; the DCI was chairman when the PRC considered intelligence matters as specified in E.O.12036. NSC Interdepartmental Groups, which dealt with specific issues at the direction of the President, were under the PRC.

- *Special Coordination Committee*: the SCC dealt with "specific, cross-cutting issues requiring coordination in the development of options and the implementation of Presidential decisions." These included "oversight of sensitive intelligence activities ... arms control evaluation; ... and crisis management" [34]. E.O. 12036 gave the SCC responsibility for sensitive foreign intelligence collection operations and counterintelligence [35]. The SCC thus replaced WASAG and the Operations Advisory Group. Unlike the PRC, the SCC was chaired by the Assistant for National Security Affairs; other members were the Vice President, the Secretaries of State and Defense, and the DCI—or their deputies—and other officials attended when appropriate. When intelligence "special activities" were being considered, the members had to attend, as had the Attorney General, the Chairman of the JCS, and the Director of the Office of Management and Budget (OMB); for counterintelligence activities, the Director of the FBI attended [36]

- The initial emphasis of the NSC's role as a policy coordinator and "think tank" represented a clear reversal of the trend that had developed under Presidents Nixon and Ford. The staff of the NSC was reduced under the Carter Administration, and National Security Adviser Zbigniew Brzezinski established a number of regional and topical offices on the NSC staff that aimed at a more "collegial" approach to staff procedures.

- Although the PRC had a wider charter than the SCC, as a result of the growing importance of crisis management functions and the increasing influence of the National Security Adviser, [37] initiative passed to the SCC and there were fewer PRC meetings.

- *Evaluation*. A rumored rivalry between Brzezinski and Secretary of State Cyrus Vance was not publicly evident during the first year of the Carter Administration, but reports of differences between the two men later increased dramatically as senior Administration officials advised different responses to such questions as Soviet and Cuban activities in Africa and the Iranian hostage question. Towards the end of the Administration, differences between Vance and Brzezinski became pronounced and were widely perceived as contributing to weak and vacillating policies. Carter's Director of Central Intelligence Stansfield Turner later wrote:

> National Security Advisers and Secretaries of State and Defense had clashed before, notably under President Nixon when Henry Kissinger was the Adviser. But because Nixon tended to follow Kissinger's advice more often than not, there was no stalemate, and foreign policy moved ahead in innovative ways. However, Jimmy Carter vacillated between Brzezinski and Vance, and they often canceled each other out [38]

Vance, who had strongly opposed the ill-fated effort to rescue the U.S. hostages in Iran, finally resigned and was succeeded by Senator Edmund Muskie in April 1980. Brzezinski's outspokenness and his public role in policymaking became an issue, and led to calls for Senate confirmation of NSC advisers and closer congressional oversight of the NSC staff.39 There were also reports of infighting between Carter loyalists on the NSC staff and those who had worked for Vice President Walter Mondale, who had been given a major policy role [40].

## The Reagan NSC, 1981-1989

Campaigning for the presidency in 1980, Ronald Reagan criticized the divisions of the Carter Administration and promised to restore Cabinet leadership (as, in the 1976 campaign, he had criticized Henry Kissinger's predominant influence in the Ford Administration). Substituting Cabinet leadership for an active NSC proved, however, to be a significant challenge.

*Organizational Changes.* After extensive delays and bureaucratic infighting, President Reagan signed a Presidential directive (NSDD-2), [41] which enhanced the role of the State Department in national security policymaking and downgraded that of the National Security Adviser. The various NSC sub-committees were to be chaired by State, Defense, and CIA officials, not NSC staff. The Reagan NSC included three Senior Interagency Groups (SIGs)— one for foreign policy, chaired by the Deputy Secretary of State; one for defense, chaired by the Deputy Secretary of Defense; and one for intelligence, chaired by the Director of Central Intelligence. There were also regional and functional interagency groups, chaired by representatives of various Cabinet departments. Crisis management formally became the direct responsibility of the Vice President [42].

This structure, however, had major limitations. Observers and participants portray an absence of orderly decisionmaking and uncertain lines of responsibility. As the Special Review Board (known as the Tower Board) appointed by the President to assess the proper role of the NSC system in the wake of the Iran-Contra revelations, pointedly noted:

> A President must at the outset provide guidelines to the members of the National Security Council, his National Security Adviser, and the National Security Council staff. These guidelines, to be effective, must include how they will relate to one another, what procedures will be followed, what the President expects of them. If his advisors are not performing as he likes, only the President can intervene [43].

The Reagan Administration had a total of six National Security Advisers. Their history is poignant. The first, Richard Allen, did not have direct access to the President, but reported to him through Presidential Counselor Edwin Meese. Allen's tenure was brief; after accusations of influence peddling, he was replaced in January 1982 by Judge William Clark, a longtime Reagan associate who had served since the beginning of the Administration as Deputy Secretary of State. Clark, in turn, resigned in October 1983 to become Secretary of the Interior and his deputy, Robert McFarlane, became National Security Adviser. McFarlane was replaced in January 1986 by his deputy, Vice Admiral John Poindexter, and subsequently pleaded guilty to withholding information from Congress. Poindexter himself was relieved in the context of the Iran-Contra scandal in November 1986, and eventually went on trial for obstructing justice. An effort was made to restore NSC effectiveness under former Ambassador Frank Carlucci, who succeeded Poindexter in December 1986. When Carlucci was appointed Secretary of Defense, he was replaced by Army General Colin Powell in November 1987.

*Evaluation.* Until the arrival of Carlucci, the Reagan NSC structure lacked a strong, politically attuned National Security Adviser that had characterized Administrations since

1961. It also lacked the administrative structure that existed under Eisenhower, Nixon, Ford, and Carter. The absence of either influential NSC Advisers or effective administrative machinery has been seen by many critics as a major factor contributing to the Iran-Contra misadventures. Allowing NSC committees to be chaired by Cabinet officials tended to reduce the possibility that all sides of a given issue would be laid before the full NSC or the President. The Tower Board noted:

> Most presidents have set up interagency committees at both a staff and policy level to surface issues, develop options, and clarify choices. There has typically been a struggle for the chairmanship of these groups between the National Security Adviser and the NSC staff on the one hand, and the cabinet secretaries and department officials on the other.
>
> Our review of the operation of the present system and that of other administrations where committee chairmen came from the Departments has led us to the conclusion that the system generally operates better when the committees are chaired by the individual with the greatest stake in making the NSC system work.
>
> We recommend that the National Security Adviser chair the senior-level committees of the NSC system [44]

The Reagan Administration, in its efforts to avoid the dominant influence wielded by previous NSC Advisers, fell victim to perpetual bureaucratic intrigues. The efforts of politically weak NSC Advisers, especially McFarlane and Poindexter, to undertake White House initiatives covertly over the strong opposition of senior Cabinet officials and congressional leaders called into question the basic competence of the Administration.

Another aspect of the Reagan NSC that came under heavy criticism was the involvement of NSC staff in covert actions. Although NSC staff efforts to manage certain crises, such as the capture of the Achille Lauro hijackers, were successful, the participation of NSC personnel, especially Lt. Col. Oliver North, in operations run apart from the traditional intelligence apparatus, including efforts to gain the release of American hostages and to supply Nicaraguan insurgents, has been widely censured. Such efforts have been criticized as undercutting the agencies with responsibilities for such operations and which are accountable to congressional oversight committees; secondly, failing to take full advantage of the professional expertise available to the Intelligence Community, and potentially involving the country in misguided ventures. The Iran- Contra Committee recommended that "the members and staff of the NSC not engage in covert actions" [45].

Reagan's final two NSC Advisers, Carlucci and Powell, brought a period of greater stability to NSC operations and both eschewed participation in covert actions. After Poindexter's departure, Carlucci created a Senior Review Group that he himself chaired and that was composed of statutory NSC members (besides the President and Vice President). He also established a Policy Review Group that was chaired by his deputy and composed of second-ranking officials of NSC agencies.

President Reagan's own role in the details of national security policymaking remains unclear. His policies on U.S.-Soviet relations, support for an aggressive struggle against international communism, and the need for strong military forces, including strategic defenses were well- known; such positions provided the overall goals for Administration officials. It is generally acknowledged, however, that unlike some of his predecessors, President Reagan did not himself engage in detailed monitoring of policy implementation. Some maintain that his NSC structure and the absence of strong NSC Advisers led directly to bureaucratic gridlock and ill-advised involvement of the NSC staff in covert actions. Others have concluded that the experience of the Reagan Administration demonstrates that a strong and efficient National Security Adviser and staff has become essential to national security policymaking, especially if the President himself does not provide detailed direction. The absence of such an Adviser, it is argued, will undermine the development and implementation of effective national security policies. Some subsequent historians, however, give Reagan higher marks for overall national security policy even if his NSC staff was often in flux.

## The George H.W. Bush NSC, 1989-1993

The Bush Administration saw the return of Brent Scowcroft as National Security Adviser. His tenure was marked by the absence of public confrontations with Cabinet officers and a close working relationship with the President. National Security Directive 1 (NSD- 1) established three NSC sub-groups. The NSC Principals Committee, was composed of the Secretaries of State and Defense, the DCI, the Chairman of the JCS, the Chief of Staff to the President, and the National Security Adviser, who was the chairman. The NSC Deputies Committee, chaired by the Deputy National Security Adviser, was composed of second-ranking officials. There were also a number of NSC Policy Coordinating Committees, chaired by senior officials of the departments most directly concerned with NSC staff members serving as executive secretaries.

The Bush NSC structure most closely resembled that of the Nixon and Ford Administrations in providing for a National Security Adviser chairing most of the key committees. The key differences lay in the personalities involved and the fact that political divisions over foreign policy, while important, lacked some of the emotional heat caused by controversies over Vietnam and Nicaragua. Secretary of State James Baker was a powerful figure in the Administration and a longtime political associate of the President; similarly, Secretary of Defense Dick Cheney himself had White House experience as chief of staff in the Ford Administration and served in a leadership post in the House of Representatives. On occasion, however, Bush did formulate policy within a narrow circle of White House aides [46].

*Evaluation.* Whether because of the personalities of NSC principals, the structure of NSC committees or the determination among political opponents to concentrate on the domestic economy, the Bush NSC did not come in for the heavy criticisms that were levied against most of its predecessors. Most observers would probably judge that the Bush Administration created a reasonably effective policymaking machinery and avoided the mistakes of some of its predecessors. Arguably, a standard NSC organization had been created. The Administration successfully addressed most issues that resulted from the breakup of the Soviet Union and the unification of Germany along with the conduct of Desert Storm.

## The Clinton NSC, 1993-2001

President Clinton came into office with a determination to focus on domestic issues. His Administration sought to emphasize connections between international concerns and the domestic economy in such areas as trade, banking, and environmental standards. Anthony Lake, who had resigned in protest from the NSC Staff in the Nixon Administration and later served in the State Department in the Carter Administration, was appointed National Security Adviser, and continued in office until he resigned in March 1997. Lake's deputy, Samuel R. Berger, succeeded him, remaining until the end of the Clinton Administration.

With the end of the Cold War, it was widely acknowledged that there was a need for closer integration of national security policy and international economic policy. A major Clinton Administration initiative was the establishment of a National Economic Council (NEC) to coordinate international economic policy which, many observers believed, had usually received short shrift from NSC staffs focused narrowly on diplomatic and security issues. The NEC, initially headed by Robert Rubin who would subsequently become Treasury Secretary in 1995, was charged with coordinating closely with the NSC. To facilitate coordination some NEC staff were "double-hatted" as NSC officials. The close relationship has been credited with enhancing policy coordination at senior White House levels, although, according to some observers, the original promise was not realized as many aspects of international economic and trade policies became parts of major political disputes such as the North American Free Trade Agreement and most-favored-nation status for China [47].

Some observers would have preferred to include a stronger international economic component within the NSC itself, but others have raised strong objections to such an approach on the grounds that national security policymaking, in significant measure the province of diplomats and military officers, is not as closely related to domestic political concerns as international economic policy. Proponents of the latter view argue that economic issues inevitably involve concerns of various domestic groups and the NSC is ill-suited to integrate them into its policymaking processes.

Presidential Decision Directive (PDD) 2, Organization of the National Security Council, issued on January 20, 1993, expanded the NSC to include, in addition to statutory members and advisers, the Secretary of the Treasury, the U.S. Representative to the United Nations, the Assistant to the President for Economic Policy, and the Chief of Staff to the President. The Attorney General attended relevant meetings including those that discuss covert actions. The National Security Adviser determined the agenda of NSC meetings and ensured the preparation of necessary papers.

The Clinton NSC continued the practice of designating the National Security Adviser as chairman of the Principals Committee of Cabinet-level officers. At a lower level, a Deputies Committee was chaired by the Deputy Assistant to the President for National Security Affairs and included representatives of the key Cabinet departments (as well as the Assistant to the Vice President for National Security Affairs). The Deputies Committee was also responsible for day-to-day crisis management.

In addition, provision was made for a system of Interagency Working Groups, (IWG) some permanent, some ad hoc, to be established by the direction of the Deputies Committee and chaired by representatives of the relevant departments, the NEC or the NSC staff. The IWGs convened on a regular basis to review and coordinate the implementation of Presidential decisions in their policy areas.

Evaluation. In general, the Clinton NSC did not see the internecine bureaucratic warfare that had surfaced in earlier administrations. PDD 2 provided for a strong NSC staff. Lake, in his writings on national security policymaking prior to becoming National Security Adviser, reflected a keen appreciation of the disadvantages of bureaucratic infighting. He subsequently recalled that when he came into office, "My model for a national security adviser was that of the behind-the-scenes consensus builder who helped present the communal views of senior advisers to the President." After some months, nonetheless, Lake

> decided to change my approach. I would stay behind the scenes.... And I would do my best always to try to achieve consensus and to make sure that my colleagues' views always had a fair hearing with the President. But I would be less hesitant in voicing my own views when they differed from those of my colleagues, even if it prevented consensus or put me more at odds with them—whether on NATO enlargement, Bosnia, Haiti, or other issues [48]

In 1999, the Clinton NSC staff played an important and influential role in shaping policy regarding Kosovo. Carefully attuned to shifts in U.S. public opinion, Berger, who succeeded Lake as National Security Adviser in March 1997, reportedly focused on the political dimension of policymaking and sought to avoid options that might lead to paralyzing debate in this country or other NATO states. He is reported to have helped the Administration steer a middle course between those who recommended a ground campaign against Serbia and those more ready to compromise with the Yugoslav leadership and, as a result, the Administration maintained a strong sense of unity throughout the Kosovo campaign. One press account suggested that "What may be Berger 's distinctive accomplishment is to have put himself so preeminently at the center of decision-making while minimizing the historic antagonisms between national security advisers and secretaries of state and defense" [49].

## The George W. Bush NSC, 2001-2009

In February 2001, President George W. Bush issued National Security Presidential Directive-1, Organization of the National Security Council System." The NSPD indicated that the NSC system was to advise and assist the President and "coordinate executive departments and agencies in the effective development and implementation" of national security policies. Among the statutory and other officials to be invited to attend NSC meetings, the Attorney General will be asked to attend meeting pertaining to his responsibilities, both matters within the Justice Department's jurisdiction and those matters arising under the Attorney General's responsibilities in accordance with 28 USC 511 to give advice and opinion on questions of law. The National Security Adviser was charged with determining the agenda, ensuring necessary papers are prepared and recording NSC actions and presidential decisions.

As has been the custom, the Principals Committee of the NSC consists of relevant department heads and relevant advisory officials, and is chaired by the National Security Adviser. When economic issues are on the agenda the National Security Adviser and the Assistant to the President for Economic Policy are to work in concert. The NSC Deputies Committees will be composed of deputy department heads, advisory officials and is chaired by the Deputy National Security Adviser. Lower-level coordination is effected by Policy Coordinating Committees which are to be chaired by appointees of the Secretary of State, another Cabinet level official or the National Security Adviser.

Subsequent to 9/11, the Intelligence Reform and Terrorism Prevention Act (P.L. 108-458) abolished the position of Director of Central Intelligence and established a new position of Director of National Intelligence (DNI) with enhanced authorities over the entire Intelligence Community. The DNI replaced the DCI in NSC-level deliberations.

Several accounts have described the key role of the NSC in undertaking a review of U.S. options in Iraq in late 2006 that resulted in the changes in tactics and force levels that have come to be known as the Surge. Although senior officials in DOD and the State Department were known to be skeptical of increasing troop levels, NSC staffers are reported to have argued that increased numbers of U.S. forces could provide the security to the Iraqi population that would encourage political stabilization. According to these reports, in the end President Bush adopted this approach [50].

*Evaluation.* Although some observers have argued that Condoleezza Rice, as National Security Adviser in President Bush's first term, allowed the Defense Department to dominate policymaking, especially in regard to Iraq, most acknowledged that she had a good working relationship with the President and was an effective public spokesman for the Administration. Hadley made fewer public appearances but emphasized the importance of the NSC staff monitoring the implementation of NSC decisions. As noted above, he is also credited with organizing a review of Iraq policy that resulted in major changes.

## The Obama NSC, 2009-

President Obama has designated retired Marine General James L. Jones to serve as National Security Adviser. Jones had previously served as Marine Corps Commandant and as NATO's Supreme Allied Commander. On February 13, 2009, the President signed Presidential Policy Directive-1, Organization of the National Security Council System. The directive lists those who will participate in NSC deliberations, including the Attorney General, the Secretary of Homeland Security, the U.S. Representative to the U.N., and the Counsel to the President. It also makes reference to officials who will be specifically invited to sessions dealing with international economic affairs, homeland security, counterterrorism, and science and technology issues. It describes the membership and duties of the Principals and Deputies Committees, which are to be chaired by the National Security Adviser and the Deputy National Security Adviser, respectively. The Principals Committee will be the "senior interagency forum for consideration of policy issues affecting national security" while the Deputies Committee will "review and monitor the work of the NSC interagency process" and "shall be responsible for day-to-day crisis management." The use of the term "monitor" may indicate a determination to enhance the NSC's ability to oversee implementation of presidential decisions on national security issues. Further management of the development and implementation of national security policies will be overseen by interagency policy committees that shall be established to address specific issues.

In May 2009 the Administration announced its intention to integrate the staffs of the National Security Council with the Homeland Security Council into a single National Security Staff, with the goal of ending "the artificial divide between White House staff who have been dealing with national security and homeland security issues" [51]. The position of Assistant to the President for Homeland Security, currently filled by John Brennan, will be retained "with direct and immediate access" to the President, but the incumbent would organizationally report to the National Security Advisor." It is anticipated that the changes will be formalized in a new Presidential Policy Directive.

*Evaluation.* In the initial months of the Obama Administration, several steps have been taken to modify and enhance the role of the National Security Council. The integration of NSC and Homeland Security Council staffs may work to overcome the intelligence and law enforcement divide that many observers believe existed prior to 9/11. It may also facilitate closer cooperation of Federal agencies and state, local, and tribal entities in dealing with homeland security issues. These relationships are, however, complex and derive from separate statutory missions; observers suggest that establishing new organizational entities can affect, but not determine the ability of different agencies to share information and cooperate on operational planning and programs. The relationships among the relevant senior officials and the role of the President will remain crucial.

## OVERVIEW OF CURRENT NSC FUNCTIONS

Largely because of the major influence in policymaking exerted by Kissinger and Brzezinski, the position of National Security Adviser has emerged as a central one. Brzezinski was even accorded Cabinet status—the only National Security Adviser to be thus designated [52]. Some observers over the years have argued that the position should be subject to Senate confirmation and that the National Security Adviser should be available to testify before congressional committees as are officials from other Government departments and agencies [53]. Others argue that a President is entitled to confidential advice from his immediate staff. They further suggest that making the position subject to confirmation would create confusion in the eyes of foreign observers as to which U.S. officials speak authoritatively on national security policy. This latter argument is arguably undercut, however, by the practice of recent National Security Advisers of appearing on television news programs.

National Security Advisers have come from various professions; not all have had extensive experience in foreign and defense policy. The report of the Committees Investigating the Iran- Contra Affair recommended that the National Security Adviser not be an active military officer, [54] although no rationale was given for this recommendation. A substantial number of NSC staff members over the years have been career military or civil servants with backgrounds in foreign policy and defense issues. A considerable number have been detailed to the NSC staff from various federal agencies, which continue to pay their salaries. This practice has been occasionally criticized as allowing the expansion of the White House staff beyond congressional authorization; nonetheless, the practice has continued with annual reports of the number of personnel involved being made to Appropriations Committees.

Beginning with the Kennedy Administration, a concerted effort was made to bring outside experts into the NSC staff in order to inject fresh perspectives and new ideas into the policymaking process. This effort has been continued to varying extents by successive Administrations. Henry Kissinger made a particular effort to hire academic experts, although some would eventually resign and become bitter critics. The Reagan NSC was occasionally criticized for filling NSC staff positions with political activists. Most of the NSC staff positions in the George H.W. Bush Administration were filled with Government officials. Anthony Lake, President Clinton's first National Security Adviser, argues that the NSC staff

> should be made up of as many career officials as possible, with as much carryover between administrations as can be managed. Its experts should be good (but not necessarily gray) bureaucrats who know how to get things done and how to fight for their views, and who are serving the national interest more than the political interests of their President.

He cautioned that:

> a political appointee whose main credential is work on national security issues in political campaigns will have learned to think about national security issues in a partisan context. The effect of his or her advice is likely to be to lengthen the period of time during which a President, at the outset of a term, tries to make policy on the basis of campaign rhetoric rather than international reality [55]

## NSC Executive and Congressional Liaison

The very composition of the NSC, its statutory members, and those who attend meetings on occasion serve to identify those agencies and departments with which the NSC has a regular working relationship. These are the Departments of State and Defense (both the civilian and military staffs), the CIA, the Treasury Department, the Council of Economic Advisers, and a number of other departments as needed. The Director of National Intelligence, who is under the NSC, is responsible for coordinating the nation's foreign intelligence effort. His regular contacts include the CIA, as well as the Defense Intelligence Agency (DIA), the National Security Agency (NSA), the State Department's Bureau of Intelligence and Research (INR), and other elements of the intelligence community. However, these groups are not represented individually in the current NSC structure.

As part of the Executive Office of the President, the NSC does not have the same regular relationship with Congress and its committees that the member departments and agencies have. Most briefings on intelligence matters are undertaken by the CIA and DIA or by the Director of National Intelligence; information on diplomatic and military matters comes primarily from the Departments of State and Defense. As noted above, the President's Assistant for National Security Affairs is not subject to confirmation by the Senate.

Over the years there have been a considerable number of congressional hearings and reports relating to the NSC. However, many have had to do with topics peculiar to a given period:

> wiretaps against NSC staff members allegedly ordered by Dr. Kissinger, the unauthorized transfer of NSC documents to officials in the Joint Chiefs of Staff, and Watergate. Annual hearings are held concerning the NSC budget, and there have been occasional hearings concerning NSC organization and procedures. Very few of these hearings and reports have served as briefings for Congress on current issues which the NSC might have been considering. NSC appropriations are handled by the Subcommittees on Financial Services and General Government of the House and Senate Appropriations Committees.

As has been noted, Congress's role in NSC matters and its relationship with the NSC are limited. The Senate does not approve the appointment of the National Security Adviser, although it does confirm statutory NSC members Congress does have authority over the designation of those positions that are to have statutory NSC membership, as well as budgetary authority over the NSC. In 2007, as part of the Energy Independence and Security Act of 2007 (P.L. 110-140, section 932) Congress added the Secretary of Energy to the NSC. However, Congress has little direct say in matters of NSC organization, procedure, role, or influence, although a number of hearings on these topics have been held.

The NSC is not a primary and regular source of national security information for Congress. National security information is for the most part provided by those departments and agencies that are represented on the NSC. The NSC, as a corporate entity, rarely testifies before or briefs Congress on substantive questions, although in some Administrations informal briefings have been provided.

The NSC is an organ devoted to the workings of the executive branch in the broad area of national security. Its role is basically that of policy analysis and coordination and, as such, it has been subject to limited oversight and legislative control by Congress. Both in its staff organization and functioning, the NSC is extremely responsive to the preferences and working methods of each President and Administration. It would be difficult to design a uniform NSC structure that would meet the requirements of chief executives who represent a wide range of backgrounds, work styles, and policy agendas although some observers believe that the general pattern established in the final years of the Reagan Administration and followed by successive Presidents is likely to endure. There is unlikely to be a desire to drastically reduce the role of the NSC staff and most observers suggest that elevating the policymaking role of the National Security Adviser at the expense of the Secretary of State leaves Presidents subject to strong criticism.

## The NSC and International Economic Issues

The NSC has traditionally focused on foreign and defense policy issues. In the aftermath of the end of the Cold War, many observers argue that the major national security concerns of the United States may no longer be centered on traditional diplomatic and military issues. They suggest, further, that international economic, banking, environmental, and health issues, among others, will be increasingly important to the country's national security. These types of concerns, however, have not been regularly part of the NSC's primary areas of responsibility. The heads of federal agencies most directly concerned with such issues have not been members of the NSC [56].

In the 1970's, Maxwell Taylor, who President Kennedy had appointed Chairman of the JCS, argued that a National Policy Council should replace the NSC and concern itself with broad areas of international and domestic policy [57] William Hyland, an NSC official in the Reagan Administration, argued in 1980 that

> ... a bad defect in the [NSC] system is that it does not have any way of addressing international economic problems. The big economic agencies are Treasury, to some extent OMB, the Council of Economic Advisers, Commerce, Labor, and Agriculture. They are not in the NSC system, but obviously energy problems, trade, and arms sales are foreign policy

issues. Every Administration tries to drag them in, usually by means of some kind of a subcommittee or a separate committee. The committee eventually runs up against some other committee. There is friction, and policies are made on a very ad hoc basis by the principal cabinet officers [58].

In early 1992, Professor Ernest May of Harvard University testified to the Senate Select Committee on Intelligence:

> In the early 1980s, the greatest foreign threat was default by Mexico and Brazil. That could have brought down the American banking system. Despite good CIA analysis and energetic efforts by some NSC staffers, the question did not get on the NSC agenda for more than two years. And then, the policy issues did not get discussed. The agencies concerned with money and banking had no natural connection with either the NSC or the intelligence community. We have no reason to suppose that agencies concerned with the new [post Cold War] policy issues will be any more receptive [59].

In the George H.W. Bush Administration, there remained a strong conviction that defense and foreign policy issues would remain vital and somewhat separate from other interests and that the NSC was the proper forum for them to be addressed. Before he became President Bush's National Security Adviser, Brent Scowcroft stated at a forum on national security policy organization:

> First of all, if there is a consensus ... that the NSC net ought to be spread ever wider, I am not a part of it. There are many things that the NSC system can do better, and it has enough on its plate now. I would not look toward its spreading its net wider [60].

As noted above, the Clinton Administration implemented its determination to coordinate foreign and domestic economic policies more closely. The National Economic Council, established by Executive Order 12835 on January 25, 1993, was designed to "coordinate the economic policy- making process with respect to domestic and international economic issues." Close linkage with the NSC were to be achieved by having the Assistant to the President for Economic Policy also sit on the NSC, supplemented by assigning staff to support both councils. The goal was to ensure that the economic dimensions of national security policy would be properly weighed in the White House decision-making process. Observers consider that cooperation between the NSC and the NEC was productive and contributed to the enhancement of both national security and economic policymaking although one senior NSC official has noted that efforts to deal with the 1997 Asian financial crisis were initially coordinated by U.S. international economic policymakers with little input from national security and foreign policy agencies [61].

## The Growing Importance of Law Enforcement Issues

The post-Cold War era has seen a much closer relationship between traditional national security concerns with international issues that have a significant law enforcement component such as terrorism and narcotics smuggling [62]. The increasing intermingling of national security and law enforcement issues could cause major difficulties for the NSC staff and the National Security Adviser who is not a law enforcement official. The Justice Department will inevitably view with concern any incursion into what is regarded as the Attorney General's constitutional responsibilities. The NSC also coordinates with the Office of Drug Control Policy whose responsibilities also encompass both law enforcement and foreign policy considerations.

In dealing with international terrorism or narcotics production and transport from foreign countries, however, diplomatic and national security issues are often involved. Apprehending a terrorist group may require cooperation from a foreign government that has its own interests and concerns. Narcotics production may be entwined in the social and economic fabric of a foreign country to an extent that precludes the country from providing the sort of cooperation that would be expected from a major ally. During the Clinton Administration, the Attorney General's representatives have been included in NSC staff deliberations when law enforcement concerns were involved. Nonetheless, observers note public disagreements between Justice Department and State Department, for instance, regarding cooperation (or the lack thereof) from Saudi Arabia or Yemen. Clearly, the President has constitutional responsibilities for both national security and law enforcement, but the status of any other official to make necessary trade-offs is unclear. Observers suggest that in some future cases the need to establish a single U.S. position may require different ways of integrating national security and law enforcement concerns. The Obama Administration took a significant step in this direction by establishing a single National Security Staff composed of the staffs of both the National Security Council and the Homeland Security Council.

Today's international terrorist threat can encompass not only physical attacks on U.S. physical structures such as the World Trade Center, but also cyber-attacks on critical infrastructures, the computerized communications and data storage systems on which U.S. society has become reliant. Since such systems are in most cases owned and operated by corporations and other commercial entities, the role of the NSC is necessarily constrained. Much depends on law enforcement as well as voluntary cooperation by the private sector. The Clinton Administration created the position of National Coordinator for Security, Infrastructure Protection, and Counterterrorism who reported to the President through the National Security Adviser [63]. The Intelligence Reform Act of 2004, however, established the National Counterterrorism Center outside the NSC structure.

In dealing with policies related to the protection of critical infrastructures, the National Security Adviser will have an important role, but one inherently different from the traditional responsibilities of the office.64 The position could involve in coordination of responses to threats both in the U.S. and from abroad and among the federal government, the states, and the private sector. It is clear to all observers that such coordination involves much uncharted territory, including a concern by some that the National Security Adviser might become overly and inappropriately involved in law enforcement matters.

## The Role of the National Security Adviser

The NSC was created by statute, and its membership has been designated and can be changed by statute. The NSC has also been subject to statutorily approved reorganization processes within the executive branch, as when it was placed in the Executive Office by a

Reorganization Plan in August 1949. Nonetheless, the NSC has been consistently regarded as a presidential entity with which Congress is rarely involved. The internal organization and roles of the NSC have been changed by Presidents and by National Security Advisers in response to their preferences and these changes have not usually been subject to congressional scrutiny.

The role of the National Security Adviser has, however, become so well established in recent years that Congress has been increasingly prepared to grant the incumbent significant statutory responsibilities. The Foreign Intelligence Surveillance Act and other legislation provides for statutory roles for the National Security Adviser. 65 Executive Orders provide other formal responsibilities. The position has become institutionalized and the exercise of its functions has remained an integral part of the conduct of national security policy in all recent administrations.

Some observers believe that these established duties which extend beyond the offering of advice and counsel to the President will inevitably lead to a determination to include the appointment of a National Security Adviser among those requiring the advice and consent of the Senate. Advice and consent by the Senate is seen as providing a role for the legislative branch in the appointment of one of the most important officials in the federal government. Another cited advantage of this proposal would be the increased order, regularity, and formalization that are involved in making appointments that are sent to the Senate. Proponents argue that this would ultimately provide greater accountability for NSC influence and decisions. Opponents on the other hand, might point to the danger of unnecessary rigidity and stratification of organization and the potential that appointments might be excessively influenced by political considerations. There is also a potential that the NSC staff might become irrelevant if it loses the trust of a future President or if its procedures become so formalized as to stultify policymaking. Should the Adviser be subject to Senate confirmation, it is argued that an important prerogative of the President to choose his immediate staff would be compromised. In addition, the incumbent could be required or expected to make routine appearances before congressional oversight committees, arguably undermining the primary purpose of the National Security Adviser which is to provide the President with candid advice on a wide range of issues, often on an informal and confidential basis.

One historian has summed up the role of the National Security Adviser:

> The entire national security system must have confidence that the [National Security Adviser] will present alternate views fairly and will not take advantage of propinquity in the coordination of papers and positions. He must be able to present bad news to the president and to sniff out and squelch misbehavior before it becomes a problem. He must be scrupulously honest in presenting presidential decisions and in monitoring the implementation process. Perhaps most important, he must impart the same sense of ethical behavior to the Staff he leads [66].

In a recent assessment, two informed observers listed tasks for which the Adviser and staff uniquely are responsible:

–   Staffing the president's daily foreign policy activity: his communications with foreign leaders and the preparation and conduct of his trips overseas;

- Managing the process of making decisions on major foreign and national security issues; -Driving the policymaking process to make real choices, in a timely manner;
- Overseeing the full implementation of the decision the president has made [67].

The increasing difficulties in separating national security issues from some law enforcement and international economic concerns has led some observers to urge that the lines separating various international staffs at the White House be erased and that a more comprehensive policymaking entity be created. It is argued that such reforms could most effectively be accomplished without legislation [68]. The Project for National Security Reform (PNSR) a nonpartisan task force that has studied the structure of national policymaking has made a number of far-reaching proposals for expanding the role of a national security director and combining the National Security Council and the Homeland Security Council [69].

As noted above, President Obama put this latter recommendation into practice in May 2009. Such initiatives raise complex questions, including the role of congressional oversight. Whereas Congress has traditionally deferred to White House leadership in national security matters, to a far greater extent than in international economic affairs, there might be serious questions about taking formal steps to place resolution of a wide range of international policies, including economic and law enforcement issues, in the hands of officials who receive little congressional oversight.

It is likely, in any event, that Congress will continue to monitor the functioning of the staff and the Adviser in the context of U.S. policymaking in a changing international environment.

## SELECTED BIBLIOGRAPHY

The most comprehensive source concerning the genesis and development of the NSC through 1960 is contained in a collection of hearings, studies, reports and recommendations complied by Senator Henry M. Jackson and published as U.S. Congress. Senate. Committee on Government Operations. Subcommittee on National Policy Machinery. Organizing for National Security, 3 Vols. 86th and 87th Congress. Washington, Government Printing Office. [1961]. Presidential memoirs are also valuable.

Other useful sources are:

Anderson, Dillon. "The President and National Security." *Atlantic Monthly*, January 1966.

Bock, Joseph G. "The National Security Assistant and the White House Staff: National Security Policy Decisionmaking and Domestic Political Considerations, 1947-1984." *Presidential Studies Quarterly*, Spring 1986. Pp. 258-279.

Bowie, Robert R. and Richard H. Immerman. Waging Peace: How Eisenhower Shaped an Enduring Cold War Strategy. New York: Oxford University Press. 1998.

Brown, Cody M. The National Security Council: A Legal History of the President's Most Powerful Advisers. Washington: Project for National Security Reform. 2008.

Brzezinski, Zbigniew. Power and Principle: Memoirs of the National Security Adviser, 19 77-1981. New York: Farrar, Straus, Giroux. 1983.

———"The NSC's Midlife Crisis". *Foreign Policy*, Winter 1987-1988. Pp. 80-99.

Bock, Joseph G., and Clarke, Duncan L. "The National Security Assistant and the White House Staff: National Security Policy Decisionmaking and Domestic Political Considerations, 1947- 1984." *Political Science Quarterly,* Spring 1986. Pp. 258-279.

Brown, Cody M. The National Security Council: A Legal History of the President's Most Powerful Advisers. Washington: Project for National Security Reform. 2008.

Bumiller, Elisabeth. Condoleezza Rice: An American Life: A Biography. New York: Random House. 2007.

Burke, John P. Honest Broker: the National Security Advisor and Presidential Decision Making. College Station, TX: Texas A & M University Press. 2009.

Caraley, Demetrios. *The Politics of Military Unification.* New York: Columbia University Press. [1966].

Clark, Keith C., and Laurence S. Legere, eds. "The President and the Management of National Security". *Report for the Institute for Defense Analyses.* New York: Praeger. [1966]. See especially pp. 55-114.

Commission on the Organization of the Executive Branch of the Government. National Security Organization. Washington: Government Printing Office. [1949].

Commission on the Organization of the Government for the Conduct of Foreign Policy. Report. Washington: Government Printing Office. [1975].

Cutler, Robert. No Time for Rest. Boston: Little, Brown. 1966.

"The Development of the National Security Council". *Foreign Affairs*, April 1956. Pp. 441- 58.

Daalder, Ivo H., and Destler, I.M. In the Shadow of the Oval Office: Profiles of the National Security Advisers and the Presidents They Served—from JFK to George W. Bush. New York: Simon and Schuster. 2009.

Destler, I.M. "Can One Man Do?" *Foreign Policy*, Winter 197 1-72. Pp. 28-40.

"National Security Advice to U.S. Presidents: Some Lessons from Thirty Years." *World Politics*, January 1977. Pp. 143-76.

Presidents, Bureaucrats and Foreign Policy: The Politics of Organization. Princeton: Princeton University Press. [1972].

Lake, Anthony; and Gelb, Leslie H. Our Own Worst Enemy: The Unmaking of American Foreign Policy. New York: Simon and Schuster. 1984.

Falk, Stanley L., and Theodore W. Bauer. *"The National Security Structure."* Washington: Industrial College of the Armed Forces. [1972].

Greenstein, Fred I. and Richard H. Immerman. "Effective National Security Advising: Recovering the Eisenhower Legacy." *Political Science Quarterly, Fall* 2000. Pp. 335-345.

Haig, Alexander M., Jr. *Caveat: Realism, Reagan, and Foreign Policy.* New York: Macmillan. 1984.

Hammond, Paul Y. "The National Security Council as a Device for Interdepartmental Coordination: An Interpretation and Appraisal". *American Political Science Review*, December 1960. Pp. 899-910.

Humphrey, David C. "NSC Meetings during the Johnson Presidency". *Diplomatic History*, Winter 1994. Pp. 29-45.

Hunter, Robert E. Organizing for National Security. Washington: Center for Strategic and International Studies. 1988.

Inderfurth, Karl F. and Johnson, Loch K., eds. Decisions of the Highest Order: Perspectives of the National Security Council. Pacific Grove, CA: Brooks/Cole Publishing Co. 1988.

Johnson, Robert H. "The National Security Council: The Relevance of its Past to its Future". *Orbis, Fall* 1969. Pp. 709-35.

Kissinger, Henry A. White House Years. Boston: Little, Brown. 1979. ——Years of Renewal. New York: Simon & Schuster. 1999. ——Years of Upheaval. Boston: Little, Brown. 1982.

Kolodziej, Edward A. "The National Security Council: Innovations and Implications". *Public Administration Review.* November/December 1969. Pp. 573-85.

Korb, Lawrence J. and Hahn, Keith D., eds. National Security Policy Organization in Perspective. Washington: American Enterprise Institute. 1981.

Laird, Melvin R. Beyond the Tower Commission. Washington: American Enterprise Institute. 1987.

Lake, Anthony. 6 Nightmares. Boston: Little, Brown. 2000. ——Somoza Failing. Boston: Houghton Mifflin. 1989.

Lay, James S., Jr. "National Security Council's Role in the U.S. Security and Peace Program". *World Affairs*, Summer 1952. Pp. 33-63.

Leacacos, John P. "Kissinger's Apparat". *Foreign Policy*, Winter 1971-72. Pp. 3-27.

Lord, Carnes. "NSC Reform for the Post-Cold War Era," Orbis, Summer 2000. Pp. 433-450. McFarlane, Robert C. "Effective Strategic Policy." *Foreign Affairs*, Fall 1988. Pp. 33-48. with Richard Saunders and Thomas C. Shull. "The National Security Council: Organization for Policy Making." *Proceedings of the Center for the Study of the Presidency.* Vol. 5. 1984. Pp. 261-273.

Head, Richard G., and Frisco W. Short. Crisis Resolution, Presidential Decision Making in the Mayaguez and Korean Confrontations. Boulder, CO: Westview Press. 1978.

Menges, Constantine C. Inside the National Security Council: The True Story of the Making and Unmaking of Reagan's Foreign Policy. New York: Simon and Schuster. 1988.

Mulcahy, Kevin V. and Crabb, Cecil V. "Presidential Management of National Security Policy Making, 1947-1987". In The Managerial Presidency, ed. by James P. Pfiffner. Pacific Grove, CA: Brooks/Cole. 1991. Pp. 250-264.

Nelson, Anna Kasten. "President Truman and the Evolution of the National Security Council." *Journal of American History*, September 1985. Pp. 360-378. "The 'Top of the Policy Hill': President Eisenhower and the National Security Council." *Diplomatic History*, Fall 1983. Pp. 307-326.

Nixon, Richard M. U.S. Foreign Policy for the 1970's: A New Strategy for Peace. Washington: Government Printing Office. [1970]. U.S. Foreign Policy for the 1970's: The Emerging Structure of Peace. Washington: Government Printing Office. [1971]. U.S. Foreign Policy for the 1970's: Building for Peace. Washington: Government Printing Office. [1972].

Powell, Colin L. "The NSC System in the Last Two Years of the Reagan Administration". *The Presidency in Transition.* Ed. by James P. Pfiffner and R. Gordon Hoxie. New York: Center for the Study of the Presidency, 1989. Pp. 204-2 18.

Prados, John. Keepers of the Keys: A History of the National Security Council from Truman to Bush. New York: William Morrow. 1991.

Rothkopf, David. *Running the World: the Inside Story of the National Security Council and the Architects of American Power*. New York: Public Affairs.2004.

Rostow, Walt Whitman. *The Diffusion of Power: An Essay in Recent History*. New York: Macmillan. 1972.

Sander, Alfred D. "Truman and the National Security Council, 1945-1947". *Journal of American History*, September 1972. Pp. 369-388.

Schlesinger, Arthur, Jr. "Effective National Security Advising: A Most Dubious Precedent." *Political Science Quarterly*, Fall 2000. Pp. 347-351.

Shoemaker, Christopher C. The NSC Staff: Counseling the Council. Boulder, CO: Westview Press. 1991.

Souers, Sidney W. "Policy Formulation for National Security". American *Political Science Review*, June 1949. Pp. 534-43.

Steiner, Barry H. "Policy Organization in American Security Affairs: An Assessment". *Public Administration Review*, July/August 1977. Pp. 357-67.

Thayer, Frederick C. "Presidential Policy Process and 'New Administration': A Search for Revised Paradigms". *Public Administration Review*, September/October 1971. Pp. 552-61.

U.S. Congress. Senate. Committee on Government Operations. Subcommittee on National Security and International Operations. The National Security Council: New role and structure. 91st Congress, 1st session. Washington: Government Printing Office. 1969.

Select Committee on Secret Military Assistance to Iran and the Nicaraguan Opposition. House of Representatives. Select Committee to Investigate Covert Arms Transactions with Iran. 100th Congress, 1st session. Report of the Congressional Committees Investigating the Iran-Contra Affair with Supplemental, Minority, and Additional Views, Senate Report 100-216/House Report 100-433. Washington: Government Printing Office. 1987.

Committee on Government Operations. Subcommittee on National Security and International Operations. The National Security Council: Comment by Henry Kissinger. March 3, 1970. 91st Congress, 2nd Session. Washington: Government Printing Office. 1970.

U.S. Department of State. "The National Security System: Responsibilities of the Department of State." *Department of State Bulletin*, February 24, 1969. Pp. 163-66.

U.S. President's Special Review Board. Report of the President's Special Review Board. Washington: Government Printing Office. 1987.

West, Bing. *The Strongest Tribe*: *War, Politics and the Endgame in Iraq*. New York. Random House. 2008.

Yost, Charles W. "The Instruments of American Foreign Policy," *Foreign Affairs,* October 1971. Pp. 59-68.

Zegart, Amy B. Flawed by Design: the Evolution of the CIA, JCS, and NSC. Stanford, CA: Stanford University Press, 1999.

*Note*: Many of the above entries contain numerous footnotes that identify a wealth of primary and secondary sources too numerous to include here. Of special interest are the oral interviews of former NSC staff personnel conducted from 1998 to 2000 as part of the National Security

Council Project undertaken by the Center for International and Security Studies at Maryland and the Brookings Institution; transcripts are available at http://w ww.cissm.umd.edu/projects/nsc.php. Also useful is the transcript of "A Forum on the Role of the National Security Adviser," cosponsored by the Woodrow Wilson International Center for Scholars and the James A. Baker III Institute for Public Policy of Rice University, available at http://wwics.si.edu/news/docs/nsa.pdf.

## APPENDIX A. NATIONAL SECURITY ADVISERS

### Table A-1. National Security Advisers, 1953-2009

| | | |
|---|---|---|
| Robert Cutler | March 23, 1953 | April 2, 1955 |
| Dillon Anderson | April 2, 1955 | September 1, 1956 |
| Robert Cutler | January 7, 1957 | June 24, 1958 |
| Gordon Gray | June 24, 1958 | January 13, 1961 |
| McGeorge Bundy | January 20, 1961 | February 28, 1966 |
| Walt W. Rostow | April 1, 1966 | January 20, 1969 |
| Henry A. Kissinger | January 20, 1969 | November 3, 1975 |
| Brent Scowcroft | November 3, 1975 | January 20, 1977 |
| Zbigniew Brzezinski | January 20, 1977 | January 21, 1981 |
| Richard V. Allen | January 21, 1981 | January 4, 1982 |
| William P. Clark | January 4, 1982 | October 17, 1983 |
| Robert C. McFarlane | October 17, 1983 | December 4, 1985 |
| John M. Poindexter | December 4, 1985 | November 25, 1986 |
| Frank C. Carlucci | December 2, 1986 | November 23, 1987 |
| Colin L. Powell | November 23, 1987 | January 20, 1989 |
| Brent Scowcroft | January 20, 1989 | January 20, 1993 |
| W. Anthony Lake | January 20, 1993 | March 14, 1997 |
| Samuel R. Berger | March 14, 1997 | January 20, 2001 |
| Condoleezza Rice | January 22, 2001 | January 25, 2005 |
| Stephen Hadley | January 26, 2005 | January 20, 2009 |
| James L. Jones | January 20, 2009 | Present |

## REFERENCES

[1] Paul Y. Hammond, "The National Security Council as a Device for Interdepartmental Coordination: An Interpretation and Appraisal," *American Political Science Review*, December, 1960, p. 899; U.S. Bureau of the Budget, *The United States at War* (Washington: Government Printing Office, 1946), p. 2.

[2]   Mark Skinner Watson, *Chief of Staff: Prewar Plans and Preparations* (Washington: Office of the Chief of Military History, 1950), pp. 89-91, 93-94.

[3]   R. Elberton Smith, *The Army and Economic Mobilization* (Washington: Office of the Chief of Military History, 1959), pp. 103-04, 109-10; Bureau of the Budget, *The United States at War*, pp. 22-25, 44, 50-51.

[4]   Ray S. Cline, *Washington Command Post: The Operations Division* (Washington: Office of the Chief of Military History, 1951), pp. 326-27; John Lewis Gaddis, *The United States and the Origins of the Cold War* (New York, Columbia University Press, 1972), p. 126; U.S. Department of State, *Foreign Relations of the United States, 1944, v. I: General* (Washington: Government Printing Office, 1966), pp. 1466-70.

[5]   One of the best studies on the creation and development of the NSC through the Eisenhower Administration, including hearings, studies, reports, recommendations and articles, can be found in U.S. Congress, Senate, 86th and 87th Congress, Committee on Government Operations, Subcommittee on National Policy Machinery, *Organizing for National Security,* 1961, 3 vols.

[6]   Demetrios Caraley, *The Politics of Military Unification* (New York: Columbia University Press, 1966), pp. 23-44; Walter Millis, ed., *The Forrestal Diaries* (New York: The Viking Press, 1951), pp. 62-63.

[7]   Caraley, *The Politics of Military Unification*, pp. 40-41; see also Jeffrey M. Dorwart, *Eberstadt and Forrestal: A National Security Partnership, 1909-1 949* (College Station, TX: Texas A & M University Press, 1991), especially pp. 90-107.

[8]   Ibid., pp. 86-87, 91; Hammond, "The NSC as a Device for Interdepartmental Coordination," pp. 900-01.

[9]   Caraley, *Politics of Military Unification*, pp. 136-37; Millis, *Forrestal Diaries*, p. 222.

[10]  The congressional debate over the National Security Act is summarized in Caraley, *Politics of Military Unification*, pp. 153-82; on the NSC, see p. 161. Examples of congressional opinion can be found throughout the lengthy debate. Some representative comments can be found in the *Congressional Record*, v. 93, July 7, 1947, p. 8299, and July 9, 1947, pp. 8496-97, 8518, 8520.

[11]  50 USC 402.

[12]  More specific information on the history of the transfers of defense mobilization and civil defense authorities may be found in Sections 402 and 404 of *U.S. Code Annotated*, Title 50 (St. Paul, MN: West Publishing Co., 1991)

[13]  The Commission on the Organization of the Executive Branch of the Government. *National Security Organization* (Washington: Government Printing Office, 1949), especially pp. 15-16, 74-76.

[14]  Walter Millis, *Arms and the State* (New York: The Twentieth Century Fund, 1958), pp. 255, 388.

[15]  Anna Kasten Nelson, "President Truman and the Evolution of the National Security Council," *Journal of American History*, September 1985, p. 377.

[16]  This position has been a continuing one, although its title has varied over the years (Special Assistant for National Security Affairs, Assistant to the President for National Security Affairs, National Security Adviser). An adviser or an assistant to the President arguably has a position of greater independence from congressional oversight than the incumbent of a position established by statute; see Richard Ehlke, "Congressional

Creation of an Office of National Security Adviser to the President," reprinted in U.S. Congress, 96th Congress, 2d session, Senate, Committee on Foreign Relations, *The National Security Adviser: Role and Accountability*, Hearing, April 17, 1980, pp. 133-135. The position of National Security Adviser is to be distinguished from the position of Executive Secretary of the NSC, which was created by statute but has, since the beginning of the Eisenhower Administration, been essentially an administrative and logistical one. National Security Adviser positions are funded not as part of the NSC but as part of the White House Office, reflecting the incumbent's status as that of an adviser to the President.

[17] Frederick C. Thayer, "Presidential Policy Processes and 'New Administration': A Search for Revised Paradigms," *Public Administration Review*, September/October 1971: 554. Robert H. Johnson, "The National Security Council: The Relevance of its Past to Its Future," *Orbis*, v. 13, Fall 1969: 715; Robert Cutler, *No Time for Rest* (Boston: Little, Brown, 1966).

[18] Some Eisenhower-era NSC documents are reprinted in the State Department's *Foreign Relations of the United States* series, especially in volumes dealing with National Security Affairs; microfilm copies of declassified NSC documents have been made available by a commercial publisher, University Publications of America, Inc. NSC documents are usually highly classified; while some are subsequently declassified and released to the public (although not necessarily in the Federal Register or other official publications series), others have been withheld. Some observers have criticized this situation; see Harold C. Relyea, "The Coming of Secret Law," *Government Information Quarterly*, May 1988, pp. 106-112; U.S. General Accounting Office, "The Use of Presidential Directives to Make and Implement U.S. Policy," Report No. GAO/NSIAD-92-72, January 1992.

[19] The hearings and reports of this study are cited in note 5.

[20] See Anna Kasten Nelson, "The 'Top of Policy Hill': President Eisenhower and the National Security Council," *Diplomatic History*, Fall 1983, p. 324; also, Stephen E. Ambrose, *The President* (New York: Simon and Schuster, 1984), pp. 345, 509.

[21] Robert R. Bowie and Richard H. Immerman, *Waging Peace: How Eisenhower Shaped an Enduring Cold War Strategy* New York: Oxford University Press, 1998), p. 258. Recent support for the Eisenhower system is given in Fred I. Greenstein and Richard H. Immerman, "Effective National Security Advising: Recovering the Eisenhower Legacy," *Political Science Quarterly*, Fall 2000; criticism is renewed in Arthur Schlesinger, Jr., "Effective National Security Advising: A Most Dangerous Precedent," *Political Science Quarterly*, Fall 2000.

[22] Thayer, "Presidential Policy Processes and 'New Administration,'" p. 555.

[23] Arthur M. Schlesinger, Jr., *A Thousand Days: John F. Kennedy in the White House* (Boston: Houghton Mifflin, 1965), pp. 406-47; see especially pp. 412-13, 426, 430-32.

[24] Kai Bird, *The Color of Truth: McGeorge Bundy and William Bundy: Brothers in Arms* (New York: Simon & Schuster, 1998), p. 186.

[25] McGeorge Bundy to Henry M. Jackson, September 4, 1961, reprinted in *Organizing for National Security*, I, 1338.

[26] Much of the documentary basis of the Nixon NSC effort is provided in U.S., Department of State, *Foreign Relations of the United States, 1969-1976*, Vol. II,

*Organization and Management of U.S. Foreign Policy, 1969-1972* (Washington, DC: Government Printing Office, 2006).

[27] Commission on the Organization of the Government for the Conduct of Foreign Policy, Report (Washington, Government Printing Office, 1975).

[28] Ibid., p. 37.

[29] Veto of a Bill to Amend the National Security Act of 1947, January 1, 1976, *Public Papers of the Presidents: Gerald R. Ford* 1976-1977 Vol. I (Washington: Government Printing Office, 1979), p. 1-2.

[30] For the Carter NSC, see Presidential Directive/NSC-1 and NSC-2, January 20, 1977; Executive Order 12036, January 24, 1978; Zbigniew Brzezinski, *Power and Principle: Memoirs of the National Security Adviser, 1977-1 981* (New York: Farrar, Straus, Giroux, 1983).

[31] Presidential Directive/NSC-2, January 20, 1977; see also Statement by White House Press Secretary, January 22, 1977, *Public Papers of the Presidents, Jimmy Carter*, 1977, Vol. I (Washington: Government Printing Office, 1977), p. 8..

[32] Presidential Directive/NSC-2.

[33] Executive Order 12036, January 24, 1978, Section 1-2.

[34] Presidential Directive/NSC-2. January 20, 1977.

[35] Executive Order 12036, January 24, 1978, Section 1-3.

[36] Executive Order 12036, January 24, 1978, Sections 1-302 to 1-304 inclusive.

[37] See Christopher C. Shoemaker, *The NSC Staff: Counseling the Council* (Boulder, CO: Westview Press, 1991), pp. 51-57.

[38] Stansfield Turner, *Terrorism and Democracy* (Boston: Houghton Mifflin, 1991), p. 58.

[39] See *National Security Adviser: Role and Accountability*.

[40] Brzezinski acknowledges but discounts the reports that Mondale had imposed certain staff members on him; see *Power and Principle*, pp. 74-78.

[41] Reprinted in *Public Papers of the Presidents, Ronald Reagan*, 1982, Vol. I (Washington: Government Printing Office, 1983), pp. 18-22.

[42] *Public Papers of the Presidents, Ronald Reagan*, 1981 (Washington: Government Printing Office, 1982), p. 285.

[43] U.S., President's Special Review Board, *Report of the President's Special Review Board* (Washington: Government Printing Office, 1987), pp. V-1-V-2. The Board consisted of former Senator John Tower, former Secretary of State Edmund Muskie and former (and future) National Security Adviser Brent Scowcroft. It is often referred to as the Tower Board.

[44] Ibid., p. V-5.

[45] U.S. Congress. Senate. Select Committee on Secret Military Assistance to Iran and the Nicaraguan Opposition. House of Representatives. Select Committee to Investigate Covert Arms Transactions with Iran. 100th Congress, 1st session. *Report of the Congressional Committees Investigating the Iran-Contra Affair with Supplemental, Minority, and Additional Views*, Senate Report 100-216/House Report 100-433, November 1987, p. 425. The Committee added that, "By statute the NSC was created to provide advice to the President on national security matters. But there is no express statutory prohibition on the NSC engaging in operational intelligence activities." Ibid.

[46] See Robert G. Sutter, "American Policy Toward Beijing, 1989-1990: the Role of President Bush and the White House Staff," *Journal of Northeast Asian Studies*, Winter 1990.

[47] The NEC was established by Executive Order 12835 on January 25, 1993; on the NEC see Kenneth I. Jester and Simon Lazarus, *Making Economic Policy: An Assessment of the National Economic Council* (Washington: Brookings Institution Press, 1997) and I.M. Destler, *The National Economic Council: A Work in Progress* (Washington: Institute for International Economics, 1996).

[48] *6 Nightmares* (Boston: Little, Brown, 2000), pp. 131,131-132.

[49] John F. Harris, "Berger's Caution Has Shaped Role of U.S. In War," *Washington Post*, May 16, 1999, p. A24.

[50] See Linda Robinson, *Tell Me How This Ends: General David Petraeus and the Search for a Way Out of Iraq* (New York: Public Affairs, 2008), pp. 26-3 6; Bing West, *The Strongest Tribe: War, Politics, and the Endgame in Iraq* (New York: Random House, 2008), pp. 197-207; Ivo H. Daalder and I.M. Destler, *In the Shadow of the Oval Office: Profiles of the National Security Advisers and the Presidents they Served from JFK to George W. Bush* (New York: Simon and Schuster, 2009), pp. 294-297.

[51] Statement by the President on the White House Organization for Homeland Security and Counterterrorism, Office of the Press Secretary, May 26, 2009.

[52] "Cabinet status" is not recognized in law, but is a distinction conferred by the President. See Ronald C. Moe, *The President's Cabinet*, CRS Report No. 86-982GOV, November 6, 1986, p. 2.

[53] There are differing views regarding linkage between Senatorial confirmation and an obligation to testify before congressional committees; see, for instance, Zbigniew Brzezinski, "NSC's Midlife Crisis," *Foreign Policy*, Winter 1987-1988, p. 95; also, the Prepared Statement of Thomas M. Franck printed in *The National Security Adviser: Role and Accountability*, pp. 40-41. For additional background, see CRS Report RL3 1351, *Presidential Advisers' Testimony Before Congressional Committees: An Overview*, by Harold C. Relyea and Todd B. Tatelman.

[54] Report of the Congressional Committees Investigating the Iran-Contra Affair, p. 426.

[55] *6 Nightmares*, pp. 261-262.

[56] There are other White House-level coordinative bodies, such as the Office of Management and Budget, the Council of Economic Advisers, the Office of the United States Trade Representative, and the Council on Environmental Quality, that do deal with such issues.

[57] Maxwell D. Taylor, *Precarious Security* (New York: W.W. Norton, 1976), pp. 113-116.

[58] Quoted in Lawrence J. Korb and Keith D. Hahn, eds., *National Security Policy Organization in Perspective* (Washington: American Enterprise Institute, 1980), p. 11.

[59] Ernest R. May, Statement for the Senate Select Committee on Intelligence, March 4, 1992; see also May's article, "Intelligence: Backing into the Future," *Foreign Affairs*, Summer 1992, especially pp. 64-66.

[60] Quoted in Korb and Hahn, eds., *National Security Policy Organization in Perspective*, p. 34.

[61] James Steinberg, "Foreign Policy: Time to Regroup," *Washington Post*, January 2, 2001, p. A15.

[62] See CRS Report RL30252, *Intelligence and Law Enforcement: Countering Transnational Threats to the U.S.*, by Richard A. Best Jr..

[63] See CRS Report RL30153, *Critical Infrastructures: Background, Policy, and Implementation*, by John D. Moteff.

[64] It has been noted that the original membership of the National Security Council included officials responsible for mobilization planning, but those offices were subsequently merged into others and are no longer represented on the NSC. The need for national mobilization to sustain a global war effort is not considered a high priority in the post-Cold War world. (See Carnes Lord, "NSC Reform in the Post-Cold War Era," Orbis, Summer 2000, pp. 449-500.) The inclusion of such officials did, nonetheless, reflect the determination of the drafters of the National Security Act that the NSC have a wide mandate in protecting the nation's security interests and one that could extend into the private sector.

[65] The Foreign Intelligence Surveillance Act of 1978, as amended, requires that applications for orders for electronic surveillance for foreign intelligence purposes include a certification regarding the need for such surveillance by the Assistant to the President for National Security Affairs (or someone else designated by the President)(50 USC 1804 (a)(7)); a similar requirement exists for applications for physical searches (50 USC 1 823(a)(7)). The Assistant to the President for National Security Affairs is also assigned as chairman of two NSC committees–the Committee on Foreign Intelligence (50 USC 402(h)(2)(D)) and the Committee on Transnational Threats (50 USC 402(i)(2)(E)). These assignments were made as part of the FY1997 Intelligence Authorization Act (P.L. 104-293); in signing it, President Clinton stated his concerns about the provisions relating to the establishment of the two NSC committees: "Such efforts to dictate the President's policy procedures unduly intrude upon Executive prerogatives and responsibilities. ("Statement on Signing the Intelligence Authorization Act for Fiscal Year 1997," October 11, 1996, *Weekly Compilation of Presidential Documents*, October 14, 1996, p. 2039). Other legislation placed the National Security Adviser on the President's Council on Counter-Narcotics (21 USC 1708(b)(1)(O)) and the Director of National Drug Control policy is required to work in conjunction with the Adviser "in any matter affecting national security interests." (21 USC 1703(b)(10)).

[66] Shoemaker, *NSC Staff: Counseling the Council*, p. 115.

[67] Ivo H. Daalder and I.M. Destler, *In the Shadow of the Oval Office: Profiles of the National Security Adviser and the Presidents They Served—From JFK to George W. Bush* (New York: Simon & Schuster, 2009), pp. 318-319.

[68] See Steinberg, "Foreign Policy: Time to Regroup."

[69] For further background, see the PNSR website, http://www.pnsr.org. See also CRS Report RL34455, *Organizing the U.S. Government for National Security: Overview of the Interagency Reform Debates,* by Catherine Dale, Nina M. Serafino, and Pat Towell.

In: U.S. Political Programs: Functions and Assessments ISBN: 978-1-61209-448-9
Editors: Julianna M. Moretti and Karen J. Chordstron © 2011 Nova Science Publishers, Inc.

*Chapter 10*

# THE GLOBAL PEACE OPERATIONS INITIATIVE: BACKGROUND AND ISSUES FOR CONGRESS\*

*Nina M. Serafino*

## ABSTRACT

In its May 2009 budget request for FY2010, the Obama Administration has requested $96.8 million for the Global Peace Operations Initiative (GPOI). GPOI was established in mid-2004 as a five-year program with intended annual funding to total $660 million from FY2005 through FY2009. (Actual funds allocated to the GPOI program from FY2005 through FY2009 totaled, as of April 2009, some $480.4 million.) The centerpiece of the Bush Administration's efforts to prepare foreign security forces to participate in international peacekeeping operations, GPOI's primary purpose has been to train and equip 75,000 military troops, a majority of them African, for peacekeeping operations by 2010. In October 2008, the National Security Council's Deputies Committee approved a five-year renewal of GPOI's mandate. Congressional approval of the FY2010 budget request would provide funding for the first year of this extension.

To date, GPOI also provides support for the Center of Excellence for Stability Police Units (CoESPU), an Italian "train-the-trainer" training center for gendarme (constabulary police) forces in Vicenza, Italy. In addition, GPOI promotes the development of an international transportation and logistics support system for peacekeepers, and encourages information exchanges to improve international coordination of peace operations training and exercises. Through GPOI, the United States supports and participates in a G\* Africa Clearinghouse and a G8++ Global Clearinghouse, both to coordinate international peacekeeping capacity building efforts.

GPOI incorporates previous capabilities-building programs for Africa. From FY1997 to FY2005, the United States spent just over $121 million on GPOI's predecessor program that was funded through the State Department Peacekeeping (PKO) account: the Clinton Administration's African Crisis Response Initiative (ACRI) and its successor, the Bush Administration's African Contingency Operations Training and Assistance (ACOTA) program. (ACOTA is now GPOI's principal training program in Africa.) Some

---

\* This is an edited, reformatted and augmented edition of a United States Congressional Research Service publication, CRS report RL32773, dated June 11, 2009.

16,000 troops from ten African nations were trained under the early ACRI/ACOTA programs. Some $33 million was provided from FY1998 to FY2005 to support classroom training of 31 foreign militaries through the Foreign Military Financing account's Enhanced International Peacekeeping Capabilities program (EIPC).

Within a year after GPOI was initiated in late 2004, the Administration began expanding its geographical scope to selected countries in Central America, Europe, and Asia. In 2006 and 2007, the program was further expanded to countries in Asia, South Asia, and the Pacific. GPOI now includes 53 "partner" countries and two partner organizations throughout the world, although the emphasis is still on Africa. According to figures provided by the State Department, almost 57,600 peacekeeper trainees and peacekeeper trainers were trained as of January 31, 2009..

Congress has tended to view the concept of the GPOI program favorably, albeit sometimes with reservations. Over the years, the State Department has addressed various congressional concerns. In a June 2008 report, the Government Accountability Office (GAO) recommended several further improvements (GAO-08-754).

In its first action on GPOI during the 111th Congress, the House passed legislation authorizing the Secretary of State to carry out and expand GPOI programs and activities (Section 1108 of the Foreign Relations Authorization Act, Fiscal Years 2010 and 2011, H.R. 2410, passed June 10, 2009).

## INTRODUCTION

As the Global Peace Operations Initiative (GPOI) completes the last of its five planned years in FY2009, the 111th Congress has begun consideration of continued funding through this program for training foreign military and police forces, and for other purposes. For FY2010, the Obama Administration has requested $96.8 million for GPOI.

This request follows the decision of the George W. Bush Administration's White House to continue the program. In October 2008, the National Security Council's Deputies Committee approved a five-year renewal of GPOI's mandate. The Obama Administration affirmed this decision once it took office, according to a State Department official.

Previous Congresses have generally endorsed the concept of this program, but also have questioned whether the program is as well-managed as possible and whether it will achieve its goals. The 111th Congress may wish to consider whether its concerns, stated in past legislation, have been met.

On June 10, 2009, the House passed the Foreign Relations Authorization Act, Fiscal Years 2010 and 2011 (H.R. 2410), which contains a provision authorizing the Secretary of State to carry out and expand GPOI programs and activities (Section 1108).

### Purposes and Goal

Established to train 75,000 international peacekeepers by 2010, GPOI was the George W. Bush Administration's signature initiative to build international peacekeeping capacity. (State Department officials express confidence that the goal of 75,000 peacekeepers-trained will be achieved by early 2010.) The Administration launched the five-year $660 million (in FY2005- FY2009 funds) initiative in mid-2004 as a means to alleviate the perceived shortage worldwide of trained peacekeepers and "gendarmes," as well as to increase available resources to transport and sustain them ("Gendarmes," also known as constabulary police or stability police, are police with a combination o f policing and military skills considered vital to the semi-stable environments of peace operations, where the potential for outbreaks of rioting and other violence creates a need for specially-trained police forces.). While the United States has provided considerable support to implement several peace processes and to support peacekeepers in the field from a variety of budget accounts for well over a decade, until GPOI it had provided relatively little funding to build up foreign military capabilities to perform peacekeeping operations [1]

In plans for GPOI after 2010, State Department officials state that the program's emphasis would shift from direct training to building the capacity of foreign nations to develop their own peacekeeping infrastructure and capabilities.

## Achievements to Date

As of the end of January 2009, GPOI funds have supported the training of 54,245 military troops as peacekeepers and of 3,350 military personnel to train others in peacekeeping skills. Of those trained, GPOI reports that as of January 30, 2009, some 46,115 troops from 21 countries were deployed to 18 peacekeeping operations and 1 election observer mission, and another 4,860 troops were in the process of being deployed [2]. In addition, GPOI has supported the training of 1,932 police trainers from 29 countries at the Italian-run Center of Excellence for Stability Police Units (CoESPU) in Vicenza, Italy.

In addition to training peacekeepers, GPOI supports a variety of institutions specializing in or contributing to peacekeeping operations. These include 22 peace operations training centers around the world, as well as the African Union and the Economic Community of West African States (ECOWAS).

GPOI also provides funds for the Transportation Logistics Support Arrangement (TLSA), which has supported troops deploying to several peacekeeping missions, [3] and other GPOI deployment equipment funding has supported troops deploying to some of these and other missions [4]. In total, as of January 30, 2009, GPOI had contributed $65.4 million to provide equipment to and transport troops deployed to seven missions, according to GPOI officials.

In total, all GPOI-funded activities helped deploy 46,115 troops from 21 countries to 18 peacekeeping operations and 1 election observer mission, as of January 30, 2009, with an additiona l4,860 troops about to deploy at that time.

## Funding to Date

Through FY2008, GPOI funding totaled $374.46 million. GPOI funding for FY2009 totals $105.95 million, plus $3.0 million in State Department International Narcotics Control and Law Enforcement (INCLE) funding. (The Bush Administration's FY2009 request called for $106.2 million in peacekeeping operations funds.)

With these funds, GPOI has provided for the training of 57,595 peacekeepers and peacekeeping trainers as of January 31, 2009 [5] (For a breakdown of this number by country, see Table 2, below.)

## Table 1. GPOI Obligations, FY2005-FY2009
## (in $ millions)

| Category | FY2005 Actuals[a] | FY2006 Actuals[b] | FY2007 Acutals | FY2008 Actuals | FY 2009 | Totals |
|---|---|---|---|---|---|---|
| African Contingency Operations Training and Assistance (ACOTA) | 28.92 | 35.00 | 40.39 | 44.00 | 49.00 | 197.28 |
| Africa Regional HQ Support: African Union (AU) and the Economic Community of West African States (ECOWAS) | 10.01 | 9.71 | 7.15 | 7.16 | 9.18 | 43.21 |
| East Asia and the Pacific | 7.74 | 11.00 | 6.55 | 9.42 | 15.13 | 49.84 |
| Europe and Eurasia | 5.05 | 6.00 | 4.00 | 5.80 | 4.10 | 24.95 |
| Near East (i.e., Jordan) | 0 | 0.65 | 1.30 | 1.00 | 1.60 | 4.55 |
| South & Central Asia | 0.93 | 5.00 | 7.36 | 10.33 | 6.60 | 30.22 |
| Western Hemisphere | 6.49 | 11.70 | 8.45 | 11.65 | 12.06 | 50.35 |
| Center of Excellence for Stability Police Units (CoESPU) | 15.00 | 0 | 0 | 0 | 0 | 15.00 |
| Transportation and Logistics Support Arrangement (TLSA) and Deployment Equipment | 21.99 | 19.77 | 5.79 | 5.69 | 4.81 | 58.05 |
| Program Management | 0.55 | 1.51 | 0 | 1.39 | 3.48 | 6.93 |
| Total | 96.66 | 100.36 | 81.00 | 96.44 | 105.95 | 480.38 |

Source: Department of State, as of April 2, 2009.

Notes: Some totals do not add due to rounding. For FY2009, GPOI also includes approximately $3 million in State Department International Narcotics Control and Law Enforcement (INCLE) funds that are not included in this table as a final amount has not been decided.

[a] As GPOI was not created until late 2004, FY2005 actuals include funds originally appropriated elsewhere: $14.88 million in Peacekeeping Account (PKO) funds for ACOTA; $1.79 million in Foreign Military Financing for Enhanced International Peacekeeping Capabilities (EIPC), and an $80 million transfer from DOD.

[b] FY2006 funding includes $57 million from FY2006 supplemental appropriations.

## BACKGROUND

Before mid-2004, the United States provided peacekeeping capacity-building assistance to foreign militaries primarily under two programs, the African Contingency Operations Training and Assistance program (ACOTA) and its predecessor program, and the Enhanced International Peacekeeping Capabilities program (EIPC). Both ACOTA and EPIC have been subsumed under the GPOI budget line. ACOTA is still the term used to refer to the Africa component of GPOI, however, and is implemented by the State Department's Africa Bureau.

## Table 2. GPOI Training Summary, FY2005-First Third, FY2009
### (#s trained to standard as of January 31, 2009)

| Region/Country/ Organization | Total # Peacekeepers Trained | Total # Peacekeeper Trainers Trained | Total # |
|---|---|---|---|
| *Sub-Saharan Africa* | | | |
| Benin | 4,260 | 195 | 4,455 |
| Botswana | 118 | 47 | 165 |
| Burkina Faso | 2,535 | 161 | 2,696 |
| Burundi | 1,291 | 0 | 1,291 |
| Cameroon | 692 | 101 | 793 |
| ECOWAS | 287 | 2 | 289 |
| Gabon | 1,212 | 161 | 1,393 |
| Ghana | 5,965 | 169 | 6,134 |
| Kenya | 189 | 5 | 194 |
| Malawi | 1,063 | 25 | 1,088 |
| Mali | 880 | 130 | 1,010 |
| Mauritania - Suspended | 284 | 20 | 304 |
| Mozambique | 868 | 161 | 1,029 |
| Namibia | 817 | 71 | 888 |
| Niger – Suspended | 1,041 | 107 | 1,121 |
| Nigeria | 9,463 | 586 | 10,049 |
| Rwanda | 4,789 | 92 | 4,881 |
| Senegal | 7,829 | 435 | 8,264 |
| South Africa | 211 | 114 | 325 |
| Tanzania | 775 | 24 | 799 |
| Uganda | 4,149 | 137 | 4,286 |
| Zambia | 563 | 113 | 676 |
| Sub-Total Africa | 49,254 | 2,856 | 52,110 |
| *Asia/South Asia/Pacific Islands/Middle East* | | | |
| Australia | 20 | 0 | 20 |
| Brunei | 47 | 5 | 52 |
| Bangladesh | 190 | 50 | 240 |
| Cambodia | 187 | 29 | 216 |
| Fiji – Suspended | 45 | 2 | 47 |
| India | 83 | 2 | 85 |
| Indonesia | 361 | 72 | 433 |
| Japan | 3 | 0 | 3 |
| Jordan | 2 | 0 | 2 |
| Korea, Republic of | 46 | 6 | 52 |
| Laos | 3 | 0 | 3 |
| Lebanon | 1 | 0 | 1 |
| Malaysia | 322 | 75 | 397 |

## Table 2. (Continued)

| Region/Country/Organization | Total # Peacekeepers Trained | Total # Peacekeeper Trainers Trained | Total # |
|---|---|---|---|
| Mongolia | 640 | 77 | 717 |
| Nepal | 372 | 35 | 407 |
| New Zealand | 5 | 0 | 5 |
| Papua New Guinea | 2 | 0 | 2 |
| Philippines | 16 | 0 | 16 |
| Singapore | 12 | 0 | 12 |
| Sri Lanka | 60 | 7 | 67 |
| Thailand | 356 | 35 | 391 |
| Tonga | 113 | 7 | 120 |
| *Subtotal Asia/Central Asia/South* | | | |
| Asia/the pacific | 2,888 | 402 | 3,290 |
| Greater Europe (Europe and Eurasia) | | | |
| Albania | 254 | 0 | 254 |
| Bosnia-Herzegovina | 3 | 0 | 3 |
| France | 3 | 0 | 3 |
| Germany | 4 | 0 | 4 |
| Italy | 1 | 0 | 1 |
| United Kingdom | 5 | 0 | 5 |
| Ukraine | 27 | 26 | 53 |
| Subtotal Greater Europe | 297 | 26 | 323 |
| Western Hemisphere | | | |
| Belize | 55 | 10 | 65 |
| Canada | 5 | 0 | 5 |
| Dominican Republic | 13 | 2 | 15 |
| El Salvador | 215 | 7 | 222 |
| Guatemala | 751 | 16 | 767 |
| Honduras | 255 | 26 | 281 |
| Nicaragua | 445 | 5 | 450 |
| Paraguay | 36 | 0 | 36 |
| Peru | 18 | 0 | 18 |
| Uruguay | 13 | 0 | 13 |
| Subtotal Western Hemisphere | 1,806 | 66 | 1,872 |
| Total | 54,245 | 3,350 | 57,595 |

*Sources:* Compiled from information provided by the U.S. Department of State, Bureau of Political-Military Affairs, February 18, 2009.

*Notes*: This table does not include soldiers trained by GPOI-trained trainers. The standard used by evaluators for inclusion was mastery of at least 80% of the coursework and an 80% or better attendance record. NA = Not Available.

This table includes countries that are not GPOI partners but participated in multilateral peacekeeping exercises or received training at GPOI-supported regional training facilities at the request of the host government. These countries include Australia, Brunei, Canada, France, Germany, Greece, India, Italy Japan, Laos, New Zealand, Papua New Guinea, Republic of Korea, and Singapore. It also includes Cameroon, which is not a GPOI partner (i.e., eligible to receive bilateral assistance). It is listed here as receiving training because it sends students to the Italian Center of Excellence for Stability Police Units (CoESPU).

# Peacekeepers = # soldiers (and occasionally gendarmes) trained in peacekeeping skills in GPOI courses in order to deploy to peacekeeping operations.

# Peacekeeper Trainers = # soldiers trained to train other military personnel in peacekeeping skills for deployment to peacekeeping operations (i.e., soldiers trained under the "train-the-trainer" program).

Overall responsibility for GPOI rests with the State Department Bureau of Political-Military Affairs' Office of Plans, Policy, and Analysis (PM/PPA). (Information about GPOI is available at http://www.state.gov/t/pm/ppa/gpoi.) PM/PPA works closely with DOD offices to plan and carry out the program.

Impetus for GPOI came from the Department of Defense (DOD), where officials in the Office of Special Operations and Low-Intensity Conflict (SO/LIC) worked with the State Department for over a year and a half to develop the proposal.

Officials in SO/LIC's section on peacekeeping developed the plan as a means to expand and improve the ACOTA program—with more and better exercises and more equipment—as well as to extend the program beyond Africa to other parts of the world. Policymakers hoped that the availability of peacekeeping training would encourage more countries to participate in peacekeeping operations, enable current donors to provide a greater number of troops, and increase the number of countries which potentially could serve as lead nations, according to some analysts.

The GPOI budget is part of the Foreign Operations Appropriations Peacekeeping (PKO) account, also known as the "voluntary" Peacekeeping account, under the Military Assistance rubric. The PKO account funds activities carried out under Section 551 of the Foreign Assistance Act of 1961, as amended (FAA) [6].

Section 551 authorizes the President to provide assistance for peacekeeping operations and other programs to further U.S. national security interests "on such terms and conditions as he may determine." (This provides some flexibility to the President, but is not tantamount to the discretion that he can exercise when funding is provided "notwithstanding any other provision of law.")

## GPOI PURPOSES AND ACTIVITIES

In his September 21, 2004 address to the opening meeting of the 59th session of the U.N. General Assembly, President Bush asserted that the world "must create permanent capabilities to respond to future crises." In particular, he pointed to a need for "more effective means to stabilize regions in turmoil, and to halt religious violence and ethnic cleansing." A similar rationale prompted the Clinton Administration to formulate the ACRI training program in 1996 and underlies the current search for new strategies and mechanisms to prevent and control conflicts [7]

### GPOI Goals and Needs

To accomplish these ends, the Bush Administration set three major GPOI goals:

- Train some 75,000 troops worldwide, with an emphasis on Africa, in peacekeeping skills by 2010.
- Support Italy in establishing a center to train international gendarme (constabulary) forces to participate in peacekeeping operations (see section below); and

- Foster an international deployment and logistics support system to transport peacekeepers to the field and maintain them there.

Through GPOI, the State Department also promotes the exchange of information among G-8 [8] donors on peace operations training and exercises in Africa. This is accomplished through donors meetings which serve as a "clearinghouse" to facilitate coordination. The first of these State Department meetings was held in Washington, D.C. on October 7-8, 2004 [9]. The United Kingdom hosted a second meeting in February 2006, the Russian Federation hosted a third in June 2006, Germany hosted a fourth in March 2007, Japan hosted the fifth in April 2008, and Italy is hosting the sixth in April 2009.

Through GPOI, the State Department also supports a G8++ Global Clearinghouse information exchange to build peacekeeping capabilities worldwide. The first Global Clearinghouse meetings was held in Washington, D.C., in October 2007, [10] and the second in the United Kingdom in December 2008.

### *Demand for Peacekeepers*

For many analysts, a continued effort to improve the peacekeeping skills of African and other military forces is an important step towards controlling devastating conflicts, particularly in Africa. In the mid-1990s, several developed nations provided most of the peacekeepers. The perception that developed nations would not be able to sustain the burden indefinitely, as well as the perception that the interests of those nations in Africa were not sufficient to ensure needed troop commitments there, led international capacity-building efforts to focus on Africa.

As of the end of December 2004, shortly after GPOI first started up, almost 25,000 of the nearly 58,000 military personnel who were participating in the current 17 U.N. peacekeeping operations were from the 22 African troop-contributing nations. (African nations provided over half of the military personnel—roughly 24,000 of 47,000—in the seven U.N. peacekeeping operations in Africa.) Africa's military contribution to U.N. peacekeeping at the end of 2004 was over double that at the end of 2000; five of the top ten African contributors, who provided some 98% of the military contribution, received training under the ACRI/ACOTA program. African contributions to the U.N. international civilian police pool (CIVPOL) remained just about the same over those four years: 1,213 in December 2004 (of a total of 6,765 from all nations) compared to 1,088 in December 2000.

African militaries also participate in regional peacekeeping operations under the auspices of the Economic Community of Western African States (ECOWAS) and the African Union (AU). (The first ECOWAS peacekeeping mission was deployed to Liberia in 1990. Subsequent missions were deployed to Liberia once again, Guinea Bissau, Sierra Leone, the Côte d'Ivoire, Sudan, and Somalia.

The AU deployed its first peacekeepers to Burundi in 2003 and Sudan in 2004. All missions eventually became U.N. operations. Both organizations are trying to develop an African stand-by peacekeeping force, comprised of contributions from five regional organizations, by 2010. Under GPOI, the United States will work to enhance and support the command structures and multilateral staff of ECOWAS and the AU.

### *Need for Gendarme/Constabulary Forces*

A second capability in short supply is the specialized units of police with military skills to handle temporary hostile situations such as unruly crowds [11] Several countries have such forces (e.g., the Italian carabinieri, the French gendarmerie, and the Spanish Guardia Civil, among others).

In the United States these forces generally have been referred to in the past as constabulary forces; in the context of peacekeeping and stabilization operations they are currently referred to as "stability police" or gendarme forces. The United Nation refers to such forces as "formed police units" or FPUs.

## U.S. Peacekeeping Training and Assistance, Pre-GPOI, in Sub- Saharan Africa

From 1996 through 2004, the United States provided field and staff training to develop military capabilities for peacekeeping through the African Crisis Response Initiative (ACRI) and its successor program, ACOTA. Early in FY2005, ACOTA was subsumed under GPOI. Under ACRI/ACOTA, the United States trained some 16,000 troops from 10 African nations: [12] Benin, Botswana, Côte d'Ivoire, Ethiopia, Ghana, Kenya, Malawi, Mali, Mozambique, Senegal, and Uganda [13]. (It also trained a small number of gendarmes who received the same training as the others.)

The United States also provided non-lethal equipment to the militaries that it trained. This included communications packages, uniforms, boots, generators, mine detectors, Global Positioning Systems (GPS), and medical and water purification equipment.

Initially, under ACRI, U.S. soldiers provided field training and oversaw classroom training provided by private contractors. Because of the demand for U.S. soldiers in Iraq and Afghanistan, private contractors also began to conduct field training. By the time GPOI was initiated, private contractors, many of whom reportedly were retired military personnel and reservists, conducted most of the training, while U.S. active duty military officers and non-commissioned officers were much less involved overall, but did provide mentoring. This remains true today.

Funding for ACRI, which like ACOTA was provided under the State Department's Peacekeeping Operations (PKO) account, totaled $83.6 million during its six fiscal years (FY1997-FY2002). (Additional support for ACRI was provided through the Foreign Military Financing program.) ACOTA was funded at $8 million in FY2003 and $15 million in FY2004.

Other support for classroom training of foreign militaries was provided through the EIPC, a "train the trainer" program which began in FY1998 and was subsumed under the GPOI rubric. EIPC provided assistance to selected countries—some 31 as of early 2005—by designing and implementing a comprehensive, country-specific peacekeeping and humanitarian assistance training and education program to enhance a nation's institutional structure to train and deploy peacekeepers. EIPC funding, provided under the Foreign Military Financing Program, totaled about $31.5 million through FY2004.

## The Transition to GPOI Training and Assistance in Sub-Saharan Africa

GPOI was designed as a program with worldwide reach, but its emphasis was always intended to remain on Africa. In FY2005, only a few hundred peacekeeper trainees were from outside Africa, and thus far the great majority of trainees are Africans. (For a detailed account of the number of trainees from each country, see Table 2 at the end of this report. This table provides the number of trainees trained using the funds from each fiscal year, not the number of trainees actually trained in that fiscal year. Because training is still being conducted with previous fiscal year funds, these numbers will change.) Training in Africa continues to be conducted under the ACOTA program, which is implemented by the State Department's Africa Bureau.

In GPOI's first funding year, during FY2005, some 12,080 African troops from 13 partners were trained using funds initially appropriated for ACOTA under the regular budget and additional funds appropriated for GPOI. This number included pre-deployment training for five battalions from Senegal that were then deployed to specific peacekeeping missions [14]. The 12 other ACOTA partners whose troops were trained using FY2005 funds were Benin, Botswana, ECO WAS, Gabon, Ghana, Malawi, Mali, Mozambique, Nigeria, Rwanda, South Africa, and Zambia.

GPOI's Africa ACOTA component now consists of 24 partners: 22 partner countries and two partner organizations. The states are Benin, Botswana, Burkina Faso, Burundi, Cameroon, Ethiopia, Gabon, Ghana, Kenya, Malawi, Mali, Mauritania, Mozambique, Namibia, Niger, Nigeria, Rwanda, Senegal, South Africa, Tanzania, Uganda, and Zambia. (However, as the State Department has suspended military assistance to Mauritania and Niger, no GPOI assistance is being provided to those countries at this time.) In addition, GPOI provides assistance to the African Union and ECOWAS, which are also partners. This assistance includes sponsoring retired U.S. Army officers contracted as advisors to these institutions.

As of February 23, 2009, GPOI funds have provided training under the ACOTA program for 55,263 peacekeepers, according to the State Department GPOI office. Of these, some 45,606 have been deployed or where in the process of deploying to a UN or other peace operation as of that date. In addition, since FY2005, ACOTA has trained 12,627 more peacekeepers from GPOI partner countries using other PKO funds and funds from the Netherlands. Of those, 12,127 have been deployed or were in the process of deploying as of February 23, 2009 [15]

In addition, GPOI supports five peace operations training centers in Sub-Saharan Africa. These are located in Ghana, Kenya, Mali, Nigeria, and South Africa.

## Development of a "Beyond Africa" Program

In July 2005, the State Department initiated a training and equipping program for countries outside of Africa (informally referred to at the time as the "Beyond Africa" program) [16] in order to extend GPOI training to three new regions: Latin America, Europe, and Asia. (As in Africa, some equipment is provided during training, but only that needed for the training itself. Trained troops are not provided with equipment needed for operations until they deploy.) The number of partner countries outside of Africa has grown to 31.

The largest number of partners outside Africa are in Asia/South Asia and the Pacific Islands, where there are 14 partner states. Eleven partner countries are in the Western Hemisphere, six in Europe and Eurasia, and one in the Middle East.

### Western Hemisphere

The Latin American program began in Central America, where GPOI funds were initially used to train and equip soldiers from El Salvador, Guatemala, Honduras, and Nicaragua, as well as to upgrade an existing facility in order to establish a peacekeeping training center in Guatemala. Through this support, Central American countries were able to stand up a battalion of about 600 Central American troops, as part of the Conferencia de Fuerzas Armadas Centroamericanas (CFAC).

There are now 11 Western Hemisphere partner countries: Belize, Bolivia, Chile, Dominican Republic, El Salvador, Guatemala, Honduras, Nicaragua, Paraguay, Peru, and Uruguay. Some 1,867 peacekeepers and trainers from Western Hemisphere partner countries and 5 from Canada (which is not a partner) received GPOI training, as of January 31, 2009. Although Bolivia is a partner country, it has not yet participated in GPOI activities.

GPOI supports eight peace operations training centers in the Western Hemisphere. These are located in Belize, the Dominican Republic, Guatemala, Honduras, Nicaragua, Paraguay, Peru, and Uruguay.

The U.S. Southern Command (SOUTHCOM) runs major peacekeeping exercises under GPOI auspices. In 2009, the PKO of the Americas will be held in multiple phases geared to the needs of each participant. Events are to be held in March and May at six locations, with additional events in June or July.

### Asia/South Asia/Pacific Islands

In Asia, the first countries to be extended train-and-equip assistance and provided some logistical support were Bangladesh, Malaysia, Mongolia, and Thailand (which was subsequently suspended because of a military coup and reinstated in February 2008). GPOI funds were also used establish and install a communications network among partner countries in the region, called the Peace Support Operations Collaboration Center (PSOCC) in Mongolia [17]

Currently, there are 14 partner countries in good standing in these regions: Bangladesh, Cambodia, Indonesia, Kazakhstan, Malaysia, Mongolia, Nepal, Pakistan, Philippines, Sri Lanka, Tajikistan, Thailand, Tonga, and Vietnam. In addition, Fiji is a partner country, but it is currently under sanctions and not eligible for GPOI assistance. India chose not to join GPOI as a partner, but Indian personnel have participated in some GPOI training events through the use of nonGPOI funds. Personnel from Australia, Brunei, Japan, Laos, Papua New Guinea, Republic of Korea, New Zealand, and Singapore have also participated in GPOI training events, although GPOI did not fund the travel and accommodations for personnel from these countries. In all, some 3,287 peacekeepers and peacekeeping trainers from those regions have been trained using GPOI funds.

GPOI supports peacekeeping operations training centers in five countries in these regions: Bangladesh, Cambodia, Indonesia, Mongolia, and Thailand.

*Greater Europe (Europe and Eurasia)*

In Europe, the first countries whose troops were offered training and other support under GPOI were Albania, Bosnia-Hercegovina, and the Ukraine. Bosnia was provided information technology support for its training center and a U.S. instructor with FY2005 funds.

Currently, GPOI has six partner countries in greater Europe: Albania, Bosnia and Herzegovina, Croatia, Romania, Macedonia, and the Ukraine. Some 323 peacekeepers and peacekeeping trainers from this area have participated in GPOI training events, including 13 from France, Germany, Italy and the United Kingdom, which are not partner countries [18]

GPOI funds supports peace operations training centers in three countries in Greater Europe: Albania, Bosnia and Ukraine. GPOI also has provided deployment equipment to SEEBRIG, the seven-member multinational South East Europe Brigade, composed of personnel from Albania, Bulgaria, Italy, Greece, Macedonia, Romania, and Turkey [19]

*Middle East*

GPOI's first and currently only Middle Eastern partner country is Jordan, which was added in FY2006. Two peacekeepers from Jordan have participated in GPOI training. (One person from Lebanon also participated in GPOI training, but his participation was not funded by GPOI.). GPOI funds support a peacekeeping operation center in Jordan.

Morocco is to be added as a GPOI partner country in FY2009.

## Foreign Contributions to Peacekeeping Capacity Building

When the Bush Administration launched GPOI in 2004, it intended it as a stimulus for increased multilateral efforts to build worldwide peacekeeping capacity, with a focus on Africa. At the time, several countries had their own significant programs supporting peacekeeping in Africa. In addition, through the G8, the major industrialized democracies had indicated increasing support for peace efforts in Africa. In June 2002, the G8 Summit at Kananaskis, Canada, adopted a broad Africa Action Plan that contained sections on conflict resolution and peace-building efforts. The more specific Joint Africa/G8 Plan to Enhance African Capabilities to Undertake Peace Support Operations was developed over the next year and presented at the June 2003 Summit at Evian-les-baines, France [20]. At their June 2004 summit meeting at Sea Island, GA, G8 leaders adopted a third Africa peacekeeping action plan: *Action Plan on Expanding Global Capability for Peace Support Operations* [21]

European and other countries continue their assistance to African peacekeeping. In addition to the United States, France and the United Kingdom (UK) conduct bilateral training programs with African militaries. Germany and the UK provided the assistance necessary to launch the regional Kofi Annan International Peacekeeping Training Center in Ghana, which opened in 2004, and Germany is providing continuing assistance. The European Union and other countries, most prominently Canada, Italy, France and the Netherlands, have also assisted the Center.

*Italian Center of Excellence for Stability Police Units (CoESPU)*

Italy supports international peacekeeping capacity building efforts with its Center of Excellence for Stability Police Units (CoESPU), an international "train the trainer" school for police to learn and transfer peacekeeping policing skills. Italian carabinieri, who are widely viewed as a leading model and have played a prominent role in providing gendarme forces to peacekeeping and stabilization operations [22] established CoESPU at Vicenza in March 2005. Italy is providing not only the facility, but also most of the staff. As of mid-2006, some 145 carabinieri were attached to CoESPU, of which about 25 were instructors and training staff. (At the same point, two U.S. military service members were attached to the center, one serving as Deputy Director. [23]) CoESPU's goal, by 2010, is to train 3,000 mid-to-high ranking personnel at Vicenza and an additional 4,000 in formed units in their home countries.

The United States is CoEPSU's primary foreign supporter. Currently, there is one U.S. service member at CoESPU, serving as the Deputy Director, and the United Sates is considering staffing additional positions through U.S. military personnel, civilian personnel, or contractors. A U.S. contribution of $10 million for the school's operation and training programs was transferred to Italy in late September 2005; its contributions through FY2009 total $15 million. (According to CoESPU officials in 2006, the U.S. contribution covers about one-third the cost of running the school.) [24]

Several other countries have contributed. Canada, France, and Russia have provided instructors for certain courses. CoESPU offers high-level courses (for staff officers ranking from Lt. Colonels to Colonels and their civilian equivalents) consisting of four-and-a-half weeks of classes (approximately 150 classroom hours) in international organizations, international law (including international humanitarian law), military arts in peace support operations, tactical doctrine, operating in mixed international environments with hybrid chains of command, and the selection, training, and organization of police units for international peace support operations.

The Center also offers a course for junior officers and senior non-commissioned officers (sergeant majors to captains) and their civilian equivalents. This course covers the materials taught in the high-level course with an emphasis on training in the more practical aspects, including checkpoint procedures, VIP security and escorts, high-risk arrests, border control, riot control, election security, and police self-defense techniques.

(The first high-level class graduated 29 officers on December 7, 2005. The first class consisted of officers from Cameroon, India, Jordan, Kenya, Morocco, and Senegal. A pilot course for the middle-management level began on January 13, 2006, and seven weeks later graduated about 100 officers. Students for this course were drawn from the same six countries as those at the first-high level course.)

CoESPU also has worked on developing a lessons-learned and doctrine writing capability in order to serve as an interactive resource for Stability Police Units (SPUs). An early intention was to develop a coherent and comprehensive SPU doctrine to promote interoperability in the field, to ensure that doctrine is the basis of training standards and methods, and to respond to questions from SPU commanders in the field, as well as to support pre-mission and in-theater training exercises. Recently, the United Nations has taken on the task of spearheading the development of SPU (or in U.N. terms, Formed Police Unit/FPU) doctrine; CoESPU is supporting this initiative.

## Administration Funding Requests and Congressional Action

### FY2005-FY2009 GPOI Funding

Funding for GPOI totaled $374.46 million from FY2005 through FY2008. Initial dedicated funding of $96.7 million in FY2005 was contained in the Consolidated Appropriations Act for FY2005 (H.R. 481 8/P.L. 108-447), split between the Department of State (almost 20%) and the DOD (80% as funds to be transferred to State) budgets.25 For FY2006, the State Department allocated $100.4 million to GPOI, which was slightly more than half of the total PKO account, but some $14 million below the President's request [26]. For FY2007, the Administration requested $102.6 million for GPOI funding. House and Senate action signaled some discontent with the program [27]. The final continuing resolution [28] that funded most government operations and programs through FY2007, including GPOI, left the decision on the amount of GPOI funding for FY2007 largely to the State Department, albeit in the context of a reduced availability of funds [29]. The State Department's FY2007 GPOI obligations totaled $81 million (i.e., $1 million less than provided for in the House-passed FY2007 Foreign Operations bill, H.R. 5522). (An earlier version of the Continuing Resolution had set the House-passed amount as the level for FY2007 GPOI funding.) For FY2008, Congress fully funded the Bush Administration's budget request for $92.5 million in GPOI funding. (This funding was contained in the omnibus Consolidated Appropriations Act, 2008 [H.R. 2764, Division J; P.L. 110-161, signed into law December 26, 2007]) [30]. The State Department allocated almost $4 million more.

State Department allocations for GPOI for FY2009 total $105.95 million from PKO funds and an expected additional amount of some $3 million from INCLE funding (see Table 1 and notes). The State Department allocated these funds from appropriations in the Omnibus Appropriations Act, 2009 (P.L. 111-8, signed into law March 11, 2009). The Bush Administration's FY2009 budget request called for $106.2 million in PKO funds for GOPI.

### FY2010 Funding Request

In its May 2009 budget request for FY2010, the Obama Administration has requested $96.8 million for the Global Peace Operations Initiative (GPOI). According to budget request documents, the FY20 10 funds "will continue to provide training, equipment, and sustainment of peacekeeping troops," but the program emphasis will shift to "strengthening partner country capabilities to train their own peacekeeping units" [31]. To that end, GPOI will focus on developing indigenous peacekeeping trainer cadres, peacekeeping training centers, and on other programs, events, and activities to encourage self-sufficiency. Through FY2010 funds, the United States will continue to provide lift and sustainment to peacekeeping troops worldwide, and to support the evaluation of GPOI, including measures of effectiveness. As in previous years, funding for GPOI is requested under the State Department Peacekeeping Operations (PKO) account.

# Congressional Action in the 111<sup>th</sup> Congress

*Foreign Relations Authorization Act, Fiscal Years 2010 and 2011 (Section 1108, H.R. 2410)*

In its first action on GPOI during the 111<sup>th</sup> Congress, the House passed legislation which would authorize the Secretary of State to carry out and to expand GPOI programs and activities. Section 1108 of the Foreign Relations Authorization Act, Fiscal Years 2010 and 2011 (H.R. 2410), as passed by the House on June 10, 2009, specifies eight GPOI functions, including five that GPOI has carried out since its inception [32] and three new functions.

In support of this proposed authorization, Section 1108 finds that the United States has "a vital interest in ensuring" that U.N. peacekeeping operations are successful because countries in conflict threaten U.S. national security and economic interests, and because conflicts result in deplorable human suffering. Section 1108 also finds that the United States benefits from U.N. peacekeeping because, in general, the costs of U.N. operations are lower than the potential cost of a similar U.S. peacekeeping operation [33]

Of the three new functions that Section 1108 would authorize, two reaffirm the State Department's concept of GPOI's future direction. These functions are (1) "enhancing the capacity of regional and sub-regional organizations to plan, train for, manage, conduct, sustain and obtain lessons-learned from" peace operations; and (2) helping partner nations become self-sufficient in developing and sustaining peacekeeping capabilities, as well as in furnishing troops and equipment for and carrying out peace operations (see Section 1108(c)(1)).

The third new GPOI function that Section 1108, as passed by the House, would authorize is financing the refurbishment of helicopters for use in U.N. peacekeeping operations or U.N. Security Council-authorized regional peacekeeping operations. A Sense of Congress statement (Section 1108(c)(2)) would direct the Secretary of State to prioritize helicopter refurbishment, to set a goal of refurbishing no fewer than three helicopters by the end of FY20 11, and to seek additional refurbishment funds from other countries.

In the report accompanying H.R. 2410 (H.Rept. 111-136), the House Foreign Affairs Committee (HFAC) states that the addition of helicopter refurbishment to GPOI's functions is intended to respond to current critical shortfalls in air assets in ongoing peacekeeping operations in Darfur, the Democratic Republic of Congo, and Chad, as well as to potential new operations "which would likely face similar shortfalls ... " (p. 167) The bill finds that a shortfall of over 50 helicopters critically hampers those three peacekeeping operations.

H.R. 2410, as reported by the committee and passed by the House, does not authorize a specific funding amount for GPOI programs and activities, including helicopter refurbishment. Instead, Section 1108 would authorize the appropriation of the funds necessary in FY2010 and FY2011 to carry out that section. In H.Rept. 111-136, HFAC encourages appropriators "to allot such funds as may be necessary above the President's request" of $96.8 million in order to refurbish helicopters. The Congressional Budget Office (CBO) estimates that the cost of refurbishing one medium-lift utility helicopter is about $2 million, and that the total cost of implementing GPOI programs and activities over the FY2010-FY2014 period, including the refurbishment of three helicopters by the end of 2011, would be about $195 billion. (H.Rept. 111-136, p. 103).

# Issues for the 111<sup>th</sup> Congress

Over the past few years, the State Department responded to concerns of the 109<sup>th</sup> and the 110<sup>th</sup> Congresses to strengthen GPOI. Its steps included producing a strategic plan (the executive summary of which is publically available), [34] facilitating procedures to speed planning and implementation, and implementing an evaluation program. As of 2008, Congress requested [35] that the Government Accountability Office (GAO) investigate a number of remaining issues: the GAO expressed several concerns about GPOI performance and management in a June 2008 report [36]

Among the points the Congress requested the GAO to address were (1) the extent to which contributing and participating countries maintain records and databases; (2) the quality and sustainability of the training of individuals and units; (3) the extent to which those trained are equipped and remain equipped to deploy in peace operations; (4) participating countries capacity to mobilize those trained; (5) the extent to which trained individuals are deployed; and (6) the extent to which contractors are used and the quality of their results. The committee also requested an assessment of whether GPOI is achieving its goals and recommendations as to whether a country's participation in GPOI "should require reciprocal participation."

In its June 2008 report, the GAO doubted, based on information available to it in its investigation, that GPOI would be able to reach its goal of training 75,000 peacekeepers by 2010. The GAO stated, however, that it could not evaluate information that the State Department subsequently provided to demonstrate that GPOI would reach its goal. As of February 2008, GPOI officials are stating that 75,000 will be trained by early 2010. GPOI officials also state that the program will, as recommended by the GAO, ensure that plans for extending GPOI activities beyond 2010 identify the necessary resources for developing long-term peacekeeping skills and infrastructure in Africa [37]. They point to plans to concentrate on building infrastructure in any post-2010 program.

The GAO made several recommendations to improve human rights vetting, program management, and training content. The following bullets note the recommendations and the steps that GPOI is taking to meet them. Congress may wish monitor progress on the GAO recommendations.

- Noting that a number of foreign military troops who received GPOI training had not been properly vetted, the GAO recommended that the Secretary of State develop a system for monitoring all GPOI vetting activities and for ensuring that all individuals are vetted. According to GPOI officials, the recommendation applies not only to GPOI, but to State Department vetting in general. To improve the vetting system, according to those officials, the Department has secured funding to establish a database that will facilitate record-keeping and access to past vetting cases. GPOI program implementers will use the system when it is available.

- Judging that GPOI was unable to account for the delivery and transfer of nonlethal training equipment to partner countries, the GAO recommended that the Secretary of State monitor implementation, on an ongoing basis, of new procedures to account for delivery and transfer of nonlethal training equipment to partner countries. According to GPOI officials, the State Department GPOI Evaluation Team had identified this accountability problem before the GAO investigation. The ACOTA program has instituted a sole-source logistics contract to improve the entire logistics process from acquisition to delivery, and is establishing a mechanism with its African partners to manage joint inventories. The State Department is developing procedures with other stakeholders to better account for equipment that is commercially acquired through the State Department's Office of Acquisition Management's regional procurement support offices. Similarly, new procedures have been developed by the State Department and the Defense Security Cooperation Agency to account for training equipment provided through the Foreign Military Sales system, with the U.S. government retaining title to and custody of defense articles until a designated U.S. government agent confirms and documents delivery of GPOI material to a recipient country's authorized representative or agent.

- In order to improve training, GAO recommended that the Secretary of State develop, in consultation with DOD a training program for GPOI that uses standard military task lists and related training standards in order to establish program-wide criteria for evaluating the quality of training and measuring trainee proficiency. According to GPOI officials, a GPOI contractor, Detica, is working in close collaboration with key stakeholders and others, including the U.N. Department of Peacekeeping Operations, to develop a set of essential tasks for peace operations [38] and corresponding training standards to improve training programs.

- In regard to U.S. support to CoESPU, GAO recommended that the State Department work with DOD in order to help Italy staff key unfilled positions in order to better evaluate progress and monitor results. GAO also suggested that GPOI provide additional guidance to U.S. missions to help the United States and Italy collect data on the training and deployment of CoESPU graduates. The State Department is looking into the possibility of using GPOI funds to provide additional staff at CoESPU who would help with evaluation and monitoring, including the development of an alumni database, outreach materials, and tracking mechanisms. Also, according to GPOI officials, U.S. Embassy staff and others have been asked to help administer a survey regarding the training activities and deployments of CoESPU graduates. The results may be available by mid-2009.

Section 1108 of H.R. 2410 calls for a report (within 180 days of enactment) that would provide information related to monitoring progress on these recommendations.

## REFERENCES

[1]  The term "peacekeeping" is used generically here. It covers the range of activities referred to elsewhere as peace operations, stability operations, or stabilization and reconstruction (S&R)operations.

[2]  These missions include the U.S.-run mission of Operation Iraqi Freedom (OIF), two NATO-run operations, two African missions, 10 United Nations operations, a joint African Union-United Nations mission, and two other operations. The NATO missions are the International Security Assistance Force (ISAF) within Operation Enduring Freedom, in Afghanistan, and the Kosovo Force (KFOR). The African Union-run

operations are AMIS in Sudan and AMISOM in Somalia. The 10 U.N. operations are MINURSO in Western Sahara,, MINUSTAH in Haiti, MONUC in the Democratic Republic of Congo, ONUB in Burundi, UNFIL in Lebanon, UNMEE in Ethiopia and Eritrea, UNMIL in Liberia, UNMIS in Sudan, UNOCI in the Ivory Coast, and UNOSIL in Sierra Leone. GPOI trained troops have also contributed to UNAMID, the joint African Union-United Nations operation in Darfur. The other two missions are the Central African Multinational Force (FOMAC) and the Regional Assistance Mission to Solomon Islands (RAMSI).

[3]   These are AMISOM, AMIS, UNAMID, and UNIFIL.

[4]   These are AMIS, AMISOM, MINUSTAH, UNMIS, and OEF/ISAF.

[5]   Information provided by Department of State, Bureau of Political-Military Affairs, e-mail of February 23, 2009.

[6]   The State Department's Peacekeeping Operations account (i.e., PKO, also known as the "voluntary" peacekeeping account) funds U.S. contributions to peacekeeping efforts other than assessed contributions to U.N. peacekeeping operations. U.N. assessed contributions are funded through the State Department's Contributions to International Peacekeeping Account (CIPA).

[7]   For more information on this topic, see CRS Report RL32862, *Peacekeeping/ Stabilization and Conflict Transitions:Background and Congressional Action on the Civilian Response/Reserve Corps and other Civilian Stabilization and Reconstruction Capabilities*, by Nina M. Serafino.

[8]   G8 refers to the "Group of 8" major industrialized democracies: Canada, France, Germany, Italy, Japan, Russia, the United Kingdom, and the United States. G8 heads of state, plus representatives from the European Union, meet at annual summits.

[9]   The United States European Command (EUCOM) held two previous "clearinghouse" meetings in May and December 2004.

[10]  This included 46 countries and organizations, according to the State Department.

[11]  Gendarme/constabulary forces are trained in both military and policing skills, but are less heavily armed than soldiers. According to the Clinton Administration's Presidential Decision Directive 71 (PDD-71), constabulary tasks include the regulation of peoples' movements when necessary to ensure safety; interventions "to stop civil violence, such as vigilante lynchings or other violent public crimes" and to "stop and deter widespread or organized looting, vandalism, riots or other mob-type action;" and the dispersal of "unruly or violent public demonstrations and civil disturbances." (*Text: The Clinton Administration White Paper on Peace Operations*, February 24, 2000, pp 9-10.) Constabulary forces often can deploy more rapidly than other international civilian police because they usually deploy as "formed units" (i.e., in previously formed working groups) instead of as individuals. They also are often equipped with their own communication and logistical support. See CRS Report RL32321, *Policing in Peacekeeping and Related Stability Operations: Problems and Proposed Solutions*, by Nina M. Serafino.

[12]  ACRI provided training in traditional peacekeeping skills where there is an existing cease-fire or peace accord. The more muscular ACOTA, initiated in 2002, has also provided training in the skills needed for African troops to perform peacekeeping tasks in more hostile environments, including force protection, light-infantry operations and small-unit tactics. Information from a State Department official and Col. Russell J.

Handy, USAF, Africa Contingency Operations Training Assistance: Developing Training Partnerships for the Future of Africa. Air and Space Power Journal, Fall 2003, as posted online at http://www.airpower.maxwell.af.mil/airchronicles/apj/apj03/fal03/handy.html. ACOTA also put greater emphasis on the "train the trainer" aspect. As of 2005, training packages included Command and Staff Operations Skills, Command Post Exercises (i.e., exercises, often computer-based, of headquarters commanders and staff) and Peace Support Operations Soldier Skills field training, according to a State Department fact sheet.

[13] Military personnel from two of these nations were trained only briefly under ACRI. Training for the Côte d'Ivoire was halted because of a military coup, and for Uganda, because of that country's involvement in the conflict in the Democratic Republic of Congo.

[14] The Senegalese were trained to participate in missions in the Democratic Republic of the Congo (DRC), the Côte d'Ivoire, Liberia, and Darfur.

[15] Department of State, Bureau of Political-Military Affairs, e-mail of February 23, 2009.

[16] The Department of Defense transferred the $80 million in P.L. 108-447 (Division J Section 117) supplemental appropriations to be used for GPOI programs in June 2005. Funds became available for obligation in mid-July, 15 days after the State Department notified Congress of its spending plans.

[17] This project was part of plans for what was formerly referred to as the Asia-Pacific Area Network (APAN).

[18] However, GPOI did not pay the individual costs of each of these participants, including travel, per diem, and any other expenses.

[19] SEEBRIG as an entity does not hold the presidential determination necessary to receive direct GPOI support, but GPOI provides support to SEEBRIG through direct assistance to Romania, which hosted the SEEBRIG headquarters. Original plans were to provide pre-deployment training for troops participating in the International Security Assistance Force (ISAF), the NATO peacekeeping operation in Afghanistan, but were changed when it was determined there was no need for it.

[20] Texts available at http://www.g8.gc.ca/2002Kananaskis/kananaskis/afraction-en.pdf and http://www.g8.gc.ca/ AFRIQUE-0 1june-en. asp.

[21] Text available at http://www.g8usa.gov/d_061004c.htm. In his September 2004 speech to the United Nations, President Bush referred to Italy as a "joint sponsor" of GPOI, because it co-sponsred with the United States the Sea Island G8 peacekeeping action plan.

[22] According to *Carabinieri* officials interviewed by the author, as of mid-November 2004, some 1,300 *carabinieri* were deployed in missions to Iraq, Afghanistan, Eritrea, Albania, and Palestine.

[23] In 2006, CoESPU officials stated they would like a commitment of five U.S. military service members, one as Deputy Director and others to assist with information, training, and studies and research efforts, including the development of doctrine. Author's interviews at CoESPU, June 2006.

[24] Author's interviews at CoESPU, June 2006.

[25] Although the initiative had long been in the works, President Bush approved GPOI in April 2004, two months after the FY2005 budget request was submitted to Congress. To fund the initiative at approximately $100 million in FY2005, the Administration

proposed that 80% be DOD funds and the remaining 20% be ACOTA State Department funds. The Armed Services committees did not back GPOI because of concerns that its inclusion in the DOD budget would divert funds from U.S. troops. GPOI's strongest support seemed to come from Senate foreign affairs authorizers and appropriators. Nevertheless, in the end, Congress divided the FY2005 GPOI funding in the Consolidated Appropriations Act for FY2005 (H.R. 4818/P.L. 108-447) as follows. Section 117 of Division J ("Other Matters") provided that "$80 million may be transferred with the concurrence of the Secretary of Defense" to the Department of State Peacekeeping Operations account, where it was allocated to GPOI. Division D of H.R. 4818/P.L. 108-447 contained $20 million in State Department PKO funding for the ACOTA account and nearly $1.8 million in EPIC Foreign Military Financing funding. Both accounts which are now subsumed under GPOI.

[26] The Bush Administration requested $114.4 million for FY2006 GPOI funding. The House FY2006 Foreign Operations appropriations bill, H.R. 3057 (as reported by the House Appropriations Committee (HAC), H.Rept. 109- 152, on June 24 and passed on June 28), contained $96.4 million for GPOI. In its report, the HAC expressed its support for GPOI as a means for the United States to "reduce the emphasis on the use of military troops for these operations." It explained that it had provided $18 million less than the request because it did not expect that all $63 million indicated for equipment and transportation outside of Africa could be obligated and spent in 2006. The Senate Foreign Relations Committee version of the State Department authorization bill for FY2006 and FY2007 (S. 600, S.Rept. 109-3 5, reported on March 10, 2005, and returned to the calendar on April 26) would have authorized $114.4 million for FY2006 and such sums as may be necessary for FY2007 for GPOI. The House version (H.R. 2601, H.Rept. 109-168, as reported by the House International Relations Committee on July 13, 2005 and passed on July 20) The Senate version of the bill (as reported June 30 and passed July 20), contained $114.0 million for GPOI. does not mention GPOI and does not detail accounts in such a way as to indicate whether GPOI is funded. There was no further action on the bill. In the end, Congress did not dedicate any funds specifically for GPOI (or for any other program in the PKO account) in the conference version of the FY2006 Foreign Operations appropriation bill (H.Rept. 109-265, P.L. 109-102, signed into law November 14, 2005), which funded the PKO account at $175 million—$20.8 million below the Administration's request of $195.8 million. The State Department eventually allocated an estimated $100.4 million for.

[27] The House was disinclined to provide full funding. Senate appropriators expressed discontent with State Department management of the program. They proposed that GPOI funding be transferred to a new FMF program and recommended that the COESPU program be either fully funded by other countries or be transferred to the State Department Bureau of International Narcotics and Law Enforcement Affairs (INL) In the Senate Appropriations Committee (SAC) version of H.R. 5522, the State, Foreign Operations and Related Programs Appropriations Bill for FY2007 (S.Rept. 109-277), approved by SAC on June 29, 2006, funding for GPOI would be transferred from the PKO account to a new program under the Foreign Military Financing Program. S.Rept. 109-277 stated that the State Department "has failed to demonstrate a requisite level of commitment to the program, instead viewing funds provided for GPOI as a funding source for other activities." [The State Department transferred $57 million

in GPOI funds to support urgent needs of the African Union Mission in Sudan (AMIS) in Darfur, Sudan, according to a State Department official.] The report also scored the State Department for ignoring committee guidance on GPOI and for its inability "to articulate any plan for the use of fiscal year 2005 funding until calendar year 2006." S.Rept. 109-277, p. 92. The SAC recommended that a Combatant Commanders Initiative Fund be created under FMF, the purpose of which would be "identical to GPOI, namely, to identify the critical shortfalls in the training, equipment, and capabilities of our allies to serve in peacekeeping and peace enforcement operations." To decide on the allocation of funds, the Assistant Secretary of State for Political-Military [Pol-Mil] Affairs would consult with commanders of the U.S. regional military commands (U.S., Pacific, Central, European, and Southern) to identify "the most critical training and equipment shortfalls of our peacekeeping partners and regional allies" in order to develop a three year plan and program to address those needs. S.Rept. 109-277, p. 92.

[28] Revised Continuing Appropriations Resolution, 2007 (H.J.Res. 20, P.L. 110-5, signed into law February 15, 2007. Amends P.L. 109-289, division B, as amended by P.L. 109-369 and P.L. 109-383.)

[29] Congress, in effect, reduced the amount of funding available for the GPOI program by funding the overall PKO budget at $223.25 million, while earmarking $50 million for peacekeeping operations in Sudan. Congress thus provided $173.25 million for other (than Sudan peacekeeping) PKO programs in FY2007, i.e., $27.25 million less than the Administration's $200.5 million PKO budget request and the same as the FY2006 PKO budget. State Department plans for FY2007 included spending for two new programs totaling some $31 million, the Trans-Sahara Counter-Terrorism Initiative (TSCTI) and Liberia, that were not included in the FY2006 budget.

[30] Although the act does not specify funding for GPOI, the Joint Explanatory Statement on the final version of the omnibus appropriations bill specifies that the executive branch is to take into account House and Senate Committee report language on bills incorporated into the omnibus when implementing the legislation. The House Report (H.Rept. 110-197) accompanying the original State Department, Foreign Operations, and Related Programs appropriations bill recommends full funding.

[31] U.S. Department of State. *Summary and Highlights, International Affairs Function 150: Fiscal Year 2010 Budget Request.* p. 42. http://www.state.gov/ documents/organization/122513.pdf.

[32] These are "training and equipping peacekeepers worldwide, with a particular focus on Africa"; "carrying out a clearinghouse function to exchange information and coordinate G-8 efforts to enhance peace operations"; "providing transportation and logistics support for deploying peacekeepers"; "developing a cached equipment program to procure and warehouse equipment for use in peace operations globally"; and "providing support to the international Center of Excellence for Stability Police Units (COESPU) in Italy to increase the capabilities and interoperability of stability police to participate in peace operations.... " See Section 1 108(c)(1).

[33] Section 1108 refers to a 2007 Government Accountability Office (GAO) report's conclusion regarding relative costs. In comparing the cost of an actual U.N. peacekeeping operation in Haiti with the potential cost of a hypothetical similar U.S. operation, the GAO judged that the U.S. operation would cost about twice as much. "A

U.S. peacekeeping operation, as illustrated by the specific example in Haiti, is likely to be much more expensive than a UN operation," according to the GAO. Although noting that the particulars of this one example "cannot be generalized across all operations," the GAO added that "many of the cost elements, such as police and military costs are likely to be more expensive for a U.S.-led operation, regardless of location." Government Accountability Office. *Peacekeeping: Observations on Costs, Strengths, and Limitations of U.S. and UN Operations*. GAO-07-998T. June 13, 2007. p. 16.

[34] U.S. Department of State. Office of Plans, Policy, and Analysis. Bureau of Political-Military Affairs. *Global Peace Operations Initiative (GPOI): Summary of GPOI Strategy for Fiscal Years 2005-2006*. September 4, 2006.

[35] In action on the FY2008 National Defense Authorization Act, the Senate Armed Services Committee (SASC), in Section 1204 of its version of the bill (S. 1547, reported June 5, 2007), called for a GAO study describing and assessing the activities and implementation of the GPOI program. This requirement was retained in the final bill (H.R. 4986, P.L. 110-181, signed into law January 28, 2008). In the SASC report accompanying the Senate version of the bill (S.Rept. 110-77), SASC stated that it wanted to "strengthen the likelihood that GPOI will be administered in such a fashion, and that there will be an expectation, if not a requirement, that GPOI training recipient countries contribute troops to U.N. missions in the near-term, and that GPOI will increase the number of peacekeepers who can remain ready via sustained training and equipping programs." SASC expressed concern as to whether the readiness of GPOI-trained troops "is being monitored or maintained" and noted that program objectives calling for the establishment of an equipment depot for and of a multilateral transportation logistics support arrangement (TLSA) have not been fulfilled.35 SASC also expressed concern that participation by other G-8 members has not met expectations.

[36] Government Accountability Office. *Peacekeeping: Thousands Trained but United States is Unlikely to Complete All Activities by 2010 and Some Improvements are Needed.* GAO-08-754, June 2008.

[37] Peacekeeping: Thousands Trained. op. cit., p. 35.

[38] "Mission essential task lists" or METLs in military terminology.

In: U.S. Political Programs: Functions and Assessments    ISBN: 978-1-61209-448-9
Editors: Julianna M. Moretti and Karen J. Chordstron    © 2011 Nova Science Publishers, Inc.

*Chapter 11*

# HEALTH CARE REFORM:
# AN INTRODUCTION*

## *Bob Lyke*

## ABSTRACT

Health care reform has become an issue in the 111th Congress, driven by growing concern about millions of people without insurance coverage, continual increases in cost and spending, and quality shortcomings. Commonly cited figures indicate that more than 45 million people have no insurance, which can limit their access to care and ability to pay for the care they receive. Costs are rising for nearly everyone, and the country now likely spends over $2.5 trillion, more than 17% of gross domestic product (GDP), on health care services and products, far more than other industrialized countries. For all this spending, the country scores but average or somewhat worse on many indicators of health care quality, and many may not get appropriate standards of care.

These concerns raise significant challenges. Each of the concerns is more complex than might first appear, which increases the difficulty of finding solutions. For example, by one statistical measure, far more than 45 million people face the risk of being uninsured for short time periods, yet by another, substantially fewer have no insurance for long periods. Insurance coverage and access to health care are not the same, and it is possible to have one without the other. Having coverage does not ensure that one can pay for care, nor does it always shield one from significant financial loss in the case of serious illness. Similarly, high levels of spending may be partly attributable to the country's wealth, while rising costs, though difficult for many, may primarily mean that less money is available for other things.

Solutions to these concerns may conflict with one another. For example, expanding coverage to most of the uninsured would likely drive up costs (as more people seek care) and expand public budgets (since additional public subsidies would be required). Cutting costs may threaten initiatives to improve quality. Other challenges include addressing the interests of stakeholders that have substantial investments in present arrangements and the unease some people have about moving from an imperfect but known system to

---

* This is an edited, reformatted and augmented edition of a United States Congressional Research Service publication. CRS Report R40517, dated June 30, 2009.

something that is potentially better but untried. How much reform might cost and how to pay for it is also an issue.

Health care reform proposals will likely rekindle debate over perennial issues in American health care policy. These include whether insurance should be public or private; whether employment- based insurance should be strengthened, weakened, or left alone; what role states might play; and whether Medicaid should be folded into new insurance arrangements. Whether changes to Medicare should occur at the same time may also be considered. Concerns about coverage, cost and spending, and quality are likely to be addressed within the context of these issues.

The committees of principal jurisdiction for health care are working on comprehensive reform proposals. The Senate HELP Committee released a draft on June 9th , while a coordinated measure by three House committees (Education and Labor, Energy and Commerce, and Ways and Means) was released on June 19th . The Senate Finance Committee has no draft available to the public, though it has released policy option documents. A dozen other comprehensive bills were introduced by the end of June.

This report does not discuss or even try to identify all of the concerns about health care in the United States that are prompting calls for reform. Other concerns may also be important, at least to some, and will likely contribute to the complexity of the reform debate.


## INTRODUCTION

Health care reform is again an issue. For the first time since 1994, when sweeping changes proposed by President Clinton and others failed to be enacted, there is demonstrable interest in reforming health care in the United States. Surveys and studies show persistent problems, political leaders are debating issues and solutions, and interest groups of all persuasions are holding conferences and staking out positions. Some states have enacted their own reforms, and others are considering doing so. The congressional committees with principal jurisdiction over health care have draft bills that may be acted on in July.

Interest in reform is being driven by three predominant concerns. One is coverage. By a commonly cited estimate, more than 45 million people were uninsured at some point in 2007— more than one-seventh of the population. The recession may have increased this number. Without private insurance or coverage under government health programs, people can have difficulty obtaining needed care and problems paying for the care they receive.

A second concern is cost and spending. Health care costs are rising for nearly everyone— employers, workers, retirees, providers, and taxpayers—sometimes in unexpected, erratic jumps. Costs are a particular source of anxiety for families that are planning for retirement or where someone is seriously ill. National health care spending now likely exceeds $2.5 trillion, more than 17% of the gross domestic product (GDP). Spending has climbed from over 12% of GDP in 1990 and 7% in 1970.

Third, there is concern about quality. Although the United States spends substantially more on health care per person than other industrialized countries, it scores only average or somewhat worse on many quality of care indicators. Medical and medication errors harm many people annually, sometimes resulting in death.

The three concerns raise significant challenges. For one thing, each is more complex than might first appear, which makes it difficult to find solutions, or at least simple or uniform solutions. Second, solutions to the three concerns may conflict with one another. Under many scenarios, for example, providing coverage to the 45 million uninsured would likely drive up costs (as more people seek care) and expand public budgets (since public subsidies would be required to help them get insurance). Attempts to restrict costs may impede efforts to increase quality, since new initiatives often require additional, not fewer, resources. It is possible, however, that cost savings might allow those initiatives to be funded. Other challenges involve significant stakeholder interests that reform might threaten, including those of insurers, hospitals and other health care facilities, and doctors and other providers, many of whom have substantial investments in present arrangements. In 2007, for example, nearly one-third of total health care expenditures occurred in hospitals (see Table C-1 in Appendix C), which cannot be quickly built, easily shut, or transformed simply by their own choice into different kinds of health care providers. In addition, if debates over the Clinton plan are still a guide, some people may be uneasy about moving from an imperfect but known system to something that is potentially better but untried.

This report provides an introduction to health care reform. It focuses on the three predominant concerns just mentioned—coverage, cost and spending, and quality—and some of the legislative issues within which they likely will be debated—the scope of reform (particularly whether Medicare and Medicaid should be included); the choice between public and private coverage; whether employment-based insurance should be strengthened, weakened, or left alone; and what role states might play. The report does not attempt to identify, let alone discuss, all the relevant concerns about health care in the United States, even though others may also be important and will likely contribute to the complexity of the reform debate. The report may be updated to include other health care reform issues as the debate in Congress unfolds.

## THREE PREDOMINANT CONCERNS

The three concerns discussed below—coverage, cost and spending, and quality—loom large in the emerging debate over health care reform. Some Members might not consider every one important, but all have been included in recent congressional debate and proposals.

Other concerns about health care in the United States that are not discussed in this report include the following:

- problems in the private insurance market, particularly for individual and small- group insurance,
- problems with shortages of health care providers,
- problems with public health programs, funding, and administrative oversight,
- problems of economic concentration among insurers and providers,
- problems of equity in access to care and the type of care received, and
- problems of equity in public subsidies.

## Coverage

In August, 2008, the U.S. Census Bureau estimated that 45.7 million people had no health insurance at a point in time in 2007. The number had declined from 47 million the previous year, largely due to increases in Medicaid and CHIP (the State Children's Health Insurance Program) enrollment [1]. The number may now be going back up due to the recession.

There are both higher and lower numbers that give different perspectives. Families USA, an advocacy group, recently estimated that 86.7 million people—one in three of those under age 65—were uninsured for some or all or the two-year period 2007-2008 [2]. The number indicates that many more than 45 million people are likely to be uninsured over a short time period, even if many have coverage at some point. On the other hand, the Agency for Healthcare Research and Quality (AHRQ) has estimated that 26.1 million people were uninsured for the entire two-year period 2004-2005, and that 17.4 million were uninsured for the preceding two years as well—four straight years [3]

Coverage is not the same as access, and it is possible to have one without the other. Some uninsured people can get care in community health clinics or from doctors providing pro bono work, even if they have no money. If people need emergency care, hospitals that participate in Medicare are required to stabilize them or provide an appropriate transfer to another facility. On the other hand, having coverage does not guarantee that one can easily find a doctor, as both Medicare and Medicaid participants sometime report. Having coverage also does not ensure that one can pay for care. People with high deductible insurance, perhaps chosen when they were healthy or because premiums were lower, may have to pay several thousand dollars out of pocket before their plan begins reimbursements [4]. For some people, including those who lose their jobs, paying for health care is a major problem [5] Even people with comprehensive plans with low deductibles may have difficulty paying the ongoing costs of chronic conditions or the major costs of serious illnesses.

Being uninsured can cause problems. According to some studies, uninsured people are more likely to postpone or do without care, including screening and preventive tests that health care practitioners commonly use. They are less likely to have regular sources of care and more likely to use emergency rooms [6]. At the same time, it is sometimes difficult to attribute differences in health status or outcomes to whether one has insurance since other unobservable factors may be important [7]

The uninsured have diverse characteristics, which suggests they may lack coverage for different reasons. As shown in Appendix B, most are employed full time or are family members of those who are, but some are in families where no one is in the labor force. Most are not poor, but many are low income. About one in eight uninsured in 2007 were in household insurance units with incomes over $50,000.

As Congress considers what to do about the uninsured, a number of issues will likely arise, including the following:

- whether it is important for everyone to have coverage,
- whether some groups (such as people between the ages of 55 and 65) should have higher priority in obtaining coverage,
- whether people should be required to have coverage (an individual mandate),

- whether coverage provided with public subsidies should meet minimum benefit and cost-sharing standards.

## Cost and Spending

According to the U.S. Department of Health and Human Services, spending on health care in the United States increased from 7.2% of GDP in 1970 to 12.3% in 1990 and 16.2% in 2007 [8]. It likely is more than 17% in 2009 [9]. Barring changes in law, the Congressional Budget Office (CBO) projected in 2008 that it would rise to 25% of GDP by 2025 and much higher levels beyond [10]. CBO has cautioned that "as health care spending consumes a greater and greater share of the nation's economic output in the future, Americans will be faced with increasingly difficult choices between health care and other priorities." [11]

The United States spends considerably more on health care than other industrialized countries: on a per capita basis, its spending is more than two times greater than the spending of the median Organization for Economic Cooperation and Development (OECD) country [12]. It has been argued that some of the higher health care spending has added real value through medical advances [13]. Some of it may be attributable to the higher per capita GDP in the United States, which simply allows Americans to spend more [14]. However, its value has been questioned in light of the mixed performance of the United States on many indicators of health care quality, as described in the next section.

"Cost" and "spending" are often used interchangeably, particularly with the issues discussed in this report. Use of one term instead of the other may reflect differences in context or perspective, not substance, though this is not always the case (for example, prices are usually described as costs, while purchases are usually described as spending). It is apparent that what are called rising costs can cause serious problems for people and entities that cannot easily absorb them. Concern about costs arises from a number of trends. The average annual rate of growth in medical care prices between 1980 and 2007 was 4.7%, in contrast to 2.5% for the entire consumer price index (CPI). Health insurance premiums on average increased by 114% from 1999 to 2007, far more than increases in workers' earnings (27%) [15]. The rising cost of health insurance likely is one reason there are increasing numbers of uninsured.

Controlling cost and spending is unlikely to be easy. Many economists argue that the principal factor driving increases in health care spending is technology, both new pharmaceuticals and other products and services and wider use of existing ones [16]. It is not obvious whether some developments can be limited or their application blocked (for example, by limiting diffusion on the basis of clinical evidence) and some would question whether they should. One challenge in controlling costs is that payers may shift burdens to others, sometimes in ways that are not clearly understood or measurable. For example, most economists argue that employer payments for health insurance are actually borne by workers through reduced wages and other forms of compensation. Attempts to limit employer-paid insurance may lead to increases in wages in ways that are difficult to predict.

One particular congressional concern is the cost of federal health insurance programs. In 2007, Medicare and Medicaid, the two largest programs, accounted for about 20% of the federal budget and over 27% of total national health care expenditures (for the latter, see Table C-2 in Appendix C). They also constituted about 5% of GDP. If past cost trends continue, it has been estimated the two programs would grow to about 20% of GDP by 2050, approximately the same share of GDP as all federal spending recently [17]. Increases of that magnitude would likely cause serious problems.

As Congress considers what to do about health care costs and spending, a number of issues will likely arise, including the following:

- whether markets in health care, if they were less regulated, would result in price reductions and quality improvements that have occurred in other markets,
- whether efforts to reduce costs for some would increase costs for others,
- whether efforts to reduce costs would adversely affect the health of consumers, and
- whether efforts to reduce spending or slow its growth would impede efforts to provide coverage to more people or to improve quality.

## Quality

Despite spending more on health care than other industrialized countries, the United States scores only average or somewhat worse on many quality of care indicators. It is near the top for some measures, such as survival rates for breast and colorectal cancer, but near the bottom for others, such as mortality and hospitalization rates for asthma [18]. A recent Centers for Disease Control and Prevention (CDC) report found that the United States ranked 29th in the world in infant mortality in 2004. The U.S. position in rankings on this measure has been declining [19]. Notwithstanding difficulties of cross-national comparisons, these indicators show that Americans do not receive the best value for their health care spending and that there is room for improvement.

Concerns about health care quality in the United States go beyond international comparisons, and they cannot be reduced simply to returns on the dollar. Medical errors appear to be one systemic shortcoming. An influential 1999 Institute of Medicine study found that at least 44,000 people, and perhaps as many as 98,000, die from in-patient hospital care every year. The study found that most medical errors do not result from individual recklessness or actions of a particular group; rather, they are attributable to "faulty systems, processes, and conditions that lead people to make mistakes or fail to prevent them" [20] A more recent study estimated that if all hospitals performed as well as the best group of hospitals for patient safety, over 44,000 deaths among Medicare beneficiaries could have been avoided during the years 2002 through 2004 [21]. Another Institute of Medicine study reported in 2006 that there were more than 400,000 preventable drug-related injuries each year in hospitals alone, and that altogether medication errors harmed at least 1.5 million people [22]

Not adhering to evidence-based practice or clinical practice guidelines is also a problem. One 2003 study found that Americans receive recommended evidence-based care only about 55% of the time. Recommended care was provided more often for conditions such as breast cancer (75.7%) and hypertension (64.7%) than it was for others such as atrial fibrillation (24.7%) or hip fracture (22.8%) [23]. A later study using the same data found that while differences among sociodemographic subgroups were relatively small, quality problems were profound and systemic [24]. Most studies of disparities have found significant differences by sociodemographic subgroups, with whites receiving better care on many core measures than racial and ethnic minorities [25]

Over the past decade, there have been numerous efforts to improve quality of care in the United States [26] Among other things, there have been attempts to improve and refine the metrics used for measuring quality, to publicly report comparative information, and, in some cases, to use quality standards as one basis for payment policies. Despite observable progress, the most recent National Healthcare Quality Report (2008) indicated that health care quality is suboptimal and continues to improve at a slow pace [27]. Among the challenges to making further improvements are disagreements about the utility or appropriateness of some measures (including concerns about how the public might interpret them), the fragmented nature of the American health care system, and barriers to access for some groups that complicate the work of providers.

As Congress considers what to do about health care quality, a number of issues will likely arise, including the following:

- whether quality improvements should be pursued for their own sake, regardless of whether they promise to save money,
- whether it is possible to improve the quality of care without reorganizing and restructuring health care delivery systems,
- whether preventive care should have a significant role in improving quality, relative to acute or chronic care services,
- whether the evidence-base is adequate for guiding quality improvement efforts, or whether the way research is organized, financed, and carried out needs to be changed, and
- whether employers and other entities that are not health care providers can play a role in improving health outcomes.

## SOME LIKELY LEGISLATIVE ISSUES

As the 111th Congress considers health care reform, some perennial issues about national policy will likely be debated. These include deep-seated disagreements about whether insurance should be public or private; whether employment-based insurance should be strengthened, weakened, or left alone; and what role states should play. The scope of reform might also be an issue, including whether Medicaid should be folded into new insurance arrangements. There already has been debate on some of these issues, both in the current and previous Congress, just as there has been in prior decades when significant health care legislation had been attempted and sometimes enacted.

The legislative issues discussed below will affect attempts to deal with the three predominant concerns discussed above. For example, even if there were a consensus that everyone should have coverage—something some Members actually might not consider a priority—that would not resolve questions of whether the coverage should be public or private, whether employer- provided coverage should in some way be favored, or whether states should have the principal responsibility for enrolling people in plans and subsidizing those who need assistance. Disputes over any of these issues could derail attempts to meet coverage goals.

Other legislative issues than those discussed below might include the following:

- how much health care reform might cost, and how it should be financed,
- whether there should be individual or employer mandates, or possibly both,
- how much individuals and families might be expected to pay for coverage from their own resources, and
- how insurance benefit standards might be set and updated.

## The Scope of Reform

The scope of reform is one of the first issues to confront proponents of change. Changing private insurance for people under age 65 through a combination of market restructuring, benefit standards, and financing reforms was the core and most controversial aspect of President Clinton's 1993 proposal, but it was only one part of a comprehensive package. His Health Security Act also would have brought about important changes in Medicare, Medicaid, long-term care, and the tax code, and it included initiatives for administrative simplification, health information privacy and security, health care quality, malpractice reform, prevention and public health, and healthcare workforce expansion.

Perhaps as a consequence of the failure of that legislation, most subsequent health care reform bills have been smaller in scope. Many proposals for insuring people under age 65 have been less sweeping, focusing on creating better options for small businesses, for example, or allowing a Medicare buy-in (i.e., allowing early retirees and others to pay premiums for coverage before age 65.)

Other parts of the Clinton proposal that got less attention at the time were addressed in legislation that followed, such as the privacy rules included in the Health Insurance Portability and Accountability Act of 1996 (HIPAA, P.L. 104-191), as were other parts of some Republican proposals of the time, such as the Health Savings Accounts included in the Medicare Prescription Drug, Improvement, and Modernization Act of 2003 (P.L. 108-173). Congress proceeded in incremental steps.

Changing the private insurance market for people under age 65 is likely once again to be the center of health care reform. Nearly all uninsured people are under that age (see Table A-1 in Appendix A), and many advocates for reform call for giving them access to coverage (and sometimes choice of coverage) that meets specified benefit and cost-sharing standards. If this could be accomplished, many advocates would consider reform initiatives to be successful.

Others would argue that reform needs to address additional problems as well. Medicare might be included since older people consume a share of health care disproportionate to the number and Medicare policies and payments significantly affect health care delivery systems. Considering the projected growth in Medicare spending, said to be unsustainable, some would argue that it should be reformed sooner rather than later.

Medicaid might be included since new public subsidies could enable lower-income families to have the same options as other Americans. It might be administratively cumbersome for these families to go from private insurance to Medicaid and then back again (or vice versa) as their economic fortunes change. However, Medicaid provides some benefits that historically private coverage has not, so some part of it might have to remain in a system that otherwise has private options.

In addition, arguments likely will be advanced that improvements in quality, public health, and other matters are needed so that people of all ages, regardless of their insured status, can receive adequate health care.

## Public or Private Insurance

Private insurance is the largest source of funding for national health expenditures, providing 34.6% of the total (see Table C-2 in Appendix C). It is somewhat larger than the combined contributions of Medicare and Medicaid (33.9%), the two largest public programs. Private insurance has always been larger than these two programs, though in the past the difference has been greater.

The distinction between public and private insurance sometimes is hard to draw. Medicare has private plan options (Medicare Advantage plans) that now enroll 20% of Medicare beneficiaries, and Medicaid has commercial managed care plans. In both cases, the private plans are publicly financed and closely regulated, but participants often have choices that are characteristic of private coverage. In turn, private insurance is regulated more than other consumer products, including requirements and restrictions on benefits, pricing, and marketing when sold as commercial insurance and tax code and ERISA rules when employers self-insure (for the latter, see "The Role of States," below). Nonetheless, important differences remain with respect to financing (public programs usually are financed largely with tax dollars, not premiums), eligibility (public programs do not use underwriting), and flexibility (private plans usually can innovate and make other changes quickly). Some people consider these differences important both for health care and for the role of government in general.

Whether public programs should be expanded is likely to be an issue in health care reform. There could be proposals to expand Medicaid to everyone below poverty, [28] for example, as well as to allow participation by some people with incomes higher than current ceilings. The categorical eligibility restrictions (for example, being a parent or dependent child) could be relaxed, perhaps in conjunction with a more limited benefit package. Similarly, there could be proposals to allow a Medicare buy-in for some under age 65.

Health insurance purchasing exchanges like the Massachusetts Connector or the Federal Employees Health Benefits Program are being considered as a way to help people find and acquire coverage [29]. Whether a public option should be allowed in the exchange, as some have proposed, already has provoked debate. Depending on what it is, a public option could provide coverage to people that private insurers do not normally seek, and it could use the government's purchasing power to control costs. With its access to public financing, however, a public plan could also compete unfairly against private plans, eventually driving them out of the market.

## Employment-Based Insurance

Employment-based insurance is the principal form of coverage for people under age 65. As shown in Table A-1 in Appendix A, more than three-fifths of that population is insured either as a worker or the spouse or dependent of a worker. Employment-based insurance has several strengths, including risk pools that are not formed on the basis of health status, ease of acquisition by workers, and tax subsidies that exceed those for individual market insurance. On the other hand, plans chosen by employers may not meet individual workers' needs, and changing jobs may require obtaining both new insurance and new doctors.

Whether employment-based insurance should be strengthened, weakened, or left alone is likely to emerge as an issue in health care reform. The issue might arise several ways. For example, if the tax exclusion for employer-paid coverage were eliminated, federal revenue receipts could increase by over $240 billion a year [30]. Some see this potential revenue as a way to finance health care reform, particularly to pay for subsidies so that all individuals and families could afford coverage. Others argue that the exclusion should be capped in order to discourage what they term as overly generous health care benefits. The former option might weaken incentives employers have to provide insurance, as might the latter depending on where the cap is set. In assessing these possible changes, one must take account of how the budget savings they generate are used in a reformed system [31]

Similarly, proposals to increase subsidies for individual market insurance (perhaps through a tax or direct premium support) might weaken employment-based insurance. If lower income people were to afford coverage, subsidies would have to cover most of its cost. (See Appendix B for the incomes of people without insurance.) However, subsidies of this size would greatly exceed tax subsidies for active workers under current law; this might lead employers to drop their own plans, especially if they largely employed low-wage workers.

## The Role of States

States have long played a significant role in health care. They are the principal regulators for insurance sold in the private market, particularly the individual and small group markets. While their authority to regulate self-insured employer plans has been preempted by the Employee Retirement Income Security Act (ERISA), they remain largely responsible for regulating business practices associated with the insurance that employers purchase [32]. (Employers that self-insure assume the risk of paying for covered services, though some limit their exposure to large losses through stop-loss insurance. A majority of people covered under employer plans are under self- insured plans.) States are also responsible for licensing of health care providers and investigating certain complaints about them, approval of health care facilities, and much of the law governing contracts, employment, and other matters. As shown in Table C-2 in Appendix C, states and their local subdivisions were also the source of $281.4 billion in health care expenditures in 2007, over 12% of the total.

An important issue for health care reform is what role states would continue to play. Conceivably one might envision a reformed system that is governed entirely by national policies and national administration, whether part of the federal government or not. However, comprehensive reform proposals that would establish nationwide health care policies typically assign some responsibilities to the states or, by their silence, allow much existing state law and regulation to continue. One important exception is the structure of the insurance market and specification of benefits, which, if a state role remains, usually must still comply with often detailed national standards. Another exception is financing and subsidies, which usually are also national in scope. However, unless the federal government is to be the sole source of public financing, states would probably be required to help.

It is possible that states might play leading roles in health care reform. If federal legislation is not enacted, some states will likely attempt to bring about change on their own. Reforms adopted in Massachusetts in 2006 might serve as a model, at least for the possibility of action, as might smaller changes adopted in other states [33]. States that act on their own may be able to tailor plans to their particular needs and preferences. However, the problems states face vary greatly, as do their fiscal capacities to pay for reforms. Massachusetts had one of the lowest uninsured rates in the country and one of the highest per capita incomes, though its health care costs are also among the highest. States might be slow to act unless they receive federal assistance. ERISA preemption might block some initiatives. State reforms could leave the country with a patchwork quilt of health care systems, though some might find this better than current arrangements or a national system not to their liking.

## THE COST OF REFORM

One of the most difficult issues of health care reform may be its cost. For many in Congress, the predominant concern will likely be the cost to the federal government, both in the near term and for many years out. Not only might new federal costs be significant, but they would come on top of large current and anticipated federal deficits, including significant projected costs for continuing federal health insurance programs (see page 5, above) [34]. However, health care reform may increase costs for others as well, including the states, employers, employees, consumers, health care providers, and taxpayers. If their expenditures do not increase, their income may go down, leaving them in a worse position financially. At the same time, reform would likely have the opposite effect for some of these parties, making them better off.

For the federal government, the largest cost component of currently-discussed proposals will likely be extending health insurance to people without coverage. Providing insurance to the uninsured will probably be expensive considering the size of this population (see page 2), their income (page 15), and the need, if the insurance is to be meaningful, to pay for most if not all of the premiums for those with low incomes. Ten-year costs for providing universal coverage, including subsidies to some who now have insurance, could approach or well exceed $1 trillion, depending on the cost of the insurance (and how that might change due to reform), the subsidy schedules, and whether premium payments in general would be considered to be part of the federal budget [35]

Federal costs for reform could be offset a number of ways, including increases in tax rates, reductions in tax subsidies, reductions in existing federal health insurance and other federal health programs, reductions in other federal programs, and increased borrowing. Considerable attention is being given to eliminating or capping the tax exclusion for employer-provided health coverage because that could raise substantial amounts of revenue [36]. (For analysis of capping the exclusion, see CRS Report R40673, *Limiting the Exclusion for Employer-Provided Health Insurance: Background and Issues*, by Bob Lyke and Chris L. Peterson.) Other proposals for offsets include increasing the excise tax on alcohol, imposing a new excise tax on sugar-sweetened beverages, changing Medicare and Medicaid graduate medical education (GME) payments, changing Medicare and Medicaid disproportionate share 9DSH) payments, and reducing Medicare reimbursements for high-growth over-valued physician services [37].

Other options have been outlined by the Congressional Budget Office [38]. (For analysis of possible tax changes that would raise revenue for reform, see CRS Report R40648, *Tax Options for Financing Health Care Reform*, by Jane G. Gravelle.)

## CONGRESSIONAL PROPOSALS

The committees of principal jurisdiction for health care are working on comprehensive reform proposals. The Senate HELP Committee released a draft on June 9th , while a coordinated measure by three House committees (Education and Labor, Energy and Commerce, and Ways and Means) was released on June 19th . The Senate Finance Committee has not yet released a public draft, though earlier it released some policy options [39]. All three measures are undergoing modification prior to final committee action, which may occur in July.

Other comprehensive reform bills introduced this Congress include H.R. 15 (Dingell), H.R. 193 (Stark), H.R. 676 (Conyers), H.R. 1200 (McDermott), H.R. 1321 (Eshoo), H.R. 2399 (Langevin), H.R. 2520 (Ryan of Wisconsin), H.R. 3000 (Lee), S. 391 (Wyden), S. 703 (Sanders), S. 1099 (Coburn), S. 1240 (DeMint), and S. 1278 (Rockefeller). In general, these bills would provide coverage for nearly all people in the United States, sometimes for everyone under new insurance plans and sometimes only for people not covered by Medicare or some other current plans and arrangements. Many would have an individual mandate, i.e., a requirement that everyone have coverage. Some would address quality, administrative simplicity, and other issues as well.

The Administration has not proposed a health reform bill of its own. However, its FY2010 budget released in February included some broad principles for reform: [40]

- protect families' financial health,
- make health coverage affordable,
- aim for universality,
- provide portability of coverage,
- guarantee choice,
- invest in prevention and wellness,
- improve patient safety and quality care, and
- maintain long-term fiscal sustainability.

If fully implemented, these objectives are likely to be expensive, costing perhaps more than $1 trillion over the next 10 years. In order to offset the cost, the budget proposed a number of tax changes that would raise over $300 billion over that period, mostly from limiting the tax rate that high income taxpayers can use to reduce their tax liability by itemized deductions [41]. It also proposed over $280 billion in Medicare savings and $22 billion in Medicaid savings [42]. On June 13th, the President announced more than $300 billion additional possible savings from Medicare [43]. According to Kathleen Sebelius, the Secretary of Health and Human Services, the President would prefer to finance reform from these sources, not by making employer-provided coverage taxable [44]

## APPENDIX A. OVERVIEW OF HEALTH INSURANCE COVERAGE

The following table provides an overview of the sources of health insurance that people have as well as estimates on the number of uninsured. Estimates for 2009 likely have changed somewhat because of additional population growth and the recession.

**Table A- 1. Health Insurance Coverage, by Type of Insurance and Age, 2007**

| Age | Population (millions) | Type of Insurance | | | | | Uninsured | |
|---|---|---|---|---|---|---|---|---|
| | | Employment based | Private Nongroup | Medicare | Medicaid or Other Public | Military or Veterans' Coverage | (percent) | (millions) |
| Under 19 | 78.7 | 60.7% | 5.3% | 0.7% | 27.6% | 2.8% | 11.3% | 8.9 |
| Under 65 | 262.3 | 64.4% | 6.5% | 2.7% | 13.8% | 3.2% | 17.1% | 45.0 |
| 65+ | 36.8 | 35.0% | 25.9% | 93.2% | 8.9% | 7.1% | 1.9% | 0.7 |
| All ages | 299.1 | 60.8% | 8.9% | 13.8% | 13.2% | 3.7% | 15.3% | 45.7 |

Source: CRS analysis of data from the March 2008 Current Population Survey (CPS). The table is a truncated version of Table 1 in CRS Report 96-891, Health Insurance Coverage: Characteristics of the Insured and Uninsured Populations in 2007, by Chris L. Peterson and April Grady.
*Note:* People may have more than one source of coverage; percentages may total to more than 100.

## APPENDIX B. CHARACTERISTICS OF THE UNINSURED

People under age 65 who were uninsured in 2007 had the following diverse characteristics: [45]

- *Age:* Young adults ages 19 to 24 represented 9.2% of this population but 16.2% of the uninsured,
- *Race and ethnicity*: Hispanics represented 16.6% of this population but 32.4% of the uninsured,
- *Citizenship:* More than one-quarter were not native-born U.S. citizens,
- *Employment:* More than half were full-time, full-year workers or their spouses and children. About a quarter were part-time or partial-year workers or their spouses or children. Less than one-fifth of the uninsured were in households with no attachment to the labor force.

- *Income:* About 57% of household insurance units had incomes below $25,000, 27% between $25,000 and $49,999, 9% between $50,000 and $74,999, and 3% between $75,000 and $99,999. About 4% had incomes of $100,000 or more.
- *Poverty status*: Three-quarters had family incomes above poverty thresholds.

Uninsurance rates for people under age 65 vary widely among the states. Based upon Current Population Survey data for 2006 and 2007, states with the highest rates were Texas (27.4%), New Mexico (25.6%), Florida (24.3%), Louisiana (23%), Arizona (21.8%), and California (20.4%). States with the lowest rates were Massachusetts (8.9%), Hawaii (9.2%), Wisconsin (9.6%), and Minnesota (9.9%) [46]

# APPENDIX C.
## DISTRIBUTION OF NATIONAL HEALTH CARE EXPENDITURES

**Table C- 1. Distribution of National Health Care Expenditures by Service, Product, and Activity, 2007**

| Type of Service, Product, or Activity | Expenditures (in billions of dollars) | Percent of Total Expenditures |
|---|---|---|
| HEALTH SERVICES AND SUPPLIES | | |
| Personal Health Care | | |
| Hospital Care | 696.5 | 31.0 |
| Professional Services | | |
| Physician and Clinical Services | 478.8 | 21.4 |
| Other Professional Services | 62.0 | 2.8 |
| Dental Services | 95.2 | 4.2 |
| Other Personal Health Care | 66.2 | 3.0 |
| Nursing Home and Home Health | 190.4 | 8.5 |
| Retail Outlet Sales of Medical Products | | |
| Prescription Drugs | 227.5 | 10.2 |
| Other Medical Products | 61.8 | 2.8 |
| Government Administration and Net Cost of Private Health Insurance | 155.7 | 6.9 |
| Government Public Health Activities | 64.1 | 2.9 |
| INVESTMENT (Research, Structures, and Equipment) | 143.1 | 6.4 |
| TOTAL | 2,241.2 | 100.0 |

Source: Centers for Medicare and Medicaid Services, U.S. Department of Health and Human Services. National Health Care Expenditures,2007. Table2. http://www.cms.hhs.gov/NationalHealthExpend Data/downloads/ tables.pdf.

Note: Data might not sum to total due to rounding.

The following table provides an overview of how the nation's $2.2 trillion in spending for health care was distributed among various services, products, and activities in 2007. The estimates were prepared by the Centers for Medicare and Medicaid Services (CMS) of the Department of Health and Human Services. CMS estimates that aggregate growth between 2007 and 2008 was 6.1%, which would bring total expenditures for the latter year to over $2.3 trillion [47]

The following table provides an overview of how the nation's $2.2 trillion in health care spending in 2007 were distributed by source of funds.

**Table C-2. Distribution of National Health Care Expenditures by Source of Funds, 2007**

| Source of Funds | Expenditures (in billions of dollars) | Percent of Total Expenditures |
|---|---|---|
| PRIVATE | | |
| Out-of-Pocket Payments | 268.6 | 12.0 |
| Private Health Insurance | 775.0 | 34.6 |
| Other Private Funds | 162.0 | 7.2 |
| PUBLIC | | |
| Federal | | |
| Medicare | 431.2 | 19.2 |
| Medicaid | 186.1 | 8.3 |
| Other Federal | 137.0 | 6.1 |
| State and Local | | |
| Medicaid | 143.3 | 6.4 |
| Other State and Local | 138.1 | 6.2 |
| TOTAL | 2,241.2 | 100.0 |

Source: Centers for Medicare and Medicaid Services, U.S. Department of Health and Human Services. National Health Care Expenditures, 2007. Table 3, http://www.cms.hhs.gov/NationalHealthExpendData/ downloads/ tables.pdf.
Notes: Data might not sum to total due to rounding.

# REFERENCES

[1]   U.S. Census Bureau, Health Insurance Coverage: 2007. http://www.census.go v/hhes/www/hlthins/hlthin07/ hlth07asc.html.

[2]   Families USA, *Americans at Risk*: One in Three Uninsured, March 2009. http://www.familiesusa.org/resources/ publications/reports/americans-at-risk.html.

[3]   Jeffrey A. Rhoades and Steven B. Cohen, *The Long-Term Uninsured in America, 2002-2005: Estimates for the U.S. Population under Age 65*, Agency for Healthcare Research and Quality, Medical Expenditure Panel Survey Statistical Brief #183, August 2007. http://www.meps.ahrq.gov/mepsweb/data_files/publications/st183/stat183.pdf.

[4]   The minimum deductible for a family plan that qualifies for a health savings account (HSA) is $2,300, though insurance reimbursements for preventive care are allowed without any deductible. Families could use funds in their HSAs to pay for some of the deductible, but some accounts may not be large enough. For additional information see

CRS Report RL33257, *Health Savings Accounts: Overview of Rules for 2009*, by Bob Lyke.

[5]   Peter Cunningham, Carolyn Miller, and Alwyn Cassel, *Living on the Edge: Health Care Expenses Strain Family Budgets*, Center for Studying Health System Change, Research Brief No. 10, December 2008. http://www.hschange.com/CONTENT/1034/1034.pdf.

[6]   See Families USA, op. cit., pp. 12-13 and the numerous studies referenced there. Also see Randall R. Bovbjerg and Jack Hadley, Why Health Insurance is Important, The Urban Institute, Health Policy Briefs DC-SPG no. 1, November 2007. http://www.urb an.org/UploadedPDF/411569_importance_of_insurance.pdf.

[7]   Helen Levy and David Meltzer, "The Impact of Health Insurance on Health," *Annual Review of Public Health*, vol. 29 (2008), pp. 399-409.

[8]   Centers for Medicare and Medicaid Services, U.S. Department of Health and Human Services. National Health Care Expenditures, 2007. Table 1. http://www.cms.hh s.gov/NationalHealthExpendData/downloads/tables.pdf.

[9]   Centers for Medicare and Medicaid Services, U.S. Department of Health and Human Services. National Health Expenditure Projections 2008 – 2018. Table 1. http://www.cms.hhs.gov/NationalHealthExpendData/downloads/ proj2008.pdf

[10]  Congressional Budget Office, Growth in Health Care Costs, CBO Testimony before the Committee on the Budget United States Senate, January 31, 2008. http://www. cbo.gov/ftpdocs/89xx/doc8948/01-31-HealthTestimony.pdf

[11]  Congressional Budget Office, The Long-Term Outlook for Health Care Spending, November, 2007. http://www.cbo.gov/ftpdocs/87xx/doc8758/11-13-LT-Health.pdf

[12]  Gerald F. Anderson and Bianca K. Frogner, "Health Spending in OECD Countries: Obtaining Value Per Dollar," *Health Affairs*, vol. 26, no. 6 (2008), pp. 17 18-1727. Also see CRS Report RL34175, *U.S. Health Care Spending: Comparison with Other OECD Countries*, by Chris L. Peterson and Rachel Burton.

[13]  David M. Cutler, Your Money or Your Life: Strong Medicine for America's Health Care System (Oxford University Press, 2005).

[14]  Uwe E. Reinhardt, Peter S. Hussey, and Gerard F. Anderson, "U.S. Health Care Spending in an International Context," *Health Affairs*, vol. 23, no. 3 (2004), pp. 10-25. Citing their previous work, the authors argue that higher prices for health care in the United States can partly be attributed to the compensation needed to attract talented professionals and the relatively greater power of the supply side versus the demand side in health care markets.

[15]  Paul B. Ginsburg, *High and Rising Health Care Costs: Demystifying U.S. Health Care Spending*, Robert Wood Johnson Foundation. The Synthesis Project, October 2008, p. 1. http://www.rwjf.org/files/research/ 101508.policysynthesis.costdrivers.rpt.pdf.

[16]  Ginsburg, op. cit., p. 1. Technology is often treated as a residual variable in studies of health care costs, so it could be overstated.

[17]  Testimony of Peter R. Orszag before the Committee on Budget, United States Senate, January 13, 2009. http://budget.senate.gov/democratic/testimony/2009/Orszag FINAL011309.pdf. Due to the recession and federal spending in response to it, some of these percentages may be changing.

[18]  Anderson and Frogner, op. cit.

[19]  Marian F. MacDorman and T.J. Mathews, *Recent Trends in Infant Mortality in the United States*, National Center for Health Statistics, Centers for Disease Control and

Prevention, October 2008. http://www.cdc.gov/nchs/data/databriefs/ db09.htm. The report notes that "international comparisons of infant mortality can be affected by differences in reporting of fetal and infant deaths. However, it appears unlikely that differences in reporting are the primary explanation for the United States' relatively low international ranking."

[20] Institute of Medicine, To Err is Human: Building A Safer Health System, November 1999.

[21] Health Grades, Third Annual Patient Safety in American Hospitals Study, April 2006, p. 4 http://www.healthgrades.com/media/dms/pdf/patientsafetyinamericanhospitals study2006.pdf.

[22] Institute of Medicine, National Academies, "Medication Errors Injure 1.5 Million People," press release, July 20, 2006, http://www8.nationalacademies.org/ onpinews/newsitem.aspx?RecordID=11623.

[23] Elizabeth A. McGlynn et al., "The Quality of Health Care Delivered to Adults in the United States," *The New England Journal of Medicine*, vol. 348, no. 26 (June 26, 2003), pp. 263 5-2646. The study was based on a random sample of adults in 12 metropolitan areas in the United States. Over 12,000 adults who received care participated in the survey.

[24] Steven M. Asch et al., "Who Is at Greatest Risk for Receiving Poor-Quality Health Care?," *New England Journal of Medicine*, vol. 354, no. 11 (March 16, 2006), pp. 1147-1156.

[25] For example, see Agency for Healthcare Research and Quality, U.S. Department of Health and Human Services, *National Healthcare Disparities Report, 2008* (May 2009). http://www.ahrq.gov/qual/nhdr08/nhdr08.pdf

[26] According to one observer, efforts to improve patient safety stemmed from the Institute of Medicine report cited above (To Err is Human) and reflected growing skepticism about the health care system after a decade of managed care. Robert M. Wachter, "The End of the Beginning: Patient Safety Five Years After 'To Err is Human'," *Health Affairs Web Exclusive*, November 30, 2004, pp. W4-534-W4-545. http://content.healt haffairs.org/cgi/reprint/hlthaff.w4.534v1?maxtoshow=&HITS=10&hits=10&RESULT FORMAT=&author1=wachter&andorexactfulltext=and&searchid=1&FIRSTINDEX=0 &resourcetype=HWCIT

[27] Agency for Healthcare Quality and Research, U.S. Department of Health and Human Services, *Key Themes and Highlights From the National Healthcare Quality Report*, 2008. (May, 2009) http://www.ahrq.gov/qual/nhqr08/ nhqr08.pdf

[28] For a discussion of issues this would raise, see CRS Report R40490, *Medicaid Checklist: Considerations in Adding a Mandatory Eligibility Group*, by Chris L. Peterson, Elicia J. Herz, and Julie Stone.

[29] The Massachusetts Connector is a state agency that helps people find insurance. For more information, see its website, http://www.mahealth connector.org/porta l/site/connector/.

[30] U.S. Congress. Joint Committee on Taxation. *Tax Expenditures for Health Care*, July 31, 2008. JCX-66-08.

[31] For a discussion of these and other issues regarding eliminating or capping the exclusion, see CRS Report RL34767, *The Tax Exclusion for Employer-Provided Health Insurance: Policy Issues Regarding the Repeal Debate*, by Bob Lyke.

[32] CRS Report RS20315, *ERISA Regulation of Health Plans: Fact Sheet*, by Hinda Chaikind.

[33] The Massachusetts plan requires everyone to have insurance, with some exceptions, and established an insurance marketplace called the Connector to help some find coverage. Premium subsidies are available depending on income and family size, and employers that do not offer coverage must pay a penalty.

[34] See CRS report CRS Report R40088, *The Federal Budget: Current and Upcoming Issues*, by D. Andrew Austin and Mindy R. Levit.

[35] Estimates in the news media and from other sources vary widely, and it usually is not clear what specific proposals are being assessed or whether similar estimates would be made by the Congressional Budget Office or the Joint Committee on Taxation. For the question of what payments and costs will likely be considered part of the federal budget, see the Congressional Budget Office, *The Budgetary Treatment of Proposals to Change the Nation's Health Insurance System* (May 27, 2009), http://www.cbo.gov/ft pdocs/102xx/doc10243/05-27-HealthInsuranceProposals.pdf.

[36] The Joint Tax Committee estimates that the exclusion reduced individuals' federal income taxes in 2008 by about $132.7 billion, and individuals' and employers' Social Security and Medicare taxes by about $93.5 billion. *Background Materials for Senate Committee on Finance Roundtable on Health Care Financing*, (JCX-27-09), May 8, 2009. http://www.jct.gov/publications.html?func=startdown&id=3557. Some argue that the exclusion should be eliminated or capped because it is an incentive for employees to obtain more insurance coverage than they otherwise would and because it often results in larger tax savings for higher income taxpayers.

[37] These and other suggestions are included in the Senate Finance Committee's descriptions of policy options for financing health care reform, discussed immediately below.

[38] Congressional Budget Office, *Budget Options Volume 1: Health Care* (December, 2008). http://www.cbo.gov/ftpdocs/99xx/doc9925/12-1 8-HealthOptions.pdf

[39] For summaries of what has been released, see Kaiser Family Foundation, *Health Care Reform Proposals*, http://www.kff.org/healthreform/upload/healthreform_tri_full.pdf.

[40] Office of Management and Budget, *A New Era of Responsibility: Renewing America's Promise*, February 26, 2009. http://www.white house.gov/omb/assets/ fy2010_new_e ra/A_New_Era_of_Responsibility2.pdf

[41] U.S. Department of the Treasury, *General Explanations of the Administration's Fiscal Year 2010 Revenue Proposals* (May 2010), p. 130.

[42] CRS Report R40587, *Medicare: FY2010 Budget Issues*, coordinated by Holly Stockdale.

[43] http://www.whitehouse.gov/MedicareFactSheetFinal/

[44] Bureau of National Affairs, *Health Care Daily*, June 30, 2009.

[45] Estimates are from CRS Report 96-891, *Health Insurance Coverage: Characteristics of the Insured and Uninsured Populations in 2007*, by Chris L. Peterson and April Grady. The estimates are based on data from the Current Population Survey.

[46]  Robert Wood Johnson Foundation and the State Health Access Data Assistance Center,
       *At the Brink: Trends in America's Uninsured, A State-by-State Analysis,* March 2009.
       http://www.rwjf.org/files/research/20090324ctuw.pdf.
[47]  Centers for Medicare and Medicaid Services, U.S. Department of Health and Human
       Services. NHE Fact Sheet. http://www.cms.hhs.gov/NationalHealthExpend Data
       /25_NHE_Fact_Sheet.asp

# INDEX

## B

## C

# E

# H

## Q

## R

## S

## T

## U

**V**

**W**